Incorporate in Delaware from Any State

INCORPORATE IN DELAWARE FROM ANY STATE

Mark Warda
Attorney at Law

SPHINX® PUBLISHING
AN IMPRINT OF SOURCEBOOKS, INC.®
NAPERVILLE, ILLINOIS
www.SphinxLegal.com

First Edition, 2002

Published by: **Sphinx® Publishing, An Imprint of Sourcebooks, Inc.®**

Naperville Office
P.O. Box 4410
Naperville, Illinois 60567-4410
630-961-3900
Fax: 630-961-2168
www.sourcebooks.com
www.SphinxLegal.com

Library of Congress Cataloging-in-Publication Data

Warda, Mark.
Incorporate in Delaware from any state / Mark Warda.-- 1st ed.
p. cm. -- (Legal survival guides)
Includes index.
ISBN 1-57248-230-3 (alk. paper)
1. Incorporation--Delaware--Popular works. I. Title. II. Series.

KFD213.5 .W37 2002
346.751'06622--dc21

2002030286

Printed and bound in the United States of America.
VHG Paperback — 10 9 8 7 6 5 4 3 2 1

Contents

Using Self-Help Law Books

Before using a self-help law book, you should realize the advantages and disadvantages of doing your own legal work and understand the challenges and diligence that this requires.

The Growing Trend

Rest assured that you won't be the first or only person handling your own legal matter. For example, in some states, more than seventy-five percent of divorces and other cases have at least one party representing him or herself. Because of the high cost of legal services, this is a major trend and many courts are struggling to make it easier for people to represent themselves. However, some courts are not happy with people who do not use attorneys and refuse to help them in any way. For some, the attitude is, "Go to the law library and figure it out for yourself."

We at Sphinx write and publish self-help law books to give people an alternative to the often complicated and confusing legal books found in most law libraries. We have made the explanations of the law as simple and easy to understand as possible. Of course, unlike an attorney advising an individual client, we cannot cover every conceivable possibility.

Cost/Value Analysis

Whenever you shop for a product or service, you are faced with various levels of quality and price. In deciding what product or service to buy, you make a cost/value analysis on the basis of your willingness to pay and the quality you desire.

When buying a car, you decide whether you want transportation, comfort, status, or sex appeal. Accordingly, you decide among such choices as a Neon, a Lincoln, a Rolls Royce, or a Porsche. Before making a decision, you usually weigh the merits of each option against the cost.

When you get a headache, you can take a pain reliever (such as aspirin) or visit a medical specialist for a neurological examination. Given this choice, most people, of course, take a pain reliever, since it costs only pennies; whereas a medical examination costs hundreds of dollars and takes a lot of time. This is usually a logical choice because it is rare to need anything more than a pain reliever for a headache. But in some cases, a headache may indicate a brain tumor and failing to see a specialist right away can result in complications. Should everyone with a headache go to a specialist? Of course not, but people treating their own illnesses must realize that they are betting on the basis of their cost/value analysis of the situation. They are taking the most logical option.

The same cost/value analysis must be made when deciding to do one's own legal work. Many legal situations are very straight forward, requiring a simple form and no complicated analysis. Anyone with a little intelligence and a book of instructions can handle the matter without outside help.

But there is always the chance that complications are involved that only an attorney would notice. To simplify the law into a book like this, several legal cases often must be condensed into a single sentence or paragraph. Otherwise, the book would be several hundred pages long and too complicated for most people. However, this simplification necessarily leaves out many details and nuances that would apply to special or unusual situations. Also, there are many ways to interpret most legal questions. Your case may come before a judge who disagrees with the analysis of our authors.

Therefore, in deciding to use a self-help law book and to do your own legal work, you must realize that you are making a cost/value analysis. You have decided that the money you will save in doing it yourself outweighs the chance that your case will not turn out to your satisfaction. Most people handling their own simple legal matters never have a problem, but occasionally people find that it ended up costing them more to have an attorney straighten out the situation than it would have if they had hired an attorney in the beginning. Keep this in mind if you decide to handle your own case, and be sure to consult an attorney if you feel you might need further guidance.

LOCAL RULES

The next thing to remember is that a book that covers the law for the entire nation, or even for an entire state, cannot possibly include every procedural difference of every county court. Whenever possible, we provide the exact form needed; however, in some areas, each county, or even each judge, may require unique forms and procedures. In our *state* books, our forms usually cover the majority of counties in the state, or provide examples of the type of form that will be required. In our *national* books, our forms are sometimes even more general in nature but are designed to give a good idea of the type of form that will be needed in most locations. Nonetheless, keep in mind that your *state,* county, or judge may have a requirement, or use a form, that is not included in this book.

You should not necessarily expect to be able to get all of the information and resources you need solely from within the pages of this book. This book will serve as your guide, giving you specific information whenever possible and helping you to find out what else you will need to know. This is just like if you decided to build your own backyard deck. You might purchase a book on how to build decks. However, such a book would not include the building codes and permit requirements of every city, town, county, and township in the nation; nor would it include the lumber, nails, saws, hammers, and other materials and tools you would need to actually build the deck. You would use the book as your guide, and then do some work and research involving such matters as whether you need a permit of some kind, what type and grade of wood are available in your area, whether to use hand tools or power tools, and how to use those tools.

Before using the forms in a book like this, you should check with your court clerk to see if there are any local rules of which you should be aware, or local forms you will need to use. Often, such forms will require the same information as the forms in the book but are merely laid out differently, use slightly different language, or use different color paper so the clerks can easily find them. They will sometimes require additional information.

Changes in the Law

Besides being subject to state and local rules and practices, the law is subject to change at any time. The courts and the legislatures of all fifty states are constantly revising the laws. It is possible that while you are reading this book, some aspect of the law is being changed or a court is interpreting a law in a different way. You should always check the most recent statutes, rules and regulations to see what, if any changes have been made.

In most cases, the change will be of minimal significance. A form will be redesigned, additional information will be required, or a waiting period will be extended. As a result, you might need to revise a form, file an extra form, or wait out a longer time period; these types of changes will not usually affect the outcome of your case. On the other hand, sometimes a major part of the law is changed, the entire law in a particular area is rewritten, or a case that was the basis of a central legal point is overruled. In such instances, your entire ability to pursue your case may be impaired.

Again, you should weigh the value of your case against the cost of an attorney and make a decision as to what you believe is in your best interest.

Introduction

For over a hundred years, Delaware has been the state of choice for the formation of business corporations. Over half the Fortune 500 corporations and nearly half the corporations on the New York Stock Exchange are incorporated in Delaware.

The reason for this is that Delaware has made being business-friendly its goal. It has laws which are favorable to corporations and its courts consistently issue rulings favorable to corporations. It does not have a corporate income tax or an inheritance tax on nonresident stockholders.

Since Delaware took the lead in enacting laws favorable to corporations in the last century, many states have followed suit and enacted similar laws. So in states which do not have a corporate income tax, there may not be as many advantages to Delaware as in the past. For example, small mom and pop businesses may find it more advantageous to form an S corporation or a limited liability corporation (LLC) in their own state. But for the business which plans to go public quickly or do national or international deals, the Delaware corporation may be the best choice. See Chapter 1 for the advantages and disadvantages of forming your business in Delaware.

The corporation has been the preferred way of doing business for hundreds of years because it offers protection from personal liability. People who wanted to participate in a risky venture, such as an expedition to the New World to seek gold, could put up a limited sum of money and not worry about being personally liable if the venture failed.

But in the last decade, the limited liability company, or LLC has become popular. This newly-devised form of business entity is a cross between a corporation and a partnership. It offers the flexibility and tax advantages of a partnership with the protection against liability of a corporation. And in some states a membership interest in an LLC is protected against the creditors of a member. Therefore, we have included both corporations and LLCs in this book to give you the choice of an entity that is best for your circumstances.

Creating a simple corporation or LLC is very easy and it is the purpose of this book to explain, in simple language, how you can do it yourself. Chapter 3 through 6 primarily focus on the start-up of such businesses. Chapters 8 and 9 focus on running such businesses. A simple corporation or LLC as used in this book is one in which there are five or fewer participants and all of them are active in the business.

If you plan to sell stock to outside investors, you should consult with a lawyer who specializes in securities laws. Selling a few thousand shares of stock to friends and neighbors may sound like an easy way to raise capital for your business, but it usually is not. Since the time just after the stock market crash of 1929, there have been federal laws regulating the sale of securities. There are harsh criminal penalties for violators, and the laws do not have many loopholes. The basic rules are explained in Chapter 7.

If your situation is in any way complicated or involves factors not mentioned in this book, you should seek the advice of an attorney practicing corporate law. The cost of a short consultation can be a lot cheaper than the consequences of violating the law. All of the appendices will give you statutes, resources, and forms that will make your time either alone or with an attorney smoother.

This book explains the basics of business taxation in Chapter 2, but you should discuss your own particular situation with your accountant before deciding what structure is best for you. He or she can also set you up with an efficient system of bookkeeping which can save both time and money.

Good luck with your new business!

1 Deciding to Incorporate in Delaware

Before you take the big step of organizing a Delaware corporation or limited liability company (LLC), you should go over the advantages of each form and the advantages and disadvantages of using the state of Delaware. For simplicity, when we say "incorporate" in the book we will be referring to forming either a corporation or an LLC.

Advantages of Corporations and LLCs

For nearly any type of business, the corporation or LLC is much preferred over the sole proprietorship or partnership. Except for the smallest home-based business, it is foolish to operate without the protections these entities offer. This section will review the advantages of using a corporation or LLC as your business entity.

Limited Liability

The main reason for forming a corporation or LLC is to limit the liability of the owners. In a sole proprietorship or partnership, the owners are personally liable for the debts and liabilities of the business, and creditors can often go after their assets to collect business debts. If a corporation or LLC is formed and operated properly, the owners can be protected from all such liability.

Example 1: If several people are in partnership and one of them makes many large extravagant purchases in the name of the partnership, the other partners can be held liable for the full amount of all such purchases. The creditors can take the bank accounts, cars, real estate, and other property of any partner to pay the debts of the partnership. If only one partner has money, he or she may have to pay all of the debts accumulated by all the other partners. When doing business in the corporate form, the corporation may go bankrupt and the shareholders may lose their initial investment, but the creditors cannot touch the assets of the owners.

Example 2: If a person runs a taxi business and one of the drivers causes a terrible accident, the owner of the taxi can be held liable for the full amount of the damages. If the taxi driver was on drugs and killed several people and the damages amount to millions of dollars more than the insurance coverage, the owner may lose everything he owns. With a corporation, only the corporation would be liable and if there was not enough money or insurance the owner still couldn't be touched. One true example was a business owner who owned hundreds of taxis. He put one or two in each of hundreds of different corporations which he owned. Each corporation only had minimum insurance and when one taxi was involved in an accident the owner only lost the assets of that corporation.

NOTE*: If a corporate officer or shareholder does something negligent himself, or signs a debt personally, or guarantees a corporate debt, the corporation will not protect him from the consequences of his own act or from the debt. Also, if a corporation does not follow the proper corporate formalities, it may be ignored by a court and the owners or officers may be held personally liable. The formalities include having separate bank accounts, holding meetings, and keeping minutes. When a court ignores a corporate structure and holds the owners or officers liable, it is called* piercing the corporate veil.

CONTINUOUS EXISTENCE

A corporation or LLC may have a *perpetual existence*. When a sole proprietor or partner dies, the assets of their business may go to their heirs but the business does not exist any longer. If the surviving spouse or other heirs of a business owner want to continue the business in their own names, they will be considered a new business even if they are using the assets of the old business. With a partnership, the death of one partner could cause a dissolution of the business.

Example 1: If a person dies owning a sole proprietorship, his or her spouse may want to continue the business. That person may inherit all of the assets but will have to start a new business. This means getting new licenses and tax numbers, registering the name and establishing credit from scratch. With a corporation or LLC, the business could continue with all of the same licenses, bank accounts, etc.

Example 2: If one partner dies and no prior agreements allow continuation of the business, the partnership may be forced to close. The heirs of the deceased partner may be able to force the sale of their share of the assets of the partnership even if the surviving partner needs them to continue the business. If he does not have the money to buy out the heirs, the business may have to be dissolved. With a corporation or properly drawn LLC agreement the surviving member could be allowed to buy out the interest of the deceased one.

EASE OF TRANSFERABILITY

A corporation and all of its assets and accounts may be transferred by the simple assignment of a stock certificate. An LLC may be transferred with an assignment of a membership interest. With a sole proprietorship, each of the individual assets must be transferred and the accounts, licenses, and permits must be individually transferred.

Example: If a sole proprietorship is sold, the new owner will have to get a new occupational license, set up his own bank account, and apply for a new taxpayer identification number. The title to any vehicles and real estate will have to be put in his name and all open accounts will have to be changed to his name. He will probably have to submit new credit applications. With a corporation, all of these items remain in the same corporate name. As the new shareholder, he would elect himself director and as director he would elect himself president, treasurer, and any other offices he wanted to hold.

NOTE: *In some cases, the new owners will have to submit personal applications for such things as credit lines or liquor licenses.*

TRANSFER OF OWNERSHIP

By distributing stock or different types of membership interests, the owner of a corporation or LLC can share the profits of a business without giving up control. This is done by keeping a majority of ownership or by issuing different classes of ownership some with voting rights and others without voting rights.

Example: If a person wants to give his children some of the profits of his business, he can give them stock and pay dividends to them without giving them any control over the management. This would not be practical with a partnership or sole proprietorship.

EASE OF RAISING CAPITAL

A corporation or LLC may raise capital by selling stock or membership interests. A corporation or LLC does not pay taxes on money it raises by the sale of stock or membership interests.

Example: If a company wants to expand, the owners can sell off ten, fifty, or ninety percent of the stock and still remain in control of the business. The people putting up the money may be more willing to invest if they know they will have a piece of the action than if they were making a loan with a limited return. They may not want to become partners in a partnership.

NOTE: *There are strict rules about the sale of stock with criminal penalties and triple damages for violators. Be sure to read Chapter 7 carefully.*

SEPARATE RECORD KEEPING

A corporation or LLC has all its own bank accounts and records. A sole proprietor may have trouble differentiating which of his expenses were for business and which were for personal items.

TAX ADVANTAGES

There are some tax advantages that are available only to corporations or LLCs. Some of these are:

- medical insurance for your family may be fully deductible;
- a tax deferred trust can be set up for a retirement plan; and,
- losses are fully deductible for a corporation, whereas an individual must prove there was a profit motive before deducting losses.

EASE OF ESTATE PLANNING

With a corporation or LLC, shares of a company can be distributed more easily than with a partnership or sole proprietorship. Different heirs can be given different percentages and control can be limited to those who are most capable.

PRESTIGE

The name of a corporation or LLC sounds more prestigious than the name of a sole proprietor to some people. John Smith d/b/a Acme Builders sounds like one lone guy. Acme Builders, Incorporated, or Acme Builders, LLC sounds like it might be a large operation. No one needs to know that it is run out of a garage. One female writer on the subject has suggested that a woman who is president of a corporation looks more successful than one doing business in her own name. This probably applies to everyone.

SEPARATE CREDIT RATING

A corporation or LLC has its own credit rating, which can be better or worse than the owner's credit rating. A corporation or LLC can go bankrupt while the owner's credit remains unaffected, or an owner's credit may be bad but the corporation may maintain a good rating.

Differences Between Corporations and LLCs

The limited liability company is the newest form of business entity and some have suggested that every business should adopt the form today. A closer look at the entities will show that while for some businesses, they may offer advantages, whereas for others, the corporate form may be better.

Advantages of Corporations

The *main* advantages that a corporation has over an LLC are:

History. The corporation has a long history and many thousands of court cases have decided the rights and obligations of the participants. Since the LLC was only invented a few years ago, there have been few court cases to spell out those rights. Thus a large business, especially one which plans to go public, might prefer the certainty of a corporation.

Taxes. The main advantage of an S corporation over an LLC is that profits taken out other than salary are not subject to social security and medicare taxes (15.3% of the first $68,400 and 2.9% of amounts over at the time of publication), whereas all profits of an LLC are subject to these taxes. However, there are proposals before Congress to end this benefit of S corporations.

For a large business where the owners take out salaries of $68,400 or more plus profits, there would not be much difference. But for a smaller business where an owner would take out a $30,000 salary and $20,000 profit, the extra taxes would be over $3,000.

Reorganizations. An S corporation is allowed under the Internal Revenue Code (IRC), Section (Sec.) 368 to have a tax-free merger or asset divestiture under certain circumstances, but an LLC is not. However, an LLC may switch to a corporate structure prior to reorganization to use these benefits.

Advantages of LLCs

The *main* advantages that an LLC has over a corporation are:

Asset protection. In some states, the interest a member owns in an LLC can be protected from the rights of that member's creditors. While corporate stock can be seized and sold by a creditor, in some states an interest in an LLC is only subject to a creditor's *charging order*. This means that the creditor only gets what the other members of the LLC decide to give him. He cannot sell the interest because the interest is not assignable. The creditor cannot vote in place of the former member and he cannot require the LLC to dissolve.

Formality. It is presumed by most legal experts that an LLC requires less formality than a corporation. While improper procedures in a corporation may allow a creditor to *pierce the corporate veil* and hold shareholders liable, the LLC is clearly meant to be a safe harbor to protect business owners from liability.

Taxes. An LLC can make special allocations of profits and losses among members (as long as the tests of Treasury Regulations Section 1.704(b) are satisfied), whereas S corporations cannot. S corporations must have one class of ownership in which profits and losses are allocated according to the percentage ownership.

In an LLC, money borrowed by the company can increase the tax basis of the owners (and lower the taxes), but in an S corporation, it does not.

Contributing property to set up an LLC is not taxable even for minority interest owners; however, for a corporation, Internal Revenue Code, Section 351 only allows it to be tax free for the contributors who have control of the business.

An S corporation may lose its favorable tax status for five years if an interest is acquired by a foreign person, another corporation, or a certain kind of trust, and it may not have more than seventy-five shareholders. An LLC has no such limitations.

When an LLC buys out a member, it may increase its basis in a portion of the receivables and tangible assets. An S corporation may not. When a third party buys the interest of a member, the LLC may make an election under Internal Revenue Code, Section 754 to increase its basis in assets. An S corporation cannot.

Upon death of an owner, the person inheriting an S corporation interest may need to pay taxes on more income than a person inheriting a similar LLC. (IRC, Sec. 691.)

Newness. Another advantage may be psychological. The LLC is a new entity and in the twenty-first century, it may look more up-to-date to be an LLC than an ordinary corporation.

Advantages of Delaware

Delaware has been the most popular state for incorporation of America's largest corporations for well over a hundred years. Some of the reasons are no longer valid, since many states have revised their corporation laws to be as advantageous as Delaware's. However, other benefits still exist and depending on the state in which your business is located, they may be great or small.

Sixty percent of the Fortune 500 companies are Delaware corporations and Delaware law is understood by most corporate lawyers dealing with national businesses. For this reason, if you are planning to take your business public, you may find the process easier as a Delaware corporation. This is especially true if you are in a state with few corporations or one with less favorable corporation laws.

Delaware has a long line of caselaw which has been favorable to corporations; also, its legislature is quick to revise its corporate laws when changes are needed to benefit businesses. The secretary of state's office is very professional and business-friendly. They can process papers within twenty-four hours and will accept them by fax with a credit card.

The following are some of the other benefits which are mentioned as reasons for incorporating in Delaware. Other states may have some of these benefits, but few, if any, have all of them.

- no income tax for corporations not doing business in the state;
- no inheritance tax on nonresident stockholders of Delaware;
- corporate statute allows more flexibility for management than some states;
- registration fees are low;
- annual fees are low;
- no minimum capital is required;
- one person can hold all of the corporate offices;
- directors can set any price on shares;
- directors can amend the bylaws; and,
- Delaware law limits hostile takeovers.

Disadvantages of Delaware

There are a few things to consider when incorporating in Delaware which may be disadvantages to your business if your business is not located in Delaware.

Delaware Registered Agent and Office

First—as a Delaware corporation, you will need to have a registered agent and registered office in the state of Delaware. If you incorporate in your own state, you can usually use your own business office as the registered agent, and you or one of your employees could be the registered agent.

However, the fee to hire a Delaware registered agent and registered office is around $100 a year so this is not a burden except for the smallest enterprise. A list of corporate agents is included in this book in Appendix B.

Home State Registration

Second—as a Delaware corporation you will need to register as a "foreign corporation" in the state in which you are actually doing business. This is usually a simple procedure of filing a form and paying a fee each year. In some states this is a small fee but in others it is considerable. A list of state offices with which you must register is included in this book in Appendix C.

LAWSUITS

A third disadvantage is that as a Delaware corporation, you can be sued in Delaware. This may be more expensive to defend than a suit in your home state if your business is a thousand or two thousand miles away.

ANNUAL FRANCHISE TAX

Delaware did not decide to offer the best corporation laws just for the good of the country. Their annual franchise tax allows the state to bring in considerable revenue and reduce the tax burden on its residents. There is one corporation registered in Delaware for each three residents.

The annual franchise tax ranges from $30 to as high as $150,000. A corporation is allowed to use either of the following two methods of calculating the tax and pay whichever is cheaper.

1. Authorized shares method:

3,000 or less shares	$30.00
3,001–5,000	50.00
5,001–10,000	90.00
each additional 10,000 or portion	50.00

2. Assumed par value capital method:

$200 per million dollars of capital per Schedule L of IRS Form 1120.

For corporations with few shareholders, the first method is best. For those with many thousands of shares outstanding, the second method works out cheapest.

DELAWARE TERMINOLOGY

The corporate terms used in Delaware are somewhat different from those used in most other states so you should learn them before beginning to use the forms or reading the statutes. The following are the most important ones of which to be aware.

Certificate of Incorporation

The document that must be filed to start a standard business corporation is called a *certificate of incorporation*. (In most other states this document is called the *articles of incorporation*.)

Stock Corporation

A stock corporation is what Delaware calls a normal business corporation which is organized to make a profit. It may be an S corporation or a C corporation and may have many options as to its capital and organizational structure.

Close Corporation

A *close corporation* is a corporation that limits its shareholders to thirty and puts restrictions on the transferability of its shares. It requires that certificates be issued for shares. It often obligates a shareholder to offer to the corporation or the shareholders the opportunity to purchase the stock before offering it to any outside purchaser. If the corporation and shareholders reject the offer, they typically must still consent to who the transferee (buyer) of the shares will be.

To become a close corporation, the certificate of incorporation must include certain provisions which are set out in the statutes. These are included in Subchapter XIV of the General Corporation Law of the State of Delaware in Appendix A. There is a **Close Corporation Certificate of Incorporation** included in Appendix D. (see form 8, p.205.)

Non-Stock Corporation

A *non-stock corporation* is what would be called a *not-for-profit corporation* in most other states. This type of entity is primarily used for organizations such as churches, schools, or social clubs. However, in recent years, more people have found that an organization they have in mind can be run as a not-for-profit and enjoy the advantages of lower taxes and postal rates.

Certificate of Formation

The document that must be filed for an LLC in Delaware is the *certificate of formation*. (In most other states, it is called the *articles of organization*.)

2 Tax Considerations

There are many tax issues when dealing with corporations and LLCs. Pay careful attention to the types of taxes you must pay, and the forms you need to file for those taxes. This chapter outlines several.

Corporation Tax Issues

A corporation has a choice of how it wants to be taxed. It can make the election at the beginning of its existence or at the beginning of a new tax year. The choices are as follows:

S Corporation

Formerly called a *Subchapter S corporation*, an *S corporation* pays no income tax and may only be used for businesses with a limited number of shareholders. All of the income or losses of the corporation for the year are passed through to the shareholders who report them on their individual returns. At the end of each year, the corporation files an *information return* listing all of its income, expenses, depreciation, etc., and sends to each shareholder a notice of his or her share as determined by percentage of stock ownership.

Advantages. Using the S corporation method avoids double taxation and allows pass-through of losses and depreciation. The business is treated like a partnership. Since many businesses have tax losses during the first years due to start-up costs, it can be advantageous to elect S status in the beginning and switch over to C corporation status in later years. Once a corporation terminates its S status, there is a five-year waiting period before it can switch back.

Disadvantages. If stockholders are in high tax brackets, their share of the profits will be taxed at those rates. Shareholders who do not "materially participate" in the business cannot deduct losses. Some fringe benefits such as health and life insurance may not be tax deductible in an S corporation, whereas they would be in a C corporation or LLC.

Requirements. To qualify for S corporation status the corporation must:

- have no more than seventy-five shareholders, none of whom are non-resident aliens or corporations, and all of whom consent to the election (shares owned by a husband and wife jointly are considered owned by one shareholder);
- have only one class of stock;
- not be a member of an "affiliated group" of companies;
- generate at least twenty percent of its income in this country and have no more than twenty percent of its income from "passive" sources (interest, rents, dividends, royalties, securities transactions); and
- file **ELECTION BY A SMALL BUSINESS CORPORATION (IRS FORM 2553)** (included in Appendix D) before the end of the fifteenth day of the third month of the tax year for which it is to be effective and have it approved by the IRS. (see form 12, p.221.)

Multiple Corporations. The IRS has approved the use of two or more S corporations in partnership to increase the number of allowable investors in a venture. It may also be possible for an S corporation to form a partnership with a C corporation.

C CORPORATION

A C *corporation* pays taxes on its net earnings at corporate tax rates. Salaries of officers, directors, and employees are deducted from income so they are not taxed to the corporation, but money paid out in dividends is taxed twice. It is taxed at the corporation's rate as part of its profit, and then the stockholders must include the amounts they receive as dividends in their income.

Advantages. If taxpayers are in a higher tax bracket than the corporation and the money will be left in the company for expansion, the taxes saved are a great advantage. Fringe benefits such as health, accident, and life insurance are deductible expenses.

Disadvantages. Double taxation of dividends by the federal government is the biggest problem with a C corporation. This tax does not apply to money taken out as salaries, and many small business owners take all profits out as salaries to avoid double taxation. But there are rules requiring that salaries be reasonable and if a stockholder's salary is deemed to be too high, relative to his or her job, the salary may be considered dividends and subject to the double taxation.

Requirements. Nothing is required. All corporations are C corporations unless they specifically elect to become S corporations.

LLC Tax Issues

When LLCs were first started a few years ago, they had to follow strict rules in order to qualify for advantageous tax treatment and single business owners could not qualify for pass-through taxation because it was not considered logical to treat a single person as a partnership.

Fortunately, common sense prevailed and there are now no hoops to jump through. You merely obtain an **Entity Classification Election (IRS Form 8832)** and check the box indicating whether you wish to be taxed like a corporation or to pass the income through to the owners and have them declare it on their personal returns. **IRS Form 8832** is included in this book in Appendix D. (see form 29, p.269.)

Since one of the reasons LLCs were developed was to allow businesses to enjoy partnership taxation with corporate protections from liability, not many LLCs will select to be taxed as corporations.

Employer Identification Number

Prior to opening a bank account, the corporation must obtain an *employer identification number* (EIN), sometimes called a *taxpayer identification number*, which is the corporate equivalent of a social security number. This is done by filing an **Application for Employer Identification Number (IRS Form SS-4)**, which is included in this book. (see form 3, p.189.) This usually takes two or three weeks, so it should be filed early.

If you need the number quickly, you may be able to obtain it by phone by calling the IRS and reading the information on your form. The telephone number depends upon the state you are in and is listed on page 2 of the form. Be sure to have your **IRS Form SS-4** complete and in front of you when you call.

When you apply for this number, you will probably be put on the mailing list for other corporate tax forms. If you do not receive these, you should call your local IRS forms number and request the forms for new businesses. These include Circular E explaining the taxes due, the W-4 forms for each employee, the tax deposit coupons, and the Form 941 quarterly return for withholding.

Sales and Use Tax Issues

If your business will be providing goods or services to the public, then in most states you will need to collect a *sales and use* tax on each sale. Most states exempt various items such as food or medicines or certain types of services. You should contact the state department of revenue in each state in which you do business to register as a collector of the tax and to obtain the rules and regulations. Your business is liable for the tax even if you do not collect it. Also, your business must remit the taxes even if the state does not send you the forms on time. If your registration materials do not arrive in time for your first filing, you may be able to get temporary forms from your local tax office to avoid a penalty for late filing.

In 1992, the United States Supreme Court safeguarded the rights of small businesses by ruling that state tax authorities cannot force them to collect sales taxes on interstate mail orders (*Quill Corporation v. North Dakota*). For example, if a business in Iowa sold something by mail to someone in New York, it does not have to figure out New York tax laws, collect New York taxes, and send them to New York tax authorities. If this case had ruled the other way, every small business would have to keep track of taxes in all fifty states (and many cities), many of which require annual fees and that a bond be posted. This would have put all but the biggest companies out of business.

Unfortunately, the court left open the possibility that Congress could allow interstate taxation of mail order sales, and several bills have since been introduced which would do so. One, introduced by Arkansas senator Dale Bumpers, was given the Orwellian "newspeak" title, *The Consumer and Main Street Protection Act*. And in 1999, the American Booksellers Association began a national campaign to force mail order and internet sellers to collect sales taxes.

Companies are currently required to collect sales taxes for states in which they *do business*. What constitutes enough business to trigger taxation is a legal question, and some try to define it as broadly as possible.

IN STATE

If you have an office in a state, clearly you are doing business there and any goods shipped to consumers in the state are subject to sales taxes. If you have a full time employee working in the state much of the year, many states will consider you doing business there. In some states, attending a two-day trade show is enough business to trigger taxation for the entire year for every order shipped to the state. One loophole that often works is to be represented at shows by persons who are not your employees.

OUT OF STATE

Because the laws are different in each state, you will have to do some research on a state-by-state basis to find out how much business you can do in a state without being subject to their taxation. You can request a state's rules from its Department of Revenue. However, keep in mind that what a Department of Revenue wants the law to be is not always what the courts will rule that it is.

Business Taxes

As mentioned above, the laws are different in each state. You will have to do some research on a state-by-state basis to find out how much business you can do in a state without being subject to their taxation. Being subject to a state's income or other business taxes is even worse than being subject to their sales taxes. For example, California charges every company doing business in the state a minimum $800 a year fee and charges income tax on a portion of the company's worldwide income. Doing a small amount of business in the state is clearly not worth getting mired in California taxation.

Some trade shows have been moved from California for this reason. This has resulted in a review of the tax policies and the creation of some "safe-harbor" guidelines to advise companies on what they can do without becoming subject to taxation.

NOTE: *Be sure to write to the Department of Revenue of any state with which you have business contacts to see what might trigger your taxation.*

Internet Taxes

State revenue departments are drooling at the prospect of taxing commerce on the Internet. Theories have already been proposed that websites available to state residents mean a company is doing business in a state.

Fortunately, Congress has passed a moratorium on taxation of the Internet. Hopefully, this will be extended and will give us a new tax-free world; however, never before has a government let a new source of revenue go untapped. It would take a tremendous outcry to keep the Internet tax-free. But perhaps the Internet can be used as a new "enterprise zone" to encourage business growth. Keep an eye out for any news stories on proposals to tax the Internet and petition your representatives against them.

If laws are passed to tax the Internet, there may still be a way around them. For many types of businesses, especially companies which can provide their goods or services over the Internet, it would be possible to set up the business on a tax-free Caribbean island. With no state presence, no taxes would be due to any state.

Canadian Taxes

The Canadian government expects American companies that sell goods by mail order to Canadians to collect taxes for them and file returns with Revenue Canada, their tax department.

Those that receive an occasional unsolicited order are not expected to register, and Canadian customers who order things from the U.S. pay the tax plus a $5 fee upon receipt of the goods. But companies that solicit Canadian orders are expected to be registered if their worldwide income is $30,000 or more per year. In some cases, a company may be required to post a bond and pay for the cost of Canadian auditors visiting its premises and auditing its books. For these reasons, you may notice that some companies decline to accept orders from Canada.

3 Your Business Name

The very first thing to do before starting a new business is to choose a great name and thoroughly check it out to be sure that no one else already has legal rights to it.

Choosing Your Business Name

While the quality of your goods or services will improve the value of your name, having a great name can give the initial image of your company the boost it needs for people to give it a try. Consider if you were looking for a flight to Paris and the two airlines you had to choose from were Air International and Barney's Airline and Baitshop! Or if you needed a repair to your office computer and two computer repair shops were called Heather's Techsters on Wheels and Micro Systems Services.

These are exaggerations of course, but you get the idea that when all you have to go on is a name, one that sounds more knowledgeable or established will probably attract more business.

Some people have started a business on a whim, used a silly name, and watched it grow so big that the name became embarrassing. You may think that if you are lucky enough to have your business explode, you will not mind changing the name. Perhaps a silly name can be used to challenge fate. You can only hope to become so big that the name has to be changed.

But changing a business name is more complicated than you would expect. After years of establishing a name and reputation, changing it can be costly in time, expense, and lost business.

GUIDELINES

In choosing a name, you should use the following guidelines:

Use the right suffix. Delaware law requires that certain words or suffixes be a part of the name of a company. In Chapter 4 is a list of those required for a corporation and in Chapter 5 is a list of those required for an LLC.

Do not use forbidden words. Certain words are not allowed to be used as part of a company name under state law. In Delaware, one cannot use the word bank or any variation unless it is licensed as a bank. In other states, it is not legal to use such words as olympic, Disney, insurance, or trust. Check with the state corporation division where you will be doing business before filing.

Do not be too similar. While there might seem to be some advantage to having your name sound like a more successful competitor, it may be more trouble than it is worth. If a name is found by a court to be confusingly similar, it can order the user to stop using it and to pay damages. The legal costs of fighting a large corporation with deep pockets can bankrupt a small business.

For example, Toys 'R' Us sues any company that it finds using "R Us" in its name (Insurance R Us, Flowers R Us). Their claim was not strong, because legally, using the same name in another field of commerce was not an infringement of a trademark. They won because little companies could not afford to spend $50,000 or $100,000 fighting them in court. However, the law now protects famous trademarks from anyone using similar names.

On the other side, if you are looking for some free publicity for your fledgling business, you're sure to get written up in the local papers if a international corporation threatens to squash you for innocently using a similar name.

Be sure it is not confusing. Many words, especially in the English language, are spelled differently from how they sound. Be sure that the name you choose is easy to spell and for people to locate. (Someone once published a list of all the remaining English words which had not yet been registered with ".com" and most of them were hard to spell or had confusing homonyms.)

SOFTWARE

There is computer software available which is claimed to be helpful in the process of choosing a name. While it is costly for a one-time use, it may be worthwhile if you plan to name several products, or you may be able to find someone who will let you use it once for a fee.

CONSULTANTS

There are consultants who offer their services in choosing an ideal name; however, for a new business, the fee is usually too high. A business magazine once ran a story about a major corporation that paid a consultant $50,000 to create a name for a new breakfast cereal. The magazine also polled its own staff for suggestions based on the criteria given to the consultant, and the magazine staff came up with the same name!

SEARCHING YOUR NAME

Once you have chosen the perfect name, you need to be sure that no one else has established legal rights to it. Many business have been forced to stop using their name after spending thousands of dollars in promotions.

Legal rights can be established by registering a name as a *trademark* or by merely using the name. Consequently, you cannot be sure no one has rights to a name just by checking registered names. You need to check to see if anyone is using the name who has not yet registered it.

The following are places you should check:

DIVISION OF CORPORATIONS

Check with the Delaware Division of Corporations to see if there is another corporation with the same name. You can call their regular line at no charge to find out if the name is available (302-739-3073). They also publicize a nine hundred number you can use to reserve up to three names for thirty days for $10 (900-420-8042).

TRADEMARKS

Next you should check the United States Patent and Trademark Office to see if anyone has registered it as a trademark. There are several ways you can do this:

Online search. The records of the trademark office were put online in 1999. You can now search every registered and pending trademark at the following site:

http://www.uspto.gov/

If you do not have access to the Internet at your home or office, you may be able to do so on a computer at a public library. If you are not familiar with how to do it, you may be able to have someone at the library perform the search either for a small fee or for free.

Federal depository libraries. You can also search trademarks at the numerous federal depository libraries around the country. These are usually connected with universities. Either your local public or university library can tell you where the nearest federal depository library is located.

Search firms. If you would rather have someone else do the search, you can hire a professional search firm. In addition to a trademark search, they can check other records around the country and give you a more accurate answer as to whether the name is being used anywhere. The cost can range from about $100 to over $500 depending on how thorough the search is and who is doing it. The following are a few firms that do searches. You can call or write to them for a quote.

Government Liaison Services, Inc.
200 North Giebe Road #321
P.O. Box 3292
Arlington, VA 22203
800-642-6564; 703-524-8200
fax: 703-525-8415
http://www.trademarkinfo.com

Thomson & Thomson
500 Victory Road
North Quincy, MA 02171-8833
800-692-8833
fax: 617-479-5398
http://www. thomson-thomson.com

Corporate Service
62 White Street
New York, NY 10013
(800) 221-2972

TELEPHONE LISTINGS

Since some businesses neglect to properly register their name (yet still may have superior rights to it), you should also check phone books and business directories. Some libraries have phone books from around the country as well as directories of trade names; however, using a computer to search the Internet is much easier.

If you have a computer with Internet access, you can search every yellow pages listing for free. Just search for "yellow pages" with any Web search engine (e.g., Yahoo, WebCrawler, Lycos, etc.). You can select a state, enter your business name, and it will tell you if any other companies are listed with that name. One site that allows you to search all states at once is:

http://www.switchboard.com

If you do not have access to a computer, you may be able to use one at your public library or have the search done at your library for a small fee.

REGISTERING YOUR NAME

Once you have chosen the right name for your new company, you should register it before someone else does.

By forming your corporation with the state of Delaware you have insured that no other person can register a company with the same name. Nonetheless, this does not stop someone from registering the name with another state or getting a trademark for it.

FEDERAL TRADEMARK

A federal trademark gives the owner the right to use the name anywhere in the United States, and to stop most others from using it.

Example: Suppose you want to start a motel chain and find that no one has registered the name Rip Van Winkle Inns as a trademark. You checked the Internet, business directories, and yellow pages listings and no one is using it. Once you register a federal trademark, you can stop anyone else from using the name except those who have previously used it. Suppose a small motel in Arizona has used the name, but it did not show up in your search. Because they used the name first, they have legal rights to it in their area. You have rights everywhere else. You cannot use the name in their immediate area in competition with them, but they cannot expand outside of their area now that you own the name.

Before attempting to register the name, you should know that the following rules apply to federal trademarks:

- You cannot register the name of a business. A trademark is a name, symbol, or other device used to identify goods; and a *service mark* is the same but used to identify services.
- You cannot be fully registered until you actually use the mark. You can file an application indicating your intent to use a mark, but you must actually use it before registration is accomplished.
- In order to qualify for federal registration, you must use your mark in commerce, which means between states or with a foreign country. The use must be *bona fide,* meaning you can't just mail a copy to a relative.
- You can register your trademark with each state. This is not necessary if you plan to get a federal trademark immediately, but if you plan to limit your business to one state or do not plan to expand out of state for a number of years, state registration is faster and cheaper than federal.

- Trademarks are registered according to classes of goods. If you plan to use your mark on such different products as tires, lubricants, and window glass, you will need to register (and pay a filing fee of $245) for each class.

Registering a federal trademark is beyond the scope of this book, but you can get more information from the USPTO website:

http://www.uspto.gov

Sub Classes

If someone else is already using a trademark you want to use in the same class, it is possible to register it if your goods are different enough.

Example: If you wanted to use the word "bud" (as in buddy) on an electronic game for boys but someone else had registered bud (picturing a rosebud) as the name of a doll, you might be able to register in the same category (#28. games and playthings) since the products are different and are aimed at different audiences. However, being so close is just inviting trouble and if you were in the same category as Bud in Budweiser®, it would be suicide.

Fictitious Names

Sometimes it seems like every good name is taken. However, name can sometimes be used if it is modified slightly or used on a different type of goods.

Example: If you want to use the name "Flowers by Freida" in San Francisco and there is already a "Flowers by Freida, Inc." in Los Angeles, you might incorporate under the name "Freida Jones, Inc." and then register the corporation as doing business under the fictitious name "Flowers by Freida." Unless "Flowers by Freida, Inc." has registered a trademark for the name either in California or nationally, you will probably be able to use the name.

NOTE: *You should realize that you might run into complications later, especially if you decide to expand into other areas of the state. One protection available would be to register the name as a trademark. This would give you exclusive use of the name anywhere that someone else was not already using it.*

4 Corporate Paperwork

This chapter explains the paperwork you must file which is specific to a corporation. If you are forming an LLC, you should skip this chapter and go on to Chapter 5. You should continue to Chapter 6 for the rest of the start-up procedures after completing the paperwork in this chapter.

Certificate of Incorporation

The act which creates the corporation is the filing of a **Certificate of Incorporation** with the Secretary of State in Dover. Some corporations have long, elaborate articles that spell out numerous powers and functions, but most of this is unnecessary. The powers of corporations are spelled out in Delaware law (See Sections 121 through 127 in Appendix A) and do not have to be repeated. The main reason to keep the articles of incorporation short is to avoid having to amend them later. By putting all but the basics in the bylaws of the corporation, you can make changes in the corporate structure much more easily. The certificates included in this book (forms 8 and 9) are as simple as possible for this reason.

Delaware law requires that only five things be included in the certificate of incorporation:

1. the name;
2. the name and address of the registered agent;
3. the nature of the business (which may be any lawful activity);
4. the amount of authorized stock; and,
5. the name of the person signing the certificate as the *incorporator*.

If the powers of the incorporator cease upon filing (such as when you hire someone to file the papers for you), the names of the first directors must also be listed. Details of these requirements follow:

Name of the corporation. The corporation name must include one of the following words or abbreviations:

- association;
- company (or co.);
- corporation (or corp.);
- club;
- foundation;
- fund;
- incorporated (or inc.);
- institute;
- limited (or ltd.);
- society;
- syndicate; or,
- union.

Substitutes for these words in other languages may be used, and if a corporation has total assets (as defined in Section 503 (i)) of $10,000,000, it does not need to use these words.

The reason for requiring these words or abbreviations is so that persons dealing with the business will be on notice that it is a corporation. This is important in protecting the shareholders from liability.

Name and address of the registered agent. The name and street address of the address in the state of Delaware of the registered agent must be provided. If you will not be using your own office in Delaware, you will need to make arrangements with a registered agent in the state. Some of those that provide this service are listed in Appendix B.

The nature of the business. The nature of the business may be stated as "any lawful act for which corporations may be organized under the General Corporation Law of Delaware."

The classes of stock. If there will be only one class of stock, the par value must be listed or a statement that the stock has no par value. If there are to be more classes, the number and par value of each class must be stated along with any preferences, qualifications, or restrictions.

In some cases, it may be advantageous to issue different classes of stock such as common and preferred, or voting and non-voting, but such matters are beyond the scope of this book and should be discussed with an attorney or accountant.

This book will explain how to form a corporation with one class of stock. It is usually advisable to authorize double or quadruple the amount of stock which will be initially issued. The unissued stock can be issued later if more capital is contributed by a shareholder or by a new member of the business.

One important point to keep in mind when issuing stock is that the full par value must be paid for the shares. If this is not done then the shareholder can later be held liable for the full par value. For more important information about issuing stock, see Chapter 7.

The name and address of the incorporator. The name provided as incorporator usually belongs to one of the parties starting the business, but it may be any person, even if that person has no future interest in the corporation. For people who need to be incorporated quickly, there are companies in Delaware that can, on a moment's notice, have someone sign and run over to the Division of Corporations to file the CERTIFICATE OF INCORPORATION which is later assigned to the real parties in interest. However, the Division now accepts credit cards and filings by fax.

If the incorporator will not be a member of the business after the certificate is filed, the names and mailing addresses of the initial directors must be listed.

EXECUTION

The **CERTIFICATE OF INCORPORATION** must be signed by the incorporator in black ink and dated.

FILING

The **CERTIFICATE OF INCORPORATION** need not be on any certain form. It can be typed on blank paper or can be on a fill-in-the-blank form. If you type the form it must be on 8-1/2 by 11 inch paper, have one inch margins on each side, two inches at the top and 1-1/5 inches at the bottom.

The forms provided by the Delaware Secretary of State for regular and close corporations (forms 8 and 9) are in Appendix D of this book. The CERTIFICATE OF INCORPORATION can be filed with the Secretary of State of Delaware by fax, mail, or courier:

Division of Corporations
John G. Townsend Building
401 Federal Street, Suite 4
Dover, DE 19901
or
Fax: 302-739-5831

FEES

You should also use the **DOCUMENT FILING SHEET**. (see form 1, p.185.) Include the following fees:

- a filing fee of $50 that covers a $15 filing, $25 receiving and indexing, and $10 certified copy, and
- a filing tax of at least $15 according to the following schedule:

Stock with no par value

First 20,000 shares, 1¢ per share

20,001 to 2,000,000 shares, 1/2¢ per share

Over 2,000,000 shares, 4/10¢ per share

Example: The fee for 10,000 shares is $100, and the fee for 1,000 shares is $10 (but the minimum fee is $15).

Stock with par value

First 20,000 shares, 2¢ per $100 par value

20,001 to 2,000,000 shares, 1¢ per $100 par value

Over 2,000,000 shares, 4/10¢ per $100 par value

Example: 10,000 shares at a par value of $100 per share would pay $200 tax and the fee for 10,000 shares with a par value of $1 would be $2 (but the minimum fee is $15).

The return time for the articles is usually a week or so. If there is a need to have them back quickly, you may request expediting for the following extra fees:

- for filing within twenty-four hours, the fee is up to $100 (call 302-739-3073 for exact fee);
- the fee is up to $200 for filing the same day (call 302-739-3073 for exact fee);
- the fee for filing within two hours is $500 and documents must be received by 7 P.M.

Bylaws and Minutes

Every corporation must have bylaws and must maintain a set of minutes of its meetings. The bylaws must be adopted at the organizational meeting of the corporation. Minutes must be kept of this meeting and of all meetings of shareholders and directors.

The bylaws are the rules for organization and operation of the corporation. Two sets of generic **BYLAWS** are included with this book—**BYLAWS** is for simple corporations. (see form 10, p.209.) The other one, **BYLAWS (PROFESSIONAL ASSOCIATIONS)** is for *professional associations.* (see form 11, p.215.) You should read the bylaws to be sure they apply to your situation and that you understand them. If you do not understand them or wish to make major changes, you should contact an attorney. To complete them, you should fill in the name of the corporation, the city of the main office of the corporation, the proposed date of the annual meeting (this can be varied each year as needed), and the number of directors to be on the board.

Delaware law allows corporate officers to execute incorporation papers without a meeting; nonetheless, it is better to have a formal meeting to prove to possible future creditors that you conducted the corporation in a formal manner.

SHAREHOLDER AGREEMENT

Whenever there are two or more shareholders in a corporation they should consider drawing up a *shareholder agreement*. This document outlines what is to happen in the event of a disagreement between them. The minority shareholders in small corporations have a risk of being locked into a long term enterprise with little or no way to withdraw their capital. A shareholder agreement is a fairly complicated document and you should consider having it drawn up by an attorney. This may be costly but the expense should be weighed against the costs of lengthy litigation should the parties split. A less expensive alternative is to sit down and decide what will happen in the event of a shareholder's death, divorce, retirement, or decision to sell out; write it up; and have everyone sign. Some of the things that may be addressed in such an agreement are as follows:

- veto by minority shareholder;
- greater than majority voting requirement;
- cumulative voting;
- deadlocks;
- arbitration;
- dissolution;
- compulsory buy-out;
- preemptive rights;
- restrictions on transfers of shares; and,
- refusal of a party to participate.

IRS Form 2553

If your corporation is to be taxed as an S corporation, you must file **IRS Form 2553** with the IRS within seventy-five days of incorporation. As a practical, matter you should sign and file this at your incorporation meeting; otherwise, you may forget. **IRS Form 2553** is included in this book. (see form 12, p.221.) To make the S corporation status "official," you should also adopt a corporate **Resolution Adopting S corporation Status** (see form 15, p.233) and keep it in your minute book.

Corporate Supplies

A corporation needs to keep a permanent record of its legal affairs. This includes the original charter; minutes of all meetings; records of the stock issued, transferred and cancelled; fictitious names registered; and any other legal matters. The records are usually kept in a ring binder. Any ring binder will do, but it is possible to purchase a specially prepared *corporate kit* that has the name of the corporation printed on it and usually contains forms such as minutes, stock certificates, etc. Most of these items are included with this book so purchasing such a kit is unnecessary unless you want to have a fancy leather binder or specially printed stock certificates. Some sources for corporate kits are:

Blumberg Excelsior
62 White Street
New York, NY 10013
800-529-6278
http://www.blumberg.com

Corpkit Legal Supplies
email: info@corpkit.com
888-888-9120
http://www.corpkit.com

Corpex
1440 Fifth Avenue
Bayshore, NY 11706
800-221-8181
email: corpex@corpexnet.com

One thing that is not included with this book is a *corporate seal*. This must be specially made for each corporation. Most corporations use a metal seal like a notary's seal to emboss the paper. These can be ordered from many office supply companies. In recent years, many have been using rubber stamps for corporate seals. These are cheaper, lighter, and easier to read. Rubber stamp seals can also be ordered from office supply stores, printers, and specialized rubber stamp companies. The corporate seal should contain the full, exact name of the corporation, the word "SEAL," and the year of incorporation. It may be round or rectangular.

Corporations are no longer required to issue stock certificates to represent shares of ownership. However, as a practical matter, it is a good idea to do so. This shows some formality and gives each person tangible evidence of ownership. If you do issue shares, the face of each certificate must show the corporate name; that the corporation was organized under Delaware law; the name of the shareholder(s); and the number, class, and series of the stock. The certificate must be signed by one or more officers designated by the bylaws or the board of directors.

If there are two or more classes or series of stock, the front or back of the certificate must disclose that upon request and without charge the corporation will provide to the shareholder the preferences, limitations, and relative rights of each class or series; the preferences of any preferred stock; and the board of directors' authority to determine rights for any subsequent classes or series. Any restrictions must be stated on the certificate, or a statement must be included that they are available without charge.

The stock certificates can be fancy, or they can be typed or even handwritten. STOCK CERTIFICATE forms are included in Appendix D of this book. (see form 18, p.239.)

NOTE: *For professional associations, the following statement should be typed on the certificate: "The transfer of the shares represented by this certificate is restricted by the bylaws of the corporation."*

LLC PAPERWORK 5

This chapter explains the paperwork you must file which is specific to a forming a limited liability company. If you are forming a corporation, you should ignore this chapter, use the instructions in Chapter 4, and go on to Chapter 6.

CERTIFICATE OF FORMATION

The act which creates a limited liability company is the filing of a CERTIFICATE OF FORMATION with the Secretary of State in Dover. (see form 28, p.267.) Some LLCs have long, elaborate certificates that spell out numerous powers and functions, but most of this is unnecessary. The powers of LLCs are spelled out in Delaware law (see Section 18-106 in Appendix A) and do not have to be repeated. The main reason to keep the CERTIFICATE OF FORMATION short is to avoid having to amend it later. By putting all but the basics in an operating agreement, you can make changes in the structure much more easily. The CERTIFICATE OF FORMATION (form 28, p.267) is as simple as possible for this reason.

Delaware law requires that only two things be included in the CERTIFICATE OF FORMATION: the name of the LLC and the name and address of the registered agent (at the registered office). Everything else can be in the management agreement. These are the requirements:

Name of the limited liability company. The company must include one of the following designations as part of the name:

- Limited Liability Company;
- L.L.C.; or,
- LLC.

It must be different from other registered companies or have permission from any to which it is too similar. It *may* contain any of the following words or their abbreviation:

- Association;
- Company;
- Club;
- Foundation;
- Fund;
- Institute;
- Limited;
- Society;
- Syndicate;
- Trust; and,
- Union.

Name and address of the registered agent. The name and street address in the state of Delaware of the registered agent must be provided. If you will not be using your own office in Delaware, you will need to make arrangements with a registered agent in the state. Some of those that provide this service are listed in Appendix B.

FORM

The CERTIFICATE OF FORMATION need not be on any certain form. It can be typed on blank paper or can be on a fill-in-the-blank form. If you type the form, it must be on 8-1/2 by 11 inch paper, have one inch margins on each side, two inches at the top, and 1-1/5 inches at the bottom. It can be filed with the Secretary of State of Delaware by fax, mail, or courier.

Division of Corporations
John G. Townsend Building
401 Federal Street, Suite 4
Dover, DE 19901
Fax: 302-739-5831

EXECUTION AND FILING

The **CERTIFICATE OF FORMATION** must be signed by the incorporator in black ink and dated. You should use the **DOCUMENT FILING SHEET.** (see form 1, p.185.)

OPERATING AGREEMENT

One thing an LLC must decide is if it will be managed by all the members or a limited number of managers. If it is to be run by managers, there may be one or more and they may or may not be members.

In either case, it is important to have a written agreement spelling out the rights and duties of the members and managers, if any. This is also a good document in which to include other rules governing the LLC. Even if an LLC has only one member, an operating agreement should be signed to formalize the LLC and make it clear that the member is not personally liable for the debts of the business.

The law of LLCs is very new. Since corporations which do not follow procedures can be pierced (and their shareholders held liable), it is possible that a court may treat an LLC similarly. Therefore, following the old formula is the safest. Of course, if you set up procedures and do not follow them, this could backfire and a court could use that as a reason to impose liability.

MEMBERSHIP OPERATING AGREEMENT

The **MEMBER-MANAGED OPERATING AGREEMENT** in Appendix D is a generic membership operating agreement. (see form 30, p.273.) Use this form if your LLC will have one member or if it will have two or more members and be managed by all the members.

This form has basic terms which can be useful to most businesses. If all of the terms apply to your business you should execute a copy and keep it with your company records.

NOTE: *If there are other terms you would like to include in your agreement, you can add them in paragraph 21 or you can draw up an addendum to the membership agreement.*

MANAGEMENT OPERATING AGREEMENT

The **MANAGEMENT OPERATING AGREEMENT** in appendix D is a generic management agreement. (see form 31, p.275.) Use this form if your LLC will have two or more members and be managed by a limited number of members or by someone who is not a member.

This form has basic terms which can be useful to most businesses. If all of the terms apply to your business, you should execute a copy and keep it with your company records.

NOTE: *If there are other terms you would like to include in your agreement, you can add them in paragraph 21 or you can draw up an addendum to the membership agreement.*

The operating agreements both use a **SCHEDULE A TO OPERATING AGREEMENT** to include the specific information for your company. (see form 32, p.277.)

IRS Form 8832

IRS FORM 8832 (form 29, p.269) is used by the IRS to allow LLCs to chose their tax status. It is basically a choice between partnership taxation and corporate taxation. For a single-member LLC, it is a choice between sole proprietorship taxation and corporate taxation.

The difference is that a sole proprietorship or partnership is not taxed at all, and a corporation is treated like a separate taxpayer. A sole proprietorship or partnership just reports its income and expenses, and the proprietor or partners report the net profit or loss on their personal tax return. A corporation files a tax return and pays tax on any profits. If it distributes any of the profits to the members, those profits are taxed again. Therefore, in most cases, it is better not to choose corporate taxation.

One way around the double taxation is if all of the profits can be paid to the members as salary; they are deductible and then the corporation has no profit on which to pay tax. The problem arises when the company makes more money than would be reasonable to pay as salaries. The IRS can then impose extra corporate taxation on the excess amounts.

If you decide to be taxed as a corporation, you should file **IRS FORM 8832** with the IRS. If you wish to pass through the income as a sole proprietor or partnership, you should fill out **IRS FORM 8832** and give a copy to each member to file with his or her annual tax return. It does not need to be filed with the IRS by the LLC if you elect *pass-through status*.

6 START-UP PROCEDURES

This chapter contains the steps to start your Delaware business after you have prepared either the corporate forms in Chapter 4 or the limited liability company forms in Chapter 5.

REGISTERING WITH YOUR HOME STATE

Once you have formed your Delaware corporation or LLC, you must register it as a foreign corporation in the state in which you will have your main office (and any other states in which you will be doing business). This usually requires filling out a simple form and paying the filing fee. You must contact your state corporation division (usually the Secretary of State) to obtain this form. The addresses of these offices for all fifty states are included in Appendix C of this book.

You can download the forms for some states from the Internet, others will send them if you call, and the more backward ones require you to send a letter. You should send for this material right away because some states take weeks to send it.

Check to see exactly what your state requires for registration (it might be a certified copy of your corporate or LLC document or a certificate of status) and be sure to get the right form from Delaware. Once your company has been successfully registered in your state, you will be legal to do business.

Organizational Meeting

The real birth of the business takes place at the organizational meeting of the corporation or LLC. This is when the payment is made for the stock or membership interests and the officers and directors or members are named.

As discussed earlier in the book, the idea behind an LLC is that not as much formality is need as for a corporation. However, the more formal an LLC conducts itself, the less likely that the members will have to face questions of liability. So it is best to use formal procedures for the LLC whenever it is not too inconvenient.

Usually minutes, tax forms, and other forms are prepared before the organizational meeting and are used as a script for the meeting. They are then signed at the end of the meeting. Otherwise, they may be forgotten until it is too late.

Agenda for a Corporation

The following is the usual agenda for a corporation:

- signing the **Waiver of Notice of Organizational Meeting** (form 13);
- noting the persons present in minutes;
- presentation and acceptance of a copy of the articles of incorporation;
- election of directors;
- adoption of bylaws (form 10 or form 11);
- election of officers;
- presentation and acceptance of corporate seal;
- presentation and acceptance of stock certificate (form 18);
- designation of bank (see **Banking Resolution,** form 4);

- acceptance of OFFER TO PURCHASE STOCK, OFFER TO SELL STOCK (form 16) (Use form 6, BILL OF SALE, if property is traded for stock.);
- RESOLUTION TO REIMBURSE EXPENSES (form 5);
- adoption of special resolutions such as S corporation status (see **IRS FORM 2553** (form 12) and RESOLUTION ADOPTING S CORPORATION STATUS (form 15); and,
- adjournment.

The stock certificates are usually issued at the end of the meeting, but in some cases, such as when a prospective shareholder does not yet have money to pay for them, they are issued when full payment is received.

To issue the stock, complete the STOCK CERTIFICATES at the end of this book by adding the name of the corporation, a statement that the corporation is organized under the laws of Delaware, the number of shares the certificate represents, and the person to whom the certificate is issued. Each certificate should be numbered in order to keep track of them. A record of the stock issuance should be made on the STOCK TRANSFER LEDGER. (see form 17, p.237.)

AGENDA FOR AN LLC

The following is the usual agenda for an LLC:

- note persons present in minutes;
- presentation and acceptance of a copy of the certificate of formation;
- presentation and acceptance of MEMBER-MANAGED OPERATING AGREEMENT or MANAGEMENT OPERATING AGREEMENT (form 30 or form 31, plus SCHEDULE A TO OPERATING AGREEMENT, form 32);
- presentation and acceptance of **IRS FORM 8832** (form 29);
- designation of bank (see BANKING RESOLUTION, form 4);
- RESOLUTION TO REIMBURSE EXPENSES (form 5); and,
- adjournment.

Records Book

After the organizational meeting, you should set up your company records book, sometimes called the minute book. As noted on page 36, this can be a fancy leather book or a simple ring binder.

CORPORATIONS

The minute book for a corporation usually contains the following:

- a title page ("Company Records of ______________");
- a table of contents;
- the letter from the Delaware Secretary of State acknowledging receipt and filing of the articles of incorporation;
- a copy of the articles of incorporation;
- the letter from the local Secretary of State acknowledging registration as a foreign company doing business in the state;
- a copy of the document filed with the local state to register as a foreign corporation able to transact business in the state;
- a copy of any fictitious name registration;
- a copy of any trademark registration;
- WAIVER OF NOTICE OF ORGANIZATIONAL MEETING;
- MINUTES OF ORGANIZATIONAL MEETING;
- bylaws;
- sample STOCK CERTIFICATE;
- offers to purchase stock;
- tax forms:
  - **IRS FORM SS-4** and Employer Identification Number certificate
  - **IRS FORM 2553** and acceptance; and,
- stock ledger.

LLCs The minute book for an LLC usually contains the following:

- a title page ("Company Records of ______________");
- a table of contents;
- the letter from the Secretary of State acknowledging receipt and filing of the certificate of formation;
- a copy of the certificate of formation;
- the letter from the local Secretary of State acknowledging registration as a foreign company doing business in the state;
- a copy of the document filed with the local state to register as a foreign LLC able to transact business;
- a copy of any fictitious name registration;
- a copy of any trademark registration;
- a copy of the operating agreement;
- tax forms:
  - **IRS Form SS-4** and Employer Identification Number certificate
  - **IRS Form 8832**; and,
- a list of members names and addresses.

Bank Accounts

A corporation must have a bank account. Checks payable to a corporation cannot be cashed—they must be deposited into an account.

Unfortunately, many banks charge ridiculous rates to corporations for the right to put their money in the bank. You can tell how much extra a corporation is being charged when you compare a corporate account to a personal account with similar activity.

For similar balance and activity, an individual might earn $6 interest for the month while a corporation pays $40 in bank fees. Surely the bank is not losing money on every personal account. Therefore, the corporate account is simply generating $46 more in profit for the bank.

Usually, there is a complicated scheme of fees with charges for each transaction. Many banks today are even bold enough to charge companies for the right to make a deposit! (Twenty-five cents for the deposit plus ten cents for each check that is deposited. Deposit thirty checks and this will cost you $3.25!) Often the customer is granted an interest credit on the balance in the account, but it is usually small and if the credit is larger than the charges, you lose the excess.

Fortunately, some banks have set up reasonable fees for small corporations such as charging no fees if a balance of $1,000 or $2,500 is maintained. Because the fees can easily amount to hundreds of dollars a year, it pays to shop around. Even if the bank is relatively far from the business, using bank-by-mail can make the distance meaningless. But don't be surprised if a bank with low fees raises them.

As the banking industry got deeper into trouble, fewer and fewer banks were offering reasonable fees for corporate checking accounts. Even with their balance sheets improving, they are not eager to give up this new source of wealth. Nonetheless, you can usually find loopholes if you use your imagination. One trick is to open a checking account and a money market account. (Money market accounts pay higher interest and do not charge for making deposits. You can only write three checks a month but you can usually make unlimited withdrawals.) Make all of your deposits into the money market account and just pay bills out of the regular checking account, transferring funds as needed. However, banks are catching on to this and starting to charge for deposits into money market accounts. You still have the option of opening one at a stock brokerage firm.

Another way to save money in bank charges is to order checks from a private source rather than through the bank. These are usually much cheaper than those the bank offers because the bank makes a profit on the check printing. If the bank officer for some reason says it cannot be done when you are opening the account, just wait until your first batch runs out and switch over without telling the bank. They probably will not even notice, as long as you get the checks printed correctly. While most "business checks" are large, there is no reason you cannot use small "personal size" checks for your business. They are easier to carry around and work just as well. (A study reported in *Business Week* in 1999 showed that attempts by banks to raise fees did not work and that when fees were raised customers switched banks, thereby lowering the banks' income.)

All you should need to open a business bank account is a copy of your certificate of incorporation (for a corporation) or certificate of formation (for an LLC) and your federal tax identification number. Some banks, however, want more, and they sometimes do not even know what it is they want. If you have trouble opening the account, you can use the **Banking Resolution** (form 4, p.197), or you can make up a similar form.

Licenses

In some states, counties and municipalities are authorized to levy a license tax on the "privilege" of doing business. Before opening your business, you should obtain a county occupational license, and if you will be working within a city, a city occupational license. Businesses that work in several cities, such as builders, must obtain a license from each city in which they work. This does not have to be done until you actually begin a job in a particular city.

County occupational licenses can usually be obtained from the tax collector in the county courthouse. City licenses are usually available at city hall. Be sure to find out if zoning allows your type of business before buying or leasing property because the licensing departments will check the zoning before issuing your license.

Home Businesses

Problems occasionally arise when persons attempt to start a business in their home. Small new businesses often cannot afford to pay rent for commercial space, and cities often try to forbid business in residential areas. Obtaining a county occupational license often gives notice to the city that a business is being conducted in a residential area.

Some people avoid the problem by starting their businesses without occupational licenses, figuring that the penalties are nowhere near the cost of office space. Others get the county license and ignore the city rules. If a person has commercial trucks and equipment parked on his property, there will probably be complaints by neighbors and the city will most likely take legal action. But if a person's business consists merely of making phone calls out of the home and keeping supplies inside the house, the problem may never arise.

If a problem does surface regarding a home business that does not disturb the neighbors, a good argument can be made that the zoning law that prohibits the business is unconstitutional. When zoning laws were first instituted they were not meant to stop people from doing things in a residence that had historically been part of the life in a residence. Consider a painter. Should a zoning law prohibit a person from sitting in his home and painting pictures? If he sells them for a living is there a difference? Can the government force him to rent commercial space?

Similar arguments can be made for many home businesses. But court battles with a city are expensive and probably not worth the effort for a small business. The best course of action is to keep a low profile. Using a post office box is sometimes helpful in diverting attention away from the residence. However, the Secretary of State and the occupational license administrator will want a street address. There should be no problem using a residential address and explaining to the city that it is merely the corporate address and that no business is conducted on the premises.

Capital Structure and Selling Stock 7

Each corporation or LLC must be funded, and there are strict federal and state laws governing that. Read this chapter carefully to help gain the background knowledge on capital and stocks.

Capital Structure

There is no hard and fast rule as to how much capital you should put into a new corporation or LLC. The more you put in as capital, the more you have at risk in the business, so you would want to put as little as possible. But if you put in too little, a court might some day say you were undercapitalized and find you personally liable for company debts, just as it could for a corporation. Also, there could be tax problems with not counting enough of your contributions as capital or for contributing appreciated property. These matters should be discussed with a tax specialist.

If you are starting a small business which does not need a lot of expensive equipment, a thousand or a few thousand dollars would be a safe amount with which to start. If you do need to buy expensive equipment, and the company can borrow the money from a third party to cover it, you would probably be safe as well. But if you need to purchase expensive equipment and personally loan the money to the company rather than contribute it as capital, you should weigh the risks of a lawsuit and consider consulting an attorney or accountant who specializes in business start-ups.

One thing to keep in mind is that if you do not put in the amount of capital you state in your initial agreement, and are later sued or file bankruptcy, you may be required to come up with any amount unpaid.

For a corporation, before any stock is issued, the purchaser should submit an **Offer to Purchase Stock.** (see form 16, p.235.) The offer states that it is made—pursuant to Internal Revenue Code, Section 1244. The advantage of this section is that in the event the business fails or the value of the stock drops, the shareholder can write off up to $50,000 ($100,000 for married couples) as ordinary income, rather than as a long term capital loss which would be limited to $3,000 a year.

Some thought should be given to the way in which the ownership of the stock or membership interests will be held. Stock owned in one person's name alone is subject to probate upon death. Making two persons joint owners of the stock (joint tenants with full rights of survivorship) would avoid probate upon the death of one of them. However, taking a joint owner's name off in the event of a disagreement (such as divorce) could be troublesome.

Where a couple jointly operates a business, joint ownership would be best. But where one person is the sole party involved in the business, the desire to avoid probate should be weighed against the risk of losing half the business in a divorce. Another way to avoid probate is to put ownership of the stock in a living trust. You are allowed to list your securities as "pay on death" or "transfer on death" in about half of the states. This avoids probate as well.

Payment for Interests

Stock or membership interests may be paid for with money, property, services, or a promissory note. The important thing to remember is that if a person fails to make the specified payment or takes return of the payment, then he or she may be liable to the company or its creditors for the full amount that should have been paid.

LLCs Some other things for an LLC to consider are:

- If a member trades services for an interest in the capital of the company, he must pay income tax on the value of interest at the time the services are exchanged for the interest. (If the interest is only a share of future profits, the tax does not have to be paid until the profits are received.)
- When appreciated property is traded to an LLC in exchange for a membership interest, the tax basis of the property carries over to the membership interest. Taxes on the appreciation are paid when the member sells his LLC interest.
- If the LLC sells the property, it may have to pay a tax on the amount received over the contributor's basis.

CORPORATIONS The most important thing for a corporation to know is that Section 351 of the IRS Code allows tax-free exchange of property for stock if the persons receiving the stock for the property or for cash *end up owning* at least eighty percent of the voting and other stock in the corporation. If more than twenty percent of the stock is issued in exchange for services instead of property and cash, the transfers of property will be taxable and treated as a sale for cash. Also, if the stock has par value and the payment is in cash, then the payment should not be less than par value but may be more.

Tax rules are complicated and ever-changing. If you will be doing creative financing you should consult with a tax expert or a tax guide.

SECURITIES LAWS

The issuance of securities is subject to both federal and state securities laws. A *security* is equity interest in a company and debt (notes, bonds, etc.). The laws covering securities are so broad that any instrument which represents an investment in an enterprise, where the investor is relying on the efforts of others for profit, is considered a security. Even a promissory note has been held to be a security. Once an investment is determined to involve a security, strict rules apply. There can be criminal penalties, and civil damages can also be awarded to purchasers, if the rules are not followed.

The rules are designed to protect people who put up money as an investment in a business. Many people lost their life savings in the stock market crash in 1929, and the government wants to be sure that it will not happen again. Unfortunately, the laws can also make it difficult to raise capital for honest businesses.

The goal of the laws covering sales of securities is that investors be given full disclosure of the risks involved in an investment. To accomplish this, the law usually requires that the securities must either be registered with the federal Securities and Exchange Commission or a similar state regulatory body, and that lengthy disclosure statements be compiled and distributed.

The law is complicated and strict compliance is required. The penalties are so harsh that most lawyers will not handle securities matters. You most likely would not be able to get through the registration process on your own. But, like your decision to form your corporation or LLC without a lawyer, you may wish to consider some alternatives when attempting to raise capital without a lawyer:

- Borrow the money as a personal loan from friends or relatives. The disadvantage is that you will have to pay them back personally if the business fails. However, you may have to do that anyway if they are close relatives or if you do not follow the securities laws.

- Tailor your stock issuance to fall within the exemptions in the securities laws. There are some exemptions in the securities laws for small businesses that may apply to your transaction. (The anti-fraud provisions always apply, even if the transaction is exempt from registration.) Some exemptions are explained below, but you should make at least one appointment with a securities lawyer to be sure you have covered everything and that there have not been any changes in the law. You can often pay for an hour or so of a securities lawyer's time for $100 or $200 and just ask questions about your plans. He or she can tell you what not to do and what your options are. You can then make an informed decision.

Federal Exemptions From Securities Laws

In most situations where one person, a husband and wife, or a few partners run a business, and all parties are active in the enterprise, securities laws do not apply to their issuance of stock to themselves. As a practical matter, you probably will not get in trouble if your father or aunt wants to put up some money for some stock in your business. They probably will not seek triple damages and criminal penalties if your business fails.

However, you may wish to obtain money from additional investors to enable your business to grow. This can be done in many circumstances as long as you follow the rules carefully. In some cases, you do not have to file anything with the SEC, but in others, you must file a notice.

Federal Private Placement Exemption

If you sell interests in your business to a small group of people without any advertising, you can fall into the private offering exemption if all of the following are true:

- offers are only made to persons who are financially astute, are participants in the business, or have a substantial net worth;
- no advertising or general solicitation is used to promote the stock;
- the number of persons to whom the offers are made is limited;
- the shares are bought for investment and not for immediate resale;
- the persons to whom the stock is offered are given all relevant information (including financial information) regarding the

issuance and the corporation. (Again, there are numerous court cases explaining each aspect of these rules, including such questions as what is a "financially astute" person.); and,

- a filing claiming the exemption is made upon the United States Securities and Exchange Commission.

FEDERAL INTRASTATE OFFERING EXEMPTION

If you only offer your securities to residents of one state, you may be exempt from federal securities laws. This is because federal laws usually only apply to interstate commerce. Intrastate offerings are covered by SEC Rule 147. If it is followed carefully, your sale will be exempt from federal registration.

In recent years, the Securities and Exchange Commission (SEC) has liberalized the rules in order to make it easier for business to grow. Under *Regulation D*, adopted by the Securities and Exchange Commission, there are three types of exemptions under rules 504, 505, and 506.

FEDERAL SMALL OFFERINGS EXEMPTIONS

Offering of securities of up to $1,000,000 in a twelve month period can be exempt under SEC Rule 504. Offers can be made to any number of persons, no specific information must be provided and investors do not have to be sophisticated.

Under SEC Rule 505 offering of up to $5,000,000 can be made in a twelvemonth period but no public advertising may be used and only thirty-five non-accredited investors may purchase stock. Any number of *accredited investors* may purchase stock. Accredited investors are sophisticated individuals with high net worth or high income, large trusts or investment companies or persons involved in the business.

SEC Rule 506 has no limit on the amount of money that may be raised but, like Rule 505, does not allow advertising and limits non-accredited investors to thirty-five.

State Securities Laws

One reason there are exemptions from federal securities laws is that there are so many state laws covering securities that additional registration is not needed. Every state has securities laws, which are called *blue sky laws*. If you wish to offer your stock in all fifty states, you must be registered in all fifty states unless you can fit into one of the exemptions. However, exemptions are very limited.

Typical State Law Private Placement Exemption

The most common one is the private placement exemption. This can apply if all of the following are true:

- there are thirty-five or fewer purchasers of shares;
- no commissions are paid to anyone to promote the stock;
- no advertising or general solicitation is used to promote the stock;
- all material information (including financial information) regarding the stock issuance and the company is given to or accessible to all shareholders; and,
- a three day right of rescission is given.

These rules may sound simple on the surface, but there are many more rules, regulations and court cases explaining each one in more detail. For example, what does "thirty-five persons" mean? Sounds simple, but it can mean more than thirty-five persons. Spouses, persons whose net worth exceeds a million dollars, and founders of the company may not be counted in some circumstances.

As you can see, the exemption does not give you much latitude in raising money. Therefore, you will have to register if you wish to raise money from a wider group of people. (To find out more about your state's requirements, you should contact the securities commission of your state. The address is in the back of this chapter.)

Another good source of information of the securities laws of all fifty states is the *Blue Sky Reporter*, a multi-volume loose leaf service which summarizes the securities laws of the states. A copy should be available in most law libraries.

Internet Stock Sales

With the advent of the Internet, promoters of business interests have a new way of reaching large numbers of people, most of whom are financially able to afford investments in securities. However, all securities laws apply to the Internet and they are being enforced. Recently, state attorneys general have issued cease and desist orders to promoters not registered in their states.

Under current law, you must be registered in a state in order to sell stock to its residents. If you are not registered in a state, you must turn down any residents from that state who want to buy your stock.

You may wonder how the famous Spring Street Brewing raised $1.6 million for its Wit Beer on the Internet. The main reason they were successful was because their president is a securities lawyer and could prepare his own prospectus to file with the SEC and the states. That would have cost anyone else about $100,000. Also, most of their stock sales were inspired by newspaper and magazine articles about them and not from the Internet.

Some Internet sites which may be helpful in raising capital are:

- America's Business Funding Directory:
  http://www.businessfinance.com
- Angel Capital Electronic Network (SBA):
  http://www.sba.gov
- FinanceHub:
  http://www.financehub.com
- NVST:
  http://www.nvst.com

State Securities Registration Offices

The following are the addresses of the offices that can supply you with information on securities registration requirements for each state.

Alabama Securities Commission
770 Washington Street, Suite 570
Montgomery, AL 36130-4700
Phone: 334-242-2984 or 800-222-1253
Fax: 334-242-0240 or 334-353-4690

Alaska Department of Commerce
and Economic Development
Division of Banking, Securities,
and Corporations
P.O. Box 110807
Juneau, AK 99811-0807
Phone: 907-465-2521
Fax: 907-465-2549
www.dced.state.ak.us/bsc

Arizona Corporation Commission
Securities Division
1300 West Washington Street, 3d Floor
Phoenix, AZ 85007
Phone: 602-542-4242
Fax: 602-542-3583
http://www.ccsd.cc.state.az.us

Arkansas Securities Department
Heritage West Building
201 East Markham, Suite 300
Little Rock, AR 72201
Phone: 501-324-9260
Fax: 501-324-9268

California Department of Corporations
Securities Regulation Division
320 West 4th Street, Suite 750
Los Angeles, California 90013-2344
Phone: 213-736-3482
Fax: 213-736-3588
http://www.corp.ca.gov/srd/security.htm

Colorado Division of Securities
1580 Lincoln Street, Suite 420
Denver, CO 80203
Phone: 303-894-2320
Fax: 303-861-2126
http://www.dora.state.co.us/securities

Connecticut Securities Division
260 Constitution Plaza
Hartford, CT 06106-1800
Phone: 806-240-8230
Fax: 860-240-8178
http://www.state.ct.us/dob/

Delaware Department of Justice
Division of Securities
820 N. French Street, 5th Floor
Wilmington, DE 19801
Phone: 302-577-2515
Fax: 302-655-0576
http://www.state.de.us/securities/index.htm

District of Columbia
Department of Insurance and Securities Regulation
810 First Street, Suite 701
Washington, DC 20002
Phone: 202-727-8000
Fax: 202-783-3571
www.disr.washingtondc.gov/main.shtm

Florida Division of Securities and Finance
101 E. Gaines Street
Tallahassee, FL 32399-0350
Phone: 850-488-9805
Fax: 850-681-2428
www.dbf.state.fl.us/licensing

Georgia Secretary of State
Securities and Business
Regulation Division
2 Martin Luther King Jr. Drive
Suite 802, West Tower
Atlanta, GA 30334
Phone: 404-656-3920
Fax: 404-657-8410
www.SOS.State.Ga.US/Securities/
or www.georgiasecurities.org

Hawaii Department of Commerce
and Consumer Affairs
Commissioner of Securities
P. O. Box 40
Honolulu, HI 96810
Phone: 808-586-2744
Fax: 808-586-2733
www.state.hi.us/dcca/breq-seu/
compliance.html

Idaho Department of Finance
700 W. State Street, 2nd Floor,
P.O. Box 83720
Boise, ID 83720-0031
Phone: 208-334-2441
Fax: 208-332-8099
www.state.id.us./finance/dof.htm

Illinois Securities Department
Lincoln Tower, Suite 200
520 South Second Street
Springfield, Illinois 62701
Phone: 217-782-2256
Fax: 217-782-8876
www.sos.state.il.us/departments/
securities/securities.html

Indiana Securities Division
302 West Washington Street, Room E-111
Indianapolis, IN 46204
Phone: 317-232-6687 or 800-223-8791
Fax: 317-233-3675
www.IN.gov/sos/securities

Iowa Securities Bureau
Lucas State Office Building, Room 214
Agency Des Moines, IA 50319
Phone: 515-281-4441
Fax: 515-281-6467
www.state.ia.us/

Kansas Securities Commissioner
Office of the Securities Commissioner
618 South Kansas Avenue
Topeka, KS 66603
Phone: 785-296-3307
Fax: 785-296-6872
www.ink.org/public/ksccom

Kentucky Department of
Financial Institutions
1025 Capital Center Drive, Suite 200
Frankfort, KY 40601-3868
Phone: 502-573-3390 or 800-223-2579
Fax: 502-573-8787
www.dfi.state.ky.us

Louisiana Office of Financial Institutions
Securities Division
P.O. Box 94095
Baton Rouge, LA 70804-9095
Phone: 225-925-4660
Fax: 225-925-4548
www.ofi.state.la.us/

Maine Securities Division
Office of Securities
121 State House Station
Bureau of Banking
Augusta, ME 04333
Phone: 207-624-8551
Fax: 207-624-8590
www.state.me.us/pfr/sec/sec_index.htm

Maryland Securities Division
200 Saint Paul Place 20th Floor
Baltimore, MD 21202
Phone: 410-576-6360
www.oaq.state.md.us/securities/index.htm

Massachusetts Securities Division
One Ashburton Place, 17th Floor
Boston, MA 02108
Phone: 617-727-3548 or 800-269-5428
Fax: 617-248-0177
www.state.ma.us/sec/sct/sctidx.htm

Michigan Department of Consumer and Industry Services
Offices of Financial and Insurance Services
P.O. Box 30222
Lansing, MI 48909-7720
Phone: 517-373-0220 or 877-999-6442
Fax: 517-335-4978
www.cis.state.mi.us/ofis

Minnesota Department of Commerce
85 7th Place East, Suite 500
St. Paul, MN 55101
Phone: 651-296-4973
www.commerce.state.mn.us/pages/securitiesmain.htm

Mississippi Securities Division
P.O. Box 136
Jackson, MS 39205
Phone: 601-359-1350
Fax: 601-359-1499
http://www.sos.state.ms.us/busserv/securities/securities.html

Office of the Missouri Secretary of State
Securities Division
600 West Main St., 2nd Floor
Jefferson City, MO 65101
www.sos.state.mo.ps/securities/default.asp

Montana Office of the State Auditor
Securities Division
P.O. Box 4009
Helena, MT 59604-4009
Phone: 406-444-5222
Fax: 406-444-5558
http://www.state.mt.us/sao/securities/properly_liscensed.htm

Nebraska Bureau of Securities
The Atrium, Suite 311
1200 N Street
P.O. Box 95006
Lincoln, NE 68509-5006
Phone: 402-471-3445
www.ndbf.org/sec.htm

Nevada Securities Division
555 E. Washington Avenue, Suite 5200
Las Vegas, NV 89101
Phone: 702-486-2440
Fax: 702-486-2452
www.sos.state.nv.us/securities/index.htm

New Hampshire Bureau of Securities Regulation
State House, Room 204
Concord, NH 03301-4989
Phone: 603-271-1463
Fax: 603-271-7933
http://webster.state.nh.us/sos/securities

New Jersey Bureau of Securities
153 Halsey Street
P.O. Box 47029
Newark, NJ 07101
Phone: 973-504-3600
http://www.state.nj.us/lps/ca/bocs.htm

New Mexico Securities Division
Regulation and Licensing Department
725 St. Michaels Drive
Santa Fe, NM 87505
Phone: 505-827-7140
http://www.rld.state.nm.us/sec/index.htm

New York State Attorney General's Office
120 Broadway, 23rd. Floor
New York, NY 10271
Phone: 212-416-8200
Fax: 212-416-8222
www.oag.state.ny.us/investors/investors.html

North Carolina Securities Division
Department of the Secretary of State
P.O. Box 29622
Raleigh, NC 27626-0622
Phone: 919-733-3924
Fax: 919-733-5172
www.secretary.state.nc.us/sec

North Dakota Securities Commission
State Capitol, 5th Floor
600 East Avenue
Bismarck, ND 58505-0510
Phone: 701-328-2910
Fax: 701-328-2946
www.state.nd.us/securities/

Ohio Department of Commerce
Division of Securities
77 South High Street, 22nd. Floor
Columbus, OH 43215
Phone: 614-644-7381
www.securities.state.oh.us/

Oklahoma Department of Securities
First National Center
120 North Robinson, Suite 860
Oklahoma City, OK 73102
Phone: 405-280-7700
Fax: 405-280-7742
www.securities.state.ok.us

Oregon Department of Consumer
and Business Services
Division of Finance and
Corporate Securities
350 Winter Street NE, Room 410
Salem, OR 97301-3880
Phone: 503-378-4140
Fax: 503-947-7862
www.cbs.state.or.us/external/dfcs

Pennsylvania Division of
Corporation Finance
Pennsylvania Securities Commission
Eastgate Office Building, 2nd Floor,
1010 North 7th Street
Harrisburg, PA 17102-1410
Phone: 717-787-8061
Fax: 717-783-5122
www.psc.state.pa.us/

Puerto Rico Commissioner of
Financial Institutions
Centro Europa Building
1492 Ponce de Leon Avenue, Suite 600
San Juan, PR 00907-4127
Phone: 787-723-8445
Fax: 787-723-3857
www.cif.gov.pr/html/securities.html

South Carolina Securities Division
P.O. Box 11350
Columbia, SC 29211
Phone: 803-734-9916
www.scsecurities.org/index.html

South Dakota Division of Securities
118 West Capital
Pierre, SD 57501
Phone: 605-773-4823
Fax: 605-773-5953
www.state.sd.us/dcr/securities/security.htm

Tennessee Department of Commerce and
Insurance Securities Division
500 James Robertson Parkway, Suite 680
Nashville, TN 37243-0583
Phone: 615-741-3187
Fax: 615-532-8375
www.state.tn.us/commerce/securdiv.html

Texas State Securities Board
P.O. Box 13167
Austin, Texas 78711-3167
Phone: 512-305-8300
Fax: 512-305-8310
www.ssb.state.tx.us

Utah Department of Commerce
Division of Securities
Box 146760
Salt Lake City, Utah 84114-6766
Phone: 801-530-6600
Fax: 801-530-6980
www.securities.state.ut.us

Vermont Securities Division
Department of Banking, Insurance, Securities and Health Care Administration
89 Main Street
Drawer 20
Montpelier, VT 05620-3101
Phone: 802-828-3420
www.bishca.state.vt.us/securitiesdiv/securindex.htm

Virginia State Corporation Commission
P.O. Box 1197
Richmond, VA 23218
Phone: 804-371-9051
Fax: 804-371-9911
www.states.va.us/scc/division/srf/webpages/homepagejavab.htm

Washington Department of Financial Institutions Securities Division
P.O. Box 9033
Olympia, Washington 98507-9033
Phone: 360-902-8766
Fax: 360-586-5068
www.dfi.wa.gov/sd/default.htm

West Virginia Securities Division
State Capitol Building 1
Room W-100
Charleston, WV 25305
Phone: 304-558-2257
Fax: 304-558-4211
www.wvauditor.com

Wisconsin Division of Securities
P.O. Box 1768
Madison, WI 53701-1768
Phone: 608-266-1064
Fax: 608-264-7979
http://www.wdfi.org/fi/securities

Wyoming Securities Division
Secretary of the State
State Capital Building
Cheyenne, WY 82002-0020
Phone: 307-777-7378
Fax: 307-777-6217
http://soswy.state.wy.us/securiti/securiti.htm

8 Running a Corporation or an LLC

Just as there are specific steps to start up a corporation or LLC, there are also steps to the day-to-day activities. Records must be kept, and certain meetings must be held. This chapter will give you the basics on these topics.

Day-to-Day Activities

There are not many differences between running a corporation, an LLC, or any other type of business. The most important point to remember is to keep the business separate from your personal affairs. Do not use company checks or credit cards to pay your personal expenses, even if you pay it back. Do not commingle your personal funds with company funds.

Another important point to remember is to always refer to the corporation as a corporation or the LLC as a limited liability company. Always use the designation "Inc." or "Corp."or "LLC" on everything. Always sign company documents with your title (president, secretary, member, etc.). If you do not, you may lose your protection from liability. (There have been many cases where a person forgot to put his title after his name and was held personally liable for a corporate debt.)

Company Records

Corporations

Delaware statutes do not contain a detailed list of what records must be maintained by a corporation, but from over a hundred years of corporate law, we can see what records are important. There are a few statutes which require that shareholders have access to records.

Minutes. Minutes should be kept of all meetings of the board of directors and the shareholders, whether they are regular meetings or special meetings.

Stockholders. Under General Corporation Law of Delaware. Section 219, an alphabetical list of stockholders who are entitled to vote must be made available at least ten days before any meeting of stockholders.

Accounting. The Internal Revenue Code requires businesses to maintain accurate accounting records.

Inspection. Under General Corporation Law of Delaware. Section 220, any stockholder or his agent or attorney has the right to inspect the records of the corporation. The stock holder can get a court order if the corporation refuses.

Form. Under General Corporation Law of Delaware. Section 224, the records of a corporation can be kept in any information storage device as long as they can be converted into legible written form within a reasonable time.

LLCs

Section 18-305(a) of the Limited Liability Company Act (LLCA) lists information which must be made available to the members upon demand. Besides any information which may be "just and reasonable" this specifically includes:

- true and full information regarding the status of the business and the financial condition;
- federal, state, and local income tax returns;
- the name and address of each member and manager;

- any written LLC agreement, certificate of formation, amendments, and any related powers of attorney; and,
- true and full information regarding the cash and agreed value of property contributed or agreed to be contributed by each member.

Meetings

While corporations are required to have annual meetings of shareholders and directors, LLCs are more flexible and can decide to forgo meetings.

Corporations A corporation must hold annual meetings of the shareholders and the directors. These meetings may be formal and held in a restaurant or they may be informal and held in the swimming pool. A sole shareholder and director can hold them in his mind without reciting all the verbiage or taking a formal vote. But the important thing is that the meetings are held and that written minutes are kept. Regular minutes and meetings are evidence that the corporation is legitimate if the issue ever comes up in court. Forms for minutes for the annual meetings are included with this book in Appendix D. (see form 21, p.253.) You can use them as master copies to photocopy each year. All that needs to be changed is the date, unless you actually change officers or directors or need to take some other corporate action.

When important decisions (such as buying a new headquarters or liquidating the business) must be made by the board or the shareholders between the annual meetings, the corporation can hold special meetings.

Subchapter VII of the statutes (in Appendix A) contains some rules regarding quorums, voting, proxies, and other matters that may come up at meetings.

LLCs LLCs have the flexibility to decide in their operating agreement if and when meetings will be held. Since LLCs are supposed to offer the ability to use less formality, an LLC may not need to ever hold meetings. However, since the law of LLCs is relatively new and to be cautious, holding meetings and keeping minutes is advisable for when big decisions are made.

Distributions

A corporation or LLC is usually free to make any distributions of money or property to its shareholders or members. The exception is if the distribution would make the company insolvent or unable to pay its debts.

Corporations

For the specific rules regarding distributions for corporations see Sections 170 through 174 of the General Corporation Law of Delaware in Appendix A.

LLCs

For specific rules regarding distributions for LLCs see the Limited Liability Company Act, Sections 18-504, 18-601, and 18-604 through 607 in Appendix A.

Annual Reports

Every corporation and LLC must file an annual report with the Secretary of State of Delaware. The form for this will be sent to you and it need only be completed and returned with the filing fee.

At the time of publication, the fee for a corporation is $20 for filing plus the franchise tax (minimum of $30 up to $150,000–see Chapter 4). The annual fee for an LLC is $100.

Employment Requirements

If you will be paying wages to anyone, even just yourself, you will need to comply with all of the employer reporting and withholding laws of both your state and the federal government. Explaining every requirement is beyond the scope of this book, but the following is a summary of most of the requirements.

New hire reporting. To improve the enforcement of child support payments, all employers must report the hiring of each new employee to an agency in the state.

Employment eligibility. To combat the hiring of illegal immigrants, employers must complete Department of Justice form I-9 for each employee.

Federal tax withholding. Social security and income taxes must be withheld from employees wages and deposited to an authorized bank quarterly, monthly, or more often depending on the amount. The initial step is to obtain a form W-4 from each employee upon hiring. (This same form can also be used to fulfill the new hire reporting law discussed previously.)

State withholding. In states that have income taxes, there is usually a withholding and reporting requirement similar to the federal one.

Local withholding. In cities that have income taxes, there is usually a withholding and reporting requirement similar to the federal one.

Unemployment compensation. There are taxes on employee wages (which employers must pay) which must be paid to the state and federal governments regularly for unemployment purposes. Also, employers are required to submit reports quarterly and annually.

Workers' compensation. Depending on the number of employees and type of work, the state may require that workers' compensation insurance be obtained by the employer.

9 Amending a Corporation or an LLC

Sometimes it is necessary to change a part of the forms filed with the secretary of state for a corporation or LLC. This chapter will help you determine how to make such changes.

Corporations

Correction of Instruments

Whenever an instrument which has been filed with the secretary of state is found to be inaccurate or defectively or erroneously executed, sealed or acknowledged, it may be corrected in either of two ways under General Corporation Law of Delaware Section 103(f):

1. by filing a certificate of correction setting out the inaccuracy and providing the correction; or
2. by filing a corrected instrument, designated as a corrected instrument in its heading, specifying the inaccuracy, and setting out the entire instrument in corrected form.

Certificate of Incorporation

Because the certificate of incorporation included in this book is so basic, it will rarely have to be amended. The only reasons for amending it would be to change the name or the number of shares of stock, or to add some special clause such as a higher than majority voting requirement for directors.

If the amendment is made before the corporation has received payment for any shares of its stock, it may be done by a majority of the incorporators if directors were not named in the certificate of incorporation or have not yet been elected. If they were named in the certificate or have been elected, the amendment can be adopted by a majority of those directors. (G.C.L.D., Sec. 241.)

If any payment has been received for the corporation's stock, the amendment must be included in a resolution of the board of directors and voted on by the shareholders. (G.C.L.D., Sec. 242.)

Bylaws. Before a corporation has received payment for any of its stock, the bylaws may be amended or repealed by the incorporators or by the directors. After payment has been received for the stock the shareholders have the power to amend or repeal the bylaws. The directors may amend or repeal the bylaws after the stock has been issued if this power is given to them in the certificate of incorporation. (G.C.L.D., Sec.109.)

In the event of an emergency, such as an attack on the United States, nuclear disaster, or other catastrophe, the board of directors may adopt emergency bylaws. These are subject to change or repeal by the shareholders. (G.C.L.D., Sec. 110.)

Registered Agent or Registered Office. To change the registered agent or registered office, a corporation a resolution to that effect must be passed by the board of directors and a certificate certifying the change, signed by an authorized officer, must be filed with the secretary of state. (G.C.L.D. Sec. 133.)

If the registered agent changes its name or address, it must follow the procedures as outlined in General Corporation Law of Delaware, Section 134.

A registered agent must follow the procedures outlined in General Corporation Law of Delaware, Section 135 if it resigns and appoints a successor.

If a registered agent resigns but does not appoint a successor, it must follow the procedures as outlined in General Corporation Law of Delaware, Section 136.

LLCs

Certificate of Formation. Because the CERTIFICATE OF FORMATION included in this book is so basic, it will rarely have to be amended. The only reasons for amending it would be to change the name, the registered agent or registered office.

Under the Limited Liability Company Act, Section 18-202, the CERTIFICATE OF FORMATION can be amended at any time by filing a *certificate of amendment* with the Secretary of State. This certificate must include the name of the LLC and the amendment. The certificate of amendment must be signed by one manager or member. Any manager or member (if there are no managers) who becomes aware of an error in a CERTIFICATE OF FORMATION is required to file an amendment under the Limited Liability Company Act, Section 18-202(b).

Registered Agent or Registered Office. The registered agent or registered office of an LLC is changed by amending the certificate of formation as explained above.

If the registered agent changes its name or address, it must follow the procedures as outlined in the Limited Liability Company Act, Section 18-104(b).

If a registered agent resigns and appoints a successor, it must follow the procedures outlined in the Limited Liability Company Act, Section 18-104(c).

If a registered agent resigns but does not appoint a successor, it must follow the procedures as outlined in the Limited Liability Company Act, Section 18-104(d).

GLOSSARY

A

annual report. A document filed by a corporation or limited liability company each year usually listing the officers, directors, and registered agent.

articles of incorporation. The document that demonstrates the organization of a corporation, called certificate of incorporation in some states.

articles of organization. The document that demonstrates the organization of a limited liability company.

B

blue sky laws. Laws governing the sales of securities.

bylaws. Rules governing the conduct of affairs of a corporation.

C

C corporation. A corporation that pays taxes on its profits.

common stock. The basic ownership shares of a corporation.

contract. An agreement between two or more parties.

corporation. An organization recognized as a person in the law that is set up to conduct a business owned by shareholders and run by officers and directors.

D

distributions. Money paid out to owners of a corporation or limited liability company.

E

employee. Person who works for another under that person's control and direction.

employer identification number. Number issued by the Internal Revenue Service to identify taxpayers who do not have social security numbers.

estate planning. Preparing such documents as a will, trust and other arrangements to control the passing of one's property at death.

exemption. The ability to sell certain limited types of securities without full compliance with securities registration laws.

F

fictitious name. A name used by a business that is not its personal or legal name.

G

general partnership. A business that is owned by two or more persons.

I

intangible property. Personal property that does not have physical presence, such as the ownership interest in a corporation.

intellectual property. Legal rights to the products of the mind, such as writings, musical compositions, formulas and designs.

L

liability. The legal responsibility to pay for an injury.

limited liability company. An entity recognized as a legal "person" that is set up to conduct a business owned and run by members.

limited liability partnership. An entity recognized as a legal "person" that is set up to conduct a business owned and run by professionals, such as attorneys or doctors.

limited partnership. A business that is owned by two or more persons of which one or more is liable for the debts of the business and one or more has no liability for the debts.

M

membership agreement. A contract controlling the operation of a limited liability company in which the company is run by members.

management agreement. A contract controlling the operation of a limited liability company in which the company is run by its managers.

minutes. Records of the proceedings of corporate meetings.

N

nonprofit corporation. An entity recognized as a legal "person" that is set up to run an operation in which none of the profits are distributed to controlling members.

O

occupational license. A government-issued permit to transact business.

operating agreement. A contract among members of a limited liability company spelling out how the company is to be run.

option. The right to buy stock at a future date, usually at a predetermined price.

organizational meeting. The meeting of the founders of a corporation or limited liability company in which the company is structured and ready to begin business.

P

par value. A value given to newly-issued stock, which used to have legal significance, but now usually does not relate to anything except, in some states, taxation.

partnership. A business formed by two or more persons.

personal property. Any type of property other than land and the structures attached to it.

piercing the corporate veil. When a court ignores the structure of a corporation and holds its owners responsible for its debts or liabilities.

professional association. An entity recognized as a legal "person" that is set up to conduct a business of professionals such as attorneys or doctors.

promoters. Persons who start a business venture and usually offer interests for sale to investors.

proprietorship. A business that is owned by one person.

R

registered agent. The person authorized to accept legal papers for a corporation or limited liability company, sometimes called a resident agent.

resident agent. *See* registered agent.

S

S corporation. A corporation in which the profits are taxed to the shareholders.

securities. Interests in a business such as stocks or bonds.

shareholder agreement. A contract among the owners of a corporation that spells out their rights.

shares. Units of stock in a corporation.

stock. Ownership interests in a corporation.

T

tangible property. Physical personal property such as desks and tables.

trademark. A name or symbol used to identify the source of goods or services.

transferability. The ability to sell shares of stock in a corporation.

U

usury. Charging an interest rate higher than that allowed by law.

W

withholding. Money taken out of an employee's salary and remitted to the government.

Z

zoning. Governmental regulation controlling the use of a piece of real property.

For Further Reference

The following books will provide valuable information to those who are starting new businesses and corporations. Some are out of print, but they are classics that are worth tracking down.

For inspiration to give you the drive to succeed:

Hill, Napoleon, *Think and Grow Rich*. New York: Fawcett Books, 1990.

Karbo, Joe, *The Lazy Man's Way to Riches*. Sunset Beach: F P Publishing, 1974.

Schwartz, David J., *The Magic of Thinking Big*. Fireside, 1987.

For hints on what it takes to be successful:

Carnegie, Dale, *How to Win Friends and Influence People*. New York: Pocket Books, 1994.

Ringer, Robert J., *Looking Out for #1*. New York: Fawcett Books, 1993.

Ringer, Robert J., *Million Dollar Habits*. New York: Fawcett Books, 1991.

Ringer, Robert J., *Winning Through Intimidation*. New York: Fawcett Books, 1993.

For advice on bookkeeping and organization:

Kamoroff, Bernard, *Small Time Operator (25th Edition)*. Bell Springs Publishing, 2000.

For a very practical guide to investing:

Tobias, Andrew, *The Only Investment Guide You'll Ever Need*. Harvest Books, 1999.

For advice on how to avoid problems with government agencies:

Browne, Harry, *How I Found Freedom in an Unfree World*. Great Falls: Liam Works, 1998.

The following are other books published by ***Sphinx Publishing*** that may be helpful to your business:

Eckert, W. Kelsea, Sartorius, Arthur, III, & Warda, Mark, *How to Form Your Own Corporation*. 2001.

Haman, Edward A., *How to Form Your Own Partnership*. 2002.

Ray, James C., *The Most Valuable Business Legal Forms You'll Ever Need*. 2001.

Ray, James C., *The Complete Book of Corporate Forms.* 2001.

Warda, Mark, *How to Form a Limited Liability Company*. 1999.

Warda, Mark, *How to Register Your Own Copyright*. 2002.

Warda, Mark, *How to Register Your Own Trademark*. 1999.

Warda, Mark, *Incorporate in Nevada from Any State*. 2001.

The following are books published by ***Sourcebooks, Inc.*** that may be helpful to your business:

Fleury, Robert E., *The Small Business Survival Guide*. 1995.

Gutman, Jean E., *Accounting Made Easy*. 1998.

Milling, Bryan E., *How to Get a Small Business Loan (2nd Edition)*. 1998.

The following websites provide information that may be useful to you in starting your business:

Internal Revenue Service: http://www.irs.gov

Small Business Administration: http://www.sba.gov

Social Security Administration: http://www.ssa.gov

U. S. Business Advisor: http://www.business.gov

Appendix A
Selected Delaware Statutes

Included in this appendix are the sections of the General Corporation Law of the State of Delaware and the Delaware Limited Liability Company Act which are most useful to new businesses.

Statutes which are italicized in the following listing are not included in this appendix. The complete statutes can be found at many libraries or on the Internet at:

http://www.michie.com/resources1.html

STATE OF DELAWARE
DEPARTMENT OF STATE

EDWARD J. FREEL
SECRETARY OF STATE

I, Edward J. Freel, Secretary of State of the State of Delaware, **DO HEREBY CERTIFY** that the "General Corporation Law of the State of Delaware" may be published by Sourcebooks under the authority granted me in accordance with the provisions of the *Delaware Code*.

Dated this 8th day of June in the year of our Lord One Thousand Nine Hundred and Ninety-nine.

Edward J. Freel
Secretary of State

401 Federal Street, Suite 3
Dover, DE 19901
(302) 739-4111
Fax: (302) 739-3811

Carvel State Office Building
820 French Street, Fourth Floor
Wilmington, DE 19801
(302) 577 - 8767
Fax: (302) 577 - 2694

General Corporation Law

Subchapter I. Formation.
101. Incorporators; how corporation formed; purposes.
102. Contents of certificate of incorporation.
103. Execution, acknowledgment, filing, recording and effective date of original certificate of incorporation and other instruments; exceptions.
104. Certificate of incorporation; definition.
105. Certificate of incorporation and other certificates; evidence.
106. Commencement of corporate existence.
107. Powers of incorporators.
108. Organization meeting of incorporators or directors named in certificate of incorporation.
109. Bylaws.
110. Emergency bylaws and other powers in emergency.
111. Interpretation and enforcement of the certificate of incorporation and bylaws.

Subchapter II. Powers.
121. General powers.
122. Specific powers.
123. Powers respecting securities of other corporations or entities.
124. Effect of lack of corporate capacity or power; ultra vires.
125. Conferring academic or honorary degrees.
126. Banking power denied.
127. Private foundation; powers and duties.

Subchapter III. Registered Office and Registered Agent.
131. Registered office in State; principal office or place of business in State.
132. Registered agent in State; resident agent.
133. Change of location of registered office; change of registered agent.
134. Change of address or name of registered agent.
135. Resignation of registered agent coupled with appointment of successor.
136. Resignation of registered agent not coupled with appointment of successor.

Subchapter IV. Directors and Officers.
141. Board of directors; powers; number, qualifications, terms and quorum; committees; classes of directors; nonprofit corporations; reliance upon books; action without meeting; removal.
142. Officers; titles, duties, selection, term; failure to elect; vacancies.
143. Loans to employees and officers; guaranty of obligations of employees and officers.
144. Interested directors; quorum.
145. Indemnification of officers, directors, employees and agents; insurance.

Subchapter V. Stock and Dividends.
151. Classes and series of stock; redemption; rights.
152. Issuance of stock; lawful consideration; fully paid stock.
153. Consideration for stock.
154. Determination of amount of capital; capital, surplus and net assets defined.
155. Fractions of shares.
156. Partly paid shares.
157. Rights and options respecting stock.
158. Stock certificates; uncertificated shares.
159. Shares of stock; personal property, transfer and taxation.
160. Corporation's powers respecting ownership, voting, etc., of its own stock; rights of stock called for redemption.
161. Issuance of additional stock; when and by whom.
162. Liability of stockholder or subscriber for stock not paid in full.
163. Payment for stock not paid in full.
164. Failure to pay for stock; remedies.
165. Revocability of preincorporation subscriptions.
166. Formalities required of stock subscriptions.
167. Lost, stolen or destroyed stock certificates; issuance of new certificate or uncertificated shares.
168. Judicial proceedings to compel issuance of new certificate or uncertificated shares.
169. Situs of ownership of stock.
170. Dividends; payment; wasting asset corporations.
171. Special purpose reserves.
172. Liability of directors and committee members as to dividends or stock redemption.
173. Declaration and payment of dividends.
174. Liability of directors for unlawful payment of dividend or unlawful stock purchase or redemption; exoneration from liability; contribution among directors; subrogation.

Subchapter VI. Stock Transfers.
201. Transfer of stock, stock certificates and uncertificated stock.
202. Restrictions on transfer and ownership of securities.
203. Business combinations with interested stockholders.

Subchapter VII. Meetings, Elections, Voting and Notice.
211. Meetings of stockholders.
212. Voting rights of stockholders; proxies; limitations.
213. Fixing date for determination of stockholders of record.
214. Cumulative voting.
215. Voting rights of members of nonstock corporations; quorum; proxies.
216. Quorum and required vote for stock corporations.
217. Voting rights of fiduciaries, pledgors and joint owners of stock.
218. Voting trusts and other voting agreements.
219. List of stockholders entitled to vote; penalty for refusal to produce; stock ledger.
220. Inspection of books and records.

221. Voting, inspection and other rights of bondholders and debenture holders.
222. Notice of meetings and adjourned meetings.
223. Vacancies and newly created directorships.
224. Form of records.
225. Contested election of directors; proceedings to determine validity.
226. Appointment of custodian or receiver of corporation on deadlock or for other cause.
227. Powers of Court in elections of directors.
228. Consent of stockholders or members in lieu of meeting.
229. Waiver of notice.
230. Exception to requirements of notice.
231. Voting procedures and inspectors of elections.
232. Notice by electronic transmission.

Subchapter VIII. Amendment of Certificate of Incorporation; Changes in Capital and Capital Stock.
241. Amendment of certificate of incorporation before receipt of payment for stock.
242. Amendment of certificate of incorporation after receipt of payment for stock; nonstock corporations.
243. Retirement of stock.
244. Reduction of capital.
245. Restated certificate of incorporation.
246. [Reserved.]

Subchapter IX. Merger, Consolidation or Conversion.
251. Merger or consolidation of domestic corporations and limited partnership.
252. Merger or consolidation of domestic and foreign corporations; service of process upon surviving or resulting corporation.
253. Merger of parent corporation and subsidiary or subsidiaries.
254. Merger or consolidation of domestic corporation and joint-stock or other association.
255. Merger or consolidation of domestic nonstock corporations.
256. Merger or consolidation of domestic and foreign nonstock corporations; service of process upon surviving or resulting corporation.
257. Merger or consolidation of domestic stock and nonstock corporations.
258. Merger or consolidation of domestic and foreign stock and nonstock corporations.
259. Status, rights, liabilities, of constituent and surviving or resulting corporations following merger or consolidation.
260. Powers of corporation surviving or resulting from merger or consolidation; issuance of stock, bonds or other indebtedness.
261. Effect of merger upon pending actions.
262. Appraisal rights.
263. Merger or consolidation of domestic corporation.
264. Merger or consolidation of domestic corporation and limited liability company.
265. Conversion of other entities to a domestic corporation.
266. Conversion of a domestic corporation to other entities.

Subchapter X. Sale of Assets, Dissolution and Winding Up.
271. Sale, lease or exchange of assets; consideration; procedure.
272. Mortgage or pledge of assets.
273. Dissolution of joint venture corporation having 2 stockholders.
274. Dissolution before issuance of shares or beginning of business; procedure.
275. Dissolution generally; procedure.
276. Dissolution of nonstock corporation; procedure.
277. Payment of franchise taxes before dissolution or merger.
278. Continuation of corporation after dissolution for purposes of suit and winding up affairs.
279. Trustees or receivers for dissolved corporations; appointment; powers; duties.
280. Notice to claimants; filing of claims.
281. Payment and distribution to claimants and stockholders.
282. Liability of stockholders of dissolved corporations.
283. Jurisdiction.
284. Revocation or forfeiture of charter; proceedings.
285. Dissolution or forfeiture of charter by decree of court; filing.

Subchapter XI. Insolvency; Receivers and Trustees.
291. Receivers for insolvent corporations; appointment and powers.
292. Title to property; filing order of appointment; exception.
293. Notices to stockholders and creditors.
294. Receivers or trustees; inventory; list of debts and report.
295. Creditors' proofs of claims; when barred; notice.
296. Adjudication of claims; appeal.
297. Sale of perishable or deteriorating property.
298. Compensation, costs and expenses of receiver or trustee.
299. Substitution of trustee or receiver as party; abatement of actions.
300. Employee's lien for wages when corporation insolvent.
301. Discontinuance of liquidation.
302. Compromise or arrangement between corporation and creditors or stockholders.
303. Reorganization under a statute of the United States; effectuation.

Subchapter XII. Renewal, Revival, Extension and Restoration of Certificate of Incorporation or Charter.
311. Revocation of voluntary dissolution.
312. Renewal, revival, extension and restoration of certificate of incorporation.
313. Renewal of certificate of incorporation or charter of religious, charitable, educational, etc., corporations.
314. Status of corporation.

Subchapter XIII. Suits Against Corporations, Directors, Officers or Stock- holders.
321. Service of process on corporations.
322. Failure of corporation to obey order of court; appointment of receiver.

18-206. Filing.
18-207. Notice.
18-208. Restated certificate.
18-209. Merger and consolidation.
18-210. Contractual appraisal rights.
18-211. Certificate of correction.
18-212. Domestication of non-United States entities.
18-213. Transfer or continuance of domestic limited liability companies.
18-214. Conversion of certain entities to a limited liability company.
18-215. Series of members, managers or limited liability company interests.
18-216. Approval of conversion of a limited liability company.

Subchapter III. Members.
18-301. Admission of members.
18-302. Classes and voting.
18-303. Liability to 3rd parties.
18-304. Events of bankruptcy.
18-305. Access to and confidentiality of information; records.
18-306. Remedies for breach of limited liability company agreement by member.

Subchapter IV. Managers.
18-401. Admission of managers.
18-402. Management of limited liability company.
18-403. Contributions by a manager.
18-404. Classes and voting.
18-405. Remedies for breach of limited liability company agreement by manager.
18-406. Reliance on reports and information by member or manager.
18-407. Delegation of rights and powers to manage.

Subchapter V. Finance.
18-501. Form of contribution.
18-502. Liability for contribution.
18-503. Allocation of profits and losses.
18-504. Allocation of distributions.
18-505. Defense of usury not available.

Subchapter VI. Distributions and Resignation.
18-601. Interim distributions.
18-602. Resignation of manager.
18-603. Resignation of member.
18-604. Distribution upon resignation.
18-605. Distribution in kind.
18-606. Right to distribution.
18-607. Limitations on distribution.

Subchapter VII. Assignment of Limited Liability Company Interests.
18-701. Nature of limited liability company interest.
18-702. Assignment of limited liability company interest.
18-703. Member's limited liability company interest subject to charging order.
18-704. Right of assignee to become member.
18-705. Powers of estate of deceased or incompetent member.

Subchapter VIII. Dissolution.
18-801. Dissolution.
18-802. Judicial dissolution.
18-803. Winding up.
18-804. Distribution of assets.

Subchapter IX. Foreign Limited Liability Companies.
18-901. Law governing.
18-902. Registration required; application.
18-903. Issuance of registration.
18-904. Name; registered office; registered agent.
18-905. Amendments to application.
18-906. Cancellation of registration.
18-907. Doing business without registration.
18-908. Foreign limited liability companies doing business without having qualified; injunctions.
18-909. Execution; liability.
18-910. Service of process on registered foreign limited liability companies.
18-911. Service of process on unregistered foreign limited liability companies.

Subchapter X. Derivative Actions.
18-1001. Right to bring action.
18-1002. Proper plaintiff.
18-1003. Complaint.
18-1004. Expenses.

Subchapter XI. Miscellaneous.
18-1101. Construction and application of chapter and limited liability company agreement.
18-1102. Short title.
18-1103. Severability.
18-1104. Cases not provided for in this chapter.
18-1105. Fees.
18-1106. Reserved power of State of Delaware to alter or repeal chapter.
18-1107. Taxation of limited liability companies.
18-1108. Cancellation of certificate of formation for failure to pay taxes.
18-1109. Revival of domestic limited liability company.

Subchapter I. Formation.

§ 101. Incorporators; how corporation formed; purposes.
(a) Any person, partnership, association or corporation, singly or jointly with others, and without regard to such person's or entity's residence, domicile or state of incorporation, may incorporate or organize a corporation under this chapter by filing with the Division of Corporations in the Department of State a certificate of incorporation which shall be executed, acknowledged and filed in accordance with § 103 of this title.
(b) A corporation may be incorporated or organized under this chapter to conduct or promote any lawful business or purposes, except as may otherwise be provided by the Constitution or other law of this State.
(c) Corporations for constructing, maintaining and operating public utilities, whether in or outside of this State, may be organized under this chapter, but corporations for constructing, maintaining and operating public utilities within this State shall be subject to, in addition to this chapter, the special provisions and requirements of Title 26 applicable to such corporations.

§ 102. Contents of certificate of incorporation.
(a) The certificate of incorporation shall set forth:
(1) The name of the corporation, which (i) shall contain 1 of the words "association," "company," "corporation," "club," "foundation," "fund," "incorporated," "institute," "society," "union," "syndicate," or "limited," (or abbreviations thereof, with or without punctuation), or words (or abbreviations thereof, with or without punctuation) of like import of foreign countries or jurisdictions (provided they are written in roman characters or letters); provided, however, that the Division of Corporations in the Department of State may waive such requirement (unless it determines that such name is, or might otherwise appear to be, that of a natural person) if such corporation executes, acknowledges and files with the Secretary of State in accordance with § 103 of this title a certificate stating that its total assets, as defined in subsection (i) of § 503 of this title, are not less than $10,000,000, (ii) shall be such as to distinguish it upon the records in the office of the Division of Corporations in the Department of State from the names on such records of other corporations, partnerships, limited partnerships, limited liability companies or business trusts organized, reserved or registered as a foreign corporation, partnership, limited partnership, limited liability company or business trust under the laws of this State, except with the written consent of such other foreign corporation or domestic or foreign partnership, limited partnership, limited liability company or business trust executed, acknowledged and filed with the Secretary of State in accordance with § 103 of this title and (iii) shall not contain the word "bank," or any variation thereof, except for the name of a bank reporting to and under the supervision of the State Bank Commissioner of this State or a subsidiary of a bank or savings association (as those terms are defined in the Federal Deposit Insurance Act, as amended, at 12 U.S.C. § 1813), or a corporation regulated under the Bank Holding Company Act of 1956, as amended, 12 U.S.C. § 1841 et seq., or the Home Owners' Loan Act, as amended, 12 U.S.C. § 1461 et seq.; provided, however, that this section shall not be construed to prevent the use of the word "bank," or any variation thereof, in a context clearly not purporting to refer to a banking business or otherwise likely to mislead the public about the nature of the business of the corporation or to lead to a pattern and practice of abuse that might cause harm to the interests of the public or the State as determined by the Division of Corporations in the Department of State;
(2) The address (which shall include the street, number, city and county) of the corporation's registered office in this State, and the name of its registered agent at such address;
(3) The nature of the business or purposes to be conducted or promoted. It shall be sufficient to state, either alone or with other businesses or purposes, that the purpose of the corporation is to engage in any lawful act or activity for which corporations may be organized under the General Corporation Law of Delaware, and by such statement all lawful acts and activities shall be within the purposes of the corporation, except for express limitations, if any;
(4) If the corporation is to be authorized to issue only 1 class of stock, the total number of shares of stock which the corporation shall have authority to issue and the par value of each of such shares, or a statement that all such shares are to be without par value. If the corporation is to be authorized to issue more than 1 class of stock, the certificate of incorporation shall set forth the total number of shares of all classes of stock which the corporation shall have authority to issue and the number of shares of each class and shall specify each class the shares of which are to be without par value and each class the shares of which are to have par value and the par value of the shares of each such class. The certificate of incorporation shall also set forth a statement of the designations and the powers, preferences and rights, and the qualifications, limitations or restrictions thereof, which are permitted by § 151 of this title in respect of any class or classes of stock or any series of any class of stock of the corporation and the fixing of which by the certificate of incorporation is desired, and an express grant of such authority as it may then be desired to grant to the board of directors to fix by resolution or resolutions any thereof that may be desired but which shall not be fixed by the certificate of incorporation. The foregoing provisions of this paragraph shall not apply to corporations which are not to have author-

ity to issue capital stock. In the case of such corporations, the fact that they are not to have authority to issue capital stock shall be stated in the certificate of incorporation. The conditions of membership of such corporations shall likewise be stated in the certificate of incorporation or the certificate may provide that the conditions of membership shall be stated in the bylaws;

(5) The name and mailing address of the incorporator or incorporators;

(6) If the powers of the incorporator or incorporators are to terminate upon the filing of the certificate of incorporation, the names and mailing addresses of the persons who are to serve as directors until the first annual meeting of stockholders or until their successors are elected and qualify.

(b) In addition to the matters required to be set forth in the certificate of incorporation by subsection (a) of this section, the certificate of incorporation may also contain any or all of the following matters:

(1) Any provision for the management of the business and for the conduct of the affairs of the corporation, and any provision creating, defining, limiting and regulating the powers of the corporation, the directors, and the stockholders, or any class of the stockholders, or the members of a nonstock corporation; if such provisions are not contrary to the laws of this State. Any provision which is required or permitted by any section of this chapter to be stated in the bylaws may instead be stated in the certificate of incorporation;

(2) The following provisions, in haec verba, viz: "Whenever a compromise or arrangement is proposed between this corporation and its creditors or any class of them and/or between this corporation and its stockholders or any class of them, any court of equitable jurisdiction within the State of Delaware may, on the application in a summary way of this corporation or of any creditor or stockholder thereof or on the application of any receiver or receivers appointed for this corporation under § 291 of Title 8 of the Delaware Code or on the application of trustees in dissolution or of any receiver or receivers appointed for this corporation under § 279 of Title 8 of the Delaware Code order a meeting of the creditors or class of creditors, and/or of the stockholders or class of stockholders of this corporation, as the case may be, to be summoned in such manner as the said court directs. If a majority in number representing three fourths in value of the creditors or class of creditors, and/or of the stockholders or class of stockholders of this corporation, as the case may be, agree to any compromise or arrangement and to any reorganization of this corporation as consequence of such compromise or arrangement, the said compromise or arrangement and the said reorganization shall, if sanctioned by the court to which the said application has been made, be binding on all the creditors or class of creditors, and/or on all the stockholders or class of stockholders, of this corporation, as the case may be, and also on this corporation";

(3) Such provisions as may be desired granting to the holders of the stock of the corporation, or the holders of any class or series of a class thereof, the preemptive right to subscribe to any or all additional issues of stock of the corporation of any or all classes or series thereof, or to any securities of the corporation convertible into such stock. No stockholder shall have any preemptive right to subscribe to an additional issue of stock or to any security convertible into such stock unless, and except to the extent that, such right is expressly granted to such stockholder in the certificate of incorporation. All such rights in existence on July 3, 1967, shall remain in existence unaffected by this paragraph unless and until changed or terminated by appropriate action which expressly provides for the change or termination;

(4) Provisions requiring for any corporate action, the vote of a larger portion of the stock or of any class or series thereof, or of any other securities having voting power, or a larger number of the directors, than is required by this chapter;

(5) A provision limiting the duration of the corporation's existence to a specified date; otherwise, the corporation shall have perpetual existence;

(6) A provision imposing personal liability for the debts of the corporation on its stockholders or members to a specified extent and upon specified conditions; otherwise, the stockholders or members of a corporation shall not be personally liable for the payment of the corporation's debts except as they may be liable by reason of their own conduct or acts;

(7) A provision eliminating or limiting the personal liability of a director to the corporation or its stockholders for monetary damages for breach of fiduciary duty as a director, provided that such provision shall not eliminate or limit the liability of a director: (i) For any breach of the director's duty of loyalty to the corporation or its stockholders; (ii) for acts or omissions not in good faith or which involve intentional misconduct or a knowing violation of law; (iii) under § 174 of this title; or (iv) for any transaction from which the director derived an improper personal benefit. No such provision shall eliminate or limit the liability of a director for any act or omission occurring prior to the date when such provision becomes effective. All references in this paragraph to a director shall also be deemed to refer (x) to a member of the governing body of a corporation which is not authorized to issue capital stock, and (y) to such other person or persons, if any, who, pursuant to a provision of the certificate of incorporation in accordance with § 141(a) of this title, exercise or perform any of the powers or duties otherwise conferred or imposed upon the board of directors by this title.

(c) It shall not be necessary to set forth in the certificate of incorporation any of the powers conferred on corporations by this chapter.

§ 103. Execution, acknowledgment, filing, recording and effective date of original certificate of incorporation and other instruments; exceptions.

(a) Whenever any instrument is to be filed with the Secretary of State or in accordance with this section or chapter, such instrument shall be executed as follows:

(1) The certificate of incorporation, and any other instrument to be filed before the election of the initial board of directors if the initial directors were not named in the certificate of incorporation, shall be signed by the incorporator or incorporators (or, in the case of any such other instrument, such incorporator's or incorporators" successors and assigns). If any incorporator is not available by reason of death, incapacity, unknown address, or refusal or neglect to act, then any such other instrument may be signed, with the same effect as if such incorporator had signed it, by any person for whom or on whose behalf such incorporator, in executing the certificate of incorporation, was acting directly or indirectly as employee or agent, provided that such other instrument shall state that such incorporator is not available and the reason therefor, that such incorporator in executing the certificate of incorporation was acting directly or indirectly as employee or agent for or on behalf of such person, and that such person's signature on such instrument is otherwise authorized and not wrongful.

(2) All other instruments shall be signed: a. By any authorized officer of the corporation; or b. If it shall appear from the instrument that there are no such officers, then by a majority of the directors or by such directors as may be designated by the board; or c. If it shall appear from the instrument that there are no such officers or directors, then by the holders of record, or such of them as may be designated by the holders of record, of a majority of all outstanding shares of stock; or d. By the holders of record of all outstanding shares of stock.

(b) Whenever this chapter requires any instrument to be acknowledged, such requirement is satisfied by either:

(1) The formal acknowledgment by the person or 1 of the persons signing the instrument that it is such person's act and deed or the act and deed of the corporation, and that the facts stated therein are true. Such acknowledgment shall be made before a person who is authorized by the law of the place of execution to take acknowledgments of deeds. If such person has a seal of office such person shall affix it to the instrument.

(2) The signature, without more, of the person or persons signing the instrument, in which case such signature or signatures shall constitute the affirmation or acknowledgment of the signatory, under penalties of perjury, that the instrument is such person's act and deed or the act and deed of the corporation, and that the facts stated therein are true.

(c) Whenever any instrument is to be filed with the Secretary of State or in accordance with this section or chapter, such requirement means that:

(1) The original signed instrument shall be delivered to the office of the Secretary of State;

(2) All taxes and fees authorized by law to be collected by the Secretary of State in connection with the filing of the instrument shall be tendered to the Secretary of State;

(3) Upon delivery of the instrument, and upon tender of the required taxes and fees, the Secretary of State shall certify that the instrument has been filed in the Secretary of State's office by endorsing upon the original signed instrument the word "Filed," and the date and hour of its filing. This endorsement is the "filing date" of the instrument, and is conclusive of the date and time of its filing in the absence of actual fraud. The Secretary of State shall thereupon file and index the endorsed instrument;

(4) The Secretary of State, acting as agent for the recorders of each of the counties, shall collect and deposit in a separate account established exclusively for that purpose a county assessment fee with respect to each filed instrument and shall thereafter weekly remit from such account to the recorder of each of the said counties the amount or amounts of such fees as provided for in paragraph (c)(5) of this section or as elsewhere provided by law. Said fees shall be for the purposes of defraying certain costs incurred by the counties in merging the information and images of such filed documents with the document information systems of each of the recorder's offices in the counties and in retrieving, maintaining and displaying such information and images in the offices of the recorders and at remote locations in each of such counties. In consideration for its acting as the agent for the recorders with respect to the collection and payment of the county assessment fees, the Secretary of State shall retain and pay over to the General Fund of the State an administrative charge of 1 percent of the total fees collected.

(5) The assessment fee to the counties shall be $24 for each 1-page instrument filed with the Secretary of State in accordance with this section and $9 for each additional page for instruments with more than 1 page. The recorder's office to receive the assessment fee shall be the recorder's office in the county in which the corporation's registered office in this State is, or is to be, located, except that an assessment fee shall not be charged for either a certificate of dissolution qualifying for treatment under § 391(a)(5)b. of this title or a document filed in accordance with subchapter XV of this chapter.

(6) The Secretary of State shall enter such information from each instrument as the Secretary deems appropriate into the Delaware Corporation Information System or

any system which is a successor thereto in the office of the Secretary of State, and such information shall be permanently maintained. A copy of each instrument shall be permanently maintained on optical disk or by other suitable medium.

(d) Any instrument filed in accordance with subsection (c) of this section shall be effective upon its filing date. Any instrument may provide that it is not to become effective until a specified time subsequent to the time it is filed, but such time shall not be later than a time on the 90th day after the date of its filing. If any instrument filed in accordance with subsection (c) of this section provides for a future effective date or time and if the transaction is terminated or its terms are amended to change the future effective date or time prior to the future effective date or time, the instrument shall be terminated or amended by the filing, prior to the future effective date or time set forth in such instrument, of a certificate of termination or amendment of the original instrument, executed in accordance with subsection (a) of this section, which shall identify the instrument which has been terminated or amended and shall state that the instrument has been terminated or the manner in which it has been amended.

(e) If another section of this chapter specifically prescribes a manner of executing, acknowledging or filing a specified instrument or a time when such instrument shall become effective which differs from the corresponding provisions of this section, then such other section shall govern.

(f) Whenever any instrument authorized to be filed with the Secretary of State under any provision of this title, has been so filed and is an inaccurate record of the corporate action therein referred to, or was defectively or erroneously executed, sealed or acknowledged, the instrument may be corrected by filing with the Secretary of State a certificate of correction of the instrument which shall be executed, acknowledged and filed in accordance with this section. The certificate of correction shall specify the inaccuracy or defect to be corrected and shall set forth the portion of the instrument in corrected form. In lieu of filing a certificate of correction the instrument may be corrected by filing with the Secretary of State a corrected instrument which shall be executed, acknowledged and filed in accordance with this section. The corrected instrument shall be specifically designated as such in its heading, shall specify the inaccuracy or defect to be corrected, and shall set forth the entire instrument in corrected form. An instrument corrected in accordance with this section shall be effective as of the date the original instrument was filed, except as to those persons who are substantially and adversely affected by the correction and as to those persons the instrument as corrected shall be effective from the filing date.

(g) Notwithstanding that any instrument authorized to be filed with the Secretary of State under this title is when filed inaccurately, defectively or erroneously executed, sealed or acknowledged, or otherwise defective in any respect, the Secretary of State shall have no liability to any person for the preclearance for filing, the acceptance for filing or the filing and indexing of such instrument by the Secretary of State.

(h) Any signature on any instrument authorized to be filed with the Secretary of State under this title may be a facsimile, a conformed signature or an electronically transmitted signature.

§ 104. Certificate of incorporation; definition.

The term "certificate of incorporation," as used in this chapter, unless the context requires otherwise, includes not only the original certificate of incorporation filed to create a corporation but also all other certificates, agreements of merger or consolidation, plans of reorganization, or other instruments, howsoever designated, which are filed pursuant to §§ 102, 133-136, 151, 241-243, 245, 251-258, 263-264, 303, or any other section of this title, and which have the effect of amending or supplementing in some respect a corporation's original certificate of incorporation.

§ 105. Certificate of incorporation and other certificates; evidence.

A copy of a certificate of incorporation, or a restated certificate of incorporation, or of any other certificate which has been filed in the office of the Secretary of State as required by any provision of this title shall, when duly certified by the Secretary of State, be received in all courts, public offices and official bodies as prima facia evidence of:

(1) Due execution, acknowledgment and filing of the instrument;

(2) Observance and performance of all acts and conditions necessary to have been observed and performed precedent to the instrument becoming effective; and

(3) Any other facts required or permitted by law to be stated in the instrument.

§ 106. Commencement of corporate existence.

Upon the filing with the Secretary of State of the certificate of incorporation, executed and acknowledged in accordance with § 103 of this title, the incorporator or incorporators who signed the certificate, and such incorporator's or incorporators' successors and assigns, shall, from the date of such filing, be and constitute a body corporate, by the name set forth in the certificate, subject to subsection (d) of § 103 of this title and subject to dissolution or other termination of its existence as provided in this chapter.

§ 107. Powers of incorporators.

If the persons who are to serve as directors until the first annual meeting of stockholders have not been named in the certificate of incorporation, the incorporator or incorporators, until the directors are elected, shall manage the affairs of the corporation and may do whatever is necessary and proper to perfect the organization of the corporation, including the adoption of the original bylaws of the corporation and the election of directors.

§ 108. Organization meeting of incorporators or directors named in certificate of incorporation.

(a) After the filing of the certificate of incorporation an organization meeting of the incorporator or incorporators, or of the board of directors if the initial directors were named in the certificate of incorporation, shall be held, either within or without this State, at the call of a majority of the incorporators or directors, as the case may be, for the purposes of adopting bylaws, electing directors (if the meeting is of the incorporators) to serve or hold office until the first annual meeting of stockholders or until their successors are elected and qualify, electing officers if the meeting is of the directors, doing any other or further acts to perfect the organization of the corporation, and transacting such other business as may come before the meeting.

(b) The persons calling the meeting shall give to each other incorporator or director, as the case may be, at least 2 days' written notice thereof by any usual means of communication, which notice shall state the time, place and purposes of the meeting as fixed by the persons calling it. Notice of the meeting need not be given to anyone who attends the meeting or who signs a waiver of notice either before or after the meeting.

(c) Any action permitted to be taken at the organization meeting of the incorporators or directors, as the case may be, may be taken without a meeting if each incorporator or director, where there is more than 1, or the sole incorporator or director where there is only 1, signs an instrument which states the action so taken.

§ 109. Bylaws.

(a) The original or other bylaws of a corporation may be adopted, amended or repealed by the incorporators, by the initial directors if they were named in the certificate of incorporation, or, before a corporation has received any payment for any of its stock, by its board of directors. After a corporation has received any payment for any of its stock, the power to adopt, amend or repeal bylaws shall be in the stockholders entitled to vote, or, in the case of a nonstock corporation, in its members entitled to vote; provided, however, any corporation may, in its certificate of incorporation, confer the power to adopt, amend or repeal bylaws upon the directors or, in the case of a nonstock corporation, upon its governing body by whatever name designated. The fact that such power has been so conferred upon the directors or governing body, as the case may be, shall not divest the stockholders or members of the power, nor limit their power to adopt, amend or repeal bylaws.

(b) The bylaws may contain any provision, not inconsistent with law or with the certificate of incorporation, relating to the business of the corporation, the conduct of its affairs, and its rights or powers or the rights or powers of its stockholders, directors, officers or employees.

§ 110. Emergency bylaws and other powers in emergency.

(a) The board of directors of any corporation may adopt emergency bylaws, subject to repeal or change by action of the stockholders, which shall notwithstanding any different provision elsewhere in this chapter or in Chapters 3 and 5 of Title 26, or in Chapter 7 of Title 5, or in the certificate of incorporation or bylaws, be operative during any emergency resulting from an attack on the United States or on a locality in which the corporation conducts its business or customarily holds meetings of its board of directors or its stockholders, or during any nuclear or atomic disaster, or during the existence of any catastrophe, or other similar emergency condition, as a result of which a quorum of the board of directors or a standing committee thereof cannot readily be convened for action. The emergency bylaws may make any provision that may be practical and necessary for the circumstances of the emergency, including provisions that:

(1) A meeting of the board of directors or a committee thereof may be called by any officer or director in such manner and under such conditions as shall be prescribed in the emergency bylaws;

(2) The director or directors in attendance at the meeting, or any greater number fixed by the emergency bylaws, shall constitute a quorum; and

(3) The officers or other persons designated on a list approved by the board of directors before the emergency, all in such order of priority and subject to such conditions and for such period of time (not longer than reasonably necessary after the termination of the emergency) as may be provided in the emergency bylaws or in the resolution approving the list, shall, to the extent required to provide a quorum at any meeting of the board of directors, be deemed directors for such meeting.

(b) The board of directors, either before or during any such emergency, may provide, and from time to time modify, lines of succession in the event that during such emergency any or all officers or agents of the corporation shall for any reason be rendered incapable of discharging their duties.

(c) The board of directors, either before or during any such emergency, may, effective in the emergency, change the head office or designate several alternative head offices or regional offices, or authorize the officers so to do.

(d) No officer, director or employee acting in accordance with any emergency bylaws shall be liable except for wilful misconduct.

(e) To the extent not inconsistent with any emergency bylaws so adopted, the bylaws of the corporation shall remain in effect during any emergency and upon its termination the emergency bylaws shall cease to be operative.

(f) Unless otherwise provided in emergency bylaws, notice of any meeting of the board of directors during such an emergency may be given only to such of the directors as it may be feasible to reach at the time and by such means as may be feasible at the time, including publication or radio.

(g) To the extent required to constitute a quorum at any meeting of the board of directors during such an emergency, the officers of the corporation who are present shall, unless otherwise provided in emergency bylaws, be deemed, in order of rank and within the same rank in order of seniority, directors for such meeting.
(h) Nothing contained in this section shall be deemed exclusive of any other provisions for emergency powers consistent with other sections of this title which have been or may be adopted by corporations created under this chapter.

§ 111. Interpretation and enforcement of the certificate of incorporation and bylaws.
Any action to interpret, apply or enforce the provisions of the certificate of incorporation or the bylaws of a corporation may be brought in the Court of Chancery.

Subchapter II. Powers.

§ 121. General powers.
(a) In addition to the powers enumerated in § 122 of this title, every corporation, its officers, directors and stockholders shall possess and may exercise all the powers and privileges granted by this chapter or by any other law or by its certificate of incorporation, together with any powers incidental thereto, so far as such powers and privileges are necessary or convenient to the conduct, promotion or attainment of the business or purposes set forth in its certificate of incorporation.
(b) Every corporation shall be governed by the provisions and be subject to the restrictions and liabilities contained in this chapter.

§ 122. Specific powers.
Every corporation created under this chapter shall have power to:

(1) Have perpetual succession by its corporate name, unless a limited period of duration is stated in its certificate of incorporation;
(2) Sue and be sued in all courts and participate, as a party or otherwise, in any judicial, administrative, arbitrative or other proceeding, in its corporate name;
(3) Have a corporate seal, which may be altered at pleasure, and use the same by causing it or a facsimile thereof, to be impressed or affixed or in any other manner reproduced;
(4) Purchase, receive, take by grant, gift, devise, bequest or otherwise, lease, or otherwise acquire, own, hold, improve, employ, use and otherwise deal in and with real or personal property, or any interest therein, wherever situated, and to sell, convey, lease, exchange, transfer or otherwise dispose of, or mortgage or pledge, all or any of its property and assets, or any interest therein, wherever situated;
(5) Appoint such officers and agents as the business of the corporation requires and to pay or otherwise provide for them suitable compensation;
(6) Adopt, amend and repeal bylaws;
(7) Wind up and dissolve itself in the manner provided in this chapter;
(8) Conduct its business, carry on its operations and have offices and exercise its powers within or without this State;
(9) Make donations for the public welfare or for charitable, scientific or educational purposes, and in time of war or other national emergency in aid thereof;
(10) Be an incorporator, promoter or manager of other corporations of any type or kind;
(11) Participate with others in any corporation, partnership, limited partnership, joint venture or other association of any kind, or in any transaction, undertaking or arrangement which the participating corporation would have power to conduct by itself, whether or not such participation involves sharing or delegation of control with or to others;
(12) Transact any lawful business which the corporation's board of directors shall find to be in aid of governmental authority;
(13) Make contracts, including contracts of guaranty and suretyship, incur liabilities, borrow money at such rates of interest as the corporation may determine, issue its notes, bonds and other obligations, and secure any of its obligations by mortgage, pledge or other encumbrance of all or any of its property, franchises and income, and make contracts of guaranty and suretyship which are necessary or convenient to the conduct, promotion or attainment of the business of

a. a corporation all of the outstanding stock of which is owned, directly or indirectly, by the contracting corporation, or
b. a corporation which owns, directly or indirectly, all of the outstanding stock of the contracting corporation, or
c. a corporation all of the outstanding stock of which is owned, directly or indirectly, by a corporation which owns, directly or indirectly, all of the outstanding stock of the contracting corporation, which contracts of guaranty and suretyship shall be deemed to be necessary or convenient to the conduct, promotion or attainment of the business of the contracting corporation, and make other contracts of guaranty and suretyship which are necessary or convenient to the conduct, promotion or attainment of the business of the contracting corporation;

(14) Lend money for its corporate purposes, invest and reinvest its funds, and take, hold and deal with real and

personal property as security for the payment of funds so loaned or invested;

(15) Pay pensions and establish and carry out pension, profit sharing, stock option, stock purchase, stock bonus, retirement, benefit, incentive and compensation plans, trusts and provisions for any or all of its directors, officers and employees, and for any or all of the directors, officers and employees of its subsidiaries;

(16) Provide insurance for its benefit on the life of any of its directors, officers or employees, or on the life of any stockholder for the purpose of acquiring at such stockholder's death shares of its stock owned by such stockholder.

(17) Renounce, in its certificate of incorporation or by action of its board of directors, any interest or expectancy of the corporation in, or in being offered an opportunity to participate in, specified business opportunities or specified classes or categories of business opportunities that are presented to the corporation or 1 or more of its officers, directors or stockholders.

§ 123. Powers respecting securities of other corporations or entities.

Any corporation organized under the laws of this State may guarantee, purchase, take, receive, subscribe for or otherwise acquire; own, hold, use or otherwise employ; sell, lease, exchange, transfer or otherwise dispose of; mortgage, lend, pledge or otherwise deal in and with, bonds and other obligations of, or shares or other securities or interests in, or issued by, any other domestic or foreign corporation, partnership, association or individual, or by any government or agency or instrumentality thereof. A corporation while owner of any such securities may exercise all the rights, powers and privileges of ownership, including the right to vote.

§ 124. Effect of lack of corporate capacity or power; ultra vires.

No act of a corporation and no conveyance or transfer of real or personal property to or by a corporation shall be invalid by reason of the fact that the corporation was without capacity or power to do such act or to make or receive such conveyance or transfer, but such lack of capacity or power may be asserted:

(1) In a proceeding by a stockholder against the corporation to enjoin the doing of any act or acts or the transfer of real or personal property by or to the corporation. If the unauthorized acts or transfer sought to be enjoined are being, or are to be, performed or made pursuant to any contract to which the corporation is a party, the court may, if all of the parties to the contract are parties to the proceeding and if it deems the same to be equitable, set aside and enjoin the performance of such contract, and in so doing may allow to the corporation or to the other parties to the contract, as the case may be, such compensation as may be equitable for the loss or damage sustained by any of them which may result from the action of the court in setting aside and enjoining the performance of such contract, but anticipated profits to be derived from the performance of the contract shall not be awarded by the court as a loss or damage sustained;

(2) In a proceeding by the corporation, whether acting directly or through a receiver, trustee or other legal representative, or through stockholders in a representative suit, against an incumbent or former officer or director of the corporation, for loss or damage due to such incumbent or former officer's or director's unauthorized act;

(3) In a proceeding by the Attorney General to dissolve the corporation, or to enjoin the corporation from the transaction of unauthorized business.

§ 125. Conferring academic or honorary degrees.

No corporation organized after April 18, 1945, shall have power to confer academic or honorary degrees unless the certificate of incorporation or an amendment thereof shall so provide and unless the certificate of incorporation or an amendment thereof prior to its being filed in the office of the Secretary of State shall have endorsed thereon the approval of the State Board of Education of this State. No corporation organized before April 18, 1945, any provision in its certificate of incorporation to the contrary notwithstanding, shall possess the power aforesaid without first filing in the office of the Secretary of State a certificate of amendment so providing, the filing of which certificate of amendment in the office of the Secretary of State shall be subject to prior approval of the State Board of Education, evidenced as hereinabove provided. Approval shall be granted only when it appears to the reasonable satisfaction of the State Board of Education that the corporation is engaged in conducting a bona fide institution of higher learning, giving instructions in arts and letters, science or the professions, or that the corporation proposes, in good faith, to engage in that field and has or will have the resources, including personnel, requisite for the conduct of an institution of higher learning. Upon dissolution, all such corporations shall comply with § 8530 of Title 14. Notwithstanding any provision herein to the contrary, no corporation shall have the power to conduct a private business or trade school unless the certificate of incorporation or an amendment thereof, prior to its being filed in the office of the Secretary of State, shall have endorsed thereon the approval of the Department of Education pursuant to Chapter 85 of Title 14. Notwithstanding the foregoing provisions, any corporation conducting a law school, which has its principal place of operation in Delaware, and which intends to meet the standards of approval of the American Bar Association, may, after it has been in actual operation for not less than 1 year, retain at its own expense a dean or dean emeritus of a law school fully approved by the American Bar Association to make an on-site inspection and report concerning the progress of the corporation toward meeting the standards for approval by the American Bar Association. Such dean or dean emeritus shall be chosen by the Attorney General from a panel of 3 deans whose names are presented to the Attorney General as being willing to serve. One such dean on this panel shall be nominated by the trustees of said law school corporation; another dean shall be nominated by a committee of the Student Bar Association of said law school; and the other dean shall be nominated by a committee of lawyers who are parents of students attending such law school. If any of the above-named groups cannot find a dean, it may substitute 2 full professors of accredited law schools for the dean it is entitled to nominate, and in such a case if the Attorney General chooses 1 of such professors, such professor shall serve the function of a dean as herein prescribed. If the dean so retained shall report in writing that, in such dean's professional judgment, the corporation is attempting, in good faith, to comply with the standards for approval of the American Bar Association and is making reasonable progress toward meeting such standards, the corporation may file a copy of the report with the Secretary of Education and with the Attorney General. Any corporation which complies with these provisions by filing such report shall be deemed to have temporary approval from the State and shall be entitled to amend its certificate of incorporation to authorize the granting of standard academic law degrees. Thereafter, until the law school operated by the corporation is approved by the American Bar Association, the corporation shall file once during each academic year a new report, in the same manner as the first report. If, at any time, the corporation fails to file such a report, or if the dean retained to render such report states that, in such dean's opinion, the corporation is not continuing to make reasonable progress toward accreditation, the Attorney General, at the request of the Secretary of Education, may file a complaint in the Court of Chancery to suspend said temporary approval and degree-granting power until a further report is filed by a dean or dean emeritus of an accredited law school that the school has resumed its progress towards meeting the standards for approval. Upon approval of the law school by the American Bar Association, temporary approval shall become final, and shall no longer be subject to suspension or vacation under this section.

§ 126. Banking power denied.

(a) No corporation organized under this chapter shall possess the power of issuing bills, notes, or other evidences of debt for circulation as money, or the power of carrying on the business of receiving deposits of money.

(b) Corporations organized under this chapter to buy, sell and otherwise deal in notes, open accounts and other similar evidences of debt, or to loan money and to take notes, open accounts and other similar evidences of debt as collateral security therefor, shall not be deemed to be engaging in the business of banking.

§ 127. Private foundation; powers and duties.

A corporation of this State which is a private foundation under the United States internal revenue laws and whose certificate of incorporation does not expressly provide that this section shall not apply to it is required to act or to refrain from acting so as not to subject itself to the taxes imposed by 26 U.S.C. § 4941 (relating to taxes on self-dealing), 4942 (relating to taxes on failure to distribute income), 4943 (relating to taxes on excess business holdings), 4944 (relating to taxes on investments which jeopardize charitable purpose), or 4945 (relating to taxable expenditures), or corresponding provisions of any subsequent United States internal revenue law.

Subchapter III. Registered Office and Registered Agent.

§ 131. Registered office in State; principal office or place of business in State.

(a) Every corporation shall have and maintain in this State a registered office which may, but need not be, the same as its place of business.

(b) Whenever the term "corporation's principal office or place of business in this State" or "principal office or place of business of the corporation in this State," or other term of like import, is or has been used in a corporation's certificate of incorporation, or in any other document, or in any statute, it shall be deemed to mean and refer to, unless the context indicates otherwise, the corporation's registered office required by this section; and it shall not be necessary for any corporation to amend its certificate of incorporation or any other document to comply with this section.

§ 132. Registered agent in State; resident agent.

(a) Every corporation shall have and maintain in this State a registered agent, which agent may be any of (i) the corporation itself, (ii) an individual resident in this State, (iii) a domestic corporation (other than the corporation itself), a domestic limited partnership, a domestic limited liability company or a domestic business trust or (iv) a foreign corporation, a foreign limited partnership or a foreign limited liability company authorized to transact business in this State, in each case, having a business office identical with the office of such registered agent which generally is open during normal business hours to accept service of process and otherwise perform the functions of a registered agent.

(b) Whenever the term "resident agent" or "resident agent in charge of a corporation's principal office or place of business in this State," or other term of like import which refers to a corporation's agent required by statute to be located in this State, is or has been used in a corporation's certificate of incorporation, or in any other document, or in any statute, it shall be deemed to mean and refer to, unless the context indicates otherwise, the corporation's registered agent required by this section; and it shall not be necessary for any corporation to amend its certificate of incorporation or any other document to comply with this section.

§ 133. Change of location of registered office; change of registered agent.

Any corporation may, by resolution of its board of directors, change the location of its registered office in this State to any other place in this State. By like resolution, the registered agent of a corporation may be changed to any other person or corporation including itself. In either such case, the resolution shall be as detailed in its statement as is required by § 102(a)(2) of this title. Upon the adoption of such a resolution, a certificate certifying the change shall be executed, acknowledged, and filed in accordance with § 103 of this title.

§ 134. Change of address or name of registered agent.
(a) A registered agent may change the address of the registered office of the corporation or corporations for which the agent is a registered agent to another address in this State by filing with the Secretary of State a certificate, executed and acknowledged by such registered agent, setting forth the address at which such registered agent has maintained the registered office for each of the corporations for which it is a registered agent, and further certifying to the new address to which each such registered office will be changed on a given day, and at which new address such registered agent will thereafter maintain the registered office for each of the corporations for which it is a registered agent. Thereafter, or until further change of address, as authorized by law, the registered office in this State of each of the corporations for which the agent is a registered agent shall be located at the new address of the registered agent thereof as given in the certificate.
(b) In the event of a change of name of any person or corporation acting as registered agent in this State, such registered agent shall file with the Secretary of State a certificate, executed and acknowledged by such registered agent, setting forth the new name of such registered agent, the name of such registered agent before it was changed, and the address at which such registered agent has maintained the registered office for each of the corporations for which it acts as a registered agent. A change of name of any person or corporation acting as a registered agent as a result of a merger or consolidation of the registered agent, with or into another person or corporation which succeeds to its assets by operation of law, shall be deemed a change of name for purposes of this section.

§ 135. Resignation of registered agent coupled with appointment of successor.
The registered agent of 1 or more corporations may resign and appoint a successor registered agent by filing a certificate with the Secretary of State, stating the name and address of the successor agent, in accordance with § 102(a)(2) of this title. There shall be attached to such certificate a statement of each affected corporation ratifying and approving such change of registered agent. Each such statement shall be executed and acknowledged in accordance with § 103 of this title. Upon such filing, the successor registered agent shall become the registered agent of such corporations as have ratified and approved such substitution and the successor registered agent's address, as stated in such certificate, shall become the address of each such corporation's registered office in this State. The Secretary of State shall then issue a certificate that the successor registered agent has become the registered agent of the corporations so ratifying and approving such change and setting out the names of such corporations.

§ 136. Resignation of registered agent not coupled with appointment of successor.
(a) The registered agent of 1 or more corporations may resign without appointing a successor by filing a certificate of resignation with the Secretary of State, but such resignation shall not become effective until 30 days after the certificate is filed. The certificate shall be executed and acknowledged by the registered agent, shall contain a statement that written notice of resignation was given to each affected corporation at least 30 days prior to the filing of the certificate by mailing or delivering such notice to the corporation at its address last known to the registered agent and shall set forth the date of such notice.
(b) After receipt of the notice of the resignation of its registered agent, provided for in subsection (a) of this section, the corporation for which such registered agent was acting shall obtain and designate a new registered agent to take the place of the registered agent so resigning in the same manner as provided in § 133 of this title for change of registered agent. If such corporation, being a corporation of this State, fails to obtain and designate a new registered agent as aforesaid prior to the expiration of the period of 30 days after the filing by the registered agent of the certificate of resignation, the Secretary of State shall declare the charter of such corporation forfeited. If such corporation, being a foreign corporation, fails to obtain and designate a new registered agent as aforesaid prior to the expiration of the period of 30 days after the filing by the registered agent of the certificate of resignation, the Secretary of State shall forfeit its authority to do business in this State.
(c) After the resignation of the registered agent shall have become effective as provided in this section and if no new registered agent shall have been obtained and designated in the time and manner aforesaid, service of legal process against the corporation for which the resigned registered agent had been acting shall thereafter be upon the Secretary of State in accordance with § 321 of this title.

Subchapter IV. Directors and Officers.

§ 141. Board of directors; powers; number, qualifications, terms and quorum; committees; classes of directors; nonprofit corporations; reliance upon books; action without meeting; removal.

(a) The business and affairs of every corporation organized under this chapter shall be managed by or under the direction of a board of directors, except as may be otherwise provided in this chapter or in its certificate of incorporation. If any such provision is made in the certificate of incorporation, the powers and duties conferred or imposed upon the board of directors by this chapter shall be exercised or performed to such extent and by such person or persons as shall be provided in the certificate of incorporation.
(b) The board of directors of a corporation shall consist of 1 or more members. The number of directors shall be fixed by, or in the manner provided in, the bylaws, unless the certificate of incorporation fixes the number of directors, in which case a change in the number of directors shall be made only by amendment of the certificate. Directors need not be stockholders unless so required by the certificate of incorporation or the bylaws. The certificate of incorporation or bylaws may prescribe other qualifications for directors. Each director shall hold office until such director's successor is elected and qualified or until such director's earlier resignation or removal. Any director may resign at any time upon notice given in writing or by electronic transmission to the corporation. A majority of the total number of directors shall constitute a quorum for the transaction of business unless the certificate of incorporation or the bylaws require a greater number. Unless the certificate of incorporation provides otherwise, the bylaws may provide that a number less than a majority shall constitute a quorum which in no case shall be less than 1/3 of the total number of directors except that when a board of 1 director is authorized under this section, then 1 director shall constitute a quorum. The vote of the majority of the directors present at a meeting at which a quorum is present shall be the act of the board of directors unless the certificate of incorporation or the bylaws shall require a vote of a greater number.
(c)
(1) All corporations incorporated prior to July 1, 1996, shall be governed by paragraph (1) of this subsection, provided that any such corporation may by a resolution adopted by a majority of the whole board elect to be governed by paragraph (2) of this subsection, in which case paragraph (1) of this subsection shall not apply to such corporation. All corporations incorporated on or after July 1, 1996, shall be governed by paragraph (2) of this subsection. The board of directors may, by resolution passed by a majority of the whole board, designate 1 or more committees, each committee to consist of 1 or more of the directors of the corporation. The board may designate 1 or more directors as alternate members of any committee, who may replace any absent or disqualified member at any meeting of the committee. The bylaws may provide that in the absence or disqualification of a member of a committee, the member or members present at any meeting and not disqualified from voting, whether or not the member or members present constitute a quorum, may unanimously appoint another member of the board of directors to act at the meeting in the place of any such absent or disqualified member. Any such committee, to the extent provided in the resolution of the board of directors, or in the bylaws of the corporation, shall have and may exercise all the powers and authority of the board of directors in the management of the business and affairs of the corporation, and may authorize the seal of the corporation to be affixed to all papers which may require it; but no such committee shall have the power or authority in reference to amending the certificate of incorporation (except that a committee may, to the extent authorized in the resolution or resolutions providing for the issuance of shares of stock adopted by the board of directors as provided in subsection (a) of § 151 of this title, fix the designations and any of the preferences or rights of such shares relating to dividends, redemption, dissolution, any distribution of assets of the corporation or the conversion into, or the exchange of such shares for, shares of any other class or classes or any other series of the same or any other class or classes of stock of the corporation or fix the number of shares of any series of stock or authorize the increase or decrease of the shares of any series), adopting an agreement of merger or consolidation under § 251, § 252, § 254, § 255, § 256, § 257, § 258, § 263 or § 264 of this title, recommending to the stockholders the sale, lease or exchange of all or substantially all of the corporation's property and assets, recommending to the stockholders a dissolution of the corporation or a revocation of a dissolution, or amending the bylaws of the corporation; and, unless the resolution, bylaws or certificate of incorporation expressly so provides, no such committee shall have the power or authority to declare a dividend, to authorize the issuance of stock or to adopt a certificate of ownership and merger pursuant to § 253 of this title.
(2) The board of directors may designate 1 or more committees, each committee to consist of 1 or more of the directors of the corporation. The board may designate 1 or more directors as alternate members of any committee, who may replace any absent or disqualified member at any meeting of the committee. The bylaws may provide that in the absence or disqualification of a member of a committee, the member or members present at any meeting and not disqualified from voting, whether or not such member or members constitute a quorum, may unanimously appoint another member of the board of directors to act at the meeting in the place of any such absent or disqualified member. Any such committee, to the extent provided in the resolution of the board of directors, or in the bylaws of the corporation, shall have and may exercise all the powers and authority of the board of directors in the management of the business and

affairs of the corporation, and may authorize the seal of the corporation to be affixed to all papers which may require it; but no such committee shall have the power or authority in reference to the following matter: (i) approving or adopting, or recommending to the stockholders, any action or matter expressly required by this chapter to be submitted to stockholders for approval or (ii) adopting, amending or repealing any bylaw of the corporation.

(d) The directors of any corporation organized under this chapter may, by the certificate of incorporation or by an initial bylaw, or by a bylaw adopted by a vote of the stockholders, be divided into 1, 2 or 3 classes; the term of office of those of the first class to expire at the annual meeting next ensuing; of the second class 1 year thereafter; of the third class 2 years thereafter; and at each annual election held after such classification and election, directors shall be chosen for a full term, as the case may be, to succeed those whose terms expire. The certificate of incorporation may confer upon holders of any class or series of stock the right to elect 1 or more directors who shall serve for such term, and have such voting powers as shall be stated in the certificate of incorporation. The terms of office and voting powers of the directors elected in the manner so provided in the certificate of incorporation may be greater than or less than those of any other director or class of directors. If the certificate of incorporation provides that directors elected by the holders of a class or series of stock shall have more or less than 1 vote per director on any matter, every reference in this chapter to a majority or other proportion of directors shall refer to a majority or other proportion of the votes of such directors.

(e) A member of the board of directors, or a member of any committee designated by the board of directors, shall, in the performance of such member's duties, be fully protected in relying in good faith upon the records of the corporation and upon such information, opinions, reports or statements presented to the corporation by any of the corporation's officers or employees, or committees of the board of directors, or by any other person as to matters the member reasonably believes are within such other person's professional or expert competence and who has been selected with reasonable care by or on behalf of the corporation.

(f) Unless otherwise restricted by the certificate of incorporation or bylaws, any action required or permitted to be taken at any meeting of the board of directors or of any committee thereof may be taken without a meeting if all members of the board or committee, as the case may be, consent thereto in writing, or by electronic transmission and the writing or writings or electronic transmission or transmissions are filed with the minutes of proceedings of the board, or committee. Such filing shall be in paper form if the minutes are maintained in paper form and shall be in electronic form if the minutes are maintained in electronic form.

(g) Unless otherwise restricted by the certificate of incorporation or bylaws, the board of directors of any corporation organized under this chapter may hold its meetings, and have an office or offices, outside of this State.

(h) Unless otherwise restricted by the certificate of incorporation or bylaws, the board of directors shall have the authority to fix the compensation of directors.

(i) Unless otherwise restricted by the certificate of incorporation or bylaws, members of the board of directors of any corporation, or any committee designated by the board, may participate in a meeting of such board, or committee by means of conference telephone or other communications equipment by means of which all persons participating in the meeting can hear each other, and participation in a meeting pursuant to this subsection shall constitute presence in person at the meeting.

(j) The certificate of incorporation of any corporation organized under this chapter which is not authorized to issue capital stock may provide that less than 1/3 of the members of the governing body may constitute a quorum thereof and may otherwise provide that the business and affairs of the corporation shall be managed in a manner different from that provided in this section. Except as may be otherwise provided by the certificate of incorporation, this section shall apply to such a corporation, and when so applied, all references to the board of directors, to members thereof, and to stockholders shall be deemed to refer to the governing body of the corporation, the members thereof and the members of the corporation, respectively.

(k) Any director or the entire board of directors may be removed, with or without cause, by the holders of a majority of the shares then entitled to vote at an election of directors, except as follows:

(1) Unless the certificate of incorporation otherwise provides, in the case of a corporation whose board is classified as provided in subsection (d) of this section, shareholders may effect such removal only for cause; or

(2) In the case of a corporation having cumulative voting, if less than the entire board is to be removed, no director may be removed without cause if the votes cast against such director's removal would be sufficient to elect such director if then cumulatively voted at an election of the entire board of directors, or, if there be classes of directors, at an election of the class of directors of which such director is a part. Whenever the holders of any class or series are entitled to elect 1 or more directors by the certificate of incorporation, this subsection shall apply, in respect to the removal without cause of a director or directors so elected, to the vote of the holders of the outstanding shares of that class or series and not to the vote of the outstanding shares as a whole.

§ 142. Officers; titles, duties, selection, term; failure to elect; vacancies.

(a) Every corporation organized under this chapter shall have such officers with such titles and duties as shall be stated in the bylaws or in a resolution of the board of directors which is not inconsistent with the bylaws and as may be necessary to enable it to sign instruments and stock certificates which comply with §§ 103(a)(2) and 158 of this title. One of the officers shall have the duty to record the proceedings of the meetings of the stockholders and directors in a book to be kept for that purpose. Any number of offices may be held by the same person unless the certificate of incorporation or bylaws otherwise provide.
(b) Officers shall be chosen in such manner and shall hold their offices for such terms as are prescribed by the bylaws or determined by the board of directors or other governing body. Each officer shall hold office until such officer's successor is elected and qualified or until such officer's earlier resignation or removal. Any officer may resign at any time upon written notice to the corporation.
(c) The corporation may secure the fidelity of any or all of its officers or agents by bond or otherwise.
(d) A failure to elect officers shall not dissolve or otherwise affect the corporation.
(e) Any vacancy occurring in any office of the corporation by death, resignation, removal or otherwise, shall be filled as the bylaws provide. In the absence of such provision, the vacancy shall be filled by the board of directors or other governing body.

§ 143. Loans to employees and officers; guaranty of obligations of employees and officers.
Any corporation may lend money to, or guarantee any obligation of, or otherwise assist any officer or other employee of the corporation or of its subsidiary, including any officer or employee who is a director of the corporation or its subsidiary, whenever, in the judgment of the directors, such loan, guaranty or assistance may reasonably be expected to benefit the corporation. The loan, guaranty or other assistance may be with or without interest, and may be unsecured, or secured in such manner as the board of directors shall approve, including, without limitation, a pledge of shares of stock of the corporation. Nothing in this section contained shall be deemed to deny, limit or restrict the powers of guaranty or warranty of any corporation at common law or under any statute.

§ 144. Interested directors; quorum.
(a) No contract or transaction between a corporation and 1 or more of its directors or officers, or between a corporation and any other corporation, partnership, association, or other organization in which 1 or more of its directors or officers, are directors or officers, or have a financial interest, shall be void or voidable solely for this reason, or solely because the director or officer is present at or participates in the meeting of the board or committee which authorizes the contract or transaction, or solely because any such director's or officer's votes are counted for such purpose, if:

(1) The material facts as to the director's or officer's relationship or interest and as to the contract or transaction are disclosed or are known to the board of directors or the committee, and the board or committee in good faith authorizes the contract or transaction by the affirmative votes of a majority of the disinterested directors, even though the disinterested directors be less than a quorum; or

(2) The material facts as to the director's or officer's relationship or interest and as to the contract or transaction are disclosed or are known to the shareholders entitled to vote thereon, and the contract or transaction is specifically approved in good faith by vote of the shareholders; or

(3) The contract or transaction is fair as to the corporation as of the time it is authorized, approved or ratified, by the board of directors, a committee or the shareholders.

(b) Common or interested directors may be counted in determining the presence of a quorum at a meeting of the board of directors or of a committee which authorizes the contract or transaction.

§ 145. Indemnification of officers, directors, employees and agents; insurance.
(a) A corporation shall have power to indemnify any person who was or is a party or is threatened to be made a party to any threatened, pending or completed action, suit or proceeding, whether civil, criminal, administrative or investigative (other than an action by or in the right of the corporation) by reason of the fact that the person is or was a director, officer, employee or agent of the corporation, or is or was serving at the request of the corporation as a director, officer, employee or agent of another corporation, partnership, joint venture, trust or other enterprise, against expenses (including attorneys' fees), judgments, fines and amounts paid in settlement actually and reasonably incurred by the person in connection with such action, suit or proceeding if the person acted in good faith and in a manner the person reasonably believed to be in or not opposed to the best interests of the corporation, and, with respect to any criminal action or proceeding, had no reasonable cause to believe the person's conduct was unlawful. The termination of any action, suit or proceeding by judgment, order, settlement, conviction, or upon a plea of nolo contendere or its equivalent, shall not, of itself, create a presumption that the person did not act in good faith and in a manner which the person reasonably believed to be in or not opposed to the best interests of the corporation, and, with respect to any criminal action or proceeding, had reasonable cause to believe that the person's conduct was unlawful.

(b) A corporation shall have power to indemnify any person who was or is a party or is threatened to be made a party to any threatened, pending or completed action or suit by or in the right of the corporation to procure a judgment in its favor by reason of the fact that the person is or was a director, officer, employee or agent of the corporation, or is or was serving at the request of the corporation as a director, officer, employee or agent of another corporation, partnership, joint venture, trust or other enterprise against expenses (including attorneys' fees) actually and reasonably incurred by the person in connection with the defense or settlement of such action or suit if the person acted in good faith and in a manner the person reasonably believed to be in or not opposed to the best interests of the corporation and except that no indemnification shall be made in respect of any claim, issue or matter as to which such person shall have been adjudged to be liable to the corporation unless and only to the extent that the Court of Chancery or the court in which such action or suit was brought shall determine upon application that, despite the adjudication of liability but in view of all the circumstances of the case, such person is fairly and reasonably entitled to indemnity for such expenses which the Court of Chancery or such other court shall deem proper.

(c) To the extent that a present or former director or officer of a corporation has been successful on the merits or otherwise in defense of any action, suit or proceeding referred to in subsections (a) and (b) of this section, or in defense of any claim, issue or matter therein, such person shall be indemnified against expenses (including attorneys' fees) actually and reasonably incurred by such person in connection therewith.

(d) Any indemnification under subsections (a) and (b) of this section (unless ordered by a court) shall be made by the corporation only as authorized in the specific case upon a determination that indemnification of the present or former director, officer, employee or agent is proper in the circumstances because the person has met the applicable standard of conduct set forth in subsections (a) and (b) of this section. Such determination shall be made, with respect to a person who is a director or officer at the time of such determination,

(1) by a majority vote of the directors who are not parties to such action, suit or proceeding, even though less than a quorum, or

(2) by a committee of such directors designated by majority vote of such directors, even though less than a quorum, or

(3) if there are no such directors, or if such directors so direct, by independent legal counsel in a written opinion, or

(4) by the stockholders.

(e) Expenses (including attorneys' fees) incurred by an officer or director in defending any civil, criminal, administrative or investigative action, suit or proceeding may be paid by the corporation in advance of the final disposition of such action, suit or proceeding upon receipt of an undertaking by or on behalf of such director or officer to repay such amount if it shall ultimately be determined that such person is not entitled to be indemnified by the corporation as authorized in this section. Such expenses (including attorneys' fees) incurred by former directors and officers or other employees and agents may be so paid upon such terms and conditions, if any, as the corporation deems appropriate.

(f) The indemnification and advancement of expenses provided by, or granted pursuant to, the other subsections of this section shall not be deemed exclusive of any other rights to which those seeking indemnification or advancement of expenses may be entitled under any bylaw, agreement, vote of stockholders or disinterested directors or otherwise, both as to action in such person's official capacity and as to action in another capacity while holding such office.

(g) A corporation shall have power to purchase and maintain insurance on behalf of any person who is or was a director, officer, employee or agent of the corporation, or is or was serving at the request of the corporation as a director, officer, employee or agent of another corporation, partnership, joint venture, trust or other enterprise against any liability asserted against such person and incurred by such person in any such capacity, or arising out of such person's status as such, whether or not the corporation would have the power to indemnify such person against such liability under this section.

(h) For purposes of this section, references to "the corporation" shall include, in addition to the resulting corporation, any constituent corporation (including any constituent of a constituent) absorbed in a consolidation or merger which, if its separate existence had continued, would have had power and authority to indemnify its directors, officers, and employees or agents, so that any person who is or was a director, officer, employee or agent of such constituent corporation, or is or was serving at the request of such constituent corporation as a director, officer, employee or agent of another corporation, partnership, joint venture, trust or other enterprise, shall stand in the same position under this section with respect to the resulting or surviving corporation as such person would have with respect to such constituent corporation if its separate existence had continued.

(i) For purposes of this section, references to "other enterprises" shall include employee benefit plans; references to "fines" shall include any excise taxes assessed on a person with respect to any employee benefit plan; and references to "serving at the request of the corporation" shall include any service as a director, officer, employee or agent of the corporation which imposes duties on, or involves services by, such director, officer, employee or agent with respect to an employee benefit plan, its participants or beneficiaries; and a person who acted in good faith and in a manner such person reasonably believed to be in the interest of the participants and beneficiaries of an employee benefit plan shall be deemed to have acted in a manner "not opposed to the best interests of the corporation" as referred to in this section.

(j) The indemnification and advancement of expenses provided by, or granted pursuant to, this section shall, unless otherwise provided when authorized or ratified, continue as to a person who has ceased to be a director, officer, employee or agent and shall inure to the benefit of the heirs, executors and administrators of such a person.

(k) The Court of Chancery is hereby vested with exclusive jurisdiction to hear and determine all actions for advancement of expenses or indemnification brought under this section or under any bylaw, agreement, vote of stockholders or disinterested directors, or otherwise. The Court of Chancery may summarily determine a corporation's obligation to advance expenses (including attorneys' fees).

Subchapter V. Stock and Dividends.

§ 151. Classes and series of stock; redemption; rights.

(a) Every corporation may issue 1 or more classes of stock or 1 or more series of stock within any class thereof, any or all of which classes may be of stock with par value or stock without par value and which classes or series may have such voting powers, full or limited, or no voting powers, and such designations, preferences and relative, participating, optional or other special rights, and qualifications, limitations or restrictions thereof, as shall be stated and expressed in the certificate of incorporation or of any amendment thereto, or in the resolution or resolutions providing for the issue of such stock adopted by the board of directors pursuant to authority expressly vested in it by the provisions of its certificate of incorporation. Any of the voting powers, designations, preferences, rights and qualifications, limitations or restrictions of any such class or series of stock may be made dependent upon facts ascertainable outside the certificate of incorporation or of any amendment thereto, or outside the resolution or resolutions providing for the issue of such stock adopted by the board of directors pursuant to authority expressly vested in it by its certificate of incorporation, provided that the manner in which such facts shall operate upon the voting powers, designations, preferences, rights and qualifications, limitations or restrictions of such class or series of stock is clearly and expressly set forth in the certificate of incorporation or in the resolution or resolutions providing for the issue of such stock adopted by the board of directors. The term "facts," as used in this subsection, includes, but is not limited to, the occurrence of any event, including a determination or action by any person or body, including the corporation. The power to increase or decrease or otherwise adjust the capital stock as provided in this chapter shall apply to all or any such classes of stock.

(b) Any stock of any class or series may be made subject to redemption by the corporation at its option or at the option of the holders of such stock or upon the happening of a specified event; provided however, that immediately following any such redemption the corporation shall have outstanding 1 or more shares of 1 or more classes or series of stock, which share, or shares together, shall have full voting powers. Notwithstanding the limitation stated in the foregoing proviso:

(1) Any stock of a regulated investment company registered under the Investment Company Act of 1940 [15 U.S.C. § 80 a-1 et seq.], as heretofore or hereafter amended, may be made subject to redemption by the corporation at its option or at the option of the holders of such stock.

(2) Any stock of a corporation which holds (directly or indirectly) a license or franchise from a governmental agency to conduct its business or is a member of a national securities exchange, which license, franchise or membership is conditioned upon some or all of the holders of its stock possessing prescribed qualifications, may be made subject to redemption by the corporation to the extent necessary to prevent the loss of such license, franchise or membership or to reinstate it. Any stock which may be made redeemable under this section may be redeemed for cash, property or rights, including securities of the same or another corporation, at such time or times, price or prices, or rate or rates, and with such adjustments, as shall be stated in the certificate of incorporation or in the resolution or resolutions providing for the issue of such stock adopted by the board of directors pursuant to subsection (a) of this section.

(c) The holders of preferred or special stock of any class or of any series thereof shall be entitled to receive dividends at such rates, on such conditions and at such times as shall be stated in the certificate of incorporation or in the resolution or resolutions providing for the issue of such stock adopted by the board of directors as hereinabove provided, payable in preference to, or in such relation to, the dividends payable on any other class or classes or of any other series of stock, and cumulative or noncumulative as shall be so stated and expressed. When dividends upon the preferred and special stocks, if any, to the extent of the preference to which such stocks are entitled, shall have been paid or declared and set apart for payment, a dividend on the remaining class or classes or series of stock may then be paid out of the remaining assets of the corporation available for dividends as elsewhere in this chapter provided.

(d) The holders of the preferred or special stock of any class or of any series thereof shall be entitled to such rights upon the dissolution of, or upon any distribution of the assets of, the corporation as shall be stated in the certificate of incorporation or in the resolution or resolutions providing for the issue of such stock adopted by the board of directors as hereinabove provided.

(e) Any stock of any class or of any series thereof may be made convertible into, or exchangeable for, at the option of either the holder or the corporation or upon the happening of a specified event, shares of any other class or classes or any other series of the same or any other class or classes of stock of the corporation, at such price or prices or at such rate or rates of exchange and with such adjustments as shall be stated in the certificate of incorporation or in the resolution or resolutions providing for the issue of such stock adopted by the board of directors as hereinabove provided.

(f) If any corporation shall be authorized to issue more than 1 class of stock or more than 1 series of any class, the powers, designations, preferences and relative, participating, optional, or other special rights of each class of stock or series thereof and the qualifications, limitations or restrictions of such preferences and/or rights shall be set forth in full or summarized on the face or back of the certificate which the corporation shall issue to represent such class or series of stock, provided that, except as otherwise provided in § 202 of this title, in lieu of the foregoing requirements, there may be set forth on the face or back of the certificate which the corporation shall issue to represent such class or series of stock, a statement that the corporation will furnish without charge to each stockholder who so requests the powers, designations, preferences and relative, participating, optional, or other special rights of each class of stock or series thereof and the qualifications, limitations or restrictions of such preferences and/or rights. Within a reasonable time after the issuance or transfer of uncertificated stock, the corporation shall send to the registered owner thereof a written notice containing the information required to be set forth or stated on certificates pursuant to this section or § 156, 202(a) or 218(a) of this title or with respect to this section a statement that the corporation will furnish without charge to each stockholder who so requests the powers, designations, preferences and relative participating, optional or other special rights of each class of stock or series thereof and the qualifications, limitations or restrictions of such preferences and/or rights. Except as otherwise expressly provided by law, the rights and obligations of the holders of uncertificated stock and the rights and obligations of the holders of certificates representing stock of the same class and series shall be identical.

(g) When any corporation desires to issue any shares of stock of any class or of any series of any class of which the powers, designations, preferences and relative, participating, optional or other rights, if any, or the qualifications, limitations or restrictions thereof, if any, shall not have been set forth in the certificate of incorporation or in any amendment thereto but shall be provided for in a resolution or resolutions adopted by the board of directors pursuant to authority expressly vested in it by the certificate of incorporation or any amendment thereto, a certificate of designations setting forth a copy of such resolution or resolutions and the number of shares of stock of such class or series as to which the resolution or resolutions apply shall be executed, acknowledged, filed and shall become effective, in accordance with § 103 of this title. Unless otherwise provided in any such resolution or resolutions, the number of shares of stock of any such series to which such resolution or resolutions apply may be increased (but not above the total number of authorized shares of the class) or decreased (but not below the number of shares thereof then outstanding) by a certificate likewise executed, acknowledged and filed setting forth a statement that a specified increase or decrease therein had been authorized and directed by a resolution or resolutions likewise adopted by the board of directors. In case the number of such shares shall be decreased the number of shares so specified in the certificate shall resume the status which they had prior to the adoption of the first resolution or resolutions. When no shares of any such class or series are outstanding, either because none were issued or because no issued shares of any such class or series remain outstanding, a certificate setting forth a resolution or resolutions adopted by the board of directors that none of the authorized shares of such class or series are outstanding, and that none will be issued subject to the certificate of designations previously filed with respect to such class or series, may be executed, acknowledged and filed in accordance with § 103 of this title and, when such certificate becomes effective, it shall have the effect of eliminating from the certificate of incorporation all matters set forth in the certificate of designations with respect to such class or series of stock. Unless otherwise provided in the certificate of incorporation, if no shares of stock have been issued of a class or series of stock established by a resolution of the board of directors, the voting powers, designations, preferences and relative, participating, optional or other rights, if any, or the qualifications, limitations or restrictions thereof, may be amended by a resolution or resolutions adopted by the board of directors. A certificate which

(1) states that no shares of the class or series have been issued,

(2) sets forth a copy of the resolution or resolutions and

(3) if the designation of the class or series is being changed, indicates the original designation and the new designation, shall be executed, acknowledged and filed and shall become effective, in accordance with § 103 of this title. When any certificate filed under this subsection becomes effective, it shall have the effect of amending the certificate of incorporation; except that neither the filing of such certificate nor the filing of a restated certificate of incorporation pursuant to § 245 of this title shall prohibit the board of directors from subsequently adopting such resolutions as authorized by this subsection.

§ 152. Issuance of stock; lawful consideration; fully paid stock.

The consideration, as determined pursuant to subsections (a) and (b) of § 153 of this title, for subscriptions to, or the purchase of, the capital stock to be issued by a corporation shall be paid in such form and in such manner as the board of directors shall determine. In the absence of actual fraud in the transaction, the judgment of the directors as to the value of such consideration shall be conclusive. The capital stock so issued shall be deemed to be fully paid and nonassessable stock, if:

(1) The entire amount of such consideration has been received by the corporation in the form of cash, services rendered, personal property, real property, leases of real property or a combination thereof; or

(2) not less than the amount of the consideration determined to be capital pursuant to § 154 of this title has been received by the corporation in such form and the corporation has received a binding obligation of the subscriber or purchaser to pay the balance of the subscription or purchase price; provided, however, nothing contained herein shall prevent the board of directors from issuing partly paid shares under § 156 of this title.

§ 153. Consideration for stock.

(a) Shares of stock with par value may be issued for such consideration, having a value not less than the par value thereof, as determined from time to time by the board of directors, or by the stockholders if the certificate of incorporation so provides.

(b) Shares of stock without par value may be issued for such consideration as is determined from time to time by the board of directors, or by the stockholders if the certificate of incorporation so provides.

(c) Treasury shares may be disposed of by the corporation for such consideration as may be determined from time to time by the board of directors, or by the stockholders if the certificate of incorporation so provides.

(d) If the certificate of incorporation reserves to the stockholders the right to determine the consideration for the issue of any shares, the stockholders shall, unless the certificate requires a greater vote, do so by a vote of a majority of the outstanding stock entitled to vote thereon.

§ 154. Determination of amount of capital; capital, surplus and net assets defined.

Any corporation may, by resolution of its board of directors, determine that only a part of the consideration which shall be received by the corporation for any of the shares of its capital stock which it shall issue from time to time shall be capital; but, in case any of the shares issued shall be shares having a par value, the amount of the part of such consideration so determined to be capital shall be in excess of the aggregate par value of the shares issued for such consideration having a par value, unless all the shares issued shall be shares having a par value, in which case the amount of the part of such consideration so determined to be capital need be only equal to the aggregate par value of such shares. In each such case the board of directors shall specify in dollars the part of such consideration which shall be capital. If the board of directors shall not have determined

(1) at the time of issue of any shares of the capital stock of the corporation issued for cash or

(2) within 60 days after the issue of any shares of the capital stock of the corporation issued for property other than cash what part of the consideration for such shares shall be capital, the capital of the corporation in respect of such shares shall be an amount equal to the aggregate par value of such shares having a par value, plus the amount of the consideration for such shares without par value. The amount of the consideration so determined to be capital in respect of any shares without par value shall be the stated capital of such shares. The capital of the corporation may be increased from time to time by resolution of the board of directors directing that a portion of the net assets of the corporation in excess of the amount so determined to be capital be transferred to the capital account. The board of directors may direct that the portion of such net assets so transferred shall be treated as capital in respect of any shares of the corporation of any designated class or classes. The excess, if any, at any given time, of the net assets of the corporation over the amount so determined to be capital shall be surplus. Net assets means the amount by which total assets exceed total liabilities. Capital and surplus are not liabilities for this purpose.

§ 155. Fractions of shares.

A corporation may, but shall not be required to, issue fractions of a share. If it does not issue fractions of a share, it shall

(1) arrange for the disposition of fractional interests by those entitled thereto,

(2) pay in cash the fair value of fractions of a share as of the time when those entitled to receive such fractions are determined or

(3) issue scrip or warrants in registered form (either represented by a certificate or uncertificated) or in bearer form (represented by a certificate) which shall entitle the holder to receive a full share upon the surrender of such scrip or warrants aggregating a full share. A certificate for a fractional share or an uncertificated fractional share shall, but scrip or warrants shall not unless otherwise provided therein, entitle the holder to exercise voting rights, to receive dividends thereon and to participate in any of the assets of the corporation in the event of liquidation. The board of directors may cause scrip or warrants to be issued subject to the conditions that they shall become void if not exchanged for certificates representing the full shares or uncertificated full shares before a specified date, or subject to the conditions that the shares for which scrip or warrants are exchangeable may be sold by

the corporation and the proceeds thereof distributed to the holders of scrip or warrants, or subject to any other conditions which the board of directors may impose.

§ 156. Partly paid shares.
Any corporation may issue the whole or any part of its shares as partly paid and subject to call for the remainder of the consideration to be paid therefor. Upon the face or back of each stock certificate issued to represent any such partly paid shares, or upon the books and records of the corporation in the case of uncertificated partly paid shares, the total amount of the consideration to be paid therefor and the amount paid thereon shall be stated. Upon the declaration of any dividend on fully paid shares, the corporation shall declare a dividend upon partly paid shares of the same class, but only upon the basis of the percentage of the consideration actually paid thereon.

§ 157. Rights and options respecting stock.
(a) Subject to any provisions in the certificate of incorporation, every corporation may create and issue, whether or not in connection with the issue and sale of any shares of stock or other securities of the corporation, rights or options entitling the holders thereof to purchase from the corporation any shares of its capital stock of any class or classes, such rights or options to be evidenced by or in such instrument or instruments as shall be approved by the board of directors.
(b) The terms upon which, including the time or times which may be limited or unlimited in duration, at or within which, and the price or prices (including a formula by which such price or prices may be determined) at which any such shares may be purchased from the corporation upon the exercise of any such right or option, shall be such as shall be stated in the certificate of incorporation, or in a resolution adopted by the board of directors providing for the creation and issue of such rights or options, and, in every case, shall be set forth or incorporated by reference in the instrument or instruments evidencing such rights or options. In the absence of actual fraud in the transaction, the judgment of the directors as to the consideration for the issuance of such rights or options and the sufficiency thereof shall be conclusive.
(c) The board of directors may, by a resolution adopted by the board, authorize 1 or more officers of the corporation to do 1 or both of the following: (i) designate officers and employees of the corporation or of any of its subsidiaries to be recipients of such rights or options created by the corporation, and (ii) determine the number of such rights or options to be received by such officers and employees; provided, however, that the resolution so authorizing such officer or officers shall specify the total number of rights or options such officer or officers may so award. The board of directors may not authorize an officer to designate himself or herself as a recipient of any such rights or options.
(d) In case the shares of stock of the corporation to be issued upon the exercise of such rights or options shall be shares having a par value, the price or prices so to be received therefor shall not be less than the par value thereof. In case the shares of stock so to be issued shall be shares of stock without par value, the consideration therefor shall be determined in the manner provided in § 153 of this title.

§ 158. Stock certificates; uncertificated shares.
The shares of a corporation shall be represented by certificates, provided that the board of directors of the corporation may provide by resolution or resolutions that some or all of any or all classes or series of its stock shall be uncertificated shares. Any such resolution shall not apply to shares represented by a certificate until such certificate is surrendered to the corporation. Notwithstanding the adoption of such a resolution by the board of directors, every holder of stock represented by certificates and upon request every holder of uncertificated shares shall be entitled to have a certificate signed by, or in the name of the corporation by the chairperson or vice-chairperson of the board of directors, or the president or vice-president, and by the treasurer or an assistant treasurer, or the secretary or an assistant secretary of such corporation representing the number of shares registered in certificate form. Any or all the signatures on the certificate may be a facsimile. In case any officer, transfer agent or registrar who has signed or whose facsimile signature has been placed upon a certificate shall have ceased to be such officer, transfer agent or registrar before such certificate is issued, it may be issued by the corporation with the same effect as if such person were such officer, transfer agent or registrar at the date of issue.

§ 159. Shares of stock; personal property, transfer and taxation.
The shares of stock in every corporation shall be deemed personal property and transferable as provided in Article 8 of subtitle I of Title 6. No stock or bonds issued by any corporation organized under this chapter shall be taxed by this State when the same shall be owned by non-residents of this State, or by foreign corporations. Whenever any transfer of shares shall be made for collateral security, and not absolutely, it shall be so expressed in the entry of transfer if, when the certificates are presented to the corporation for transfer or uncertificated shares are requested to be transferred, both the transferor and transferee request the corporation to do so.

§ 160. Corporation's powers respecting ownership, voting, etc., of its own stock; rights of stock called for redemption.
(a) Every corporation may purchase, redeem, receive, take or otherwise acquire, own and hold, sell, lend, exchange, transfer or otherwise dispose of, pledge, use and otherwise

deal in and with its own shares; provided, however, that no corporation shall:

(1) Purchase or redeem its own shares of capital stock for cash or other property when the capital of the corporation is impaired or when such purchase or redemption would cause any impairment of the capital of the corporation, except that a corporation may purchase or redeem out of capital any of its own shares which are entitled upon any distribution of its assets, whether by dividend or in liquidation, to a preference over another class or series of its stock, or, if no shares entitled to such a preference are outstanding, any of its own shares, if such shares will be retired upon their acquisition and the capital of the corporation reduced in accordance with §§ 243 and 244 of this title. Nothing in this subsection shall invalidate or otherwise affect a note, debenture or other obligation of a corporation given by it as consideration for its acquisition by purchase, redemption or exchange of its shares of stock if at the time such note, debenture or obligation was delivered by the corporation its capital was not then impaired or did not thereby become impaired;

(2) Purchase, for more than the price at which they may then be redeemed, any of its shares which are redeemable at the option of the corporation; or

(3) Redeem any of its shares unless their redemption is authorized by subsection (b) of § 151 of this title and then only in accordance with such section and the certificate of incorporation.

(b) Nothing in this section limits or affects a corporation's right to resell any of its shares theretofore purchased or redeemed out of surplus and which have not been retired, for such consideration as shall be fixed by the board of directors.

(c) Shares of its own capital stock belonging to the corporation or to another corporation, if a majority of the shares entitled to vote in the election of directors of such other corporation is held, directly or indirectly, by the corporation, shall neither be entitled to vote nor be counted for quorum purposes. Nothing in this section shall be construed as limiting the right of any corporation to vote stock, including but not limited to its own stock, held by it in a fiduciary capacity.

(d) Shares which have been called for redemption shall not be deemed to be outstanding shares for the purpose of voting or determining the total number of shares entitled to vote on any matter on and after the date on which written notice of redemption has been sent to holders thereof and a sum sufficient to redeem such shares has been irrevocably deposited or set aside to pay the redemption price to the holders of the shares upon surrender of certificates therefor.

§ 161. Issuance of additional stock; when and by whom.

The directors may, at any time and from time to time, if all of the shares of capital stock which the corporation is authorized by its certificate of incorporation to issue have not been issued, subscribed for, or otherwise committed to be issued, issue or take subscriptions for additional shares of its capital stock up to the amount authorized in its certificate of incorporation.

§ 162. Liability of stockholder or subscriber for stock not paid in full.

(a) When the whole of the consideration payable for shares of a corporation has not been paid in, and the assets shall be insufficient to satisfy the claims of its creditors, each holder of or subscriber for such shares shall be bound to pay on each share held or subscribed for by such holder or subscriber the sum necessary to complete the amount of the unpaid balance of the consideration for which such shares were issued or are to be issued by the corporation.

(b) The amounts which shall be payable as provided in subsection (a) of this section may be recovered as provided in § 325 of this title, after a writ of execution against the corporation has been returned unsatisfied as provided in said § 325.

(c) Any person becoming an assignee or transferee of shares or of a subscription for shares in good faith and without knowledge or notice that the full consideration therefor has not been paid shall not be personally liable for any unpaid portion of such consideration, but the transferor shall remain liable therefor.

(d) No person holding shares in any corporation as collateral security shall be personally liable as a stockholder but the person pledging such shares shall be considered the holder thereof and shall be so liable. No executor, administrator, guardian, trustee or other fiduciary shall be personally liable as a stockholder, but the estate or funds held by such executor, administrator, guardian, trustee or other fiduciary in such fiduciary capacity shall be liable.

(e) No liability under this section or under § 325 of this title shall be asserted more than 6 years after the issuance of the stock or the date of the subscription upon which the assessment is sought.

(f) In any action by a receiver or trustee of an insolvent corporation or by a judgment creditor to obtain an assessment under this section, any stockholder or subscriber for stock of the insolvent corporation may appear and contest the claim or claims of such receiver or trustee.

§ 163. Payment for stock not paid in full.

The capital stock of a corporation shall be paid for in such amounts and at such times as the directors may require. The directors may, from time to time, demand payment, in respect of each share of stock not fully paid, of such sum of money as the necessities of the business may, in the judgment of the board of directors, require, not exceeding in the whole the balance remaining unpaid on said stock, and such sum so demanded shall be paid to the corporation at such times and by such installments as the directors shall direct. The directors shall give written notice of the time and place of such payments, which notice shall be mailed at least 30 days before the time for such payment, to each holder of or subscriber for stock which is not fully paid at such holder's or subscriber's last known post-office address.

§ 164. Failure to pay for stock; remedies.
When any stockholder fails to pay any installment or call upon such stockholder's stock which may have been properly demanded by the directors, at the time when such payment is due, the directors may collect the amount of any such installment or call or any balance thereof remaining unpaid, from the said stockholder by an action at law, or they shall sell at public sale such part of the shares of such delinquent stockholder as will pay all demands then due from such stockholder with interest and all incidental expenses, and shall transfer the shares so sold to the purchaser, who shall be entitled to a certificate therefor. Notice of the time and place of such sale and of the sum due on each share shall be given by advertisement at least 1 week before the sale, in a newspaper of the county in this State where such corporation's registered office is located, and such notice shall be mailed by the corporation to such delinquent stockholder at such stockholder's last known post-office address, at least 20 days before such sale. If no bidder can be had to pay the amount due on the stock, and if the amount is not collected by an action at law, which may be brought within the county where the corporation has its registered office, within 1 year from the date of the bringing of such action at law, the said stock and the amount previously paid in by the delinquent stockholder on the stock shall be forfeited to the corporation.

§ 165. Revocability of preincorporation subscriptions.
Unless otherwise provided by the terms of the subscription, a subscription for stock of a corporation to be formed shall be irrevocable, except with the consent of all other subscribers or the corporation, for a period of 6 months from its date.

§ 166. Formalities required of stock subscriptions.
A subscription for stock of a corporation, whether made before or after the formation of a corporation, shall not be enforceable against a subscriber, unless in writing and signed by the subscriber or by such subscriber's agent.

§ 167. Lost, stolen or destroyed stock certificates; issuance of new certificate or uncertificated shares.
A corporation may issue a new certificate of stock or uncertificated shares in place of any certificate theretofore issued by it, alleged to have been lost, stolen or destroyed, and the corporation may require the owner of the lost, stolen or destroyed certificate, or such owner's legal representative to give the corporation a bond sufficient to indemnify it against any claim that may be made against it on account of the alleged loss, theft or destruction of any such certificate or the issuance of such new certificate or uncertificated shares.

§ 168. Judicial proceedings to compel issuance of new certificate or uncertificated shares.
(a) If a corporation refuses to issue new uncertificated shares or a new certificate of stock in place of a certificate theretofore issued by it, or by any corporation of which it is the lawful successor, alleged to have been lost, stolen or destroyed, the owner of the lost, stolen or destroyed certificate or such owner's legal representatives may apply to the Court of Chancery for an order requiring the corporation to show cause why it should not issue new uncertificated shares or a new certificate of stock in place of the certificate so lost, stolen or destroyed. Such application shall be by a complaint which shall state the name of the corporation, the number and date of the certificate, if known or ascertainable by the plaintiff, the number of shares of stock represented thereby and to whom issued, and a statement of the circumstances attending such loss, theft or destruction. Thereupon the court shall make an order requiring the corporation to show cause at a time and place therein designated, why it should not issue new uncertificated shares or a new certificate of stock in place of the one described in the complaint. A copy of the complaint and order shall be served upon the corporation at least 5 days before the time designated in the order.
(b) If, upon hearing, the court is satisfied that the plaintiff is the lawful owner of the number of shares of capital stock, or any part thereof, described in the complaint, and that the certificate therefor has been lost, stolen or destroyed, and no sufficient cause has been shown why new uncertificated shares or a new certificate should not be issued in place thereof, it shall make an order requiring the corporation to issue and deliver to the plaintiff new uncertificated shares or a new certificate for such shares. In its order the court shall direct that, prior to the issuance and delivery to the plaintiff of such new uncertificated shares or a new certificate, the plaintiff give the corporation a bond in such form and with such security as to the court appears sufficient to indemnify the corporation against any claim that may be made against it on account of the alleged loss, theft or destruction of any such certificate or the issuance of such new uncertificated shares or new certificate. No corporation which has issued uncertificated shares or a certificate pursuant to an order of the court entered hereunder shall be liable in an amount in excess of the amount specified in such bond.

§ 169. Situs of ownership of stock.
For all purposes of title, action, attachment, garnishment and jurisdiction of all courts held in this State, but not for

the purpose of taxation, the situs of the ownership of the capital stock of all corporations existing under the laws of this State, whether organized under this chapter or otherwise, shall be regarded as in this State.

§ 170. Dividends; payment; wasting asset corporations.
(a) The directors of every corporation, subject to any restrictions contained in its certificate of incorporation, may declare and pay dividends upon the shares of its capital stock, or to its members if the corporation is a nonstock corporation, either

(1) out of its surplus, as defined in and computed in accordance with §§ 154 and 244 of this title, or

(2) in case there shall be no such surplus, out of its net profits for the fiscal year in which the dividend is declared and/or the preceding fiscal year. If the capital of the corporation, computed in accordance with §§ 154 and 244 of this title, shall have been diminished by depreciation in the value of its property, or by losses, or otherwise, to an amount less than the aggregate amount of the capital represented by the issued and outstanding stock of all classes having a preference upon the distribution of assets, the directors of such corporation shall not declare and pay out of such net profits any dividends upon any shares of any classes of its capital stock until the deficiency in the amount of capital represented by the issued and outstanding stock of all classes having a preference upon the distribution of assets shall have been repaired. Nothing in this subsection shall invalidate or otherwise affect a note, debenture or other obligation of the corporation paid by it as a dividend on shares of its stock, or any payment made thereon, if at the time such note, debenture or obligation was delivered by the corporation, the corporation had either surplus or net profits as provided in clause (1) or (2) of this subsection from which the dividend could lawfully have been paid.

(b) Subject to any restrictions contained in its certificate of incorporation, the directors of any corporation engaged in the exploitation of wasting assets (including but not limited to a corporation engaged in the exploitation of natural resources or other wasting assets, including patents, or engaged primarily in the liquidation of specific assets) may determine the net profits derived from the exploitation of such wasting assets or the net proceeds derived from such liquidation without taking into consideration the depletion of such assets resulting from lapse of time, consumption, liquidation or exploitation of such assets.

§ 171. Special purpose reserves.
The directors of a corporation may set apart out of any of the funds of the corporation available for dividends a reserve or reserves for any proper purpose and may abolish any such reserve.

§ 172. Liability of directors and committee members as to dividends or stock redemption.
A member of the board of directors, or a member of any committee designated by the board of directors, shall be fully protected in relying in good faith upon the records of the corporation and upon such information, opinions, reports or statements presented to the corporation by any of its officers or employees, or committees of the board of directors, or by any other person as to matters the director reasonably believes are within such other person's professional or expert competence and who has been selected with reasonable care by or on behalf of the corporation, as to the value and amount of the assets, liabilities and/or net profits of the corporation or any other facts pertinent to the existence and amount of surplus or other funds from which dividends might properly be declared and paid, or with which the corporation's stock might properly be purchased or redeemed.

§ 173. Declaration and payment of dividends.
No corporation shall pay dividends except in accordance with this chapter. Dividends may be paid in cash, in property, or in shares of the corporation's capital stock. If the dividend is to be paid in shares of the corporation's theretofore unissued capital stock the board of directors shall, by resolution, direct that there be designated as capital in respect of such shares an amount which is not less than the aggregate par value of par value being declared as a dividend and, in the case of shares without par value being declared as a dividend, such amount as shall be determined by the board of directors. No such designation as capital shall be necessary if shares are being distributed by a corporation pursuant to a split-up or division of its stock rather than as payment of a dividend declared payable in stock of the corporation.

§ 174. Liability of directors for unlawful payment of dividend or unlawful stock purchase or redemption; exoneration from liability; contribution among directors; subrogation.
(a) In case of any wilful or negligent violation of § 160 or 173 of this title, the directors under whose administration the same may happen shall be jointly and severally liable, at any time within 6 years after paying such unlawful dividend or after such unlawful stock purchase or redemption, to the corporation, and to its creditors in the event of its dissolution or insolvency, to the full amount of the dividend unlawfully paid, or to the full amount unlawfully paid for the purchase or redemption of the corporation's stock, with interest from the time such liability accrued. Any director who may have been absent when the same was done, or who may have dissented from the act or resolution by which the same was done, may be exonerated from such liability by causing his or her dissent to be entered on the books containing the minutes of the proceedings of the

directors at the time the same was done, or immediately after such director has notice of the same.

(b) Any director against whom a claim is successfully asserted under this section shall be entitled to contribution from the other directors who voted for or concurred in the unlawful dividend, stock purchase or stock redemption.

(c) Any director against whom a claim is successfully asserted under this section shall be entitled, to the extent of the amount paid by such director as a result of such claim, to be subrogated to the rights of the corporation against stockholders who received the dividend on, or assets for the sale or redemption of, their stock with knowledge of facts indicating that such dividend, stock purchase or redemption was unlawful under this chapter, in proportion to the amounts received by such stockholders respectively.

Subchapter VI. Stock Transfers.

§ 201. Transfer of stock, stock certificates and uncertificated stock.

Except as otherwise provided in this chapter, the transfer of stock and the certificates of stock which represent the stock or uncertificated stock shall be governed by Article 8 of subtitle I of Title 6. To the extent that any provision of this chapter is inconsistent with any provision of subtitle I of Title 6, this chapter shall be controlling.

§ 202. Restrictions on transfer and ownership of securities.

(a) A written restriction or restrictions on the transfer or registration of transfer of a security of a corporation, or on the amount of the corporation's securities that may be owned by any person or group of persons, if permitted by this section and noted conspicuously on the certificate or certificates representing the security or securities so restricted or, in the case of uncertificated shares, contained in the notice or notices sent pursuant to § 151(f) of this title, may be enforced against the holder of the restricted security or securities or any successor or transferee of the holder including an executor, administrator, trustee, guardian or other fiduciary entrusted with like responsibility for the person or estate of the holder. Unless noted conspicuously on the certificate or certificates representing the security or securities so restricted or, in the case of uncertificated shares, contained in the notice or notices sent pursuant to § 151(f) of this title, a restriction, even though permitted by this section, is ineffective except against a person with actual knowledge of the restriction.

(b) A restriction on the transfer or registration of transfer of securities of a corporation, or on the amount of a corporation's securities that may be owned by any person or group of persons, may be imposed by the certificate of incorporation or by the bylaws or by an agreement among any number of security holders or among such holders and the corporation. No restrictions so imposed shall be binding with respect to securities issued prior to the adoption of the restriction unless the holders of the securities are parties to an agreement or voted in favor of the restriction.

(c) A restriction on the transfer or registration of transfer of securities of a corporation or on the amount of such securities that may be owned by any person or group of persons is permitted by this section if it:

(1) Obligates the holder of the restricted securities to offer to the corporation or to any other holders of securities of the corporation or to any other person or to any combination of the foregoing, a prior opportunity, to be exercised within a reasonable time, to acquire the restricted securities; or

(2) Obligates the corporation or any holder of securities of the corporation or any other person or any combination of the foregoing, to purchase the securities which are the subject of an agreement respecting the purchase and sale of the restricted securities; or

(3) Requires the corporation or the holders of any class or series of securities of the corporation to consent to any proposed transfer of the restricted securities or to approve the proposed transferee of the restricted securities, or to approve the amount of securities of the corporation that may be owned by any person or group of persons; or

(4) Obligates the holder of the restricted securities to sell or transfer an amount of restricted securities to the corporation or to any other holders of securities of the corporation or to any other person or to any combination of the foregoing, or causes or results in the automatic sale or transfer of an amount of restricted securities to the corporation or to any other holders of securities of the corporation or to any other person or to any combination of the foregoing; or

(5) Prohibits or restricts the transfer of the restricted securities to, or the ownership of restricted securities by, designated persons or classes of persons or groups of persons, and such designation is not manifestly unreasonable.

(d) Any restriction on the transfer or the registration of transfer of the securities of a corporation, or on the amount of securities of a corporation that may be owned by a person or group of persons, for any of the following purposes shall be conclusively presumed to be for a reasonable purpose:

(1) Maintaining any local, state, federal or foreign tax advantage to the corporation or its stockholders, including without limitation: a. Maintaining the corporation's status as an electing small business corporation under subchapter S of the United States Internal Revenue Code [26 U.S.C. § 1371 et seq.], or b. Maintaining or preserving any tax attribute (including without limitation net operating losses), or c. Qualifying or maintaining the qualification of the corporation as a real estate investment trust pursuant to the United States Internal Revenue Code or regulations adopted pursuant to the United States Internal Revenue Code, or

(2) Maintaining any statutory or regulatory advantage or complying with any statutory or regulatory requirements under applicable local, state, federal or foreign law.

(e) Any other lawful restriction on transfer or registration of transfer of securities, or on the amount of securities that may be owned by any person or group of persons, is permitted by this section.

§ 203. Business combinations with interested stockholders. (a) Notwithstanding any other provisions of this chapter, a corporation shall not engage in any business combination with any interested stockholder for a period of 3 years following the time that such stockholder became an interested stockholder, unless:

(1) Prior to such time the board of directors of the corporation approved either the business combination or the transaction which resulted in the stockholder becoming an interested stockholder;

(2) Upon consummation of the transaction which resulted in the stockholder becoming an interested stockholder, the interested stockholder owned at least 85% of the voting stock of the corporation outstanding at the time the transaction commenced, excluding for purposes of determining the number of shares outstanding those shares owned (i) by persons who are directors and also officers and (ii) employee stock plans in which employee participants do not have the right to determine confidentially whether shares held subject to the plan will be tendered in a tender or exchange offer; or

(3) At or subsequent to such time the business combination is approved by the board of directors and authorized at an annual or special meeting of stockholders, and not by written consent, by the affirmative vote of at least 662/3% of the outstanding voting stock which is not owned by the interested stockholder.

(b) The restrictions contained in this section shall not apply if:

(1) The corporation's original certificate of incorporation contains a provision expressly electing not to be governed by this section;

(2) The corporation, by action of its board of directors, adopts an amendment to its bylaws within 90 days of February 2, 1988, expressly electing not to be governed by this section, which amendment shall not be further amended by the board of directors;

(3) The corporation, by action of its stockholders, adopts an amendment to its certificate of incorporation or bylaws expressly electing not to be governed by this section; provided that, in addition to any other vote required by law, such amendment to the certificate of incorporation or bylaws must be approved by the affirmative vote of a majority of the shares entitled to vote. An amendment adopted pursuant to this paragraph shall be effective immediately in the case of a corporation that both (i) has never had a class of voting stock that falls within any of the 3 categories set out in subsection (b)(4) hereof, and (ii) has not elected by a provision in its original certificate of incorporation or any amendment thereto to be governed by this section. In all other cases, an amendment adopted pursuant to this paragraph shall not be effective until 12 months after the adoption of such amendment and shall not apply to any business combination between such corporation and any person who became an interested stockholder of such corporation on or prior to such adoption. A bylaw amendment adopted pursuant to this paragraph shall not be further amended by the board of directors;

(4) The corporation does not have a class of voting stock that is: (i) Listed on a national securities exchange; (ii) authorized for quotation on The NASDAQ Stock Market; or (iii) held of record by more than 2,000 stockholders, unless any of the foregoing results from action taken, directly or indirectly, by an interested stockholder or from a transaction in which a person becomes an interested stockholder;

(5) A stockholder becomes an interested stockholder inadvertently and (i) as soon as practicable divests itself of ownership of sufficient shares so that the stockholder ceases to be an interested stockholder; and (ii) would not, at any time within the 3-year period immediately prior to a business combination between the corporation and such stockholder, have been an interested stockholder but for the inadvertent acquisition of ownership;

(6) The business combination is proposed prior to the consummation or abandonment of and subsequent to the earlier of the public announcement or the notice required hereunder of a proposed transaction which (i) constitutes one of the transactions described in the 2nd sentence of this paragraph; (ii) is with or by a person who either was not an interested stockholder during the previous 3 years or who became an interested stockholder with the approval of the corporation's board of directors or during the period described in paragraph

(7) of this subsection (b); and (iii) is approved or not opposed by a majority of the members of the board of directors then in office (but not less than 1) who were directors prior to any person becoming an interested stockholder during the previous 3 years or were recommended for election or elected to succeed such directors by a majority of such directors. The proposed transactions referred to in the preceding sentence are limited to (x) a merger or consolidation of the corporation (except for a merger in respect of which, pursuant to § 251(f) of this title, no vote of the stockholders of the corporation is required); (y) a sale, lease, exchange, mortgage, pledge, transfer or other disposition (in 1 transaction or a series of transactions), whether as part of a dissolution or otherwise, of assets of the corporation or of any direct or indirect majority-owned subsidiary of the corporation (other than to any direct or indirect wholly-owned sub-

sidiary or to the corporation) having an aggregate market value equal to 50% or more of either that aggregate market value of all of the assets of the corporation determined on a consolidated basis or the aggregate market value of all the outstanding stock of the corporation; or (z) a proposed tender or exchange offer for 50% or more of the outstanding voting stock of the corporation. The corporation shall give not less than 20 days' notice to all interested stockholders prior to the consummation of any of the transactions described in clause (x) or (y) of the 2nd sentence of this paragraph; or (7) The business combination is with an interested stockholder who became an interested stockholder at a time when the restrictions contained in this section did not apply by reason of any of paragraphs (1) through (4) of this subsection (b), provided, however, that this paragraph (7) shall not apply if, at the time such interested stockholder became an interested stockholder, the corporation's certificate of incorporation contained a provision authorized by the last sentence of this subsection (b). Notwithstanding paragraphs (1), (2), (3) and (4) of this subsection, a corporation may elect by a provision of its original certificate of incorporation or any amendment thereto to be governed by this section; provided that any such amendment to the certificate of incorporation shall not apply to restrict a business combination between the corporation and an interested stockholder of the corporation if the interested stockholder became such prior to the effective date of the amendment.

(c) As used in this section only, the term:

(1) "Affiliate" means a person that directly, or indirectly through 1 or more intermediaries, controls, or is controlled by, or is under common control with, another person.

(2) "Associate," when used to indicate a relationship with any person, means: (i) Any corporation, partnership, unincorporated association or other entity of which such person is a director, officer or partner or is, directly or indirectly, the owner of 20% or more of any class of voting stock; (ii) any trust or other estate in which such person has at least a 20% beneficial interest or as to which such person serves as trustee or in a similar fiduciary capacity; and (iii) any relative or spouse of such person, or any relative of such spouse, who has the same residence as such person.

(3) "Business combination," when used in reference to any corporation and any interested stockholder of such corporation, means: (i) Any merger or consolidation of the corporation or any direct or indirect majority-owned subsidiary of the corporation with

(A) the interested stockholder, or

(B) with any other corporation, partnership, unincorporated association or other entity if the merger or consolidation is caused by the interested stockholder and as a result of such merger or consolidation subsection (a) of this section is not applicable to the surviving entity; (ii) Any sale, lease, exchange, mortgage, pledge, transfer or other disposition (in 1 transaction or a series of transactions), except proportionately as a stockholder of such corporation, to or with the interested stockholder, whether as part of a dissolution or otherwise, of assets of the corporation or of any direct or indirect majority-owned subsidiary of the corporation which assets have an aggregate market value equal to 10% or more of either the aggregate market value of all the assets of the corporation determined on a consolidated basis or the aggregate market value of all the outstanding stock of the corporation; (iii) Any transaction which results in the issuance or transfer by the corporation or by any direct or indirect majority-owned subsidiary of the corporation of any stock of the corporation or of such subsidiary to the interested stockholder, except: (A) Pursuant to the exercise, exchange or conversion of securities exercisable for, exchangeable for or convertible into stock of such corporation or any such subsidiary which securities were outstanding prior to the time that the interested stockholder became such; (B) pursuant to a merger under § 251(g) of this title; (C) pursuant to a dividend or distribution paid or made, or the exercise, exchange or conversion of securities exercisable for, exchangeable for or convertible into stock of such corporation or any such subsidiary which security is distributed, pro rata to all holders of a class or series of stock of such corporation subsequent to the time the interested stockholder became such; (D) pursuant to an exchange offer by the corporation to purchase stock made on the same terms to all holders of said stock; or (E) any issuance or transfer of stock by the corporation; provided however, that in no case under items (C)-(E) of this subparagraph shall there be an increase in the interested stockholder's proportionate share of the stock of any class or series of the corporation or of the voting stock of the corporation; (iv) Any transaction involving the corporation or any direct or indirect majority-owned subsidiary of the corporation which has the effect, directly or indirectly, of increasing the proportionate share of the stock of any class or series, or securities convertible into the stock of any class or series, of the corporation or of any such subsidiary which is owned by the interested stockholder, except as a result of immaterial changes due to fractional share adjustments or as a result of any purchase or redemption of any shares of stock not caused, directly or indirectly, by the interested stockholder; or (v) Any receipt by the interested stockholder of the benefit, directly or indirectly (except proportionately as a stockholder of such corporation), of any loans, advances, guarantees, pledges or other financial benefits (other than those expressly permitted in subparagraphs (i)-(iv) of this paragraph) provided by or through the corporation or any direct or indirect majority-owned subsidiary.

(4) "Control," including the terms "controlling," "controlled by" and "under common control with," means the possession, directly or indirectly, of the power to direct or cause the direction of the management and policies of a person, whether through the ownership of voting stock, by contract or otherwise. A person who is the owner of 20% or more of the outstanding voting stock of any corporation, partnership, unincorporated association or other entity shall be presumed to have control of such entity, in the absence of proof by a preponderance of the evidence to the contrary; Notwithstanding the foregoing, a presumption of control shall not apply where such person holds voting stock, in good faith and not for the purpose of circumventing this section, as an agent, bank, broker, nominee, custodian or trustee for 1 or more owners who do not individually or as a group have control of such entity.

(5) "Interested stockholder" means any person (other than the corporation and any direct or indirect majority-owned subsidiary of the corporation) that (i) is the owner of 15% or more of the outstanding voting stock of the corporation, or (ii) is an affiliate or associate of the corporation and was the owner of 15% or more of the outstanding voting stock of the corporation at any time within the 3-year period immediately prior to the date on which it is sought to be determined whether such person is an interested stockholder; and the affiliates and associates of such person; provided, however, that the term "interested stockholder" shall not include (x) any person who (A) owned shares in excess of the 15% limitation set forth herein as of, or acquired such shares pursuant to a tender offer commenced prior to, December 23, 1987, or pursuant to an exchange offer announced prior to the aforesaid date and commenced within 90 days thereafter and either (I) continued to own shares in excess of such 15% limitation or would have but for action by the corporation or (II) is an affiliate or associate of the corporation and so continued (or so would have continued but for action by the corporation) to be the owner of 15% or more of the outstanding voting stock of the corporation at any time within the 3-year period immediately prior to the date on which it is sought to be determined whether such a person is an interested stockholder or (B) acquired said shares from a person described in item (A) of this paragraph by gift, inheritance or in a transaction in which no consideration was exchanged; or (y) any person whose ownership of shares in excess of the 15% limitation set forth herein is the result of action taken solely by the corporation; provided that such person shall be an interested stockholder if thereafter such person acquires additional shares of voting stock of the corporation, except as a result of further corporate action not caused, directly or indirectly, by such person. For the purpose of determining whether a person is an interested stockholder, the voting stock of the corporation deemed to be outstanding shall include stock deemed to be owned by the person through application of paragraph (8) of this subsection but shall not include any other unissued stock of such corporation which may be issuable pursuant to any agreement, arrangement or understanding, or upon exercise of conversion rights, warrants or options, or otherwise.

(6) "Person" means any individual, corporation, partnership, unincorporated association or other entity.

(7) "Stock" means, with respect to any corporation, capital stock and, with respect to any other entity, any equity interest.

(8) "Voting stock" means, with respect to any corporation, stock of any class or series entitled to vote generally in the election of directors and, with respect to any entity that is not a corporation, any equity interest entitled to vote generally in the election of the governing body of such entity.

(9) "Owner," including the terms "own" and "owned," when used with respect to any stock, means a person that individually or with or through any of its affiliates or associates: (i) Beneficially owns such stock, directly or indirectly; or (ii) Has (A) the right to acquire such stock (whether such right is exercisable immediately or only after the passage of time) pursuant to any agreement, arrangement or understanding, or upon the exercise of conversion rights, exchange rights, warrants or options, or otherwise; provided, however, that a person shall not be deemed the owner of stock tendered pursuant to a tender or exchange offer made by such person or any of such person's affiliates or associates until such tendered stock is accepted for purchase or exchange; or (B) the right to vote such stock pursuant to any agreement, arrangement or understanding; provided, however, that a person shall not be deemed the owner of any stock because of such person's right to vote such stock if the agreement, arrangement or understanding to vote such stock arises solely from a revocable proxy or consent given in response to a proxy or consent solicitation made to 10 or more persons; or (iii) Has any agreement, arrangement or understanding for the purpose of acquiring, holding, voting (except voting pursuant to a revocable proxy or consent as described in item (B) of subparagraph (ii) of this paragraph), or disposing of such stock with any other person that beneficially owns, or whose affiliates or associates beneficially own, directly or indirectly, such stock.

(d) No provision of a certificate of incorporation or bylaw shall require, for any vote of stockholders required by this section, a greater vote of stockholders than that specified in this section.

(e) The Court of Chancery is hereby vested with exclusive jurisdiction to hear and determine all matters with respect to this section.

Subchapter VII. Meetings, Elections, Voting and Notice.

§ 211. Meetings of stockholders.

(a)

(1) Meetings of stockholders may be held at such place, either within or without this State as may be designated by or in the manner provided in the certificate of incorporation or bylaws, or if not so designated, as determined by the board of directors. If, pursuant to this paragraph or the certificate of incorporation or the bylaws of the corporation, the board of directors is authorized to determine the place of a meeting of stockholders, the board of directors may, in its sole discretion, determine that the meeting shall not be held at any place, but may instead be held solely by means of remote communication as authorized by paragraph (a)(2) of this section.

(2) If authorized by the board of directors in its sole discretion, and subject to such guidelines and procedures as the board of directors may adopt, stockholders and proxyholders not physically present at a meeting of stockholders may, by means of remote communication: a. Participate in a meeting of stockholders; and b. Be deemed present in person and vote at a meeting of stockholders, whether such meeting is to be held at a designated place or solely by means of remote communication, provided that (i) the corporation shall implement reasonable measures to verify that each person deemed present and permitted to vote at the meeting by means of remote communication is a stockholder or proxyholder, (ii) the corporation shall implement reasonable measures to provide such stockholders and proxyholders a reasonable opportunity to participate in the meeting and to vote on matters submitted to the stockholders, including an opportunity to read or hear the proceedings of the meeting substantially concurrently with such proceedings, and (iii) if any stockholder or proxyholder votes or takes other action at the meeting by means of remote communication, a record of such vote or other action shall be maintained by the corporation.

(b) Unless directors are elected by written consent in lieu of an annual meeting as permitted by this subsection, an annual meeting of stockholders shall be held for the election of directors on a date and at a time designated by or in the manner provided in the bylaws. Stockholders may, unless the certificate of incorporation otherwise provides, act by written consent to elect directors; provided, however, that, if such consent is less than unanimous, such action by written consent may be in lieu of holding an annual meeting only if all of the directorships to which directors could be elected at an annual meeting held at the effective time of such action are vacant and are filled by such action. Any other proper business may be transacted at the annual meeting.

(c) A failure to hold the annual meeting at the designated time or to elect a sufficient number of directors to conduct the business of the corporation shall not affect otherwise valid corporate acts or work a forfeiture or dissolution of the corporation except as may be otherwise specifically provided in this chapter. If the annual meeting for election of directors is not held on the date designated therefor or action by written consent to elect directors in lieu of an annual meeting has not been taken, the directors shall cause the meeting to be held as soon as is convenient. If there be a failure to hold the annual meeting or to take action by written consent to elect directors in lieu of an annual meeting for a period of 30 days after the date designated for the annual meeting, or if no date has been designated, for a period of 13 months after the latest to occur of the organization of the corporation, its last annual meeting or the last action by written consent to elect directors in lieu of an annual meeting, the Court of Chancery may summarily order a meeting to be held upon the application of any stockholder or director. The shares of stock represented at such meeting, either in person or by proxy, and entitled to vote thereat, shall constitute a quorum for the purpose of such meeting, notwithstanding any provision of the certificate of incorporation or bylaws to the contrary. The Court of Chancery may issue such orders as may be appropriate, including, without limitation, orders designating the time and place of such meeting, the record date for determination of stockholders entitled to vote, and the form of notice of such meeting.

(d) Special meetings of the stockholders may be called by the board of directors or by such person or persons as may be authorized by the certificate of incorporation or by the bylaws.

(e) All elections of directors shall be by written ballot unless otherwise provided in the certificate of incorporation; if authorized by the board of directors, such requirement of a written ballot shall be satisfied by a ballot submitted by electronic transmission, provided that any such electronic transmission must either set forth or be submitted with information from which it can be determined that the electronic transmission was authorized by the stockholder or proxy holder.

§ 212. Voting rights of stockholders; proxies; limitations.

(a) Unless otherwise provided in the certificate of incorporation and subject to § 213 of this title, each stockholder shall be entitled to 1 vote for each share of capital stock held by such stockholder. If the certificate of incorporation provides for more or less than 1 vote for any share, on any matter, every reference in this chapter to a majority or other proportion of stock shall refer to such majority or other proportion of the votes of such stock.

(b) Each stockholder entitled to vote at a meeting of stockholders or to express consent or dissent to corporate action in writing without a meeting may authorize another person or persons to act for such stockholder by proxy, but no such proxy shall be voted or acted upon after 3 years from its date, unless the proxy provides for a longer period.

(c) Without limiting the manner in which a stockholder may authorize another person or persons to act for such stockholder as proxy pursuant to subsection (b) of this section, the following shall constitute a valid means by which a stockholder may grant such authority:

(1) A stockholder may execute a writing authorizing another person or persons to act for such stockholder as proxy. Execution may be accomplished by the stockholder or such stockholder's authorized officer, director, employee or agent signing such writing or causing such person's signature to be affixed to such writing by any reasonable means including, but not limited to, by facsimile signature.

(2) A stockholder may authorize another person or persons to act for such stockholder as proxy by transmitting or authorizing the transmission of a telegram, cablegram, or other means of electronic transmission to the person who will be the holder of the proxy or to a proxy solicitation firm, proxy support service organization or like agent duly authorized by the person who will be the holder of the proxy to receive such transmission, provided that any such telegram, cablegram or other means of electronic transmission must either set forth or be submitted with information from which it can be determined that the telegram, cablegram or other electronic transmission was authorized by the stockholder. If it is determined that such telegrams, cablegrams or other electronic transmissions are valid, the inspectors or, if there are no inspectors, such other persons making that determination shall specify the information upon which they relied.

(d) Any copy, facsimile telecommunication or other reliable reproduction of the writing or transmission created pursuant to subsection (c) of this section may be substituted or used in lieu of the original writing or transmission for any and all purposes for which the original writing or transmission could be used, provided that such copy, facsimile telecommunication or other reproduction shall be a complete reproduction of the entire original writing or transmission.

(e) A duly executed proxy shall be irrevocable if it states that it is irrevocable and if, and only as long as, it is coupled with an interest sufficient in law to support an irrevocable power. A proxy may be made irrevocable regardless of whether the interest with which it is coupled is an interest in the stock itself or an interest in the corporation generally.

§ 213. Fixing date for determination of stockholders of record.

(a) In order that the corporation may determine the stockholders entitled to notice of or to vote at any meeting of stockholders or any adjournment thereof, the board of directors may fix a record date, which record date shall not precede the date upon which the resolution fixing the record date is adopted by the board of directors, and which record date shall not be more than 60 nor less than 10 days before the date of such meeting. If no record date is fixed by the board of directors, the record date for determining stockholders entitled to notice of or to vote at a meeting of stockholders shall be at the close of business on the day next preceding the day on which notice is given, or, if notice is waived, at the close of business on the day next preceding the day on which the meeting is held. A determination of stockholders of record entitled to notice of or to vote at a meeting of stockholders shall apply to any adjournment of the meeting; provided, however, that the board of directors may fix a new record date for the adjourned meeting.

(b) In order that the corporation may determine the stockholders entitled to consent to corporate action in writing without a meeting, the board of directors may fix a record date, which record date shall not precede the date upon which the resolution fixing the record date is adopted by the board of directors, and which date shall not be more than 10 days after the date upon which the resolution fixing the record date is adopted by the board of directors. If no record date has been fixed by the board of directors, the record date for determining stockholders entitled to consent to corporate action in writing without a meeting, when no prior action by the board of directors is required by this chapter, shall be the first date on which a signed written consent setting forth the action taken or proposed to be taken is delivered to the corporation by delivery to its registered office in this State, its principal place of business or an officer or agent of the corporation having custody of the book in which proceedings of meetings of stockholders are recorded. Delivery made to a corporation's registered office shall be by hand or by certified or registered mail, return receipt requested. If no record date has been fixed by the board of directors and prior action by the board of directors is required by this chapter, the record date for determining stockholders entitled to consent to corporate action in writing without a meeting shall be at the close of business on the day on which the board of directors adopts the resolution taking such prior action.

(c) In order that the corporation may determine the stockholders entitled to receive payment of any dividend or other distribution or allotment of any rights or the stockholders entitled to exercise any rights in respect of any change, conversion or exchange of stock, or for the purpose of any other lawful action, the board of directors may fix a record date, which record date shall not precede the date upon which the resolution fixing the record date is adopted, and which record date shall be not more than 60 days prior to such action. If no record date is fixed, the record date for determining stockholders for any such purpose shall be at the close of business on the day on which the board of directors adopts the resolution relating thereto.

§ 214. Cumulative voting.
The certificate of incorporation of any corporation may provide that at all elections of directors of the corporation, or at elections held under specified circumstances, each holder of stock or of any class or classes or of a series or series thereof shall be entitled to as many votes as shall equal the number of votes which (except for such provision as to cumulative voting) such holder would be entitled to cast for the election of directors with respect to such holder's shares of stock multiplied by the number of directors to be elected by such holder, and that such holder may cast all of such votes for a single director or may distribute them among the number to be voted for, or for any 2 or more of them as such holder may see fit.

§ 215. Voting rights of members of nonstock corporations; quorum; proxies.
(a) Sections 211 through 214 and 216 of this title shall not apply to corporations not authorized to issue stock, except that § 211(a) of this title and § 212(c) and (d) of this title shall apply to such corporations, and, when so applied, all references therein to stockholders and to the board of directors shall be deemed to refer to the members and the governing body of a nonstock corporation, respectively.
(b) Unless otherwise provided in the certificate of incorporation of a nonstock corporation, each member shall be entitled at every meeting of members to 1 vote in person or by proxy, but no proxy shall be voted on after 3 years from its date, unless the proxy provides for a longer period.
(c) Unless otherwise provided in this chapter, the certificate of incorporation or bylaws of a nonstock corporation may specify the number of members having voting power who shall be present or represented by proxy at any meeting in order to constitute a quorum for, and the votes that shall be necessary for, the transaction of any business. In the absence of such specification in the certificate of incorporation or bylaws of a nonstock corporation:

(1) One-third of the members of such corporation shall constitute a quorum at a meeting of such members;

(2) In all matters other than the election of the governing body of such corporation, the affirmative vote of a majority of such members present in person or represented by proxy at the meeting and entitled to vote on the subject matter shall be the act of the members, unless the vote of a greater number is required by this chapter; and

(3) Members of the governing body shall be elected by a plurality of the votes of the members of the corporation present in person or represented by proxy at the meeting and entitled to vote thereon.

(d) If the election of the governing body of any nonstock corporation shall not be held on the day designated by the bylaws, the governing body shall cause the election to be held as soon thereafter as convenient. The failure to hold such an election at the designated time shall not work any forfeiture or dissolution of the corporation, but the Court of Chancery may summarily order such an election to be held upon the application of any member of the corporation. At any election pursuant to such order the persons entitled to vote in such election who shall be present at such meeting, either in person or by proxy, shall constitute a quorum for such meeting, notwithstanding any provision of the certificate of incorporation or the bylaws of the corporation to the contrary.
(e) If authorized by the governing body, any requirement of a written ballot shall be satisfied by a ballot submitted by electronic transmission, provided that any such electronic transmission must either set forth or be submitted with information from which it can be determined that the electronic transmission was authorized by the member or proxy holder.

§ 216. Quorum and required vote for stock corporations.
Subject to this chapter in respect of the vote that shall be required for a specified action, the certificate of incorporation or bylaws of any corporation authorized to issue stock may specify the number of shares and/or the amount of other securities having voting power the holders of which shall be present or represented by proxy at any meeting in order to constitute a quorum for, and the votes that shall be necessary for, the transaction of any business, but in no event shall a quorum consist of less than one-third of the shares entitled to vote at the meeting, except that, where a separate vote by a class or series or classes or series is required, a quorum shall consist of no less than one-third of the shares of such class or series or classes or series. In the absence of such specification in the certificate of incorporation or bylaws of the corporation:

(1) A majority of the shares entitled to vote, present in person or represented by proxy, shall constitute a quorum at a meeting of stockholders;

(2) In all matters other than the election of directors, the affirmative vote of the majority of shares present in person or represented by proxy at the meeting and entitled to vote on the subject matter shall be the act of the stockholders;

(3) Directors shall be elected by a plurality of the votes of the shares present in person or represented by proxy at the meeting and entitled to vote on the election of directors; and

(4) Where a separate vote by a class or series or classes or series is required, a majority of the outstanding shares of such class or series or classes or series, present in person

or represented by proxy, shall constitute a quorum entitled to take action with respect to that vote on that matter and the affirmative vote of the majority of shares of such class or series or classes or series present in person or represented by proxy at the meeting shall be the act of such class or series or classes or series.

§ 217. Voting rights of fiduciaries, pledgors and joint owners of stock.

(a) Persons holding stock in a fiduciary capacity shall be entitled to vote the shares so held. Persons whose stock is pledged shall be entitled to vote, unless in the transfer by the pledgor on the books of the corporation such person has expressly empowered the pledgee to vote thereon, in which case only the pledgee, or such pledgee's proxy, may represent such stock and vote thereon.

(b) If shares or other securities having voting power stand of record in the names of 2 or more persons, whether fiduciaries, members of a partnership, joint tenants, tenants in common, tenants by the entirety or otherwise, or if 2 or more persons have the same fiduciary relationship respecting the same shares, unless the secretary of the corporation is given written notice to the contrary and is furnished with a copy of the instrument or order appointing them or creating the relationship wherein it is so provided, their acts with respect to voting shall have the following effect:

(1) If only 1 votes, such person's act binds all;

(2) If more than 1 vote, the act of the majority so voting binds all;

(3) If more than 1 vote, but the vote is evenly split on any particular matter, each faction may vote the securities in question proportionally, or any person voting the shares, or a beneficiary, if any, may apply to the Court of Chancery or such other court as may have jurisdiction to appoint an additional person to act with the persons so voting the shares, which shall then be voted as determined by a majority of such persons and the person appointed by the Court. If the instrument so filed shows that any such tenancy is held in unequal interests, a majority or even split for the purpose of this subsection shall be a majority or even split in interest.

§ 218. Voting trusts and other voting agreements.

(a) One stockholder or 2 or more stockholders may by agreement in writing deposit capital stock of an original issue with or transfer capital stock to any person or persons, or entity or entities authorized to act as trustee, for the purpose of vesting in such person or persons, entity or entities, who may be designated voting trustee, or voting trustees, the right to vote thereon for any period of time determined by such agreement, upon the terms and conditions stated in such agreement. The agreement may contain any other lawful provisions not inconsistent with such purpose. After the filing of a copy of the agreement in the registered office of the corporation in this State, which copy shall be open to the inspection of any stockholder of the corporation or any beneficiary of the trust under the agreement daily during business hours, certificates of stock or uncertificated stock shall be issued to the voting trustee or trustees to represent any stock of an original issue so deposited with such voting trustee or trustees, and any certificates of stock or uncertificated stock so transferred to the voting trustee or trustees shall be surrendered and cancelled and new certificates or uncertificated stock shall be issued therefore to the voting trustee or trustees. In the certificate so issued, if any, it shall be stated that it is issued pursuant to such agreement, and that fact shall also be stated in the stock ledger of the corporation. The voting trustee or trustees may vote the stock so issued or transferred during the period specified in the agreement. Stock standing in the name of the voting trustee or trustees may be voted either in person or by proxy, and in voting the stock, the voting trustee or trustees shall incur no responsibility as stockholder, trustee or otherwise, except for their own individual malfeasance. In any case where 2 or more persons or entities are designated as voting trustees, and the right and method of voting any stock standing in their names at any meeting of the corporation are not fixed by the agreement appointing the trustees, the right to vote the stock and the manner of voting it at the meeting shall be determined by a majority of the trustees, or if they be equally divided as to the right and manner of voting the stock in any particular case, the vote of the stock in such case shall be divided equally among the trustees.

(b) Any amendment to a voting trust agreement shall be made by a written agreement, a copy of which shall be filed in the registered office of the corporation in this State.

(c) An agreement between 2 or more stockholders, if in writing and signed by the parties thereto, may provide that in exercising any voting rights, the shares held by them shall be voted as provided by the agreement, or as the parties may agree, or as determined in accordance with a procedure agreed upon by them.

(d) This section shall not be deemed to invalidate any voting or other agreement among stockholders or any irrevocable proxy which is not otherwise illegal.

§ 219. List of stockholders entitled to vote; penalty for refusal to produce; stock ledger.

(a) The officer who has charge of the stock ledger of a corporation shall prepare and make, at least 10 days before every meeting of stockholders, a complete list of the stockholders entitled to vote at the meeting, arranged in alphabetical order, and showing the address of each stockholder and the number of shares registered in the name of each stockholder. Nothing contained in this section shall require the corporation to include electronic mail addresses or other electronic contact information on such list. Such list shall be open to the examination of any stockholder for any purpose germane to the meeting for a period of at least 10

days prior to the meeting: (i) on a reasonably accessible electronic network, provided that the information required to gain access to such list is provided with the notice of the meeting, or (ii) during ordinary business hours, at the principal place of business of the corporation. In the event that the corporation determines to make the list available on an electronic network, the corporation may take reasonable steps to ensure that such information is available only to stockholders of the corporation. If the meeting is to be held at a place, then the list shall be produced and kept at the time and place of the meeting during the whole time thereof and may be inspected by any stockholder who is present. If the meeting is to be held solely by means of remote communication, then the list shall also be open to the examination of any stockholder during the whole time of the meeting on a reasonably accessible electronic network, and the information required to access such list shall be provided with the notice of the meeting.
(b) Upon the wilful neglect or refusal of the directors to produce such a list at any meeting for the election of directors held at a place, or to open such a list to examination on a reasonably accessible electronic network during any meeting for the election of directors held solely by means of remote communication, they shall be ineligible for election to any office at such meeting.
(c) The stock ledger shall be the only evidence as to who are the stockholders entitled to examine the stock ledger, the list required by this section or the books of the corporation, or to vote in person or by proxy at any meeting of stockholders.

§ 220. Inspection of books and records.
(a) As used in this section, "stockholder" means a stockholder of record of stock in a stock corporation and also a member of a nonstock corporation as reflected on the records of the nonstock corporation. As used in this section, the term "list of stockholders" includes lists of members in a nonstock corporation.
(b) Any stockholder, in person or by attorney or other agent, shall, upon written demand under oath stating the purpose thereof, have the right during the usual hours for business to inspect for any proper purpose the corporation's stock ledger, a list of its stockholders, and its other books and records, and to make copies or extracts therefrom. A proper purpose shall mean a purpose reasonably related to such person's interest as a stockholder. In every instance where an attorney or other agent shall be the person who seeks the right to inspection, the demand under oath shall be accompanied by a power of attorney or such other writing which authorizes the attorney or other agent to so act on behalf of the stockholder. The demand under oath shall be directed to the corporation at its registered office in this State or at its principal place of business.
(c) If the corporation, or an officer or agent thereof, refuses to permit an inspection sought by a stockholder or attorney or other agent acting for the stockholder pursuant to subsection (b) of this section or does not reply to the demand within 5 business days after the demand has been made, the stockholder may apply to the Court of Chancery for an order to compel such inspection. The Court of Chancery is hereby vested with exclusive jurisdiction to determine whether or not the person seeking inspection is entitled to the inspection sought. The Court may summarily order the corporation to permit the stockholder to inspect the corporation's stock ledger, an existing list of stockholders, and its other books and records, and to make copies or extracts therefrom; or the Court may order the corporation to furnish to the stockholder a list of its stockholders as of a specific date on condition that the stockholder first pay to the corporation the reasonable cost of obtaining and furnishing such list and on such other conditions as the Court deems appropriate. Where the stockholder seeks to inspect the corporation's books and records, other than its stock ledger or list of stockholders, such stockholder shall first establish

(1) that such stockholder has complied with this section respecting the form and manner of making demand for inspection of such documents; and

(2) that the inspection such stockholder seeks is for a proper purpose. Where the stockholder seeks to inspect the corporation's stock ledger or list of stockholders and such stockholder has complied with this section respecting the form and manner of making demand for inspection of such documents, the burden of proof shall be upon the corporation to establish that the inspection such stockholder seeks is for an improper purpose. The Court may, in its discretion, prescribe any limitations or conditions with reference to the inspection, or award such other or further relief as the Court may deem just and proper. The Court may order books, documents and records, pertinent extracts therefrom, or duly authenticated copies thereof, to be brought within this State and kept in this State upon such terms and conditions as the order may prescribe.

(d) Any director (including a member of the governing body of a nonstock corporation) shall have the right to examine the corporation's stock ledger, a list of its stockholders and its other books and records for a purpose reasonably related to the director's position as a director. The Court of Chancery is hereby vested with the exclusive jurisdiction to determine whether a director is entitled to the inspection sought. The Court may summarily order the corporation to permit the director to inspect any and all books and records, the stock ledger and the list of stockholder's and to make copies or extracts therefrom. The Court may, in its discretion, prescribe any limitations or conditions with reference to the inspection, or award such other and further relief as the Court may deem just and proper.

§ 221. Voting, inspection and other rights of bondholders and debenture holders.

Every corporation may in its certificate of incorporation confer upon the holders of any bonds, debentures or other obligations issued or to be issued by the corporation the power to vote in respect to the corporate affairs and management of the corporation to the extent and in the manner provided in the certificate of incorporation and may confer upon such holders of bonds, debentures or other obligations the same right of inspection of its books, accounts and other records, and also any other rights, which the stockholders of the corporation have or may have by reason of this chapter or of its certificate of incorporation. If the certificate of incorporation so provides, such holders of bonds, debentures or other obligations shall be deemed to be stockholders, and their bonds, debentures or other obligations shall be deemed to be shares of stock, for the purpose of any provision of this chapter which requires the vote of stockholders as a prerequisite to any corporate action and the certificate of incorporation may divest the holders of capital stock, in whole or in part, of their right to vote on any corporate matter whatsoever, except as set forth in paragraph (2) of subsection (b) of § 242 of this title.

§ 222. Notice of meetings and adjourned meetings.

(a) Whenever stockholders are required or permitted to take any action at a meeting, a written notice of the meeting shall be given which shall state the place, if any, date and hour of the meeting, the means of remote communications, if any, by which stockholders and proxy holders may be deemed to be present in person and vote at such meeting, and, in the case of a special meeting, the purpose or purposes for which the meeting is called.

(b) Unless otherwise provided in this chapter, the written notice of any meeting shall be given not less than 10 nor more than 60 days before the date of the meeting to each stockholder entitled to vote at such meeting. If mailed, notice is given when deposited in the United States mail, postage prepaid, directed to the stockholder at such stockholder's address as it appears on the records of the corporation. An affidavit of the secretary or an assistant secretary or of the transfer agent or other agent of the corporation that the notice has been given shall, in the absence of fraud, be prima facie evidence of the facts stated therein.

(c) When a meeting is adjourned to another time or place, unless the bylaws otherwise require, notice need not be given of the adjourned meeting if the time, place, if any, thereof, and the means of remote communications, if any, by which stockholders and proxy holders may be deemed to be present in person and vote at such adjourned meeting are announced at the meeting at which the adjournment is taken. At the adjourned meeting the corporation may transact any business which might have been transacted at the original meeting. If the adjournment is for more than 30 days, or if after the adjournment a new record date is fixed for the adjourned meeting, a notice of the adjourned meeting shall be given to each stockholder of record entitled to vote at the meeting.

§ 223. Vacancies and newly created directorships.

(a) Unless otherwise provided in the certificate of incorporation or bylaws:

(1) Vacancies and newly created directorships resulting from any increase in the authorized number of directors elected by all of the stockholders having the right to vote as a single class may be filled by a majority of the directors then in office, although less than a quorum, or by a sole remaining director;

(2) Whenever the holders of any class or classes of stock or series thereof are entitled to elect 1 or more directors by the certificate of incorporation, vacancies and newly created directorships of such class or classes or series may be filled by a majority of the directors elected by such class or classes or series thereof then in office, or by a sole remaining director so elected. If at any time, by reason of death or resignation or other cause, a corporation should have no directors in office, then any officer or any stockholder or an executor, administrator, trustee or guardian of a stockholder, or other fiduciary entrusted with like responsibility for the person or estate of a stockholder, may call a special meeting of stockholders in accordance with the certificate of incorporation or the bylaws, or may apply to the Court of Chancery for a decree summarily ordering an election as provided in § 211 of this title.

(b) In the case of a corporation the directors of which are divided into classes, any directors chosen under subsection (a) of this section shall hold office until the next election of the class for which such directors shall have been chosen, and until their successors shall be elected and qualified.

(c) If, at the time of filling any vacancy or any newly created directorship, the directors then in office shall constitute less than a majority of the whole board (as constituted immediately prior to any such increase), the Court of Chancery may, upon application of any stockholder or stockholders holding at least 10 percent of the total number of the shares at the time outstanding having the right to vote for such directors, summarily order an election to be held to fill any such vacancies or newly created directorships, or to replace the directors chosen by the directors then in office as aforesaid, which election shall be governed by § 211 of this title as far as applicable.

(d) Unless otherwise provided in the certificate of incorporation or bylaws, when 1 or more directors shall resign from the board, effective at a future date, a majority of the directors then in office, including those who have so resigned, shall have power to fill such vacancy or vacancies, the vote thereon to take effect when such resignation or resignations shall become effective, and each director so chosen shall hold office as provided in this section in the filling of other vacancies.

§ 224. Form of records.
Any records maintained by a corporation in the regular course of its business, including its stock ledger, books of account, and minute books, may be kept on, or by means of, or be in the form of, any information storage device, or method provided that the records so kept can be converted into clearly legible paper form within a reasonable time. Any corporation shall so convert any records so kept upon the request of any person entitled to inspect such records pursuant to any provision of this chapter. When records are kept in such manner, a clearly legible paper form produced from or by means of the information storage device or method shall be admissible in evidence, and accepted for all other purposes, to the same extent as an original paper record of the same information would have been, provided the paper form accurately portrays the record.

§ 225. Contested election of directors; proceedings to determine validity.
(a) Upon application of any stockholder or director, or any officer whose title to office is contested, or any member of a corporation without capital stock, the Court of Chancery may hear and determine the validity of any election of any director, member of the governing body, or officer of any corporation, and the right of any person to hold such office, and, in case any such office is claimed by more than 1 person, may determine the person entitled thereto; and to that end make such order or decree in any such case as may be just and proper, with power to enforce the production of any books, papers and records of the corporation relating to the issue. In case it should be determined that no valid election has been held, the Court of Chancery may order an election to be held in accordance with § 211 or 215 of this title. In any such application, service of copies of the application upon the registered agent of the corporation shall be deemed to be service upon the corporation and upon the person whose title to office is contested and upon the person, if any, claiming such office; and the registered agent shall forward immediately a copy of the application to the corporation and to the person whose title to office is contested and to the person, if any, claiming such office, in a postpaid, sealed, registered letter addressed to such corporation and such person at their post-office addresses last known to the registered agent or furnished to the registered agent by the applicant stockholder. The Court may make such order respecting further or other notice of such application as it deems proper under the circumstances.
(b) Upon application of any stockholder or any member of a corporation without capital stock, the Court of Chancery may hear and determine the result of any vote of stockholders or members, as the case may be, upon matters other than the election of directors, officers or members of the governing body. Service of the application upon the registered agent of the corporation shall be deemed to be service upon the corporation, and no other party need be joined in order for the Court to adjudicate the result of the vote. The Court may make such order respecting notice of the application as it deems proper under the circumstances.

§ 226. Appointment of custodian or receiver of corporation on deadlock or for other cause.
(a) The Court of Chancery, upon application of any stockholder, may appoint 1 or more persons to be custodians, and, if the corporation is insolvent, to be receivers, of and for any corporation when:
(1) At any meeting held for the election of directors the stockholders are so divided that they have failed to elect successors to directors whose terms have expired or would have expired upon qualification of their successors; or
(2) The business of the corporation is suffering or is threatened with irreparable injury because the directors are so divided respecting the management of the affairs of the corporation that the required vote for action by the board of directors cannot be obtained and the stockholders are unable to terminate this division; or
(3) The corporation has abandoned its business and has failed within a reasonable time to take steps to dissolve, liquidate or distribute its assets.
(b) A custodian appointed under this section shall have all the powers and title of a receiver appointed under § 291 of this title, but the authority of the custodian is to continue the business of the corporation and not to liquidate its affairs and distribute its assets, except when the Court shall otherwise order and except in cases arising under paragraph (3) of subsection (a) of this section or paragraph (2) of subsection (a) of § 352 of this title.

§ 227. Powers of Court in elections of directors.
(a) The Court of Chancery, in any proceeding instituted under § 211, 215 or 225 of this title may determine the right and power of persons claiming to own stock, or in the case of a corporation without capital stock, of the persons claiming to be members, to vote at any meeting of the stockholders or members.
(b) The Court of Chancery may appoint a Master to hold any election provided for in § 211, 215 or 225 of this title under such orders and powers as it deems proper; and it may punish any officer or director for contempt in case of disobedience of any order made by the Court; and, in case of disobedience by a corporation of any order made by the Court, may enter a decree against such corporation for a penalty of not more than $5,000.

§ 228. Consent of stockholders or members in lieu of meeting.

(a) Unless otherwise provided in the certificate of incorporation, any action required by this chapter to be taken at any annual or special meeting of stockholders of a corporation, or any action which may be taken at any annual or special meeting of such stockholders, may be taken without a meeting, without prior notice and without a vote, if a consent or consents in writing, setting forth the action so taken, shall be signed by the holders of outstanding stock having not less than the minimum number of votes that would be necessary to authorize or take such action at a meeting at which all shares entitled to vote thereon were present and voted and shall be delivered to the corporation by delivery to its registered office in this State, its principal place of business or an officer or agent of the corporation having custody of the book in which proceedings of meetings of stockholders are recorded. Delivery made to a corporation's registered office shall be by hand or by certified or registered mail, return receipt requested.

(b) Unless otherwise provided in the certificate of incorporation, any action required by this chapter to be taken at a meeting of the members of a nonstock corporation, or any action which may be taken at any meeting of the members of a nonstock corporation, may be taken without a meeting, without prior notice and without a vote, if a consent or consents in writing, setting forth the action so taken, shall be signed by members having not less than the minimum number of votes that would be necessary to authorize or take such action at a meeting at which all members having a right to vote thereon were present and voted and shall be delivered to the corporation by delivery to its registered office in this State, its principal place of business or an officer or agent of the corporation having custody of the book in which proceedings of meetings of members are recorded. Delivery made to a corporation's registered office shall be by hand or by certified or registered mail, return receipt requested.

(c) Every written consent shall bear the date of signature of each stockholder or member who signs the consent, and no written consent shall be effective to take the corporate action referred to therein unless, within 60 days of the earliest dated consent delivered in the manner required by this section to the corporation, written consents signed by a sufficient number of holders or members to take action are delivered to the corporation by delivery to its registered office in this State, its principal place of business or an officer or agent of the corporation having custody of the book in which proceedings of meetings of stockholders or members are recorded. Delivery made to a corporation's registered office shall be by hand or by certified or registered mail, return receipt requested.

(d)

(1) A telegram, cablegram or other electronic transmission consenting to an action to be taken and transmitted by a stockholder, member or proxyholder, or by a person or persons authorized to act for a stockholder, member or proxyholder, shall be deemed to be written, signed and dated for the purposes of this section, provided that any such telegram, cablegram or other electronic transmission sets forth or is delivered with information from which the corporation can determine (A) that the telegram, cablegram or other electronic transmission was transmitted by the stockholder, member or proxyholder or by a person or persons authorized to act for the stockholder, member or proxyholder and (B) the date on which such stockholder, member or proxyholder or authorized person or persons transmitted such telegram, cablegram or electronic transmission. The date on which such telegram, cablegram or electronic transmission is transmitted shall be deemed to be the date on which such consent was signed. No consent given by telegram, cablegram or other electronic transmission shall be deemed to have been delivered until such consent is reproduced in paper form and until such paper form shall be delivered to the corporation by delivery to its registered office in this State, its principal place of business or an officer or agent of the corporation having custody of the book in which proceedings of meetings of stockholders or members are recorded. Delivery made to a corporation's registered office shall be made by hand or by certified or registered mail, return receipt requested. Notwithstanding the foregoing limitations on delivery, consents given by telegram, cablegram or other electronic transmission, may be otherwise delivered to the principal place of business of the corporation or to an officer or agent of the corporation having custody of the book in which proceedings of meetings of stockholders or members are recorded if, to the extent and in the manner provided by resolution of the board of directors or governing body of the corporation.

(2) Any copy, facsimile or other reliable reproduction of a consent in writing may be substituted or used in lieu of the original writing for any and all purposes for which the original writing could be used, provided that such copy, facsimile or other reproduction shall be a complete reproduction of the entire original writing.

(e) Prompt notice of the taking of the corporate action without a meeting by less than unanimous written consent shall be given to those stockholders or members who have not consented in writing and who, if the action had been taken at a meeting, would have been entitled to notice of the meeting if the record date for such meeting had been the date that written consents signed by a sufficient number of holders or members to take the action were delivered to the corporation as provided in subsection (c) of this section. In the event that the action which is consented to is such as would have required the filing of a certificate under any other section of this title, if such action had been voted on by stockholders or by members at a meeting thereof, the certificate filed under such other section shall state, in lieu of any statement required by such section concerning any vote of stockholders or members, that written consent has been given in accordance with this section.

§ 229. Waiver of notice.

Whenever notice is required to be given under any provision of this chapter or the certificate of incorporation or bylaws, a written waiver, signed by the person entitled to notice, or a waiver by electronic transmission by the person entitled to notice, whether before or after the time stated therein, shall be deemed equivalent to notice. Attendance of a person at a meeting shall constitute a waiver of notice of such meeting, except when the person attends a meeting for the express purpose of objecting at the beginning of the meeting, to the transaction of any business because the meeting is not lawfully called or convened. Neither the business to be transacted at, nor the purpose of, any regular or special meeting of the stockholders, directors or members of a committee of directors need be specified in any written waiver of notice or any waiver by electronic transmission unless so required by the certificate of incorporation or the bylaws.

§ 230. Exception to requirements of notice.

(a) Whenever notice is required to be given, under any provision of this chapter or of the certificate of incorporation or bylaws of any corporation, to any person with whom communication is unlawful, the giving of such notice to such person shall not be required and there shall be no duty to apply to any governmental authority or agency for a license or permit to give such notice to such person. Any action or meeting which shall be taken or held without notice to any such person with whom communication is unlawful shall have the same force and effect as if such notice had been duly given. In the event that the action taken by the corporation is such as to require the filing of a certificate under any of the other sections of this title, the certificate shall state, if such is the fact and if notice is required, that notice was given to all persons entitled to receive notice except such persons with whom communication is unlawful.

(b) Whenever notice is required to be given, under any provision of this title or the certificate of incorporation or bylaws of any corporation, to any stockholder or, if the corporation is a nonstock corporation, to any member, to whom

(1) notice of 2 consecutive annual meetings, and all notices of meetings or of the taking of action by written consent without a meeting to such person during the period between such 2 consecutive annual meetings, or

(2) all, and at least 2, payments (if sent by first-class mail) of dividends or interest on securities during a 12-month period, have been mailed addressed to such person at such person's address as shown on the records of the corporation and have been returned undeliverable, the giving of such notice to such person shall not be required.

Any action or meeting which shall be taken or held without notice to such person shall have the same force and effect as if such notice had been duly given. If any such person shall deliver to the corporation a written notice setting forth such person's then current address, the requirement that notice be given to such person shall be reinstated. In the event that the action taken by the corporation is such as to require the filing of a certificate under any of the other sections of this title, the certificate need not state that notice was not given to persons to whom notice was not required to be given pursuant to this subsection.

(c) The exception in paragraph (b)(1) of this section to the requirement that notice be given shall not be applicable to any notice returned as undeliverable if the notice was given by electronic transmission.

§ 231. Voting procedures and inspectors of elections.

(a) The corporation shall, in advance of any meeting of stockholders, appoint 1 or more inspectors to act at the meeting and make a written report thereof. The corporation may designate 1 or more persons as alternate inspectors to replace any inspector who fails to act. If no inspector or alternate is able to act at a meeting of stockholders, the person presiding at the meeting shall appoint 1 or more inspectors to act at the meeting. Each inspector, before entering upon the discharge of the duties of inspector, shall take and sign an oath faithfully to execute the duties of inspector with strict impartiality and according to the best of such inspector's ability.

(b) The inspectors shall:

(1) Ascertain the number of shares outstanding and the voting power of each;

(2) Determine the shares represented at a meeting and the validity of proxies and ballots;

(3) Count all votes and ballots;

(4) Determine and retain for a reasonable period a record of the disposition of any challenges made to any determination by the inspectors; and

(5) Certify their determination of the number of shares represented at the meeting, and their count of all votes and ballots. The inspectors may appoint or retain other persons or entities to assist the inspectors in the performance of the duties of the inspectors.

(c) The date and time of the opening and the closing of the polls for each matter upon which the stockholders will vote at a meeting shall be announced at the meeting. No ballot, proxies or votes, nor any revocations thereof or changes thereto, shall be accepted by the inspectors after the closing of the polls unless the Court of Chancery upon application by a stockholder shall determine otherwise.

(d) In determining the validity and counting of proxies and ballots, the inspectors shall be limited to an examination of the proxies, any envelopes submitted with those proxies, any information provided in accordance with § 211(e) or §

212(c)(2) of this title, or any information provided pursuant to § 211(a)(2)(B)(i) or (iii) of this title, ballots and the regular books and records of the corporation, except that the inspectors may consider other reliable information for the limited purpose of reconciling proxies and ballots submitted by or on behalf of banks, brokers, their nominees or similar persons which represent more votes than the holder of a proxy is authorized by the record owner to cast or more votes than the stockholder holds of record. If the inspectors consider other reliable information for the limited purpose permitted herein, the inspectors at the time they make their certification pursuant to subsection (b)(5) of this section shall specify the precise information considered by them including the person or persons from whom they obtained the information, when the information was obtained, the means by which the information was obtained and the basis for the inspectors' belief that such information is accurate and reliable.

(e) Unless otherwise provided in the certificate of incorporation or bylaws, this section shall not apply to a corporation that does not have a class of voting stock that is:

(1) Listed on a national securities exchange;

(2) Authorized for quotation on an interdealer quotation system of a registered national securities association; or

(3) Held of record by more than 2,000 stockholders.

§ 232. Notice by electronic transmission.

(a) Without limiting the manner by which notice otherwise may be given effectively to stockholders, any notice to stockholders given by the corporation under any provision of this chapter, the certificate of incorporation, or the bylaws shall be effective if given by a form of electronic transmission consented to by the stockholder to whom the notice is given. Any such consent shall be revocable by the stockholder by written notice to the corporation. Any such consent shall be deemed revoked if

(1) the corporation is unable to deliver by electronic transmission 2 consecutive notices given by the corporation in accordance with such consent and

(2) such inability becomes known to the secretary or an assistant secretary of the corporation or to the transfer agent, or other person responsible for the giving of notice; provided, however, the inadvertent failure to treat such inability as a revocation shall not invalidate any meeting or other action.

(b) Notice given pursuant to subsection (a) of this section shall be deemed given:

(1) if by facsimile telecommunication, when directed to a number at which the stockholder has consented to receive notice;

(2) if by electronic mail, when directed to an electronic mail address at which the stockholder has consented to receive notice;

(3) if by a posting on an electronic network together with separate notice to the stockholder of such specific posting, upon the later of (A) such posting and (B) the giving of such separate notice; and

(4) if by any other form of electronic transmission, when directed to the stockholder. An affidavit of the secretary or an assistant secretary or of the transfer agent or other agent of the corporation that the notice has been given by a form of electronic transmission shall, in the absence of fraud, be prima facie evidence of the facts stated therein.

(c) For purposes of this chapter, "electronic transmission" means any form of communication, not directly involving the physical transmission of paper, that creates a record that may be retained, retrieved and reviewed by a recipient thereof, and that may be directly reproduced in paper form by such a recipient through an automated process.

(d) This section shall apply to a corporation organized under this chapter that is not authorized to issue capital stock, and when so applied, all references to stockholders shall be deemed to refer to members of such a corporation.

(e) This section shall not apply to § 164, 296, 311, 312, or 324 of this title.

Subchapter VIII. Amendment of Certificate of Incorporation; Changes in Capital and Capital Stock.

§ 241. Amendment of certificate of incorporation before receipt of payment for stock.

(a) Before a corporation has received any payment for any of its stock, it may amend its certificate of incorporation at any time or times, in any and as many respects as may be desired, so long as its certificate of incorporation as amended would contain only such provisions as it would be lawful and proper to insert in an original certificate of incorporation filed at the time of filing the amendment.

(b) The amendment of a certificate of incorporation authorized by this section shall be adopted by a majority of the incorporators, if directors were not named in the original certificate of incorporation or have not yet been elected, or, if directors were named in the original certificate of incorporation or have been elected and have qualified, by a majority of the directors. A certificate setting forth the amendment and certifying that the corporation has not received any payment for any of its stock and that the amendment has been duly adopted in accordance with this section shall be executed, acknowledged and filed in accordance with § 103 of this title. Upon such filing, the corporation's certificate of incorporation shall be deemed to be amended accordingly as of the date on which the original certificate of incorporation became effective, except as to those persons who are substantially and adversely affected by the amendment and as to those persons the amendment shall be effective from the filing date.

§ 242. Amendment of certificate of incorporation after receipt of payment for stock; nonstock corporations.

(a) After a corporation has received payment for any of its capital stock, it may amend its certificate of incorporation, from time to time, in any and as many respects as may be desired, so long as its certificate of incorporation as amended would contain only such provisions as it would be lawful and proper to insert in an original certificate of incorporation filed at the time of the filing of the amendment; and, if a change in stock or the rights of stockholders, or an exchange, reclassification, subdivision, combination or cancellation of stock or rights of stockholders is to be made, such provisions as may be necessary to effect such change, exchange, reclassification, subdivision, combination or cancellation. In particular, and without limitation upon such general power of amendment, a corporation may amend its certificate of incorporation, from time to time, so as:

(1) To change its corporate name; or

(2) To change, substitute, enlarge or diminish the nature of its business or its corporate powers and purposes; or

(3) To increase or decrease its authorized capital stock or to reclassify the same, by changing the number, par value, designations, preferences, or relative, participating, optional, or other special rights of the shares, or the qualifications, limitations or restrictions of such rights, or by changing shares with par value into shares without par value, or shares without par value into shares with par value either with or without increasing or decreasing the number of shares, or by subdividing or combining the outstanding shares of any class or series of a class of shares into a greater or lesser number of outstanding shares; or

(4) To cancel or otherwise affect the right of the holders of the shares of any class to receive dividends which have accrued but have not been declared; or

(5) To create new classes of stock having rights and preferences either prior and superior or subordinate and inferior to the stock of any class then authorized, whether issued or unissued; or

(6) To change the period of its duration. Any or all such changes or alterations may be effected by 1 certificate of amendment.

(b) Every amendment authorized by subsection (a) of this section shall be made and effected in the following manner:

(1) If the corporation has capital stock, its board of directors shall adopt a resolution setting forth the amendment proposed, declaring its advisability, and either calling a special meeting of the stockholders entitled to vote in respect thereof for the consideration of such amendment or directing that the amendment proposed be considered at the next annual meeting of the stockholders. Such special or annual meeting shall be called and held upon notice in accordance with § 222 of this title. The notice shall set forth such amendment in full or a brief summary of the changes to be effected thereby, as the directors shall deem advisable. At the meeting a vote of the stockholders entitled to vote thereon shall be taken for and against the proposed amendment. If a majority of the outstanding stock entitled to vote thereon, and a majority of the outstanding stock of each class entitled to vote thereon as a class has been voted in favor of the amendment, a certificate setting forth the amendment and certifying that such amendment has been duly adopted in accordance with this section shall be executed, acknowledged and filed and shall become effective in accordance with § 103 of this title.

(2) The holders of the outstanding shares of a class shall be entitled to vote as a class upon a proposed amendment, whether or not entitled to vote thereon by the certificate of incorporation, if the amendment would increase or decrease the aggregate number of authorized shares of such class, increase or decrease the par value of the shares of such class, or alter or change the powers, preferences, or special rights of the shares of such class so as to affect them adversely. If any proposed amendment would alter or change the powers, preferences, or special rights of 1 or more series of any class so as to affect them adversely, but shall not so affect the entire class, then only the shares of the series so affected by the amendment shall be considered a separate class for the purposes of this paragraph. The number of authorized shares of any such class or classes of stock may be increased or decreased (but not below the number of shares thereof then outstanding) by the affirmative vote of the holders of a majority of the stock of the corporation entitled to vote irrespective of this subsection, if so provided in the original certificate of incorporation, in any amendment thereto which created such class or classes of stock or which was adopted prior to the issuance of any shares of such class or classes of stock, or in any amendment thereto which was authorized by a resolution or resolutions adopted by the affirmative vote of the holders of a majority of such class or classes of stock.

(3) If the corporation has no capital stock, then the governing body thereof shall adopt a resolution setting forth the amendment proposed and declaring its advisability. If a majority of all the members of the governing body shall vote in favor of such amendment, a certificate thereof shall be executed, acknowledged and filed and shall become effective in accordance with § 103 of this title. The certificate of incorporation of any such corporation without capital stock may contain a provision requiring any amendment thereto to be approved by a specified number or percentage of the members or of any specified class of members of such corporation in which event such proposed amendment shall be submitted to the members or to any specified class of members of such corporation without capital stock in the same manner, so far as applicable, as is provided in this section for an amendment to the certificate of incorporation of a stock corporation; and in the event of the adoption thereof by such members, a certificate evidencing such amendment shall be

executed, acknowledged and filed and shall become effective in accordance with § 103 of this title.

(4) Whenever the certificate of incorporation shall require for action by the board of directors, by the holders of any class or series of shares or by the holders of any other securities having voting power the vote of a greater number or proportion than is required by any section of this title, the provision of the certificate of incorporation requiring such greater vote shall not be altered, amended or repealed except by such greater vote.

(c) The resolution authorizing a proposed amendment to the certificate of incorporation may provide that at any time prior to the effectiveness of the filing of the amendment with the Secretary of State, notwithstanding authorization of the proposed amendment by the stockholders of the corporation or by the members of a nonstock corporation, the board of directors or governing body may abandon such proposed amendment without further action by the stockholders or members.

§ 243. Retirement of stock.

(a) A corporation, by resolution of its board of directors, may retire any shares of its capital stock that are issued but are not outstanding.

(b) Whenever any shares of the capital stock of a corporation are retired, they shall resume the status of authorized and unissued shares of the class or series to which they belong unless the certificate of incorporation otherwise provides. If the certificate of incorporation prohibits the reissuance of such shares, or prohibits the reissuance of such shares as a part of a specific series only, a certificate stating that reissuance of the shares (as part of the class or series) is prohibited identifying the shares and reciting their retirement shall be executed, acknowledged and filed and shall become effective in accordance with § 103 of this title. When such certificate becomes effective, it shall have the effect of amending the certificate of incorporation so as to reduce accordingly the number of authorized shares of the class or series to which such shares belong or, if such retired shares constitute all of the authorized shares of the class or series to which they belong, of eliminating from the certificate of incorporation all reference to such class or series of stock.

(c) If the capital of the corporation will be reduced by or in connection with the retirement of shares, the reduction of capital shall be effected pursuant to § 244 of this title.

§ 244. Reduction of capital.

(a) A corporation, by resolution of its board of directors, may reduce its capital in any of the following ways:

(1) By reducing or eliminating the capital represented by shares of capital stock which have been retired;

(2) By applying to an otherwise authorized purchase or redemption of outstanding shares of its capital stock some or all of the capital represented by the shares being purchased or redeemed, or any capital that has not been allocated to any particular class of its capital stock;

(3) By applying to an otherwise authorized conversion or exchange of outstanding shares of its capital stock some or all of the capital represented by the shares being converted or exchanged, or some or all of any capital that has not been allocated to any particular class of its capital stock, or both, to the extent that such capital in the aggregate exceeds the total aggregate par value or the stated capital of any previously unissued shares issuable upon such conversion or exchange; or (4) By transferring to surplus (i) some or all of the capital not represented by any particular class of its capital stock; (ii) some or all of the capital represented by issued shares of its par value capital stock, which capital is in excess of the aggregate par value of such shares; or (iii) some of the capital represented by issued shares of its capital stock without par value.

(b) Notwithstanding the other provisions of this section, no reduction of capital shall be made or effected unless the assets of the corporation remaining after such reduction shall be sufficient to pay any debts of the corporation for which payment has not been otherwise provided. No reduction of capital shall release any liability of any stockholder whose shares have not been fully paid.

(c) [Repealed.]

§ 245. Restated certificate of incorporation.

(a) A corporation may, whenever desired, integrate into a single instrument all of the provisions of its certificate of incorporation which are then in effect and operative as a result of there having theretofore been filed with the Secretary of State 1 or more certificates or other instruments pursuant to any of the sections referred to in § 104 of this title, and it may at the same time also further amend its certificate of incorporation by adopting a restated certificate of incorporation.

(b) If the restated certificate of incorporation merely restates and integrates but does not further amend the certificate of incorporation, as theretofore amended or supplemented by any instrument that was filed pursuant to any of the sections mentioned in § 104 of this title, it may be adopted by the board of directors without a vote of the stockholders, or it may be proposed by the directors and submitted by them to the stockholders for adoption, in which case the procedure and vote required by § 242 of this title for amendment of the certificate of incorporation shall be applicable. If the restated certificate of incorporation restates and integrates and also further amends in any respect the certificate of incorporation, as theretofore amended or supplemented, it shall be proposed by the directors and adopted by the stockholders in the manner and by the vote prescribed by § 242 of this title or, if the corporation has not received any payment for any of its stock, in the manner and by the vote prescribed by § 241 of this title.

(c) A restated certificate of incorporation shall be specifically designated as such in its heading. It shall state, either in its heading or in an introductory paragraph, the corporation's present name, and, if it has been changed, the name under which it was originally incorporated, and the date of filing of its original certificate of incorporation with the Secretary of State. A restated certificate shall also state that it was duly adopted in accordance with this section. If it was adopted by the board of directors without a vote of the stockholders (unless it was adopted pursuant to § 241 of this title), it shall state that it only restates and integrates and does not further amend the provisions of the corporation's certificate of incorporation as theretofore amended or supplemented, and that there is no discrepancy between those provisions and the provisions of the restated certificate. A restated certificate of incorporation may omit (a) such provisions of the original certificate of incorporation which named the incorporator or incorporators, the initial board of directors and the original subscribers for shares, and (b) such provisions contained in any amendment to the certificate of incorporation as were necessary to effect a change, exchange, reclassification, subdivision, combination or cancellation of stock, if such change, exchange, reclassification, subdivision, combination or cancellation has become effective. Any such omissions shall not be deemed a further amendment.

(d) A restated certificate of incorporation shall be executed, acknowledged and filed in accordance with § 103 of this title. Upon its filing with the Secretary of State, the original certificate of incorporation, as theretofore amended or supplemented, shall be superseded; thenceforth, the restated certificate of incorporation, including any further amendments or changes made thereby, shall be the certificate of incorporation of the corporation, but the original date of incorporation shall remain unchanged.

(e) Any amendment or change effected in connection with the restatement and integration of the certificate of incorporation shall be subject to any other provision of this chapter, not inconsistent with this section, which would apply if a separate certificate of amendment were filed to effect such amendment or change.

§ 246. [Reserved.].

Subchapter XIV. Close Corporations; Special Provisions.

§ 341. Law applicable to close corporation.

(a) This subchapter applies to all close corporations, as defined in § 342 of this title. Unless a corporation elects to become a close corporation under this subchapter in the manner prescribed in this subchapter, it shall be subject in all respects to this chapter, except this subchapter.

(b) This chapter shall be applicable to all close corporations, as defined in § 342 of this title, except insofar as this subchapter otherwise provides.

§ 342. Close corporation defined; contents of certificate of incorporation.

(a) A close corporation is a corporation organized under this chapter whose certificate of incorporation contains the provisions required by § 102 of this title and, in addition, provides that:

(1) All of the corporation's issued stock of all classes, exclusive of treasury shares, shall be represented by certificates and shall be held of record by not more than a specified number of persons, not exceeding 30; and

(2) All of the issued stock of all classes shall be subject to 1 or more of the restrictions on transfer permitted by § 202 of this title; and

(3) The corporation shall make no offering of any of its stock of any class which would constitute a "public offering" within the meaning of the United States Securities Act of 1933 [15 U.S.C. § 77a et seq.] as it may be amended from time to time.

(b) The certificate of incorporation of a close corporation may set forth the qualifications of stockholders, either by specifying classes of persons who shall be entitled to be holders of record of stock of any class, or by specifying classes of persons who shall not be entitled to be holders of stock of any class or both.

(c) For purposes of determining the number of holders of record of the stock of a close corporation, stock which is held in joint or common tenancy or by the entireties shall be treated as held by 1 stockholder.

§ 343. Formation of a close corporation.

A close corporation shall be formed in accordance with §§ 101, 102 and 103 of this title, except that:

(1) Its certificate of incorporation shall contain a heading stating the name of the corporation and that it is a close corporation; and

(2) Its certificate of incorporation shall contain the provisions required by § 342 of this title.

§ 344. Election of existing corporation to become a close corporation.

Any corporation organized under this chapter may become a close corporation under this subchapter by executing, acknowledging and filing, in accordance with § 103 of this title, a certificate of amendment of its certificate of incorporation which shall contain a statement that it elects to become a close corporation, the provisions required by § 342 of this title to appear in the certificate of incorporation of a close corporation, and a heading stating the name of the corporation and that it is a close corporation. Such amendment shall be adopted in accordance with the requirements of § 241 or 242 of this title, except that it must be approved by a vote of the holders of record of at least two thirds of the shares of each class of stock of the corporation which are outstanding.

§ 345. Limitations on continuation of close corporation status.

A close corporation continues to be such and to be subject to this subchapter until:

(1) It files with the Secretary of State a certificate of amendment deleting from its certificate of incorporation the provisions required or permitted by § 342 of this title to be stated in the certificate of incorporation to qualify it as a close corporation; or

(2) Any 1 of the provisions or conditions required or permitted by § 342 of this title to be stated in a certificate of incorporation to qualify a corporation as a close corporation has in fact been breached and neither the corporation nor any of its stockholders takes the steps required by § 348 of this title to prevent such loss of status or to remedy such breach.

§ 346. Voluntary termination of close corporation status by amendment of certificate of incorporation; vote required.

(a) A corporation may voluntarily terminate its status as a close corporation and cease to be subject to this subchapter by amending its certificate of incorporation to delete therefrom the additional provisions required or permitted by § 342 of this title to be stated in the certificate of incorporation of a close corporation. Any such amendment shall be adopted and shall become effective in accordance with § 242 of this title, except that it must be approved by a vote of the holders of record of at least two-thirds of the shares of each class of stock of the corporation which are outstanding.

(b) The certificate of incorporation of a close corporation may provide that on any amendment to terminate its status as a close corporation, a vote greater than two-thirds or a vote of all shares of any class shall be required; and if the certificate of incorporation contains such a provision, that provision shall not be amended, repealed or modified by any vote less than that required to terminate the corporation's status as a close corporation.

§ 347. Issuance or transfer of stock of a close corporation in breach of qualifying conditions.

(a) If stock of a close corporation is issued or transferred to any person who is not entitled under any provision of the certificate of incorporation permitted by subsection (b) of § 342 of this title to be a holder of record of stock of such corporation, and if the certificate for such stock conspicuously notes the qualifications of the persons entitled to be holders of record thereof, such person is conclusively presumed to have notice of the fact of such person's ineligibility to be a stockholder.

(b) If the certificate of incorporation of a close corporation states the number of persons, not in excess of 30, who are entitled to be holders of record of its stock, and if the certificate for such stock conspicuously states such number, and if the issuance or transfer of stock to any person would cause the stock to be held by more than such number of persons, the person to whom such stock is issued or transferred is conclusively presumed to have notice of this fact.

(c) If a stock certificate of any close corporation conspicuously notes the fact of a restriction on transfer of stock of the corporation, and the restriction is one which is permitted by § 202 of this title, the transferee of the stock is conclusively presumed to have notice of the fact that such person has acquired stock in violation of the restriction, if such acquisition violates the restriction.

(d) Whenever any person to whom stock of a close corporation has been issued or transferred has, or is conclusively presumed under this section to have, notice either

(1) that such person is a person not eligible to be a holder of stock of the corporation, or

(2) that transfer of stock to such person would cause the stock of the corporation to be held by more than the number of persons permitted by its certificate of incorporation to hold stock of the corporation, or

(3) that the transfer of stock is in violation of a restriction on transfer of stock, the corporation may, at its option, refuse to register transfer of the stock into the name of the transferee.

(e) Subsection (d) of this section shall not be applicable if the transfer of stock, even though otherwise contrary to subsection (a), (b) or (c), of this section has been consented to by all the stockholders of the close corporation, or if the close corporation has amended its certificate of incorporation in accordance with § 346 of this title.

(f) The term "transfer," as used in this section, is not limited to a transfer for value.

(g) The provisions of this section do not in any way impair any rights of a transferee regarding any right to rescind the transaction or to recover under any applicable warranty express or implied.

§ 348. Involuntary termination of close corporation status; proceeding to prevent loss of status.

(a) If any event occurs as a result of which 1 or more of the provisions or conditions included in a close corporation's certificate of incorporation pursuant to § 342 of this title to qualify it as a close corporation has been breached, the corporation's status as a close corporation under this subchapter shall terminate unless:

(1) Within 30 days after the occurrence of the event, or within 30 days after the event has been discovered, whichever is later, the corporation files with the Secretary of State a certificate, executed and acknowledged in accordance with § 103 of this title, stating that a specified provision or condition included in its certifi-

cate of incorporation pursuant to § 342 of this title to qualify it as a close corporation has ceased to be applicable, and furnishes a copy of such certificate to each stockholder; and

(2) The corporation concurrently with the filing of such certificate takes such steps as are necessary to correct the situation which threatens its status as a close corporation, including, without limitation, the refusal to register the transfer of stock which has been wrongfully transferred as provided by § 347 of this title, or a proceeding under subsection (b) of this section.

(b) The Court of Chancery, upon the suit of the corporation or any stockholder, shall have jurisdiction to issue all orders necessary to prevent the corporation from losing its status as a close corporation, or to restore its status as a close corporation by enjoining or setting aside any act or threatened act on the part of the corporation or a stockholder which would be inconsistent with any of the provisions or conditions required or permitted by § 342 of this title to be stated in the certificate of incorporation of a close corporation, unless it is an act approved in accordance with § 346 of this title. The Court of Chancery may enjoin or set aside any transfer or threatened transfer of stock of a close corporation which is contrary to the terms of its certificate of incorporation or of any transfer restriction permitted by § 202 of this title, and may enjoin any public offering, as defined in § 342 of this title, or threatened public offering of stock of the close corporation.

§ 349. Corporate option where a restriction on transfer of a security is held invalid.
If a restriction on transfer of a security of a close corporation is held not to be authorized by § 202 of this title, the corporation shall nevertheless have an option, for a period of 30 days after the judgment setting aside the restriction becomes final, to acquire the restricted security at a price which is agreed upon by the parties, or if no agreement is reached as to price, then at the fair value as determined by the Court of Chancery. In order to determine fair value, the Court may appoint an appraiser to receive evidence and report to the Court such appraiser's findings and recommendation as to fair value.

§ 350. Agreements restricting discretion of directors.
A written agreement among the stockholders of a close corporation holding a majority of the outstanding stock entitled to vote, whether solely among themselves or with a party not a stockholder, is not invalid, as between the parties to the agreement, on the ground that it so relates to the conduct of the business and affairs of the corporation as to restrict or interfere with the discretion or powers of the board of directors. The effect of any such agreement shall be to relieve the directors and impose upon the stockholders who are parties to the agreement the liability for managerial acts or omissions which is imposed on directors to the extent and so long as the discretion or powers of the board in its management of corporate affairs is controlled by such agreement.

§ 351. Management by stockholders.
The certificate of incorporation of a close corporation may provide that the business of the corporation shall be managed by the stockholders of the corporation rather than by a board of directors. So long as this provision continues in effect:

(1) No meeting of stockholders need be called to elect directors;

(2) Unless the context clearly requires otherwise, the stockholders of the corporation shall be deemed to be directors for purposes of applying provisions of this chapter; and

(3) The stockholders of the corporation shall be subject to all liabilities of directors. Such a provision may be inserted in the certificate of incorporation by amendment if all incorporators and subscribers or all holders of record of all of the outstanding stock, whether or not having voting power, authorize such a provision. An amendment to the certificate of incorporation to delete such a provision shall be adopted by a vote of the holders of a majority of all outstanding stock of the corporation, whether or not otherwise entitled to vote. If the certificate of incorporation contains a provision authorized by this section, the existence of such provision shall be noted conspicuously on the face or back of every stock certificate issued by such corporation.

§ 352. Appointment of custodian for close corporation.
(a) In addition to § 226 of this title respecting the appointment of a custodian for any corporation, the Court of Chancery, upon application of any stockholder, may appoint 1 or more persons to be custodians, and, if the corporation is insolvent, to be receivers, of any close corporation when:

(1) Pursuant to § 351 of this title the business and affairs of the corporation are managed by the stockholders and they are so divided that the business of the corporation is suffering or is threatened with irreparable injury and any remedy with respect to such deadlock provided in the certificate of incorporation or bylaws or in any written agreement of the stockholders has failed; or

(2) The petitioning stockholder has the right to the dissolution of the corporation under a provision of the certificate of incorporation permitted by § 355 of this title.

(b) In lieu of appointing a custodian for a close corporation under this section or § 226 of this title the Court of Chancery may appoint a provisional director, whose powers and status shall be as provided in § 353 of this title if the Court determines that it would be in the best interest of the corporation. Such appointment shall not preclude any subsequent order of the Court appointing a custodian for such corporation.

§ 353. Appointment of a provisional director in certain cases.

(a) Notwithstanding any contrary provision of the certificate of incorporation or the bylaws or agreement of the stockholders, the Court of Chancery may appoint a provisional director for a close corporation if the directors are so divided respecting the management of the corporation's business and affairs that the votes required for action by the board of directors cannot be obtained with the consequence that the business and affairs of the corporation can no longer be conducted to the advantage of the stockholders generally.

(b) An application for relief under this section must be filed

(1) by at least one half of the number of directors then in office,

(2) by the holders of at least one third of all stock then entitled to elect directors, or,

(3) if there be more than 1 class of stock then entitled to elect 1 or more directors, by the holders of two thirds of the stock of any such class; but the certificate of incorporation of a close corporation may provide that a lesser proportion of the directors or of the stockholders or of a class of stockholders may apply for relief under this section.

(c) A provisional director shall be an impartial person who is neither a stockholder nor a creditor of the corporation or of any subsidiary or affiliate of the corporation, and whose further qualifications, if any, may be determined by the Court of Chancery. A provisional director is not a receiver of the corporation and does not have the title and powers of a custodian or receiver appointed under §§ 226 and 291 of this title. A provisional director shall have all the rights and powers of a duly elected director of the corporation, including the right to notice of and to vote at meetings of directors, until such time as such person shall be removed by order of the Court of Chancery or by the holders of a majority of all shares then entitled to vote to elect directors or by the holders of two thirds of the shares of that class of voting shares which filed the application for appointment of a provisional director. A provisional director's compensation shall be determined by agreement between such person and the corporation subject to approval of the Court of Chancery, which may fix such person's compensation in the absence of agreement or in the event of disagreement between the provisional director and the corporation.

(d) Even though the requirements of subsection (b) of this section relating to the number of directors or stockholders who may petition for appointment of a provisional director are not satisfied, the Court of Chancery may nevertheless appoint a provisional director if permitted by subsection (b) of § 352 of this title.

§ 354. Operating corporation as partnership.

No written agreement among stockholders of a close corporation, nor any provision of the certificate of incorporation or of the bylaws of the corporation, which agreement or provision relates to any phase of the affairs of such corporation, including but not limited to the management of its business or declaration and payment of dividends or other division of profits or the election of directors or officers or the employment of stockholders by the corporation or the arbitration of disputes, shall be invalid on the ground that it is an attempt by the parties to the agreement or by the stockholders of the corporation to treat the corporation as if it were a partnership or to arrange relations among the stockholders or between the stockholders and the corporation in a manner that would be appropriate only among partners.

§ 355. Stockholders' option to dissolve corporation.

(a) The certificate of incorporation of any close corporation may include a provision granting to any stockholder, or to the holders of any specified number or percentage of shares of any class of stock, an option to have the corporation dissolved at will or upon the occurrence of any specified event or contingency. Whenever any such option to dissolve is exercised, the stockholders exercising such option shall give written notice thereof to all other stockholders. After the expiration of 30 days following the sending of such notice, the dissolution of the corporation shall proceed as if the required number of stockholders having voting power had consented in writing to dissolution of the corporation as provided by § 228 of this title.

(b) If the certificate of incorporation as originally filed does not contain a provision authorized by subsection (a) of this section, the certificate may be amended to include such provision if adopted by the affirmative vote of the holders of all the outstanding stock, whether or not entitled to vote, unless the certificate of incorporation specifically authorizes such an amendment by a vote which shall be not less than two thirds of all the outstanding stock whether or not entitled to vote.

(c) Each stock certificate in any corporation whose certificate of incorporation authorizes dissolution as permitted by this section shall conspicuously note on the face thereof the existence of the provision. Unless noted conspicuously on the face of the stock certificate, the provision is ineffective.

§ 356. Effect of this subchapter on other laws.

This subchapter shall not be deemed to repeal any statute or rule of law which is or would be applicable to any corporation which is organized under this chapter but is not a close corporation.

Subchapter XVII. Miscellaneous Provisions.

§ 391. Taxes and fees payable to Secretary of State upon filing certificate or other paper.

(a) The following taxes and fees shall be collected by and paid to the Secretary of State, for the use of the State:

(1) Upon the receipt for filing of an original certificate of incorporation, the tax shall be computed on the basis of 2 cents for each share of authorized capital stock having par value up to and including 20,000 shares, 1 cent for each share in excess of 20,000 shares up to and including 200,000 shares, and two-fifths of a cent for each share in excess of 200,000 shares; 1 cent for each share of authorized capital stock without par value up to and including 20,000 shares, one-half of a cent for each share in excess of 20,000 shares up to and including 2,000,000 shares, and two-fifths of a cent for each share in excess of 2,000,000 shares. In no case shall the amount paid be less than $15. For the purpose of computing the tax on par value stock each $100 unit of the authorized capital stock shall be counted as 1 taxable share.

(2) Upon the receipt for filing of a certificate of amendment of certificate of incorporation, or a certificate of amendment of certificate of incorporation before payment of capital, or a restated certificate of incorporation, increasing the authorized capital stock of a corporation, the tax shall be an amount equal to the difference between the tax computed at the foregoing rates upon the total authorized capital stock of the corporation including the proposed increase, and the tax computed at the foregoing rates upon the total authorized capital stock excluding the proposed increase. In no case shall the amount paid be less than $30.

(3) Upon the receipt for filing of a certificate of amendment of certificate of incorporation before payment of capital and not involving an increase of authorized capital stock, or an amendment to the certificate of incorporation not involving an increase of authorized capital stock, or a restated certificate of incorporation not involving an increase of authorized capital stock, or a certificate of retirement of stock, the tax to be paid shall be $30. For all other certificates relating to corporations, not otherwise provided for, the tax to be paid shall be $5. In case of corporations created solely for religious or charitable purposes no tax shall be paid.

(4) Upon the receipt for filing of a certificate of merger or consolidation of 2 or more corporations, the tax shall be an amount equal to the difference between the tax computed at the foregoing rates upon the total authorized capital stock of the corporation created by the merger or consolidation, and the tax so computed upon the aggregate amount of the total authorized capital stock of the constituent corporations. In no case shall the amount paid be less than $75. The foregoing tax shall be in addition to any tax or fee required under any other law of this State to be paid by any constituent entity that is not a corporation in connection with the filing of the certificate of merger or consolidation.

(5) Upon the receipt for filing of a certificate of dissolution, there shall be paid to and collected by the Secretary of State a tax of: a. Forty dollars ($40); or b. Ten dollars ($10) in the case of a certificate of dissolution which certifies that: 1. The corporation has no assets and has ceased transacting business; and 2. The corporation, for each year since its incorporation in this State, has been required to pay only the minimum franchise tax then prescribed by § 503 of this title; and 3. The corporation has paid all franchise taxes and fees due to or assessable by this State through the end of the year in which said certificate of dissolution is filed.

(6) Upon the receipt for filing of a certificate or other paper of surrender and withdrawal from the State by a foreign corporation, there shall be collected by and paid to the Secretary of State a tax of $10.

(7) For receiving and filing and/or indexing any certificate, affidavit, agreement or any other paper provided for by this chapter, for which no different fee is specifically prescribed, a fee of $50 in each case shall be paid to the Secretary of State. The fee in the case of a certificate of incorporation filed as required by § 102 of this title shall be $25. For entering information from each instrument into the Delaware Corporation Information System in accordance with § 103(c)(6) of this title, the fee shall be $20, except the fee for entering such information for a certificate of incorporation filed as required by § 102 of this title shall be $10. a. A certificate of dissolution which meets the criteria stated in paragraph (5)b. of this subsection shall not be subject to such fee; and b. A certificate of incorporation filed in accordance with § 102 of this title shall be subject to a fee of $25.

(8) For receiving and filing and/or indexing the annual report of a foreign corporation doing business in this State, a fee of $50 shall be paid. In the event of neglect, refusal or failure on the part of any foreign corporation to file the annual report with the Secretary of State on or before the 30th day of June each year, the corporation shall pay a penalty of $50.

(9) For recording and indexing articles of association and other papers required by this chapter to be recorded by the Secretary of State, a fee computed on the basis of 1 cent a line shall be paid.

(10) For certifying copies of any paper on file provided by this chapter, a fee of $20 shall be paid for each copy certified. In addition, a fee of $1 per page shall be paid in each instance where the Secretary of State provides the copies of the document to be certified.

(11) For issuing any certificate of the Secretary of State other than a certification of a copy under paragraph (10) of this subsection, or a certificate that recites all of a corporation's filings with the Secretary of State, a fee of $20 shall be paid for each certificate. For issuing any certifi-

cate of the Secretary of State that recites all of a corporation's filings with the Secretary of State, a fee of $100 shall be paid for each certificate.
(12) For filing in the office of the Secretary of State any certificate of change of address or change of name of registered agent, as provided in § 134 of this title, there shall be collected by and paid to the Secretary of State a fee of $50, plus the same fees for receiving, filing, indexing, copying and certifying the same as are charged in the case of filing a certificate of incorporation.
(13) For filing in the office of the Secretary of State any certificate of resignation of a registered agent and appointment of a successor, as provided in § 135 of this title, there shall be collected by and paid to the Secretary of State a fee of $50 and a further fee of $2 for each corporation whose registered agent is changed by such certificate.
(14) For filing in the office of the Secretary of State, any certificate of resignation of a registered agent without appointment of a successor, as provided in §§ 136 and 377 of this title, there shall be collected by and paid to the Secretary of State a fee of $2.50 for each corporation whose registered agent has resigned by such certificate.
(15) For preparing and providing a written report of a record search, a fee of $30 shall be paid.
(16) For preclearance of any document for filing, a fee of $250 shall be paid.
(17) For receiving and filing and/or indexing an annual franchise tax report of a corporation provided for by § 502 of this title, a fee of $20 shall be paid.
(18) For receiving and filing and/or indexing by the Secretary of State of a certificate of domestication and certificate of incorporation prescribed in § 388(d) of this title, a fee of $100, plus the tax and fee payable upon the receipt for filing of an original certificate of incorporation, shall be paid.
(19) For receiving, reviewing and filing and/or indexing by the Secretary of State of the documents prescribed in § 389(c) of this title, a fee of $10,000 shall be paid.
(20) For receiving, reviewing and filing and/or indexing by the Secretary of State of the documents prescribed in § 389(d) of this title, an annual fee of $2,500 shall be paid.
(21) Except as provided in this section, the fees of the Secretary of State shall be as provided for in § 2315 of Title 29.
(22) In the case of nonstock corporations and of religious, charitable or other nonprofit corporations organized under the laws of the State, the total fees payable to the Secretary of State upon the filing of a Certificate of Change of Registered Agent and/or Registered Office shall be $5.
(23) For accepting a corporate name reservation via telephone, mail or hand delivery, there shall be collected by and paid to the Secretary of State a fee of $10.
(24) For receiving and filing and/or indexing by the Secretary of State of a certificate of transfer or a certificate of continuance prescribed in § 390 of this title, a fee of $1,000 shall be paid.
(25) For receiving and filing and/or indexing by the Secretary of State of a certificate of conversion and certificate of incorporation prescribed in § 265 of this title, a fee of $50, plus the tax and fee payable upon the receipt for filing of an original certificate of incorporation, shall be paid.
(26) For receiving and filing and/or indexing by the Secretary of State of a certificate of conversion prescribed in § 266 of this title, a fee of $50 shall be paid. (b) (1) For the purpose of computing the taxes prescribed in paragraphs (1), (2) and (4) of subsection (a) of this section the authorized capital stock of a corporation shall be considered to be the total number of shares which the corporation is authorized to issue, whether or not the total number of shares that may be outstanding at any one time be limited to a less number. (2) For the purpose of computing the taxes prescribed in paragraphs (2) and (3) of subsection (a) of this section, a certificate of amendment of certificate of incorporation, or an amended certificate of incorporation before payment of capital, or a restated certificate of incorporation, shall be considered as increasing the authorized capital stock of a corporation provided it involves an increase in the number of shares, or an increase in the par value of shares, or a change of shares with par value into shares without par value, or a change of shares without par value into shares with par value, or any combination of 2 or more of the above changes, and provided further that the tax computed at the rates set forth in paragraph (1) of subsection (a) of this section upon the total authorized capital stock of the corporation including the proposed change or changes exceeds the tax so computed upon the total authorized stock of the corporation excluding such change or changes.
(c) The Secretary of State may issue photocopies or electronic image copies of instruments on file, as well as instruments, documents and other papers not on file, and for all such photocopies or electronic image copies which are not certified by the Secretary of State, a fee of $5 shall be paid for the first page and $1 for each additional page. The Secretary of State may also issue microfiche copies of instruments on file as well as instruments, documents and other papers not on file, and for each such microfiche a fee of $2 shall be paid therefor. Notwithstanding Delaware's Freedom of Information Act or other provision of this Code granting access to public records, the Secretary of State shall issue only photocopies, microfiche or electronic image copies of records in exchange for the fees described above.
(d) No fees for the use of the State shall be charged or collected from any corporation incorporated for the drainage

and reclamation of lowlands or for the amendment or renewal of the charter of such corporation.
(e) The Secretary of State may in the Secretary of State's discretion permit the extension of credit for the taxes or fees required by this section upon such terms as the Secretary of State shall deem to be appropriate.
(f) The Secretary of State shall retain from the revenue collected from the taxes or fees required by this section a sum sufficient to provide at all times a fund of at least $500, but not more than $1,500, from which the Secretary of State may refund any payment made pursuant to this section to the extent that it exceeds the taxes or fees required by this section. The fund shall be deposited in the financial institution which is the legal depository of state moneys to the credit of the Secretary of State and shall be disbursable on order of the Secretary of State.
(g) The Secretary of State may in the Secretary of State's discretion charge a fee of $25 for each check received for payment of any fee or tax under Chapter 1 or Chapter 6 of this title that is returned due to insufficient funds or as the result of a stop payment order.
(h) In addition to those fees charged under subsections (a) and (c) of this section, there shall be collected by and paid to the Secretary of State the following: (1) For all services described in subsections (a) and (c) of this section that are requested to be completed within 2 hours on the same day as the day of the request, an additional sum of up to $500; and (2) For all services described in subsections (a) and (c) of this section that are requested to be completed within the same day as the day of the request, an additional sum of up to $200; and (3) For all services described in subsections (a) and (c) of this section that are requested to be completed within a 24-hour period from the time of the request, an additional sum of up to $100. The Secretary of State shall establish (and may from time to time alter or amend) a schedule of specific fees payable pursuant to this subsection.
(i) A domestic corporation or a foreign corporation registered to do business in this State that files with the Secretary of State any instrument or certificate, and in connection therewith, neglects, refuses or fails to pay any fee or tax under Chapter 1 or Chapter 6 of this title shall, after written demand therefor by the Secretary of State by mail addressed to such domestic corporation or foreign corporation in care of its registered agent in this State, cease to be in good standing as a domestic corporation or registered as a foreign corporation in this State on the 90th day following the date of mailing of such demand, unless such fee or tax and, if applicable, the fee provided for in subsection (g) of this section are paid in full prior to the 90th day following the date of mailing of such demand. A domestic corporation that has ceased to be in good standing or a foreign corporation that has ceased to be registered by reason of the neglect, refusal or failure to pay any such fee or tax shall be restored to and have the status of a domestic corporation in good standing or a foreign corporation that is registered in this State upon the payment of the fee or tax which such domestic corporation or foreign corporation neglected, refused or failed to pay together with the fee provided for in subsection (g) of this section, if applicable. The Secretary of State shall not accept for filing any instrument authorized to be filed with the Secretary of State under this title in respect of any domestic corporation that is not in good standing or any foreign corporation that has ceased to be registered by reason of the neglect, refusal or failure to pay any such fee or tax, and shall not issue any certificate of good standing with respect to such domestic corporation or foreign corporation, unless and until such domestic corporation or foreign corporation shall have been restored to and have the status of a domestic corporation in good standing or a foreign corporation duly registered in this State.

§ 392. [Reserved.].

§ 393. Rights, liabilities and duties under prior statutes.
All rights, privileges and immunities vested or accrued by and under any laws enacted prior to the adoption or amendment of this chapter, all suits pending, all rights of action conferred, and all duties, restrictions, liabilities and penalties imposed or required by and under laws enacted prior to the adoption or amendment of this chapter, shall not be impaired, diminished or affected by this chapter.

§ 394. Reserved power of State to amend or repeal chapter; chapter part of corporation's charter or certificate of incorporation.
This chapter may be amended or repealed, at the pleasure of the General Assembly, but any amendment or repeal shall not take away or impair any remedy under this chapter against any corporation or its officers for any liability which shall have been previously incurred. This chapter and all amendments thereof shall be a part of the charter or certificate of incorporation of every corporation except so far as the same are inapplicable and inappropriate to the objects of the corporation.

§ 395. Corporations using "trust" in name, advertisements and otherwise; restrictions; violations and penalties; exceptions.
(a) Every corporation of this State using the word "trust" as part of its name, except a corporation regulated under the Bank Holding Company Act of 1956, 12 U.S.C. § 1841 et seq., or the Savings and Loan Holding Company Act, 12 U.S.C. § 1730a et seq., as those statutes shall from time to time be amended, shall be under the supervision of the State Bank Commissioner of this State and shall make not less than 2 reports during each year to the Commissioner, according to the form which shall be prescribed by the Commissioner, verified by the oaths or affirmations of the

president or vice-president, and the treasurer or secretary of the corporation, and attested by the signatures of at least 3 directors.

(b) No corporation of this State shall use the word "trust" as part of its name, except a corporation reporting to and under the supervision of the State Bank Commissioner of this State or a corporation regulated under the Bank Holding Company Act of 1956, 12 U.S.C. § 1841 et seq., or the Savings and Loan Holding Company Act, 12 U.S.C. § 1730a et seq., as those statutes shall from time to time be amended. The name of any such corporation shall not be amended so as to include the word "trust" unless such corporation shall report to and be under the supervision of the Commissioner, or unless it is regulated under the Bank Holding Company Act of 1956 or the Savings and Loan Holding Act.

(c) No person, firm, association of persons, or corporation of this State, except corporations reporting to and under the supervision of the State Bank Commissioner of this State or corporations regulated under the Bank Holding Company Act of 1956, 12 U.S.C. § 1841 et seq., or the Savings and Loan Holding Company Act, 12 U.S.C. § 1730a et seq., as those statutes shall from time to time be amended, shall advertise or put forth any sign as a trust company, or in any way solicit or receive deposits or transact business as a trust company, or use the word "trust" as a part of such person's or entity's name.

§ 396. Publication of chapter by Secretary of State; distribution.

The Secretary of State may have printed, from time to time as the Secretary of State deems necessary, pamphlet copies of this chapter, and the Secretary of State shall dispose of the copies to persons and corporations desiring the same for a sum not exceeding the cost of printing. The money received from the sale of the copies shall be disposed of as are other fees of the office of the Secretary of State. Nothing in this section shall prevent the free distribution of single pamphlet copies of this chapter by the Secretary of State, for the printing of which provision is made from time to time by joint resolution of the General Assembly.

§ 397. Penalty for unauthorized publication of chapter.

Whoever prints or publishes this chapter without the authority of the Secretary of State of this State, shall be fined not more than $500 or imprisoned not more than 3 months, or both.

§ 398. Short title.

This chapter shall be known and may be identified and referred to as the "General Corporation Law of the State of Delaware."

§ 18-101. Definitions.

As used in this chapter unless the context otherwise requires:

(1) "Bankruptcy" means an event that causes a person to cease to be a member as provided in § 18-304 of this title.

(2) "Certificate of formation" means the certificate referred to in § 18-201 of this title, and the certificate as amended.

(3) "Contribution" means any cash, property, services rendered or a promissory note or other obligation to contribute cash or property or to perform services, which a person contributes to a limited liability company in the person's capacity as a member.

(4) "Foreign limited liability company" means a limited liability company formed under the laws of any state or under the laws of any foreign country or other foreign jurisdiction and denominated as such under the laws of such state or foreign country or other foreign jurisdiction.

(5) "Knowledge" means a person's actual knowledge of a fact, rather than the person's constructive knowledge of the fact.

(6) "Limited liability company" and "domestic limited liability company" means a limited liability company formed under the laws of the State of Delaware and having 1 or more members.

(7) "Limited liability company agreement" means any agreement, written or oral, of the member or members as to the affairs of a limited liability company and the conduct of its business. A limited liability company agreement of a limited liability company having only 1 member shall not be unenforceable by reason of there being only 1 person who is a party to the limited liability company agreement. A written limited liability company agreement or another written agreement or writing: a. May provide that a person shall be admitted as a member of a limited liability company, or shall become an assignee of a limited liability company interest or other rights or powers of a member to the extent assigned, and shall become bound by the limited liability company agreement:

1. If such person (or a representative authorized by such person orally, in writing or by other action such as payment for a limited liability company interest) executes the limited liability company agreement or any other writing evidencing the intent of such person to become a member or assignee; or

2. Without such execution, if such person (or a representative authorized by such person orally, in writing or by other action such as payment for a limited liability company interest) complies with the conditions for becoming a member or assignee as set forth in the limited liability company agreement or any other writing; and b. Shall not be unenforceable by reason of its not having been signed by a person being admitted as a member or becoming an assignee as provided in sub-

paragraph a. of this paragraph, or by reason of its having been signed by a representative as provided in this chapter.

(8) "Limited liability company interest" means a member's share of the profits and losses of a limited liability company and a member's right to receive distributions of the limited liability company's assets.

(9) "Liquidating trustee" means a person carrying out the winding up of a limited liability company.

(10) "Manager" means a person who is named as a manager of a limited liability company in, or designated as a manager of a limited liability company pursuant to, a limited liability company agreement or similar instrument under which the limited liability company is formed.

(11) "Member" means a person who has been admitted to a limited liability company as a member as provided in § 18-301 of this title or, in the case of a foreign limited liability company, in accordance with the laws of the state or foreign country or other foreign jurisdiction under which the foreign limited liability company is organized.

(12) "Person" means a natural person, partnership (whether general or limited), trust, estate, association, corporation, custodian, nominee or any other individual or entity in its own or any representative capacity, in each case, whether domestic or foreign, and a limited liability company or foreign limited liability company.

(13) "Personal representative" means, as to a natural person, the executor, administrator, guardian, conservator or other legal representative thereof and, as to a person other than a natural person, the legal representative or successor thereof.

(14) "State" means the District of Columbia or the Commonwealth of Puerto Rico or any state, territory, possession or other jurisdiction of the United States other than the State of Delaware.

§ 18-102. Name set forth in certificate.

The name of each limited liability company as set forth in its certificate of formation:

(1) Shall contain the words "Limited Liability Company" or the abbreviation "L.L.C." or the designation "LLC";

(2) May contain the name of a member or manager;

(3) Must be such as to distinguish it upon the records in the office of the Secretary of State from the name on such records of any corporation, partnership, limited partnership, business trust or limited liability company reserved, registered, formed or organized under the laws of the State of Delaware or qualified to do business or registered as a foreign corporation, foreign limited partnership, foreign business trust, foreign partnership, or foreign limited liability company in the State of Delaware; provided however, that a limited liability company may register under any name which is not such as to distinguish it upon the records in the office of the Secretary of State from the name on such records of any domestic or foreign corporation, partnership, limited partnership, business trust or limited liability company reserved, registered, formed or organized under the laws of the State of Delaware with the written consent of the other corporation, partnership, limited partnership, business trust or limited liability company, which written consent shall be filed with the Secretary of State; and

(4) May contain the following words: "Company," "Association," "Club," "Foundation," "Fund," "Institute," "Society," "Union," "Syndicate," "Limited" or "Trust" (or abbreviations of like import).

§ 18-103. Reservation of name.

(a) The exclusive right to the use of a name may be reserved by:

(1) Any person intending to organize a limited liability company under this chapter and to adopt that name;

(2) Any domestic limited liability company or any foreign limited liability company registered in the State of Delaware which, in either case, proposes to change its name;

(3) Any foreign limited liability company intending to register in the State of Delaware and adopt that name; and

(4) Any person intending to organize a foreign limited liability company and intending to have it register in the State of Delaware and adopt that name.

(b) The reservation of a specified name shall be made by filing with the Secretary of State an application, executed by the applicant, specifying the name to be reserved and the name and address of the applicant. If the Secretary of State finds that the name is available for use by a domestic or foreign limited liability company, the Secretary shall reserve the name for the exclusive use of the applicant for a period of 120 days. Once having so reserved a name, the same applicant may again reserve the same name for successive 120-day periods. The right to the exclusive use of a reserved name may be transferred to any other person by filing in the office of the Secretary of State a notice of the transfer, executed by the applicant for whom the name was reserved, specifying the name to be transferred and the name and address of the transferee. The reservation of a specified name may be cancelled by filing with the Secretary of State a notice of cancellation, executed by the applicant or transferee, specifying the name reservation to be cancelled and the name and address of the applicant or transferee. Unless the Secretary of State finds that any application, notice of transfer, or notice of cancellation filed with the Secretary of State as required by this subsection does not conform to law, upon receipt of all filing fees required by law the Secretary shall prepare and return to the person who filed such instrument a copy of the filed instrument with a notation thereon of the action taken by the Secretary of State.

(c) A fee as set forth in § 18-1105(a)(1) of this title shall be paid at the time of the initial reservation of any name, at the time of the renewal of any such reservation and at the time of the filing of a notice of the transfer or cancellation of any such reservation.

§ 18-104. Registered office; registered agent.
(a) Each limited liability company shall have and maintain in the State of Delaware:

(1) A registered office, which may but need not be a place of its business in the State of Delaware; and
(2) A registered agent for service of process on the limited liability company, which agent may be either an individual resident of the State of Delaware whose business office is identical with the limited liability company's registered office, or a domestic corporation, or a domestic limited partnership, or a domestic limited liability company, or a domestic business trust, or a foreign corporation, or a foreign limited partnership, or a foreign limited liability company authorized to do business in the State of Delaware having a business office identical with such registered office, which is generally open during normal business hours to accept service of process and otherwise perform the functions of a registered agent, or the limited liability company itself.

(b) A registered agent may change the address of the registered office of the limited liability company(ies) for which it is registered agent to another address in the State of Delaware by paying a fee as set forth in § 18-1105(a)(2) of this title and filing with the Secretary of State a certificate, executed by such registered agent, setting forth the address at which such registered agent has maintained the registered office for each of the limited liability companies for which it is a registered agent, and further certifying to the new address to which each such registered office will be changed on a given day, and at which new address such registered agent will thereafter maintain the registered office for each of the limited liability companies for which it is a registered agent. Upon the filing of such certificate, the Secretary of State shall furnish to the registered agent a certified copy of the same under the Secretary's hand and seal of office, and thereafter, or until further change of address, as authorized by law, the registered office in the State of Delaware of each of the limited liability companies for which the agent is a registered agent shall be located at the new address of the registered agent thereof as given in the certificate. In the event of a change of name of any person acting as a registered agent of a limited liability company, such registered agent shall file with the Secretary of State a certificate executed by such registered agent setting forth the new name of such registered agent, the name of such registered agent before it was changed, and the address at which such registered agent has maintained the registered office for each of the limited liability companies for which it is a registered agent, and shall pay a fee as set forth in § 18-1105(a)(2) of this title. Upon the filing of such certificate, the Secretary of State shall furnish to the registered agent a certified copy of the certificate under his or her hand and seal of office. A change of name of any person acting as a registered agent of a limited liability company as a result of a merger or consolidation of the registered agent with or into another person which succeeds to its assets and liabilities by operation of law shall be deemed a change of name for purposes of this section. Filing a certificate under this section shall be deemed to be an amendment of the certificate of formation of each limited liability company affected thereby, and each such limited liability company shall not be required to take any further action with respect thereto to amend its certificate of formation under § 18-202 of this title. Any registered agent filing a certificate under this section shall promptly, upon such filing, deliver a copy of any such certificate to each limited liability company affected thereby.

(c) The registered agent of 1 or more limited liability companies may resign and appoint a successor registered agent by paying a fee as set forth in § 18-1105(a)(2) of this title and filing a certificate with the Secretary of State stating that it resigns and the name and address of the successor registered agent. There shall be attached to such certificate a statement of each affected limited liability company ratifying and approving such change of registered agent. Upon such filing, the successor registered agent shall become the registered agent of such limited liability companies as have ratified and approved such substitution, and the successor registered agent's address, as stated in such certificate, shall become the address of each such limited liability company's registered office in the State of Delaware. The Secretary of State shall then issue a certificate that the successor registered agent has become the registered agent of the limited liability companies so ratifying and approving such change and setting out the names of such limited liability companies. Filing of such certificate of resignation shall be deemed to be an amendment of the certificate of formation of each limited liability company affected thereby, and each such limited liability company shall not be required to take any further action with respect thereto to amend its certificate of formation under § 18-202 of this title.

(d) The registered agent of 1 or more limited liability companies may resign without appointing a successor registered agent by paying a fee as set forth in § 18-1105(a)(2) of this title and filing a certificate of resignation with the Secretary of State, but such resignation shall not become effective until 30 days after the certificate is filed. The certificate shall contain a statement that written notice of resignation was given to each affected limited liability company at least 30 days prior to the filing of the certificate by mailing or delivering such notice to the limited liability company at its address last known to the registered agent and shall set forth the date of such notice. After receipt of the notice of the resignation of its registered agent, the limited liability company for which such registered agent was acting shall obtain and designate a new registered agent, to take the place of the registered agent so resigning. If such limited liability company fails to obtain and designate a new registered agent as aforesaid prior to the expiration of the period of 30 days after the filing by the registered agent of the certificate of resignation, the certificate of formation of such limited liability company shall be deemed to be canceled. After the resignation of the registered agent shall have become effective as provided in this section and if no new registered agent shall have been obtained and designated in the time and manner aforesaid, service of legal process against each limited liability company for which the resigned registered agent had been acting shall thereafter be upon the Secretary of State in accordance with § 18-105 of this title.

§ 18-105. Service of process on domestic limited liability companies.

(a) Service of legal process upon any domestic limited liability company shall be made by delivering a copy personally to any manager of the limited liability company in the State of Delaware or the registered agent of the limited liability company in the State of Delaware, or by leaving it at the dwelling house or usual place of abode in the State of Delaware of any such manager or registered agent (if the registered agent be an individual), or at the registered office or other place of business of the limited liability company in the State of Delaware. If the registered agent be a corporation, service of process upon it as such may be made by serving, in the State of Delaware, a copy thereof on the president, vice-president, secretary, assistant secretary or any director of the corporate registered agent. Service by copy left at the dwelling house or usual place of abode of a manager or registered agent, or at the registered office or other place of business of the limited liability company in the State of Delaware, to be effective, must be delivered thereat at least 6 days before the return date of the process, and in the presence of an adult person, and the officer serving the process shall distinctly state the manner of service in the officer's return thereto. Process returnable forthwith must be delivered personally to the manager or registered agent.

(b) In case the officer whose duty it is to serve legal process cannot by due diligence serve the process in any manner provided for by subsection (a) of this section, it shall be lawful to serve the process against the limited liability company upon the Secretary of State, and such service shall be as effectual for all intents and purposes as if made in any of the ways provided for in subsection (a) of this section. In the event that service is effected through the Secretary of State in accordance with this subsection, the Secretary of State shall forthwith notify the limited liability company by letter, certified mail, return receipt requested, directed to the limited liability company at its address as it appears on the records relating to such limited liability company on file with the Secretary of State or, if no such address appears, at its last registered office. Such letter shall enclose a copy of the process and any other papers served on the Secretary of State pursuant to this subsection. It shall be the duty of the plaintiff in the event of such service to serve process and any other papers in duplicate, to notify the Secretary of State that service is being effected pursuant to this subsection, and to pay the Secretary of State the sum of $50 for the use of the State of Delaware, which sum shall be taxed as part of the costs in the proceeding if the plaintiff shall prevail therein. The Secretary of State shall maintain an alphabetical record of any such service setting forth the name of the plaintiff and defendant, the title, docket number and nature of the proceeding in which process has been served upon the Secretary, the fact that service has been effected pursuant to this subsection, the return date thereof, and the day and hour when the service was made. The Secretary of State shall not be required to retain such information for a period longer than 5 years from the Secretary's receipt of the service of process.

§ 18-106. Nature of business permitted; powers.

(a) A limited liability company may carry on any lawful business, purpose or activity, whether or not for profit, with the exception of the business of granting policies of insurance, or assuming insurance risks or banking as defined in § 126 of Title 8.

(b) A limited liability company shall possess and may exercise all the powers and privileges granted by this chapter or by any other law or by its limited liability company agreement, together with any powers incidental thereto, including such powers and privileges as are necessary or convenient to the conduct, promotion or attainment of the business, purposes or activities of the limited liability company.

§ 18-107. Business transactions of member or manager with the limited liability company.

Except as provided in a limited liability company agreement, a member or manager may lend money to, borrow money from, act as a surety, guarantor or endorser for, guarantee or assume 1 or more obligations of, provide collateral for, and transact other business with, a limited liability company and, subject to other applicable law, has the same rights and obligations with respect to any such matter as a person who is not a member or manager.

§ 18-108. Indemnification.

Subject to such standards and restrictions, if any, as are set forth in its limited liability company agreement, a limited liability company may, and shall have the power to, indemnify and hold harmless any member or manager or other person from and against any and all claims and demands whatsoever.

§ 18-109. Service of process on managers and liquidating trustees.

(a) A manager or a liquidating trustee of a limited liability company may be served with process in the manner prescribed in this section in all civil actions or proceedings brought in the State of Delaware involving or relating to the business of the limited liability company or a violation by the manager or the liquidating trustee of a duty to the limited liability company, or any member of the limited liability company, whether or not the manager or the liquidating trustee is a manager or a liquidating trustee at the time suit is commenced. A manager's or a liquidating trustee's serving as such constitutes such person's consent to the appointment of the registered agent of the limited liability company (or, if there is none, the Secretary of State) as such person's agent upon whom service of process may be made as provided in this section. Such service as a manager or a liquidating trustee shall signify the consent of such manager or liquidating trustee that any process when so served shall be of the same legal force and validity as if served upon such manager or liquidating trustee within the State of Delaware and such appointment of the registered agent (or, if there is none, the Secretary of State) shall be irrevocable. As used in this subsection (a) and in subsections (b), (c) and (d) of this section, the term "manager" refers (i) to a person who is a manager as defined in § 18-101(10) of this title and (ii) to a person, whether or not a member of a limited liability company, who, although not a manager as defined in § 18-101(10) of this title, participates materially in the management of the limited liability company; provided however, that the power to elect or otherwise select or to participate in the election or selection of a person to be a manager as defined in § 18-101(10) of this title shall not, by itself, constitute participation in the management of the limited liability company.

(b) Service of process shall be effected by serving the registered agent (or, if there is none, the Secretary of State) with 1 copy of such process in the manner provided by law for service of writs of summons. In the event service is made under this subsection upon the Secretary of State, the plaintiff shall pay to the Secretary of State the sum of $50 for the use of the State of Delaware, which sum shall be taxed as part of the costs of the proceeding if the plaintiff shall prevail therein. In addition, the Prothonotary or the Register in Chancery of the court in which the civil action or proceeding is pending shall, within 7 days of such service, deposit in the United States mails, by registered mail, postage prepaid, true and attested copies of the process, together with a statement that service is being made pursuant to this section, addressed to such manager or liquidating trustee at the registered office of the limited liability company and at the manager's or liquidating trustee's address last known to the party desiring to make such service.

(c) In any action in which any such manager or liquidating trustee has been served with process as hereinabove provided, the time in which a defendant shall be required to appear and file a responsive pleading shall be computed from the date of mailing by the Prothonotary or the Register in Chancery as provided in subsection (b) of this section; however, the court in which such action has been commenced may order such continuance or continuances as may be necessary to afford such manager or liquidating trustee reasonable opportunity to defend the action.

(d) In a written limited liability company agreement or other writing, a manager or member may consent to be subject to the nonexclusive jurisdiction of the courts of, or arbitration in, a specified jurisdiction, or the exclusive jurisdiction of the courts of the State of Delaware, or the exclusivity of arbitration in a specified jurisdiction or the State of Delaware, and to be served with legal process in the manner prescribed in such limited liability company agreement or other writing. Except by agreeing to arbitrate any arbitrable matter in a specified jurisdiction or in the State of Delaware, a member who is not a manager may not waive its right to maintain a legal action or proceeding in the courts of the State of Delaware with respect to matters relating to the organization or internal affairs of a limited liability company.

(e) Nothing herein contained limits or affects the right to serve process in any other manner now or hereafter provided by law. This section is an extension of and not a limitation upon the right otherwise existing of service of legal process upon nonresidents.

(f) The Court of Chancery and the Superior Court may make all necessary rules respecting the form of process, the manner of issuance and return thereof and such other rules which may be necessary to implement this section and are not inconsistent with this section.

§ 18-110. Contested matters relating to managers; contested votes.

(a) Upon application of any member or manager, the Court of Chancery may hear and determine the validity of any admission, election, appointment, removal or resignation of a manager of a limited liability company, and the right of any person to become or continue to be a manager of a limited liability company, and, in case the right to serve as a manager is claimed by more than 1 person, may determine the person or persons entitled to serve as managers; and to that end make such order or decree in any such case as may be just and proper, with power to enforce the production of any books, papers and records of the limited liability company relating to the issue. In any such application, the limited liability company shall be named as a party and service of copies of the application upon the registered agent of the limited liability company shall be deemed to be service upon the limited liability company and upon the person or persons whose right to serve as a manager is contested and upon the person or persons, if any, claiming to be a manager or claiming the right to be a manager; and the registered agent shall forward immediately a copy of the application to the limited liability company and to the person or persons whose right to serve as a manager is contested and to the person or persons, if any, claiming to be a manager or the right to be a manager, in a postpaid, sealed, registered letter addressed to such limited liability company and such person or persons at their post-office addresses last known to the registered agent or furnished to the registered agent by the applicant member or manager. The Court may make such order respecting further or other notice of such application as it deems proper under these circumstances.

(b) Upon application of any member or manager, the Court of Chancery may hear and determine the result of any vote of members or managers upon matters as to which the members or managers of the limited liability company, or any class or group of members or managers, have the right to vote pursuant to the limited liability company agreement or other agreement or this chapter (other than the admission, election, appointment, removal or resignation of managers). In any such application, the limited liability company shall be named as a party and service of the application upon the registered agent of the limited liability company shall be deemed to be service upon the limited liability company, and no other party need be joined in order for the Court to adjudicate the result of the vote. The Court may make such order respecting further or other notice of such application as it deems proper under these circumstances.

(c) Nothing herein contained limits or affects the right to serve process in any other manner now or hereafter provided by law. This section is an extension of and not a limitation upon the right otherwise existing of service of legal process upon nonresidents.

§ 18-111. Interpretation and enforcement of limited liability company agreement.

Any action to interpret, apply or enforce the provisions of a limited liability company agreement, or the duties, obligations or liabilities of a limited liability company to the members or managers of the limited liability company, or the duties, obligations or liabilities among members or managers and of members or managers to the limited liability company, or the rights or powers of, or restrictions on, the limited liability company, members or managers, may be brought in the Court of Chancery.

Subchapter II. Formation; Certificate of Formation.

§ 18-201. Certificate of formation.

(a) In order to form a limited liability company, 1 or more authorized persons must execute a certificate of formation. The certificate of formation shall be filed in the office of the Secretary of State and set forth:

(1) The name of the limited liability company;

(2) The address of the registered office and the name and address of the registered agent for service of process required to be maintained by § 18-104 of this title; and

(3) Any other matters the members determine to include therein.

(b) A limited liability company is formed at the time of the filing of the initial certificate of formation in the office of the Secretary of State or at any later date or time specified in the certificate of formation if, in either case, there has been substantial compliance with the requirements of this section. A limited liability company formed under this chapter shall be a separate legal entity, the existence of which as a separate legal entity shall continue until cancellation of the limited liability company's certificate of formation.

(c) The filing of the certificate of formation in the office of the Secretary of State shall make it unnecessary to file any other documents under Chapter 31 of this title.

(d) A limited liability company agreement may be entered into either before, after or at the time of the filing of a certificate of formation and, whether entered into before, after or at the time of such filing, may be made effective as of the formation of the limited liability company or at such other time or date as provided in the limited liability company agreement.

§ 18-202. Amendment to certificate of formation.

(a) A certificate of formation is amended by filing a certificate of amendment thereto in the office of the Secretary of State. The certificate of amendment shall set forth:

(1) The name of the limited liability company; and

(2) The amendment to the certificate of formation.

(b) A manager or, if there is no manager, then any member who becomes aware that any statement in a certificate of formation was false when made, or that any matter described has changed making the certificate of formation false in any material respect, shall promptly amend the certificate of formation.

(c) A certificate of formation may be amended at any time for any other proper purpose.

(d) Unless otherwise provided in this chapter or unless a later effective date or time (which shall be a date or time certain) is provided for in the certificate of amendment, a certificate of amendment shall be effective at the time of its filing with the Secretary of State.

§ 18-203. Cancellation of certificate.

A certificate of formation shall be cancelled upon the dissolution and the completion of winding up of a limited liability company, or as provided in § 18-104(d) or § 18-1108 of this chapter, or upon the filing of a certificate of merger or consolidation if the limited liability company is not the surviving or resulting entity in a merger or consolidation. A certificate of cancellation shall be filed in the office of the Secretary of State to accomplish the cancellation of a certificate of formation upon the dissolution and the completion of winding up of a limited liability company and shall set forth:

(1) The name of the limited liability company;
(2) The date of filing of its certificate of formation;
(3) The reason for filing the certificate of cancellation;
(4) The future effective date or time (which shall be a date or time certain) of cancellation if it is not to be effective upon the filing of the certificate; and
(5) Any other information the person filing the certificate of cancellation determines.

§ 18-204. Execution.
(a) Each certificate required by this subchapter to be filed in the office of the Secretary of State shall be executed by 1 or more authorized persons.
(b) Unless otherwise provided in a limited liability company agreement, any person may sign any certificate or amendment thereof or enter into a limited liability company agreement or amendment thereof by an agent, including an attorney-in-fact. An authorization, including a power of attorney, to sign any certificate or amendment thereof or to enter into a limited liability company agreement or amendment thereof need not be in writing, need not be sworn to, verified or acknowledged, and need not be filed in the office of the Secretary of State, but if in writing, must be retained by the limited liability company.
(c) The execution of a certificate by an authorized person constitutes an oath or affirmation, under the penalties of perjury in the third degree, that, to the best of the authorized person's knowledge and belief, the facts stated therein are true.

§ 18-205. Execution, amendment or cancellation by judicial order.
(a) If a person required to execute a certificate required by this subchapter fails or refuses to do so, any other person who is adversely affected by the failure or refusal may petition the Court of Chancery to direct the execution of the certificate. If the Court finds that the execution of the certificate is proper and that any person so designated has failed or refused to execute the certificate, it shall order the Secretary of State to record an appropriate certificate.
(b) If a person required to execute a limited liability company agreement or amendment thereof fails or refuses to do so, any other person who is adversely affected by the failure or refusal may petition the Court of Chancery to direct the execution of the limited liability company agreement or amendment thereof. If the Court finds that the limited liability company agreement or amendment thereof should be executed and that any person required to execute the limited liability company agreement or amendment thereof has failed or refused to do so, it shall enter an order granting appropriate relief.

§ 18-206. Filing.
(a) The original signed copy of the certificate of formation and of any certificates of amendment, correction, amendment of a certificate with a future effective date or time, termination of a certificate with a future effective date or time or cancellation (or of any judicial decree of amendment or cancellation), and of any certificate of merger or consolidation, any restated certificate, any corrected certificate, any certificate of conversion to limited liability company, any certificate of transfer, any certificate of transfer and continuance, any certificate of limited liability company domestication, and of any certificate of revival shall be delivered to the Secretary of State. A person who executes a certificate as an agent or fiduciary need not exhibit evidence of that person's authority as a prerequisite to filing. Any signature on any certificate authorized to be filed with the Secretary of State under any provision of this chapter may be a facsimile, a conformed signature or an electronically transmitted signature. Unless the Secretary of State finds that any certificate does not conform to law, upon receipt of all filing fees required by law the Secretary of State shall:

(1) Certify that the certificate of formation, the certificate of amendment, the certificate of correction, the certificate of amendment of a certificate with a future effective date or time, the certificate of termination of a certificate with a future effective date or time, the certificate of cancellation (or of any judicial decree of amendment or cancellation), the certificate of merger or consolidation, the restated certificate, the corrected certificate, the certificate of conversion to limited liability company, the certificate of transfer, the certificate of transfer and continuance, the certificate of limited liability company domestication or the certificate of revival has been filed in the Secretary of State's office by endorsing upon the original certificate the word "Filed," and the date and hour of the filing. This endorsement is conclusive of the date and time of its filing in the absence of actual fraud;
(2) File and index the endorsed certificate; and
(3) Prepare and return to the person who filed it or that person's representative a copy of the original signed instrument, similarly endorsed, and shall certify such copy as a true copy of the original signed instrument.

(b) Upon the filing of a certificate of amendment (or judicial decree of amendment), certificate of correction, corrected certificate or restated certificate in the office of the Secretary of State, or upon the future effective date or time of a certificate of amendment (or judicial decree thereof) or restated certificate, as provided for therein, the certificate of formation shall be amended, corrected or restated as set forth therein. Upon the filing of a certificate of cancellation (or a judicial decree thereof), or a certificate of merger or consolidation which acts as a certificate of cancellation or a certificate of transfer, or upon the future effective date or time of a certificate of cancellation (or a judicial decree thereof) or of a certificate of merger or consolidation which acts as a certificate of cancellation or a certificate of transfer, as provided for therein, or as specified in § 18-104(d) of this title, the certificate of formation is cancelled. Upon the filing of a certificate of limited liability company domestication or upon the future effective date or time of a certificate of limited liability company domestication, the entity filing the certificate of limited liability company domestication is domesticated as a limited liability company with the effect provided in § 18-212 of this title. Upon the filing of a certificate of conversion to limited liability company or upon the future effective date or time of a certificate of conversion to limited liability company, the entity filing the certificate of conversion to limited liability company is converted to a limited liability company with the effect provided in § 18-214 of this title. Upon the filing of a certificate of revival, the limited liability company is revived with the effect provided in § 18-1109 of this title. Upon the filing of a certificate of transfer and continuance, or upon the future effective date or time of a certificate of transfer and continuance, as provided for therein, the limited liability company filing the certificate of transfer and continuance shall continue to exist as a limited liability company of the State of Delaware with the effect provided in § 18-213 of this title.

(c) If any certificate filed in accordance with this chapter provides for a future effective date or time and if, prior to such future effective date or time set forth in such certificate, the transaction is terminated or its terms are amended to change the future effective date or time or any other matter described in such certificate so as to make such certificate false or inaccurate in any respect, such certificate shall, prior to the future effective date or time set forth in such certificate, be terminated or amended by the filing of a certificate of termination or certificate of amendment of such certificate, executed in accordance with § 18-204 of this title, which shall identify the certificate which has been terminated or amended and shall state that the certificate has been terminated or the manner in which it has been amended. Upon the filing of a certificate of amendment of a certificate with a future effective date or time, the certificate identified in such certificate of amendment is amended. Upon the filing of a certificate of termination of a certificate with a future effective date or time, the certificate identified in such certificate of termination is terminated.

(d) A fee as set forth in § 18-1105(a)(3) of this title shall be paid at the time of the filing of a certificate of formation, a certificate of amendment, a certificate of correction, a certificate of amendment of a certificate with a future effective date or time, a certificate of termination of a certificate with a future effective date or time, a certificate of cancellation, a certificate of merger or consolidation, a restated certificate, a corrected certificate, a certificate of conversion to limited liability company, a certificate of transfer, a certificate of transfer and continuance, a certificate of limited liability company domestication or a certificate of revival.

(e) A fee as set forth in § 18-1105(a)(4) of this title shall be paid for a certified copy of any paper on file as provided for by this chapter, and a fee as set forth in § 18-1105(a)(5) of this title shall be paid for each page copied.

§ 18-207. Notice.

The fact that a certificate of formation is on file in the office of the Secretary of State is notice that the entity formed in connection with the filing of the certificate of formation is a limited liability company formed under the laws of the State of Delaware and is notice of all other facts set forth therein which are required to be set forth in a certificate of formation by § 18-201(a)(1) and (2) of this title and which are permitted to be set forth in a certificate of formation by § 18-215(b) of this title.

§ 18-208. Restated certificate.

(a) A limited liability company may, whenever desired, integrate into a single instrument all of the provisions of its certificate of formation which are then in effect and operative as a result of there having theretofore been filed with the Secretary of State 1 or more certificates or other instruments pursuant to any of the sections referred to in this subchapter, and it may at the same time also further amend its certificate of formation by adopting a restated certificate of formation.

(b) If a restated certificate of formation merely restates and integrates but does not further amend the initial certificate of formation, as theretofore amended or supplemented by any instrument that was executed and filed pursuant to any of the sections in this subchapter, it shall be specifically designated in its heading as a "Restated Certificate of Formation" together with such other words as the limited liability company may deem appropriate and shall be executed by an authorized person and filed as provided in § 18-206 of this title in the office of the Secretary of State. If a restated certificate restates and integrates and also further amends in any respect the certificate of formation, as theretofore amended or supplemented, it shall be specifically designated in its heading as an "Amended and Restated Certificate of Formation" together with such other words as the limited liability company may deem appropriate and shall be executed by at least 1 authorized person, and filed as provided in § 18-206 of this title in the office of the Secretary of State.

(c) A restated certificate of formation shall state, either in its heading or in an introductory paragraph, the limited liability company's present name, and, if it has been changed, the name under which it was originally filed, and the date of filing of its original certificate of formation with the Secretary of State, and the future effective date or time

(which shall be a date or time certain) of the restated certificate if it is not to be effective upon the filing of the restated certificate. A restated certificate shall also state that it was duly executed and is being filed in accordance with this section. If a restated certificate only restates and integrates and does not further amend a limited liability company's certificate of formation as theretofore amended or supplemented and there is no discrepancy between those provisions and the restated certificate, it shall state that fact as well.
(d) Upon the filing of a restated certificate of formation with the Secretary of State, or upon the future effective date or time of a restated certificate of formation as provided for therein, the initial certificate of formation, as theretofore amended or supplemented, shall be superseded; thenceforth, the restated certificate of formation, including any further amendment or changes made thereby, shall be the certificate of formation of the limited liability company, but the original effective date of formation shall remain unchanged.
(e) Any amendment or change effected in connection with the restatement and integration of the certificate of formation shall be subject to any other provision of this chapter, not inconsistent with this section, which would apply if a separate certificate of amendment were filed to effect such amendment or change.

§ 18-209. Merger and consolidation.
(a) As used in this section, "other business entity" means a corporation, or a business trust or association, a real estate investment trust, a common-law trust, or any other unincorporated business, including a partnership (whether general (including a limited liability partnership) or limited (including a limited liability limited partnership)), and a foreign limited liability company, but excluding a domestic limited liability company.
(b) Pursuant to an agreement of merger or consolidation, 1 or more domestic limited liability companies may merge or consolidate with or into 1 or more domestic limited liability companies or 1 or more other business entities formed or organized under the laws of the State of Delaware or any other state or the United States or any foreign country or other foreign jurisdiction, or any combination thereof, with such domestic limited liability companies or other business entity as the agreement shall provide being the surviving or resulting domestic limited liability companies or other business entity. Unless otherwise provided in the limited liability company agreement, a merger or consolidation shall be approved by each domestic limited liability company which is to merge or consolidate by the members or, if there is more than one class or group of members, then by each class or group of members, in either case, by members who own more than 50 percent of the then current percentage or other interest in the profits of the domestic limited liability company owned by all of the members or by the members in each class or group, as appropriate. In connection with a merger or consolidation hereunder, rights or securities of, or interests in, a domestic limited liability company or other business entity which is a constituent party to the merger or consolidation may be exchanged for or converted into cash, property, rights or securities of, or interests in, the surviving or resulting domestic limited liability company or other business entity or, in addition to or in lieu thereof, may be exchanged for or converted into cash, property, rights or securities of, or interests in, a domestic limited liability company or other business entity which is not the surviving or resulting limited liability company or other business entity in the merger or consolidation. Notwithstanding prior approval, an agreement of merger or consolidation may be terminated or amended pursuant to a provision for such termination or amendment contained in the agreement of merger or consolidation.
(c) If a domestic limited liability company is merging or consolidating under this section, the domestic limited liability company or other business entity surviving or resulting in or from the merger or consolidation shall file a certificate of merger or consolidation executed by 1 or more authorized persons on behalf of the domestic limited liability company when it is the surviving or resulting entity in the office of the Secretary of State. The certificate of merger or consolidation shall state:

(1) The name and jurisdiction of formation or organization of each of the domestic limited liability companies and other business entities which is to merge or consolidate;
(2) That an agreement of merger or consolidation has been approved and executed by each of the domestic limited liability companies and other business entities which is to merge or consolidate;
(3) The name of the surviving or resulting domestic limited liability company or other business entity;
(4) The future effective date or time (which shall be a date or time certain) of the merger or consolidation if it is not to be effective upon the filing of the certificate of merger or consolidation;
(5) That the agreement of merger or consolidation is on file at a place of business of the surviving or resulting domestic limited liability company or other business entity, and shall state the address thereof;
(6) That a copy of the agreement of merger or consolidation will be furnished by the surviving or resulting domestic limited liability company or other business entity, on request and without cost, to any member of any domestic limited liability company or any person holding an interest in any other business entity which is to merge or consolidate; and
(7) If the surviving or resulting entity is not a domestic limited liability company, or a corporation or limited partnership organized under the laws of the State of

Delaware, or a business trust organized under Chapter 38 of Title 12, a statement that such surviving or resulting other business entity agrees that it may be served with process in the State of Delaware in any action, suit or proceeding for the enforcement of any obligation of any domestic limited liability company which is to merge or consolidate, irrevocably appointing the Secretary of State as its agent to accept service of process in any such action, suit or proceeding and specifying the address to which a copy of such process shall be mailed to it by the Secretary of State. In the event of service hereunder upon the Secretary of State, the procedures set forth in § 18-911(c) of this title shall be applicable, except that the plaintiff in any such action, suit or proceeding shall furnish the Secretary of State with the address specified in the certificate of merger or consolidation provided for in this section and any other address which the plaintiff may elect to furnish, together with copies of such process as required by the Secretary of State, and the Secretary of State shall notify such surviving or resulting other business entity at all such addresses furnished by the plaintiff in accordance with the procedures set forth in § 18-911(c) of this title.

(d) Unless a future effective date or time is provided in a certificate of merger or consolidation, in which event a merger or consolidation shall be effective at any such future effective date or time, a merger or consolidation shall be effective upon the filing in the office of the Secretary of State of a certificate of merger or consolidation.

(e) A certificate of merger or consolidation shall act as a certificate of cancellation for a domestic limited liability company which is not the surviving or resulting entity in the merger or consolidation. Whenever this section requires the filing of a certificate of merger or consolidation, such requirement shall be deemed satisfied by the filing of an agreement of merger or consolidation containing the information required by this section to be set forth in the certificate of merger or consolidation.

(f) An agreement of merger or consolidation approved in accordance with subsection (b) of this section may:

(1) Effect any amendment to the limited liability company agreement; or

(2) Effect the adoption of a new limited liability company agreement, for a limited liability company if it is the surviving or resulting limited liability company in the merger or consolidation. Any amendment to a limited liability company agreement or adoption of a new limited liability company agreement made pursuant to the foregoing sentence shall be effective at the effective time or date of the merger or consolidation. The provisions of this subsection shall not be construed to limit the accomplishment of a merger or of any of the matters referred to herein by any other means provided for in a limited liability company agreement or other agreement or as otherwise permitted by law, including that the limited liability company agreement of any constituent limited liability company to the merger or consolidation (including a limited liability company formed for the purpose of consummating a merger or consolidation) shall be the limited liability company agreement of the surviving or resulting limited liability company.

(g) When any merger or consolidation shall have become effective under this section, for all purposes of the laws of the State of Delaware, all of the rights, privileges and powers of each of the domestic limited liability companies and other business entities that have merged or consolidated, and all property, real, personal and mixed, and all debts due to any of said domestic limited liability companies and other business entities, as well as all other things and causes of action belonging to each of such domestic limited liability companies and other business entities, shall be vested in the surviving or resulting domestic limited liability company or other business entity, and shall thereafter be the property of the surviving or resulting domestic limited liability company or other business entity as they were of each of the domestic limited liability companies and other business entities that have merged or consolidated, and the title to any real property vested by deed or otherwise, under the laws of the State of Delaware, in any of such domestic limited liability companies and other business entities, shall not revert or be in any way impaired by reason of this chapter; but all rights of creditors and all liens upon any property of any of said domestic limited liability companies and other business entities shall be preserved unimpaired, and all debts, liabilities and duties of each of the said domestic limited liability companies and other business entities that have merged or consolidated shall thenceforth attach to the surviving or resulting domestic limited liability company or other business entity, and may be enforced against it to the same extent as if said debts, liabilities and duties had been incurred or contracted by it. Unless otherwise agreed, a merger or consolidation of a domestic limited liability company, including a domestic limited liability company which is not the surviving or resulting entity in the merger or consolidation, shall not require such domestic limited liability company to wind up its affairs under § 18-803 of this title or pay its liabilities and distribute its assets under § 18-804 of this title.

§ 18-210. Contractual appraisal rights.

A limited liability company agreement or an agreement of merger or consolidation may provide that contractual appraisal rights with respect to a limited liability company interest or another interest in a limited liability company shall be available for any class or group of members or limited liability company interests in connection with any amendment of a limited liability company agreement, any merger or consolidation in which the limited liability company is a constituent party to the merger or consolidation, or the sale of all or substantially all of the limited liability company's assets. The Court of Chancery shall have jurisdiction to hear and determine any matter relating to any such appraisal rights.

§ 18-211. Certificate of correction.

(a) Whenever any certificate authorized to be filed with the office of the Secretary of State under any provision of this chapter has been so filed and is an inaccurate record of the action therein referred to, or was defectively or erroneously executed, such certificate may be corrected by filing with the office of the Secretary of State a certificate of correction of such certificate. The certificate of correction shall specify the inaccuracy or defect to be corrected, shall set forth the portion of the certificate in corrected form, and shall be executed and filed as required by this chapter. The certificate of correction shall be effective as of the date the original certificate was filed, except as to those persons who are substantially and adversely affected by the correction, and as to those persons the certificate of correction shall be effective from the filing date.

(b) In lieu of filing a certificate of correction, a certificate may be corrected by filing with the Secretary of State a corrected certificate which shall be executed and filed as if the corrected certificate were the certificate being corrected, and a fee equal to the fee payable to the Secretary of State if the certificate being corrected were then being filed shall be paid and collected by the Secretary of State for the use of the State of Delaware in connection with the filing of the corrected certificate. The corrected certificate shall be specifically designated as such in its heading, shall specify the inaccuracy or defect to be corrected and shall set forth the entire certificate in corrected form. A certificate corrected in accordance with this section shall be effective as of the date the original certificate was filed, except as to those persons who are substantially and adversely affected by the correction and as to those persons the certificate as corrected shall be effective from the filing date.

§ 18-212. Domestication of non-United States entities.

(a) As used in this section, "non-United States entity" means a foreign limited liability company (other than one formed under the laws of a state) or a corporation, a business trust or association, a real estate investment trust, a common-law trust or any other unincorporated business, including a partnership (whether general (including a limited liability partnership) or limited (including a limited liability limited partnership)) formed, incorporated, created or that otherwise came into being under the laws of any foreign country or other foreign jurisdiction (other than any state).

(b) Any non-United States entity may become domesticated as a limited liability company in the State of Delaware by complying with subsection (g) of this section and filing in the office of the Secretary of State in accordance with § 18-206 of this title:

(1) A certificate of limited liability company domestication that has been executed by 1 or more authorized persons in accordance with § 18-204 of this title; and

(2) A certificate of formation that complies with § 18-201 of this title and has been executed by 1 or more authorized persons in accordance with § 18-204 of this title.

(c) The certificate of limited liability company domestication shall state:

(1) The date on which and jurisdiction where the non-United States entity was first formed, incorporated, created or otherwise came into being;

(2) The name of the non-United States entity immediately prior to the filing of the certificate of limited liability company domestication;

(3) The name of the limited liability company as set forth in the certificate of formation filed in accordance with subsection (b) of this section;

(4) The future effective date or time (which shall be a date or time certain) of the domestication as a limited liability company if it is not to be effective upon the filing of the certificate of limited liability company domestication and the certificate of formation; and

(5) The jurisdiction that constituted the seat, siege social, or principal place of business or central administration of the non-United States entity, or any other equivalent thereto under applicable law, immediately prior to the filing of the certificate of limited liability company domestication.

(d) Upon the filing in the office of the Secretary of State of the certificate of limited liability company domestication and the certificate of formation or upon the future effective date or time of the certificate of limited liability company domestication and the certificate of formation, the non-United States entity shall be domesticated as a limited liability company in the State of Delaware and the limited liability company shall thereafter be subject to all of the provisions of this chapter, except that notwithstanding § 18-201 of this title, the existence of the limited liability company shall be deemed to have commenced on the date the non-United States entity commenced its existence in the jurisdiction in which the non-United States entity was first formed, incorporated, created or otherwise came into being.

(e) The domestication of any non-United States entity as a limited liability company in the State of Delaware shall not be deemed to affect any obligations or liabilities of the non-United States entity incurred prior to its domestication as a limited liability company in the State of Delaware, or the personal liability of any person therefor.

(f) The filing of a certificate of limited liability company domestication shall not affect the choice of law applicable to the non-United States entity, except that from the effective date or time of the domestication, the law of the State of Delaware, including the provisions of this chapter, shall apply to the non-United States entity to the same extent as if the non-United States entity had been formed as a limited liability company on that date.

(g) Prior to filing a certificate of limited liability company domestication with the Office of the Secretary of State, the domestication shall be approved in the manner provided for by the document, instrument, agreement or other writing, as the case may be, governing the internal affairs of the non-United States entity and the conduct of its business or by applicable non-Delaware law, as appropriate, and a limited liability company agreement shall be approved by the same authorization required to approve the domestication.

(h) When any domestication shall have become effective under this section, for all purposes of the laws of the State of Delaware, all of the rights, privileges and powers of the non-United States entity that has been domesticated, and all property, real, personal and mixed, and all debts due to such non-United States entity, as well as all other things and causes of action belonging to such non-United States entity, shall remain vested in the domestic limited liability company to which such non-United States entity has been domesticated and shall be the property of such domestic limited liability company, and the title to any real property vested by deed or otherwise in such non-United States entity shall not revert or be in any way impaired by reason of this chapter; but all rights of creditors and all liens upon any property of such non-United States entity shall be preserved unimpaired, and all debts, liabilities and duties of the non-United States entity that has been domesticated shall remain attached to the domestic limited liability company to which such non-United States entity has been domesticated, and may be enforced against it to the same extent as if said debts, liabilities and duties had originally been incurred or contracted by it in its capacity as a domestic limited liability company. The rights, privileges, powers and interests in property of the non-United States entity, as well as the debts, liabilities and duties of the non-United States entity, shall not be deemed, as a consequence of the domestication, to have been transferred to the domestic limited liability company to which such non-United States entity has domesticated for any purpose of the laws of the State of Delaware.

(i) When a non-United States entity has become domesticated as a limited liability company pursuant to this section, the limited liability company shall, for all purposes of the laws of the State of Delaware, be deemed to be the same entity as the domesticating non-United States entity. Unless otherwise agreed, or as required under applicable non-Delaware law, the domesticating non-United States entity shall not be required to wind up its affairs or pay its liabilities and distribute its assets, and the domestication shall not be deemed to constitute a dissolution of such non-United States entity and shall constitute a continuation of the existence of the domesticating non-United States entity in the form of a domestic limited liability company. If, following domestication, a non-United States entity that has become domesticated as a limited liability company continues its existence in the foreign country or other foreign jurisdiction in which it was existing immediately prior to domestication, the limited liability company and such non-United States entity shall, for all purposes of the laws of the State of Delaware, constitute a single entity formed, incorporated, created or otherwise having come into being, as applicable, and existing under the laws of the State of Delaware and the laws of such foreign country or other foreign jurisdiction.

(j) In connection with a domestication hereunder, rights or securities of, or interests in, the non-United States entity that is to be domesticated as a domestic limited liability company may be exchanged for or converted into cash, property, rights or securities of, or interests in, such domestic limited liability company or, in addition to or in lieu thereof, may be exchanged for or converted into cash, property, rights or securities of, or interests in, another domestic limited liability company or other entity.

§ 18-213. Transfer or continuance of domestic limited liability companies.

(a) Upon compliance with this section, any limited liability company may transfer to or domesticate in any jurisdiction, other than any state, that permits the transfer to or domestication in such jurisdiction of a limited liability company and, in connection therewith, may elect to continue its existence as a limited liability company in the State of Delaware.

(b) Unless otherwise provided in a limited liability company agreement, a transfer or domestication or continuance described in subsection (a) of this section shall be approved in writing by all of the managers and all of the members. If all of the managers and all of the members of the limited liability company or such other vote as may be stated in a limited liability company agreement shall approve the transfer or domestication described in subsection (a) of this section, a certificate of transfer if the limited liability company's existence as a limited liability company of the State of Delaware is to cease, or a certificate of transfer and continuance if the limited liability company's existence as a limited liability company in the State of Delaware is to continue, executed in accordance with § 18-204 of this title, shall be filed in the office of the Secretary of State in accordance with § 18-206 of this title. The certificate of transfer or the certificate of transfer and continuance shall state:

(1) The name of the limited liability company and, if it has been changed, the name under which its certificate of formation was originally filed;

(2) The date of the filing of its original certificate of formation with the Secretary of State;

(3) The jurisdiction to which the limited liability company shall be transferred or in which it shall be domesticated;

(4) The future effective date or time (which shall be a date or time certain) of the transfer or domestication to the jurisdiction specified in subsection (b)(3) of this section if it is not to be effective upon the filing of the certificate of transfer or the certificate of transfer and continuance;

(5) That the transfer or domestication or continuance of the limited liability company has been approved in accordance with this section;

(6) In the case of a certificate of transfer, (i) that the existence of the limited liability company as a limited liability company of the State of Delaware shall cease when the certificate of transfer becomes effective, and (ii) the agreement of the limited liability company that it may be served with process in the State of Delaware in any action, suit or proceeding for enforcement of any obligation of the limited liability company arising while it was a limited liability company of the State of Delaware, and that it irrevocably appoints the Secretary of State as its agent to accept service of process in any such action, suit or proceeding;

(7) The address to which a copy of the process referred to in subsection (b)(6) of this section shall be mailed to it by the Secretary of State. In the event of service hereunder upon the Secretary of State, the procedures set forth in § 18-911(c) of this title shall be applicable, except that the plaintiff in any such action, suit or proceeding shall furnish the Secretary of State with the address specified in this subsection and any other address that the plaintiff may elect to furnish, together with copies of such process as required by the Secretary of State, and the Secretary of State shall notify the limited liability company that has transferred or domesticated out of the State of Delaware at all such addresses furnished by the plaintiff in accordance with the procedures set forth in § 18-911(c) of this title; and

(8) In the case of a certificate of transfer and continuance, that the limited liability company will continue to exist as a limited liability company of the State of Delaware after the certificate of transfer and continuance becomes effective.

(c) Upon the filing in the office of the Secretary of State of the certificate of transfer or upon the future effective date or time of the certificate of transfer and payment to the Secretary of State of all fees prescribed in this chapter, the Secretary of State shall certify that the limited liability company has filed all documents and paid all fees required by this chapter, and thereupon the limited liability company shall cease to exist as a limited liability company of the State of Delaware. Such certificate of the Secretary of State shall be prima facie evidence of the transfer or domestication by such limited liability company out of the State of Delaware.

(d) The transfer or domestication of a limited liability company out of the State of Delaware in accordance with this section and the resulting cessation of its existence as a limited liability company of the State of Delaware pursuant to a certificate of transfer shall not be deemed to affect any obligations or liabilities of the limited liability company incurred prior to such transfer or domestication or the personal liability of any person incurred prior to such transfer or domestication, nor shall it be deemed to affect the choice of law applicable to the limited liability company with respect to matters arising prior to such transfer or domestication. Unless otherwise agreed, the transfer or domestication of a limited liability company out of the State of Delaware in accordance with this section shall not require such limited liability company to wind up its affairs under § 18-803 of this title or pay its liabilities and distribute its assets under § 18-804 of this title.

(e) If a limited liability company files a certificate of transfer and continuance, after the time the certificate of transfer and continuance becomes effective, the limited liability company shall continue to exist as a limited liability company of the State of Delaware, and the laws of the State of Delaware, including this chapter, shall apply to the limited liability company to the same extent as prior to such time. So long as a limited liability company continues to exist as a limited liability company of the State of Delaware following the filing of a certificate of transfer and continuance, the continuing domestic limited liability company and the entity formed, incorporated, created or that otherwise came into being as a consequence of the transfer of the limited liability company to, or its domestication in, a foreign country or other foreign jurisdiction shall, for all purposes of the laws of the State of Delaware, constitute a single entity formed, incorporated, created or otherwise having come into being, as applicable, and existing under the laws of the State and the laws of such foreign country or other foreign jurisdiction.

(f) In connection with a transfer or domestication of a domestic limited liability company to or in another jurisdiction pursuant to subsection (a) of this section, rights or securities of, or interests in, such limited liability company may be exchanged for or converted into cash, property, rights or securities of, or interests in, the business form in which the limited liability company will exist in such other jurisdiction as a consequence of the transfer or domestication or, in addition to or in lieu thereof, may be exchanged for or converted into cash, property, rights or securities of, or interests in, another business form.

§ 18-214. Conversion of certain entities to a limited liability company.

(a) As used in this section, the term "other entity" means a corporation, business trust or association, a real estate investment trust, a common-law trust or any other unincorporated business, including a partnership (whether general (including a limited liability partnership) or limited (including a limited liability limited partnership)) or a foreign limited liability company.

(b) Any other entity may convert to a domestic limited liability company by complying with subsection (h) of this section and filing in the office of the Secretary of State in accordance with § 18-206 of this title:

(1) A certificate of conversion to limited liability company that has been executed by 1 or more authorized persons in accordance with § 18-204 of this title; and

(2) A certificate of formation that complies with § 18-201 of this title and has been executed by 1 or more authorized persons in accordance with § 18-204 of this title.

(c) The certificate of conversion to limited liability company shall state:

(1) The date on which and jurisdiction where the other entity was first created, incorporated, formed or otherwise came into being and, if it has changed, its jurisdiction immediately prior to its conversion to a domestic limited liability company;

(2) The name of the other entity immediately prior to the filing of the certificate of conversion to limited liability company;

(3) The name of the limited liability company as set forth in its certificate of formation filed in accordance with subsection (b) of this section; and

(4) The future effective date or time (which shall be a date or time certain) of the conversion to a limited liability company if it is not to be effective upon the filing of the certificate of conversion to limited liability company and the certificate of formation.

(d) Upon the filing in the office of the Secretary of State of the certificate of conversion to limited liability company and the certificate of formation or upon the future effective date or time of the certificate of conversion to limited liability company and the certificate of formation, the other entity shall be converted into a domestic limited liability company and the limited liability company shall thereafter be subject to all of the provisions of this chapter, except that notwithstanding § 18-201 of this title, the existence of the limited liability company shall be deemed to have commenced on the date the other entity commenced its existence in the jurisdiction in which the other entity was first created, formed, incorporated or otherwise came into being.

(e) The conversion of any other entity into a domestic limited liability company shall not be deemed to affect any obligations or liabilities of the other entity incurred prior to its conversion to a domestic limited liability company or the personal liability of any person incurred prior to such conversion.

(f) When any conversion shall have become effective under this section, for all purposes of the laws of the State of Delaware, all of the rights, privileges and powers of the other entity that has converted, and all property, real, personal and mixed, and all debts due to such other entity, as well as all other things and causes of action belonging to such other entity, shall remain vested in the domestic limited liability company to which such other entity has converted and shall be the property of such domestic limited liability company, and the title to any real property vested by deed or otherwise in such other entity shall not revert or be in any way impaired by reason of this chapter; but all rights of creditors and all liens upon any property of such other entity shall be preserved unimpaired, and all debts, liabilities and duties of the other entity that has converted shall remain attached to the domestic limited liability company to which such other entity has converted, and may be enforced against it to the same extent as if said debts, liabilities and duties had originally been incurred or contracted by it in its capacity as a domestic limited liability company. The rights, privileges, powers and interests in property of the other entity, as well as the debts, liabilities and duties of the other entity, shall not be deemed, as a consequence of the conversion, to have been transferred to the domestic limited liability company to which such other entity has converted for any purpose of the laws of the State of Delaware.

(g) Unless otherwise agreed, or as required under applicable non-Delaware law, the converting other entity shall not be required to wind up its affairs or pay its liabilities and distribute its assets, and the conversion shall not be deemed to constitute a dissolution of such other entity and shall constitute a continuation of the existence of the converting other entity in the form of a domestic limited liability company. When an other entity has been converted to a limited liability company pursuant to this section, the limited liability company shall, for all purposes of the laws of the State of Delaware, be deemed to be the same entity as the converting other entity.

(h) Prior to filing a certificate of conversion to limited liability company with the office of the Secretary of State, the conversion shall be approved in the manner provided for by the document, instrument, agreement or other writing, as the case may be, governing the internal affairs of the other entity and the conduct of its business or by applicable law, as appropriate and a limited liability company agreement shall be approved by the same authorization required to approve the conversion.

(i) In connection with a conversion hereunder, rights or securities of or interests in the other entity which is to be converted to a domestic limited liability company may be exchanged for or converted into cash, property, or rights or securities of or interests in such domestic limited liability company or, in addition to or in lieu thereof, may be exchanged for or converted into cash, property, or rights or securities of or interests in another domestic limited liability company or other entity.

(j) The provisions of this section shall not be construed to limit the accomplishment of a change in the law governing, or the domicile of, an other entity to the State of Delaware by any other means provided for in a limited liability company agreement or other agreement or as otherwise permitted by law, including by the amendment of a limited liability company agreement or other agreement.

§ 18-215. Series of members, managers or limited liability company interests.

(a) A limited liability company agreement may establish or provide for the establishment of designated series of members, managers or limited liability company interests having separate rights, powers or duties with respect to specified property or obligations of the limited liability company or profits and losses associated with specified property or obligations, and, to the extent provided in the limited liability company agreement, any such series may have a separate business purpose or investment objective.

(b) Notwithstanding anything to the contrary set forth in this chapter or under other applicable law, in the event that a limited liability company agreement creates 1 or more series, and if separate and distinct records are maintained for any such series and the assets associated with any such series are held (directly or indirectly, including through a nominee or otherwise) and accounted for separately from the other assets of the limited liability company, or any other series thereof, and if the limited liability company agreement so provides, and notice of the limitation on liabilities of a series as referenced in this subsection is set forth in the certificate of formation of the limited liability company, then the debts, liabilities and obligations incurred, contracted for or otherwise existing with respect to a particular series shall be enforceable against the assets of such series only, and not against the assets of the limited liability company generally or any other series thereof, and, unless otherwise provided in the limited liability company agreement, none of the debts, liabilities, obligations and expenses incurred, contracted for or otherwise existing with respect to the limited liability company generally or any other series thereof shall be enforceable against the assets of such series. The fact that a certificate of formation that contains the foregoing notice of the limitation on liabilities of a series is on file in the office of the Secretary of State shall constitute notice of such limitation on liabilities of a series.

(c) Notwithstanding § 18-303(a) of this title, under a limited liability company agreement or under another agreement, a member or manager may agree to be obligated personally for any or all of the debts, obligations and liabilities of one or more series.

(d) A limited liability company agreement may provide for classes or groups of members or managers associated with a series having such relative rights, powers and duties as the limited liability company agreement may provide, and may make provision for the future creation in the manner provided in the limited liability company agreement of additional classes or groups of members or managers associated with the series having such relative rights, powers and duties as may from time to time be established, including rights, powers and duties senior to existing classes and groups of members or managers associated with the series. A limited liability company agreement may provide for the taking of an action, including the amendment of the limited liability company agreement, without the vote or approval of any member or manager or class or group of members or managers, including an action to create under the provisions of the limited liability company agreement a class or group of the series of limited liability company interests that was not previously outstanding. A limited liability company agreement may provide that any member or class or group of members associated with a series shall have no voting rights.

(e) A limited liability company agreement may grant to all or certain identified members or managers or a specified class or group of the members or managers associated with a series the right to vote separately or with all or any class or group of the members or managers associated with the series, on any matter. Voting by members or managers associated with a series may be on a per capita, number, financial interest, class, group or any other basis.

(f) Unless otherwise provided in a limited liability company agreement, the management of a series shall be vested in the members associated with such series in proportion to the then current percentage or other interest of members in the profits of the series owned by all of the members associated with such series, the decision of members owning more than 50 percent of the said percentage or other interest in the profits controlling; provided, however, that if a limited liability company agreement provides for the management of the series, in whole or in part, by a manager, the management of the series, to the extent so provided, shall be vested in the manager who shall be chosen in the manner provided in the limited liability company agreement. The manager of the series shall also hold the offices and have the responsibilities accorded to the manager as set forth in a limited liability company agreement. A series may have more than 1 manager. Subject to § 18-602 of this title, a manager shall cease to be a manager with respect to a series as provided in a limited liability company agreement. Except as otherwise provided in a limited liability company agreement, any event under this chapter or in a limited liability company agreement that causes a manager to cease to be a manager with respect to a series shall not, in itself, cause such manager to cease to be a manager of the limited liability company or with respect to any other series thereof.

(g) Notwithstanding § 18-606 of this title, but subject to subsections (h) and (k) of this section, and unless otherwise provided in a limited liability company agreement, at the time a member associated with a series that has been established in accordance with subsection (b) of this section becomes entitled to receive a distribution with respect to such series, the member has the status of, and is entitled to all remedies available to, a creditor of the series, with respect to the distribution. A limited liability company agreement may provide for the establishment of a record date with respect to allocations and distributions with respect to a series.

(h) Notwithstanding § 18-607(a) of this title, a limited liability company may make a distribution with respect to a series that has been established in accordance with subsection (b) of this section. A limited liability company shall not make a distribution with respect to a series that has been established in accordance with subsection (b) of this section to a member to the extent that at the time of the distribution, after giving effect to the distribution, all liabilities of such series, other than liabilities to members on account of their limited liability company interests with respect to such series and liabilities for which the recourse of creditors is limited to specified property of such series, exceed the fair value of the assets associated with such series, except that the fair value of property of the series that is subject to a liability for which the recourse of creditors is limited shall be included in the assets associated with such series only to the extent that the fair value of that property exceeds that liability. For purposes of the immediately preceding sentence, the term "distribution" shall not include amounts constituting reasonable compensation for present or past services or reasonable payments made in the ordinary course of business pursuant to a bona fide retirement plan or other benefits program. A member who receives a distribution in violation of this subsection, and who knew at the time of the distribution that the distribution violated this subsection, shall be liable to a series for the amount of the distribution. A member who receives a distribution in violation of this subsection, and who did not know at the time of the distribution that the distribution violated this subsection, shall not be liable for the amount of the distribution. Subject to § 18-607(c) of this title, which shall apply to any distribution made with respect to a series under this subsection, this subsection shall not affect any obligation or liability of a member under an agreement or other applicable law for the amount of a distribution.

(i) Unless otherwise provided in the limited liability company agreement, a member shall cease to be associated with a series and to have the power to exercise any rights or powers of a member with respect to such series upon the assignment of all of the member's limited liability company interest with respect to such series. Except as otherwise provided in a limited liability company agreement, any event under this chapter or a limited liability company agreement that causes a member to cease to be associated with a series shall not, in itself, cause such member to cease to be associated with any other series or terminate the continued membership of a member in the limited liability company or cause the termination of the series, regardless of whether such member was the last remaining member associated with such series.

(j) Subject to § 18-801 of this title, except to the extent otherwise provided in the limited liability company agreement, a series may be terminated and its affairs wound up without causing the dissolution of the limited liability company. The termination of a series established in accordance with subsection (b) of this section shall not affect the limitation on liabilities of such series provided by subsection (b) of this section. A series is terminated and its affairs shall be wound up upon the dissolution of the limited liability company under § 18-801 of this title or otherwise upon the first to occur of the following:

(1) At the time specified in the limited liability company agreement;

(2) Upon the happening of events specified in the limited liability company agreement;

(3) Unless otherwise provided in the limited liability company agreement, upon the affirmative vote or written consent of the members of the limited liability company associated with such series or, if there is more than 1 class or group of members associated with such series, then by each class or group of members associated with such series, in either case, by members associated with such series who own more than two-thirds of the then-current percentage or other interest in the profits of the series of the limited liability company owned by all of the members associated with such series or by the members in each class or group of such series, as appropriate; or

(4) The termination of such series under subsection (l) of this section.

(k) Notwithstanding § 18-803(a) of this title, unless otherwise provided in the limited liability company agreement, a manager associated with a series who has not wrongfully terminated the series or, if none, the members associated with the series or a person approved by the members associated with the series or, if there is more than 1 class or group of members associated with the series, then by each class or group of members associated with the series, in either case, by members who own more than 50 percent of the then current percentage or other interest in the profits of the series owned by all of the members associated with the series or by the members in each class or group associated with the series, as appropriate, may wind up the affairs of the series; but, if the series has been established in accordance with subsection (b) of this section, the Court of Chancery, upon cause shown, may wind up the affairs of the series upon application of any member associated with the series, the member's personal representative or assignee, and in connection therewith, may appoint a liquidating trustee. The persons winding up the affairs of a series may, in the name of the limited liability company and for and on behalf of the limited liability company and such series, take all actions with respect to the series as are permitted under § 18-803(b) of this title. The persons winding up the affairs of a series shall provide for the claims and obligations of the series and distribute the assets of the series as provided in § 18-804 of this title, which section shall apply to the winding up and distribution of assets of a series. Actions taken in accordance with this subsection shall not affect the liability of members and shall not impose liability on a liquidating trustee.

(l) On application by or for a member or manager associated with a series established in accordance with subsection (b) of this section, the Court of Chancery may decree termination of such series whenever it is not reasonably practicable to carry on the business of the series in conformity with a limited liability company agreement.

(m) If a foreign limited liability company that is registering to do business in the State of Delaware in accordance with § 18-902 of this title is governed by a limited liability company agreement that establishes or provides for the establishment of designated series of members, managers or limited liability company interests having separate rights, powers or duties with respect to specified property or obligations of the foreign limited liability company or profits and losses associated with specified property or obligations, that fact shall be so stated on the application for registration as a foreign limited liability company. In addition, the foreign limited liability company shall state on such application whether the debts, liabilities and obligations incurred, contracted for or otherwise existing with respect to a particular series, if any, shall be enforceable against the assets of such series only, and not against the assets of the foreign limited liability company generally or any other series thereof, and, unless otherwise provided in the limited liability company agreement, none of the debts, liabilities, obligations and expenses incurred, contracted for or otherwise existing with respect to the foreign limited liability company generally or any other series thereof shall be enforceable against the assets of such series.

§ 18-216. Approval of conversion of a limited liability company.

A domestic limited liability company may convert to a corporation, business trust or association, a real estate investment trust, a common-law trust, a general partnership (including a limited liability partnership) or a limited partnership (including a limited liability limited partnership), organized, formed or created under the laws of the State of Delaware, upon the authorization of such conversion in accordance with this section. If the limited liability company agreement specifies the manner of authorizing a conversion of the limited liability company, the conversion shall be authorized as specified in the limited liability company agreement. If the limited liability company agreement does not specify the manner of authorizing a conversion of the limited liability company and does not prohibit a conversion of the limited liability company, the conversion shall be authorized in the same manner as is specified in the limited liability company agreement for authorizing a merger or consolidation that involves the limited liability company as a constituent party to the merger or consolidation. If the limited liability company agreement does not specify the manner of authorizing a conversion of the limited liability company or a merger or consolidation that involves the limited liability company as a constituent party and does not prohibit a conversion of the limited liability company, the conversion shall be authorized by the approval by the members or, if there is more than 1 class or group of members, then by each class or group of members, in either case, by members who own more than 50 percent of the then current percentage or other interest in the profits of the domestic limited liability company owned by all of the members or by the members in each class or group, as appropriate. Unless otherwise agreed, the conversion of a domestic limited liability company to another business form pursuant to this section shall not require such limited liability company to wind up its affairs under § 18-803 of this title or pay its liabilities and distribute its assets under § 18-804 of this title. In connection with a conversion of a domestic limited liability company to another business form pursuant to this section, rights or securities of or interests in the domestic limited liability company which is to be converted may be exchanged for or converted into cash, property, rights or securities of or interests in the business form into which the domestic limited liability company is being converted or, in addition to or in lieu thereof, may be exchanged for or converted into cash, property, rights or securities of or interests in another business form.

Subchapter III. Members.

§ 18-301. Admission of members.

(a) In connection with the formation of a limited liability company, a person is admitted as a member of the limited liability company upon the later to occur of:

(1) The formation of the limited liability company; or

(2) The time provided in and upon compliance with the limited liability company agreement or, if the limited liability company agreement does not so provide, when the person's admission is reflected in the records of the limited liability company.

(b) After the formation of a limited liability company, a person is admitted as a member of the limited liability company:

(1) In the case of a person who is not an assignee of a limited liability company interest, including a person acquiring a limited liability company interest directly from the limited liability company and a person to be admitted as a member of the limited liability company without acquiring a limited liability company interest in the limited liability company at the time provided in and upon compliance with the limited liability company agreement or, if the limited liability company agreement does not so

provide, upon the consent of all members and when the person's admission is reflected in the records of the limited liability company;

(2) In the case of an assignee of a limited liability company interest, as provided in § 18-704(a) of this title and at the time provided in and upon compliance with the limited liability company agreement or, if the limited liability company agreement does not so provide, when any such person's permitted admission is reflected in the records of the limited liability company; or

(3) Unless otherwise provided in an agreement of merger or consolidation, in the case of a person acquiring a limited liability company interest in a surviving or resulting limited liability company pursuant to a merger or consolidation approved in accordance with § 18-209(b) of this title, at the time provided in and upon compliance with the limited liability company agreement of the surviving or resulting limited liability company.

(c) In connection with the domestication of a non-United States entity (as defined in § 18-212 of this title) as a limited liability company in the State of Delaware in accordance with § 18-212 of this title or the conversion of an other entity (as defined in § 18-214 of this title) to a domestic limited liability company in accordance with § 18-214 of this title, a person is admitted as a member of the limited liability company at the time provided in and upon compliance with the limited liability company agreement.

(d) A person may be admitted to a limited liability company as a member of the limited liability company and may receive a limited liability company interest in the limited liability company without making a contribution or being obligated to make a contribution to the limited liability company. Unless otherwise provided in a limited liability company agreement, a person may be admitted to a limited liability company as a member of the limited liability company without acquiring a limited liability company interest in the limited liability company. Unless otherwise provided in a limited liability company agreement, a person may be admitted as the sole member of a limited liability company without making a contribution or being obligated to make a contribution to the limited liability company or without acquiring a limited liability company interest in the limited liability company.

§ 18-302. Classes and voting.

(a) A limited liability company agreement may provide for classes or groups of members having such relative rights, powers and duties as the limited liability company agreement may provide, and may make provision for the future creation in the manner provided in the limited liability company agreement of additional classes or groups of members having such relative rights, powers and duties as may from time to time be established, including rights, powers and duties senior to existing classes and groups of members. A limited liability company agreement may provide for the taking of an action, including the amendment of the limited liability company agreement, without the vote or approval of any member or class or group of members, including an action to create under the provisions of the limited liability company agreement a class or group of limited liability company interests that was not previously outstanding. A limited liability company agreement may provide that any member or class or group of members shall have no voting rights.

(b) A limited liability company agreement may grant to all or certain identified members or a specified class or group of the members the right to vote separately or with all or any class or group of the members or managers, on any matter. Voting by members may be on a per capita, number, financial interest, class, group or any other basis.

(c) A limited liability company agreement may set forth provisions relating to notice of the time, place or purpose of any meeting at which any matter is to be voted on by any members, waiver of any such notice, action by consent without a meeting, the establishment of a record date, quorum requirements, voting in person or by proxy, or any other matter with respect to the exercise of any such right to vote.

(d) Unless otherwise provided in a limited liability company agreement, on any matter that is to be voted on, consented to or approved by members, the members may take such action without a meeting, without prior notice and without a vote if a consent or consents in writing, setting forth the action so taken, shall be signed by the members having not less than the minimum number of votes that would be necessary to authorize or take such action at a meeting at which all members entitled to vote thereon were present and voted. Unless otherwise provided in a limited liability company agreement, on any matter that is to be voted on by members, the members may vote in person or by proxy, and such proxy may be granted in writing, by means of electronic transmission or as otherwise permitted by applicable law. Unless otherwise provided in a limited liability company agreement, a consent transmitted by electronic transmission by a member or by a person or persons authorized to act for a member shall be deemed to be written and signed for purposes of this subsection. For purposes of this subsection, the term "electronic transmission" means any form of communication not directly involving the physical transmission of paper that creates a record that may be retained, retrieved and reviewed by a recipient thereof and that may be directly reproduced in paper form by such a recipient through an automated process.

§ 18-303. Liability to 3rd parties.

(a) Except as otherwise provided by this chapter, the debts, obligations and liabilities of a limited liability company, whether arising in contract, tort or otherwise, shall be solely the debts, obligations and liabilities of the limited liability company, and no member or manager of a limited liability company shall be obligated personally for any such debt, obligation or liability of the limited liability company solely by reason of being a member or acting as a manager of the limited liability company.

(b) Notwithstanding the provisions of subsection (a) of this section, under a limited liability company agreement or under another agreement, a member or manager may agree to be obligated personally for any or all of the debts, obligations and liabilities of the limited liability company.

§ 18-304. Events of bankruptcy.

A person ceases to be a member of a limited liability company upon the happening of any of the following events:

(1) Unless otherwise provided in a limited liability company agreement, or with the written consent of all members, a member: a. Makes an assignment for the benefit of creditors; b. Files a voluntary petition in bankruptcy; c. Is adjudged a bankrupt or insolvent, or has entered against the member an order for relief, in any bankruptcy or insolvency proceeding; d. Files a petition or answer seeking for the member any reorganization, arrangement, composition, readjustment, liquidation, dissolution or similar relief under any statute, law or regulation; e. Files an answer or other pleading admitting or failing to contest the material allegations of a petition filed against the member in any proceeding of this nature; f. Seeks, consents to or acquiesces in the appointment of a trustee, receiver or liquidator of the member or of all or any substantial part of the member's properties; or

(2) Unless otherwise provided in a limited liability company agreement, or with the written consent of all members, 120 days after the commencement of any proceeding against the member seeking reorganization, arrangement, composition, readjustment, liquidation, dissolution or similar relief under any statute, law or regulation, if the proceeding has not been dismissed, or if within 90 days after the appointment without the member's consent or acquiescence of a trustee, receiver or liquidator of the member or of all or any substantial part of the member's properties, the appointment is not vacated or stayed, or within 90 days after the expiration of any such stay, the appointment is not vacated.

§ 18-305. Access to and confidentiality of information; records.

(a) Each member of a limited liability company has the right, subject to such reasonable standards (including standards governing what information and documents are to be furnished at what time and location and at whose expense) as may be set forth in a limited liability company agreement or otherwise established by the manager or, if there is no manager, then by the members, to obtain from the limited liability company from time to time upon reasonable demand for any purpose reasonably related to the member's interest as a member of the limited liability company:

(1) True and full information regarding the status of the business and financial condition of the limited liability company;

(2) Promptly after becoming available, a copy of the limited liability company's federal, state and local income tax returns for each year;

(3) A current list of the name and last known business, residence or mailing address of each member and manager;

(4) A copy of any written limited liability company agreement and certificate of formation and all amendments thereto, together with executed copies of any written powers of attorney pursuant to which the limited liability company agreement and any certificate and all amendments thereto have been executed;

(5) True and full information regarding the amount of cash and a description and statement of the agreed value of any other property or services contributed by each member and which each member has agreed to contribute in the future, and the date on which each became a member; and

(6) Other information regarding the affairs of the limited liability company as is just and reasonable.

(b) Each manager shall have the right to examine all of the information described in subsection (a) of this section for a purpose reasonably related to the position of manager.

(c) The manager of a limited liability company shall have the right to keep confidential from the members, for such period of time as the manager deems reasonable, any information which the manager reasonably believes to be in the nature of trade secrets or other information the disclosure of which the manager in good faith believes is not in the best interest of the limited liability company or could damage the limited liability company or its business or which the limited liability company is required by law or by agreement with a 3rd party to keep confidential.

(d) A limited liability company may maintain its records in other than a written form if such form is capable of conversion into written form within a reasonable time.

(e) Any demand by a member under this section shall be in writing and shall state the purpose of such demand.

(f) Any action to enforce any right arising under this section shall be brought in the Court of Chancery. If the limited liability company refuses to permit a member to obtain or a manager to examine the information described in subsection (a)(3) of this section or does not reply to the demand that has been made within 5 business days after the demand has been made, the demanding member or manager may apply to the Court of Chancery for an order to compel such disclosure. The Court of Chancery is hereby vested with exclusive jurisdiction to determine whether or not the person seeking such information is entitled to the information sought. The Court of Chancery may summarily order the limited liability company to permit the demanding member to obtain or manager to examine the information described in subsection (a)(3) of this section and to make copies or abstracts therefrom, or the Court of Chancery may summarily order the limited liability company to furnish to the demanding member or manager the information described in subsection (a)(3) of this section on the condition that the demanding member or manager first pay to the limited liability company the reasonable cost of obtaining and furnishing such information and on such other conditions as the Court of Chancery deems appropriate. When a demanding member seeks to obtain or a manager seeks to examine the information described in subsection (a)(3) of this section, the demanding member or manager shall first establish

(1) that the demanding member or manager has complied with the provisions of this section respecting the form and manner of making demand for obtaining or examining of such information, and

(2) that the information the demanding member or manager seeks is reasonably related to the member's interest as a member or the manager's position as a manager, as the case may be. The Court of Chancery may, in its discretion, prescribe any limitations or conditions with reference to the obtaining or examining of information, or award such other or further relief as the Court of Chancery may deem just and proper. The Court of Chancery may order books, documents and records, pertinent extracts therefrom, or duly authenticated copies thereof, to be brought within the State of Delaware and kept in the State of Delaware upon such terms and conditions as the order may prescribe.

(g) The rights of a member or manager to obtain information as provided in this section may be restricted in an original limited liability company agreement or in any subsequent amendment approved or adopted by all of the members and in compliance with any applicable requirements of the limited liability company agreement. The provisions of this subsection shall not be construed to limit the ability to impose restrictions on the rights of a member or manager to obtain information by any other means permitted under this section.

§ 18-306. Remedies for breach of limited liability company agreement by member.

A limited liability company agreement may provide that:

(1) A member who fails to perform in accordance with, or to comply with the terms and conditions of, the limited liability company agreement shall be subject to specified penalties or specified consequences; and

(2) At the time or upon the happening of events specified in the limited liability company agreement, a member shall be subject to specified penalties or specified consequences. Such specified penalties or specified consequences may include and take the form of any penalty or consequence set forth in § 18-502(c) of this title.

Subchapter IV. Managers.

§ 18-401. Admission of managers.

A person may be named or designated as a manager of the limited liability company as provided in § 18-101(10) of this title.

§ 18-402. Management of limited liability company.

Unless otherwise provided in a limited liability company agreement, the management of a limited liability company shall be vested in its members in proportion to the then current percentage or other interest of members in the profits of the limited liability company owned by all of the members, the decision of members owning more than 50 percent of the said percentage or other interest in the profits controlling; provided however, that if a limited liability company agreement provides for the management, in whole or in part, of a limited liability company by a manager, the management of the limited liability company, to the extent so provided, shall be vested in the manager who shall be chosen in the manner provided in the limited liability company agreement. The manager shall also hold the offices and have the responsibilities accorded to the manager by or in the manner provided in a limited liability company agreement. Subject to § 18-602 of this title, a manager shall cease to be a manager as provided in a limited liability company agreement. A limited liability company may have more than 1 manager. Unless otherwise provided in a limited liability company agreement, each member and manager has the authority to bind the limited liability company.

§ 18-403. Contributions by a manager.

A manager of a limited liability company may make contributions to the limited liability company and share in the profits and losses of, and in distributions from, the limited liability company as a member. A person who is both a manager and a member has the rights and powers, and is subject to the restrictions and liabilities, of a manager and, except as provided in a limited liability company agreement, also has the rights and powers, and is subject to the restrictions and liabilities, of a member to the extent of the manager's participation in the limited liability company as a member.

§ 18-404. Classes and voting.

(a) A limited liability company agreement may provide for classes or groups of managers having such relative rights, powers and duties as the limited liability company agreement may provide, and may make provision for the future creation in the manner provided in the limited liability company agreement of additional classes or groups of managers having such relative rights, powers and duties as may from time to time be established, including rights, powers and duties senior to existing classes and groups of managers.

A limited liability company agreement may provide for the taking of an action, including the amendment of the limited liability company agreement, without the vote or approval of any manager or class or group of managers, including an action to create under the provisions of the limited liability company agreement a class or group of limited liability company interests that was not previously outstanding.

(b) A limited liability company agreement may grant to all or certain identified managers or a specified class or group of the managers the right to vote, separately or with all or any class or group of managers or members, on any matter. Voting by managers may be on a per capita, number, financial interest, class, group or any other basis.

(c) A limited liability company agreement may set forth provisions relating to notice of the time, place or purpose of any meeting at which any matter is to be voted on by any manager or class or group of managers, waiver of any such notice, action by consent without a meeting, the establishment of a record date, quorum requirements, voting in person or by proxy, or any other matter with respect to the exercise of any such right to vote.

(d) Unless otherwise provided in a limited liability company agreement, on any matter that is to be voted on, consented to or approved by managers, the managers may take such action without a meeting, without prior notice and without a vote if a consent or consents in writing, setting forth the action so taken, shall be signed by the managers having not less than the minimum number of votes that would be necessary to authorize or take such action at a meeting at which all managers entitled to vote thereon were present and voted. Unless otherwise provided in a limited liability company agreement, on any matter that is to be voted on by managers, the managers may vote in person or by proxy, and such proxy may be granted in writing, by means of electronic transmission or as otherwise permitted by applicable law. Unless otherwise provided in a limited liability company agreement, a consent transmitted by electronic transmission by a manager or by a person or persons authorized to act for a manager shall be deemed to be written and signed for purposes of this subsection. For purposes of this subsection, the term "electronic transmission" means any form of communication not directly involving the physical transmission of paper that creates a record that may be retained, retrieved and reviewed by a recipient thereof and that may be directly reproduced in paper form by such a recipient through an automated process.

§ 18-405. Remedies for breach of limited liability company agreement by manager.

A limited liability company agreement may provide that:

(1) A manager who fails to perform in accordance with, or to comply with the terms and conditions of, the limited liability company agreement shall be subject to specified penalties or specified consequences; and

(2) At the time or upon the happening of events specified in the limited liability company agreement, a manager shall be subject to specified penalties or specified consequences.

§ 18-406. Reliance on reports and information by member or manager.

A member or manager of a limited liability company shall be fully protected in relying in good faith upon the records of the limited liability company and upon such information, opinions, reports or statements presented to the limited liability company by any of its other managers, members, officers, employees or committees of the limited liability company, or by any other person, as to matters the member or manager reasonably believes are within such other person's professional or expert competence and who has been selected with reasonable care by or on behalf of the limited liability company, including information, opinions, reports or statements as to the value and amount of the assets, liabilities, profits or losses of the limited liability company or any other facts pertinent to the existence and amount of assets from which distributions to members might properly be paid.

§ 18-407. Delegation of rights and powers to manage.

Unless otherwise provided in the limited liability company agreement, a member or manager of a limited liability company has the power and authority to delegate to 1 or more other persons the member's or manager's, as the case may be, rights and powers to manage and control the business and affairs of the limited liability company, including to delegate to agents, officers and employees of a member or manager or the limited liability company, and to delegate by a management agreement or another agreement with, or otherwise to, other persons. Unless otherwise provided in the limited liability company agreement, such delegation by a member or manager of a limited liability company shall not cause the member or manager to cease to be a member or manager, as the case may be, of the limited liability company.

Subchapter V. Finance.

§ 18-501. Form of contribution.

The contribution of a member to a limited liability company may be in cash, property or services rendered, or a promissory note or other obligation to contribute cash or property or to perform services.

§ 18-502. Liability for contribution.

(a) Except as provided in a limited liability company agreement, a member is obligated to a limited liability company to perform any promise to contribute cash or property or to perform services, even if the member is unable to perform because of death, disability or any other reason. If a member does not make the required contribution of property or services, the member is obligated at the option of the limited liability company to contribute cash equal to that portion of the agreed value (as stated in the records of the limited liability company) of the contribution that has not been made. The foregoing option shall be in addition to, and not in lieu of, any other rights, including the right to specific performance, that the limited liability company may have against such member under the limited liability company agreement or applicable law.

(b) Unless otherwise provided in a limited liability company agreement, the obligation of a member to make a contribution or return money or other property paid or distributed in violation of this chapter may be compromised only by consent of all the members. Notwithstanding the compromise, a creditor of a limited liability company who extends credit, after the entering into of a limited liability company agreement or an amendment thereto which, in either case, reflects the obligation, and before the amendment thereof to reflect the compromise, may enforce the original obligation to the extent that, in extending credit, the creditor reasonably relied on the obligation of a member to make a contribution or return. A conditional obligation of a member to make a contribution or return money or other property to a limited liability company may not be enforced unless the conditions of the obligation have been satisfied or waived as to or by such member. Conditional obligations include contributions payable upon a discretionary call of a limited liability company prior to the time the call occurs.

(c) A limited liability company agreement may provide that the interest of any member who fails to make any contribution that the member is obligated to make shall be subject to specified penalties for, or specified consequences of, such failure. Such penalty or consequence may take the form of reducing or eliminating the defaulting member's proportionate interest in a limited liability company, subordinating the member's limited liability company interest to that of nondefaulting members, a forced sale of that limited liability company interest, forfeiture of his or her limited liability company interest, the lending by other members of the amount necessary to meet the defaulting member's commitment, a fixing of the value of his or her limited liability company interest by appraisal or by formula and redemption or sale of the limited liability company interest at such value, or other penalty or consequence.

§ 18-503. Allocation of profits and losses.

The profits and losses of a limited liability company shall be allocated among the members, and among classes or groups of members, in the manner provided in a limited liability company agreement. If the limited liability company agreement does not so provide, profits and losses shall be allocated on the basis of the agreed value (as stated in the records of the limited liability company) of the contributions made by each member to the extent they have been received by the limited liability company and have not been returned.

§ 18-504. Allocation of distributions.

Distributions of cash or other assets of a limited liability company shall be allocated among the members, and among classes or groups of members, in the manner provided in a limited liability company agreement. If the limited liability company agreement does not so provide, distributions shall be made on the basis of the agreed value (as stated in the records of the limited liability company) of the contributions made by each member to the extent they have been received by the limited liability company and have not been returned.

§ 18-505. Defense of usury not available.

No obligation of a member or manager of a limited liability company to the limited liability company arising under the limited liability company agreement or a separate agreement or writing, and no note, instrument or other writing evidencing any such obligation of a member or manager, shall be subject to the defense of usury, and no member or manager shall interpose the defense of usury with respect to any such obligation in any action.

Subchapter VI. Distributions and Resignation.

§ 18-601. Interim distributions.

Except as provided in this subchapter, to the extent and at the times or upon the happening of the events specified in a limited liability company agreement, a member is entitled to receive from a limited liability company distributions before the member's resignation from the limited liability company and before the dissolution and winding up thereof.

§ 18-602. Resignation of manager.

A manager may resign as a manager of a limited liability company at the time or upon the happening of events specified in a limited liability company agreement and in accordance with the limited liability company agreement. A limited liability company agreement may provide that a manager shall not have the right to resign as a manager of a limited liability company. Notwithstanding that a limited liability company agreement provides that a manager does not have the right to resign as a manager of a limited liability company, a manager may resign as a manager of a limited liability company at any time by giving written notice to the members and other managers. If the resignation of a manager violates a limited liability company agreement, in addition to any remedies otherwise available under applicable law, a limited liability company may recover from the resigning manager damages for breach of the limited liability company agreement and offset the damages against the amount otherwise distributable to the resigning manager.

§ 18-603. Resignation of member.
A member may resign from a limited liability company only at the time or upon the happening of events specified in a limited liability company agreement and in accordance with the limited liability company agreement. Notwithstanding anything to the contrary under applicable law, unless a limited liability company agreement provides otherwise, a member may not resign from a limited liability company prior to the dissolution and winding up of the limited liability company. Notwithstanding anything to the contrary under applicable law, a limited liability company agreement may provide that a limited liability company interest may not be assigned prior to the dissolution and winding up of the limited liability company. Unless otherwise provided in a limited liability company agreement, a limited liability company whose original certificate of formation was filed with the Secretary of State and effective on or prior to July 31, 1996, shall continue to be governed by this section as in effect on July 31, 1996, and shall not be governed by this section.

§ 18-604. Distribution upon resignation.
Except as provided in this subchapter, upon resignation any resigning member is entitled to receive any distribution to which such member is entitled under a limited liability company agreement and, if not otherwise provided in a limited liability company agreement, such member is entitled to receive, within a reasonable time after resignation, the fair value of such member's limited liability company interest as of the date of resignation based upon such member's right to share in distributions from the limited liability company.

§ 18-605. Distribution in kind.
Except as provided in a limited liability company agreement, a member, regardless of the nature of the member's contribution, has no right to demand and receive any distribution from a limited liability company in any form other than cash. Except as provided in a limited liability company agreement, a member may not be compelled to accept a distribution of any asset in kind from a limited liability company to the extent that the percentage of the asset distributed exceeds a percentage of that asset which is equal to the percentage in which the member shares in distributions from the limited liability company. Except as provided in the limited liability company agreement, a member may be compelled to accept a distribution of any asset in kind from a limited liability company to the extent that the percentage of the asset distributed is equal to a percentage of that asset which is equal to the percentage in which the member shares in distributions from the limited liability company.

§ 18-606. Right to distribution.
Subject to §§ 18-607 and 18-804 of this title, and unless otherwise provided in a limited liability company agreement, at the time a member becomes entitled to receive a distribution, the member has the status of, and is entitled to all remedies available to, a creditor of a limited liability company with respect to the distribution. A limited liability company agreement may provide for the establishment of a record date with respect to allocations and distributions by a limited liability company.

§ 18-607. Limitations on distribution.
(a) A limited liability company shall not make a distribution to a member to the extent that at the time of the distribution, after giving effect to the distribution, all liabilities of the limited liability company, other than liabilities to members on account of their limited liability company interests and liabilities for which the recourse of creditors is limited to specified property of the limited liability company, exceed the fair value of the assets of the limited liability company, except that the fair value of property that is subject to a liability for which the recourse of creditors is limited shall be included in the assets of the limited liability company only to the extent that the fair value of that property exceeds that liability. For purposes of this subsection (a), the term "distribution" shall not include amounts constituting reasonable compensation for present or past services or reasonable payments made in the ordinary course of business pursuant to a bona fide retirement plan or other benefits program.

(b) A member who receives a distribution in violation of subsection (a) of this section, and who knew at the time of the distribution that the distribution violated subsection (a) of this section, shall be liable to a limited liability company for the amount of the distribution. A member who receives a distribution in violation of subsection (a) of this section, and who did not know at the time of the distribution that the distribution violated subsection (a) of this section, shall not be liable for the amount of the distribution. Subject to subsection (c) of this section, this subsection shall not affect any obligation or liability of a member under an agreement or other applicable law for the amount of a distribution.

(c) Unless otherwise agreed, a member who receives a distribution from a limited liability company shall have no liability under this chapter or other applicable law for the amount of the distribution after the expiration of 3 years from the date of the distribution unless an action to recover the distribution from such member is commenced prior to the expiration of the said 3-year period and an adjudication of liability against such member is made in the said action.

Subchapter VII. Assignment of Limited Liability Company Interests.

§ 18-701. Nature of limited liability company interest.
A limited liability company interest is personal property. A member has no interest in specific limited liability company property.

§ 18-702. Assignment of limited liability company interest.
(a) A limited liability company interest is assignable in whole or in part except as provided in a limited liability company agreement. The assignee of a member's limited liability company interest shall have no right to participate in the management of the business and affairs of a limited liability company except as provided in a limited liability company agreement and upon:

(1) The approval of all of the members of the limited liability company other than the member assigning the limited liability company interest; or

(2) Compliance with any procedure provided for in the limited liability company agreement.

(b) Unless otherwise provided in a limited liability company agreement:

(1) An assignment of a limited liability company interest does not entitle the assignee to become or to exercise any rights or powers of a member;

(2) An assignment of a limited liability company interest entitles the assignee to share in such profits and losses, to receive such distribution or distributions, and to receive such allocation of income, gain, loss, deduction, or credit or similar item to which the assignor was entitled, to the extent assigned; and

(3) A member ceases to be a member and to have the power to exercise any rights or powers of a member upon assignment of all of the member's limited liability company interest. Unless otherwise provided in a limited liability company agreement, the pledge of, or granting of a security interest, lien or other encumbrance in or against, any or all of the limited liability company interest of a member shall not cause the member to cease to be a member or to have the power to exercise any rights or powers of a member.

(c) Unless otherwise provided in a limited liability company agreement, a member's interest in a limited liability company may be evidenced by a certificate of limited liability company interest issued by the limited liability company. A limited liability company agreement may provide for the assignment or transfer of any limited liability company interest represented by such a certificate and make other provisions with respect to such certificates.

(d) Unless otherwise provided in a limited liability company agreement and except to the extent assumed by agreement, until an assignee of a limited liability company interest becomes a member, the assignee shall have no liability as a member solely as a result of the assignment.

(e) Unless otherwise provided in the limited liability company agreement, a limited liability company may acquire, by purchase, redemption or otherwise, any limited liability company interest or other interest of a member or manager in the limited liability company. Unless otherwise provided in the limited liability company agreement, any such interest so acquired by the limited liability company shall be deemed canceled.

§ 18-703. Member's limited liability company interest subject to charging order.
(a) On application by a judgment creditor of a member or of a member's assignee, a court having jurisdiction may charge the limited liability company interest of the judgment debtor to satisfy the judgment. The court may appoint a receiver of the share of the distributions due or to become due to the judgment debtor in respect of the limited liability company, which receiver shall have only the rights of an assignee, and the court may make all other orders, directions, accounts and inquiries the judgment debtor might have made or which the circumstances of the case may require.

(b) A charging order constitutes a lien on the judgment debtor's limited liability company interest. The court may order a foreclosure of the limited liability company interest subject to the charging order at any time. The purchaser at the foreclosure sale has only the rights of an assignee.

(c) Unless otherwise provided in a limited liability company agreement, at any time before foreclosure, a limited liability company interest charged may be redeemed:

(1) By the judgment debtor;

(2) With property other than limited liability company property, by 1 or more of the other members; or

(3) By the limited liability company with the consent of all of the members whose interests are not so charged.

(d) This chapter does not deprive a member of a right under exemption laws with respect to the member's limited liability company interest.

(e) This section provides the exclusive remedy by which a judgment creditor of a member or member's assignee may satisfy a judgment out of the judgment debtor's limited liability company interest.

(f) No creditor of a member shall have any right to obtain possession of, or otherwise exercise legal or equitable remedies with respect to, the property of the limited liability company.

§ 18-704. Right of assignee to become member.
(a) An assignee of a limited liability company interest may become a member as provided in a limited liability company agreement and upon:

(1) The approval of all of the members of the limited liability company other than the member assigning limited liability company interest; or

(2) Compliance with any procedure provided for in the limited liability company agreement.

(b) An assignee who has become a member has, to the extent assigned, the rights and powers, and is subject to the restrictions and liabilities, of a member under a limited liability company agreement and this chapter. Notwithstanding the foregoing, unless otherwise provided in a limited liability company agreement, an assignee who becomes a member is liable for the obligations of the assignor to make contributions as provided in § 18-502 of this title, but shall not be liable for the obligations of the assignor under subchapter VI of this chapter. However, the assignee is not obligated for liabilities, including the obligations of the assignor to make contributions as provided in § 18-502 of this title, unknown to the assignee at the time the assignee became a member and which could not be ascertained from a limited liability company agreement.

(c) Whether or not an assignee of a limited liability company interest becomes a member, the assignor is not released from liability to a limited liability company under subchapters V and VI of this chapter.

§ 18-705. Powers of estate of deceased or incompetent member.

If a member who is an individual dies or a court of competent jurisdiction adjudges the member to be incompetent to manage the member's person or property, the member's personal representative may exercise all of the member's rights for the purpose of settling the member's estate or administering the member's property, including any power under a limited liability company agreement of an assignee to become a member. If a member is a corporation, trust or other entity and is dissolved or terminated, the powers of that member may be exercised by its personal representative.

Subchapter XI. Miscellaneous.

§ 18-1101. Construction and application of chapter and limited liability company agreement.

(a) The rule that statutes in derogation of the common law are to be strictly construed shall have no application to this chapter.

(b) It is the policy of this chapter to give the maximum effect to the principle of freedom of contract and to the enforceability of limited liability company agreements.

(c) To the extent that, at law or in equity, a member or manager or other person has duties (including fiduciary duties) and liabilities relating thereto to a limited liability company or to another member or manager or to an other person that is a party to or is otherwise bound by a limited liability company agreement:

(1) Any such member or manager or other person acting under the limited liability company agreement shall not be liable to the limited liability company or to any such other member or manager or to any such other person for the member's or manager's or other person's good faith reliance on the provisions of the limited liability company agreement; and

(2) The member's or manager's or other person's duties and liabilities may be expanded or restricted by provisions in the limited liability company agreement.

(d) Unless the context otherwise requires, as used herein, the singular shall include the plural and the plural may refer to only the singular. The use of any gender shall be applicable to all genders. The captions contained herein are for purposes of convenience only and shall not control or affect the construction of this chapter.

§ 18-1102. Short title.

This chapter may be cited as the "Delaware Limited Liability Company Act."

§ 18-1103. Severability.

If any provision of this chapter or its application to any person or circumstances is held invalid, the invalidity does not affect other provisions or applications of the chapter which can be given effect without the invalid provision or application, and to this end, the provisions of this chapter are severable.

§ 18-1104. Cases not provided for in this chapter.

In any case not provided for in this chapter, the rules of law and equity, including the law merchant, shall govern.

§ 18-1105. Fees.

(a) No document required to be filed under this chapter shall be effective until the applicable fee required by this section is paid. The following fees shall be paid to and collected by the Secretary of State for the use of the State of Delaware:

(1) Upon the receipt for filing of an application for reservation of name, an application for renewal of reservation or a notice of transfer or cancellation of reservation pursuant to § 18-103(b) of this title, a fee in the amount of $75.

(2) Upon the receipt for filing of a certificate under § 18-104(b) of this title, a fee in the amount of $50, upon the receipt for filing of a certificate under § 18-104(c) of this title, a fee in the amount of $50 and a further fee of $2 for each limited liability company affected by such certificate, and upon the receipt for filing of a certificate under § 18-104(d) of this title, a fee in the amount of $2.50.

(3) Upon the receipt for filing of a certificate of limited liability company domestication under § 18-212 of this title, a certificate of transfer or a certificate of transfer and continuance under § 18-213 of this title, a certificate of conversion to limited liability company under § 18-214 of this title, a certificate of formation under § 18-201 of

this title, a certificate of amendment under § 18-202 of this title, a certificate of cancellation under § 18-203 of this title, a certificate of merger or consolidation under § 18-209 of this title, a restated certificate of formation under § 18-208 of this title, a certificate of amendment of a certificate with a future effective date or time under § 18-206(c) of this title, a certificate of termination of a certificate with a future effective date or time under § 18-206(c) of this title, a certificate of correction under § 18-211 of this title, or a certificate of revival under § 18-1109 of this title, and upon the restoration of a domestic limited liability company or a foreign limited liability company under § 18-1107(i) of this title, a fee in the amount of $50.

(4) For certifying copies of any paper on file as provided for by this chapter, a fee in the amount of $20 for each copy certified.

(5) The Secretary of State may issue photocopies or electronic image copies of instruments on file, as well as instruments, documents and other papers not on file, and for all such photocopies or electronic image copies, whether certified or not, a fee of $5 shall be paid for the 1st page and $1 for each additional page. The Secretary of State may also issue microfiche copies of instruments on file as well as instruments, documents and other papers not on file, and for each such microfiche a fee of $2 shall be paid therefor. Notwithstanding the State of Delaware's Freedom of Information Act or other provision of this Code granting access to public records, the Secretary of State shall issue only photocopies, microfiche or electronic image copies of records in exchange for the fees described above.

(6) Upon the receipt for filing of an application for registration as a foreign limited liability company under § 18-902 of this title, a certificate under § 18-905 of this title or a certificate of cancellation under § 18-906 of this title, a fee in the amount of $50.

(7) Upon the receipt for filing of a certificate under § 18-904(c) of this title, a fee in the amount of $50, upon the receipt for filing of a certificate under § 18-904(d) of this title, a fee in the amount of $50 and a further fee of $2 for each foreign limited liability company affected by such certificate, and upon the receipt for filing of a certificate under § 18-904(e) of this title, a fee in the amount of $2.50.

(8) For preclearance of any document for filing, a fee in the amount of $250.

(9) For preparing and providing a written report of a record search, a fee in the amount of $30.

(10) For issuing any certificate of the Secretary of State, including but not limited to a certificate of good standing, other than a certification of a copy under paragraph (4) of this subsection, a fee in the amount of $20, except that for issuing any certificate of the Secretary of State that recites all of a limited liability company's filings with the Secretary of State, a fee of $100 shall be paid for each such certificate.

(11) For receiving and filing and/or indexing any certificate, affidavit, agreement or any other paper provided for by this chapter, for which no different fee is specifically prescribed, a fee in the amount of $25.

(12) The Secretary of State may in his or her discretion charge a fee of $25 for each check received for payment of any fee that is returned due to insufficient funds or the result of a stop payment order.

(b) In addition to those fees charged under subsection (a) of this section, there shall be collected by and paid to the Secretary of State the following:

(1) For all services described in subsection (a) of this section that are requested to be completed within 2 hours on the same day as the day of the request, an additional sum of up to $500;

(2) For all services described in subsection (a) of this section that are requested to be completed within the same day as the day of the request, an additional sum of up to $200; and

(3) For all services described in subsection (a) of this section that are requested to be completed within a 24-hour period from the time of the request, an additional sum of up to $100. The Secretary of State shall establish (and may from time to time amend) a schedule of specific fees payable pursuant to this subsection.

(c) The Secretary of State may in his or her discretion permit the extension of credit for the fees required by this section upon such terms as the secretary shall deem to be appropriate.

(d) The Secretary of State shall retain from the revenue collected from the fees required by this section a sum sufficient to provide at all times a fund of at least $500, but not more than $1,500, from which the secretary may refund any payment made pursuant to this section to the extent that it exceeds the fees required by this section. The funds shall be deposited in a financial institution which is a legal depository of State of Delaware moneys to the credit of the Secretary of State and shall be disbursable on order of the Secretary of State.

(e) Except as provided in this section, the fees of the Secretary of State shall be as provided in § 2315 of Chapter 29.

§ 18-1106. Reserved power of State of Delaware to alter or repeal chapter.

All provisions of this chapter may be altered from time to time or repealed and all rights of members and managers are subject to this reservation. Unless expressly stated to the contrary in this chapter, all amendments of this chapter shall apply to limited liability companies and members and managers whether or not existing as such at the time of the enactment of any such amendment.

§ 18-1107. Taxation of limited liability companies.

(a) For purposes of any tax imposed by the State of Delaware or any instrumentality, agency or political subdivision of the State of Delaware, a limited liability company formed under this chapter or qualified to do business in the State of Delaware as a foreign limited liability company shall be classified as a partnership unless classified otherwise for federal income tax purposes, in which case the limited liability company shall be classified in the same manner as it is classified for federal income tax purposes. For purposes of any tax imposed by the State of Delaware or any instrumentality, agency or political subdivision of the State of Delaware, a member or an assignee of a member of a limited liability company formed under this chapter or qualified to do business in the State of Delaware as a foreign limited liability company shall be treated as either a resident or nonresident partner unless classified otherwise for federal income tax purposes, in which case the member or assignee of a member shall have the same status as such member or assignee of a member has for federal income tax purposes.

(b) Every domestic limited liability company and every foreign limited liability company registered to do business in the State of Delaware shall pay an annual tax, for the use of the State of Delaware, in the amount of $100.

(c) The annual tax shall be due and payable on the first day of June following the close of the calendar year or upon the cancellation of a certificate of formation. The Secretary of State shall receive the annual tax and pay over all taxes collected to the Department of Finance of the State of Delaware. If the annual tax remains unpaid after the due date, the tax shall bear interest at the rate of 1 and one-half percent for each month or portion thereof until fully paid.

(d) The Secretary of State shall, at least 60 days prior to the first day of June of each year, cause to be mailed to each domestic limited liability company and each foreign limited liability company required to comply with the provisions of this section in care of its registered agent in the State of Delaware an annual statement for the tax to be paid hereunder.

(e) In the event of neglect, refusal or failure on the part of any domestic limited liability company or foreign limited liability company to pay the annual tax to be paid hereunder on or before the 1st day of June in any year, such domestic limited liability company or foreign limited liability company shall pay the sum of $100 to be recovered by adding that amount to the annual tax and such additional sum shall become a part of the tax and shall be collected in the same manner and subject to the same penalties.

(f) In case any domestic limited liability company or foreign limited liability company shall fail to pay the annual tax due within the time required by this section, and in case the agent in charge of the registered office of any domestic limited liability company or foreign limited liability company upon whom process against such domestic limited liability company or foreign limited liability company may be served shall die, resign, refuse to act as such, remove from the State of Delaware or cannot with due diligence be found, it shall be lawful while default continues to serve process against such domestic limited liability company or foreign limited liability company upon the Secretary of State. Such service upon the Secretary of State shall be made in the manner and shall have the effect stated in § 18-105 of this title in the case of a domestic limited liability company and § 18-910 of this title in the case of a foreign limited liability company and shall be governed in all respects by said sections.

(g) The annual tax shall be a debt due from a domestic limited liability company or foreign limited liability company to the State of Delaware, for which an action at law may be maintained after the same shall have been in arrears for a period of 1 month. The tax shall also be a preferred debt in the case of insolvency.

(h) A domestic limited liability company or foreign limited liability company that neglects, refuses or fails to pay the annual tax when due shall cease to be in good standing as a domestic limited liability company or registered as a foreign limited liability company in the State of Delaware.

(i) A domestic limited liability company that has ceased to be in good standing or a foreign limited liability company that has ceased to be registered by reason of the failure to pay an annual tax shall be restored to and have the status of a domestic limited liability company in good standing or a foreign limited liability company that is registered in the State of Delaware upon the payment of the annual tax and all penalties and interest thereon for each year for which such domestic limited liability company or foreign limited liability company neglected, refused or failed to pay an annual tax. A fee as set forth in § 18-1105(a)(3) of this title shall be paid at the time of restoration.

(j) On the motion of the Attorney General or upon request of the Secretary of State, whenever any annual tax due under this chapter from any domestic limited liability company or foreign limited liability company shall have remained in arrears for a period of 3 months after the tax shall have become payable, the Attorney General may apply to the Court of Chancery, by petition in the name of the State of Delaware, on 5 days' notice to such domestic limited liability company or foreign limited liability company, which notice may be served in such manner as the Court may direct, for an injunction to restrain such domestic limited liability company or foreign limited liability company from the transaction of any business within the State of Delaware or elsewhere, until the payment of the annual tax, and all penalties and interest due thereon and the cost of the application which shall be fixed by the Court. The Court of Chancery may grant the injunction, if a proper case appears, and upon granting and service of the injunction, such domestic limited liability company or foreign limited liability company thereafter shall not transact any business until the injunction shall be dissolved.

(k) A domestic limited liability company that has ceased to be in good standing by reason of its neglect, refusal or failure to pay an annual tax shall remain a domestic limited liability company formed under this chapter. The Secretary of State shall not accept for filing any certificate (except a certificate of resignation of a registered agent when a successor registered agent is not being appointed) required or permitted by this chapter to be filed in respect of any domestic limited liability company or foreign limited liability company which has neglected, refused or failed to pay an annual tax, and shall not issue any certificate of good standing with respect to such domestic limited liability company or foreign limited liability company, unless or until such domestic limited liability company or foreign limited liability company shall have been restored to and have the status of a domestic limited liability company in good standing or a foreign limited liability company duly registered in the State of Delaware.

(l) A domestic limited liability company that has ceased to be in good standing or a foreign limited liability company that has ceased to be registered in the State of Delaware by reason of its neglect, refusal or failure to pay an annual tax may not maintain any action, suit or proceeding in any court of the State of Delaware until such domestic limited liability company or foreign limited liability company has been restored to and has the status of a domestic limited liability company or foreign limited liability company in good standing or duly registered in the State of Delaware. An action, suit or proceeding may not be maintained in any court of the State of Delaware by any successor or assignee of such domestic limited liability company or foreign limited liability company on any right, claim or demand arising out the transaction of business by such domestic limited liability company after it has ceased to be in good standing or a foreign limited liability company that has ceased to be registered in the State of Delaware until such domestic limited liability company or foreign limited liability company, or any person that has acquired all or substantially all of its assets, has paid any annual tax then due and payable, together with penalties and interest thereon.

(m) The neglect, refusal or failure of a domestic limited liability company or foreign limited liability company to pay an annual tax shall not impair the validity on any contract, deed, mortgage, security interest, lien or act or such domestic limited liability company or foreign limited liability company or prevent such domestic limited liability company or foreign limited liability company from defending any action, suit or proceeding with any court of the State of Delaware.

(n) A member or manager of a domestic limited liability company or foreign limited liability company is not liable for the debts, obligations or liabilities of such domestic limited liability company or foreign limited liability company solely by reason of the neglect, refusal or failure of such domestic limited liability company or foreign limited liability company to pay an annual tax or by reason of such domestic limited liability company or foreign limited liability company ceasing to be in good standing or duly registered.

§ 18-1108. Cancellation of certificate of formation for failure to pay taxes.

(a) The certificate of formation of a domestic limited liability company shall be deemed to be canceled if the domestic limited liability company shall fail to pay the annual tax due under § 18-1107 of this title for a period of 3 years from the date it is due, such cancellation to be effective on the third anniversary of such due date.

(b) On or before October 31 of each calendar year, the Secretary of State shall publish once in at least 1 newspaper of general circulation in the State of Delaware a list of those domestic limited liability companies whose certificates of formation were canceled on June 1 of such calendar year pursuant to § 18-1108(a) of this title.

§ 18-1109. Revival of domestic limited liability company.

(a) A domestic limited liability company whose certificate of formation has been canceled pursuant to § 18-104(d) or § 18-1108(a) of this title may be revived by filing in the office of the Secretary of State a certificate of revival accompanied by the payment of the fee required by § 18-1105(a)(3) of this title and payment of the annual tax due under § 18-1107 of this title and all penalties and interest thereon for each year for which such domestic limited liability company neglected, refused or failed to pay such annual tax, including each year between the cancellation of its certificate of formation and its revival. The certificate of revival shall set forth:

(1) The name of the limited liability company at the time its certificate of formation was canceled and, if such name is not available at the time of revival, the name under which the limited liability company is to be revived;

(2) The date of filing of the original certificate of formation of the limited liability company;

(3) The address of the limited liability company's registered office in the State of Delaware and the name and address of the limited liability company's registered agent in the State of Delaware;

(4) A statement that the certificate of revival is filed by 1 or more persons authorized to execute and file the certificate of revival to revive the limited liability company; and

(5) Any other matters the persons executing the certificate of revival determine to include therein.

(b) The certificate of revival shall be deemed to be an amendment to the certificate of formation of the limited liability company, and the limited liability company shall

not be required to take any further action to amend its certificate of formation under § 18-202 of this title with respect to the matters set forth in the certificate of revival.
(c) Upon the filing of a certificate of revival, a limited liability company shall be revived with the same force and effect as if its certificate of formation had not been canceled pursuant to § 18-104(d) or § 18-1108(a) of this title. Such revival shall validate all contracts, acts, matters and things made, done and performed by the limited liability company, its members, managers, employees and agents during the time when its certificate of formation was canceled pursuant to § 18-104(d) or § 18-1108(a) of this title, with the same force and effect and to all intents and purposes as if the certificate of formation had remained in full force and effect. All real and personal property, and all rights and interests, which belonged to the limited liability company at the time its certificate of formation was canceled pursuant to § 18-104(d) or § 18-1108(a) of this title or which were acquired by the limited liability company following the cancellation of its certificate of formation pursuant to § 18-104(d) or § 18-1108(a) of this title, and which were not disposed of prior to the time of its revival, shall be vested in the limited liability company after its revival as fully as they were held by the limited liability company at, and after, as the case may be, the time its certificate of formation was canceled pursuant to § 18-104(d) or § 18-1108(a) of this title. After its revival, the limited liability company shall be as exclusively liable for all contracts, acts, matters and things made, done or performed in its name and on its behalf by its members, managers, employees and agents prior to its revival as if its certificate of formation had at all times remained in full force and effect.

Appendix B
Delaware Registered Agents

The following is a list of companies which can serve as a registered agent for your Delaware corporation or LLC.

AAA-Self Filer's Incorporation Services, Corp.
25 Greystone Manor
Lewes, DE 19958-9776
Sussex County
Tel: 800-345-2677
Tel: 302-645-7400
Fax: 302-645-1280
Email: rickbell@delawareinc.com
Website: http://www.delawareinc.com

ABD Corporate Services, Inc.
851 Watkins Way
Newark, DE 19702
New Castle County
Tel: 302-832-7144
Tel: (toll free) 877-768-0459
Fax 302-832-7146
E-mail: abdcorpserv@dca.net
Website: http://www.abdcorpservices.com

AccuCorp Incorporators, Ltd.
Suite 300A, Two Greenville Crossing
4001 Kennett Pike
P.O. Box 4477
Wilmington, DE 19807-0477
New Castle County
Tel: 800-318-7407
Tel: 302-652-4800
Fax: 302-652-6760

Acme Filings Corp.
709 Woodside Avenue
Wilmington, DE 19809
New Castle County
Tel: 302-777-0650
Tel: (toll free) 866-345-3267 (filecorp)
Fax: 866-329-2677 (toll free)
E-mail: sales@incorporatedelawareonline.com
Website: http://www.incorporatedelawareonline.com

Advance Corporate Service, Inc.
2213 Concord Pike
Wilmington, DE 19803
New Castle County
Tel: 302-652-2100

Agents and Corporations, Inc.
Suite 600, One Commerce Center
12th & Orange Streets
Suite 600, One Commerce Center
Wilmington, DE 19801
New Castle County
Tel: 800-759-2248
Tel: 302-575-0877
Fax: 302-575-1642
Email: agents@WHW-De.com
Website: http://www.incnow.com

Agents for Delaware Corporations, Inc.
15 Loockerman Street
P.O. Box 841
Dover, DE 19903-0841
Kent County
Tel: 800-227-3906
Fax: 302-734-5164

American Business Group, Inc.
25 Greystone Manor
Lewes, DE 19958
Sussex County
Tel: 302-645-2526

American Guaranty & Trust Company
Christiana Executive Campus
220 Continental Drive
Newark, DE 19713
New Castle County
Tel: 800-441-7698
Tel: 302-456-1010
Fax: 302-731-5157

American Incorporators Ltd.
1220 North Market Street
Suite 606
Wilmington, DE 19801
New Castle County
Tel: 800-421-2661
Tel: 302-421-5752
Fax: 302-421-5753
Email: inc@ailcorp.com
Website: http://www.ailcorp.com

Aradel, Inc.
16 West Main Street
Christiana, DE 19702
New Castle County
Tel: 302-737-5511

ATA Corporate Services, Inc.
222 Delaware Avenue, Suite 1200
Wilmington, DE 19801
New Castle County
302-421-6820
Fax 302-421-5866

Bancroft Service Corp.
1020 North Bancroft Parkway
P.O. Box 429
Wilmington DE 19805-0429
New Castle County
Tel: 302-571-1782
Fax: 302-571-1638

Barros, McNamara, Scanlon, Malkiewicz & Taylor, P.A.
2 West Loockerman Street
P.O. Box 1298
Dover, DE 19903
Kent County
Tel: 302-734-8400
Fax: 302-734-4349

Bayard, Handelman & Murdoch, P.A.
Mellon Bank Center, 15th Floor
919 North Market Street
P.O. Box 25130
Wilmington, DE 19899
New Castle County
Tel: 302-655-5000
Fax: 302-658-6395

Brown, Shiels & Chasanov
108 East Water Street
P.O. Drawer F
Dover, DE 19903
Kent County
Tel: 302-734-4766

Business Filings Incorporated
9 E. Loockerman Street, Suite 205
Dover, DE 19904
Kent County
Tel: 800-981-7183
Fax: 608-251-6907

Business Incorporators, Inc.
1019 Cypress Road
Wilmington, DE 19810
New Castle County
Tel: 800-695-6596
Tel: 302-475-6596
Fax: 302-529-7426

Capitol Corporate Services, Inc.
314 South State Street
P.O. Box 741
Dover, DE 19903
Kent County
Tel: 302-736-0156
Fax: 302-736-0336
E-mail: juhrden@duanemorris.com

Capitol Services, Inc.
615 South DuPont Highway
Dover, DE 19901
Kent County
Tel: 800-345-4647
Fax: 800-432-3622
Website: http://www.capitolservices.com

Central Delaware Corporate Services, Inc.
12260 Willow Grove Road
Bldg. #2
Camden, DE 19934
Kent County
Tel: 800-637-2327
Tel: 302-698-0118
Fax 302-698-0443
Fax 302-698-0297
E-mail: cdcs19934@aol.com

Charles Snyderman, Esq.
5301 Limestone Road Suite 214
Wilmington, DE 19808
New Castle County
Tel: 302-239-1104
Fax: 302-239-2124
E-mail: charsynderman@rcn.com

Christiana Incorporators, Inc.
508 Main Street
Wilmington, DE 19804
New Castle County
Tel: 302-998-2008

Colby Attorneys Service Co., Inc.
9 East Loockerman Street
Dover, DE 19901
Kent County
Tel: 800-832-1220
Fax: 518-434-2574

Colonial Charter Company
300 Delaware Avenue
Suite 1130
Wilmington, DE 19801
New Castle County
Tel: 302-656-9850
Fax: 302-656-9836

The Company Corporation
1013 Centre Road, Suite 400
Wilmington, DE 19805
New Castle County
Tel: 800-877-4224
Tel: 302-636-5440
Fax: 302-636-5454
Website: http://www.corporate.com

Company Express (Delaware) Limited
3505 Silverside Road
208 H Plaza Centre
Wilmington, DE 19810
New Castle County
Tel: 302-478-4460
Fax: 302-478-4467
E-mail: delaware@com-exp.com
Website: http://www.company-express.net
Contact: Christy Buchanan

Concord Assets Finance Corporation
12th & Orange Streets
One Commerce Center
Wilmington, DE 19801
New Castle County
Tel: 302-573-2521

Cooch & Taylor, A Professional Assoc.
Suite 1000, Marine Midland Plaza
824 North Market Street
P.O. Box 1680
Wilmington, DE 19899-1680
New Castle County
Tel: 302-652-3641
Fax: 302-652-5379

CorpAmerica, Inc.
30 Old Rudnick Lane
Dover, DE 19901
Kent County
Tel: 888-736-4300
Tel: 302-736-4300
Fax: 302-736-5620
E-mail: info@corpamerica.com
Website: http://www.CorpAmerica.com

CorpoMax Inc.
220 East Delaware Avenue
Newark, DE 19711
New Castle County
Tel: 866-950-5500 (U.S. and Canada - Toll Free)
Tel: 302-266-8200 (International)
Fax: 302-266-8226
E-mail: info@corpomax.com
Website: http://www.corpomax.com

Corporate Agents, Inc.
2711 Centerville Road, Suite 400
Wilmington, DE 19805
New Castle County
Tel: 800-877-4224
Tel: 302-636-5440
Fax: 302-636-5454
Website: http://www.corporate.com

Corporate Consulting Ltd.
701 Renner Road
Wilmington, DE 19810
New Castle County
Tel: 800-546-8607
Tel: 302-529-0500
Fax: 302-529-9005
E-mail: corporate_consulting@msn.com
Website: http://www.IncorporateDelawareUSA.com

Corporate Creations Network Inc.
2530 Channin Drive
Wilmington, DE 19810
New Castle County
Tel: 800-672-9110
Fax: 302-424-4866
E-mail: info@corpcreations.com
Website: http://www.CorporateCreations.com

Corporate Excel, Inc.
501 Silverside Road, Suite 142
Wilmington, DE 19809
New Castle County
Tel: 877-932-3923
Fax: 877-881-2008

Corporate Holding Services, Inc.
818 Washington Street
Wilmington, DE 19801
New Castle County
Tel: 302-428-0515
Fax: 302-428-0642

Corporate Service Bureau, Inc.
15 East North Street
Dover, DE 19901
Kent County
Tel: 518-463-8550
Fax: 518-463-3752

Corporate Systems Inc.
101 North Fairfield Drive
Dover, DE 19901
Kent County
Tel: 800-331-7040
Tel: 302-697-2139
Fax: 302-697-2130

Corporation Guarantee & Trust Company
11th Floor, Rodney Square North
11th & Market Streets
Wilmington, DE 19801
New Castle County
Tel: 302-655-2325
Tel: 800-563-6131
Fax: 215-633-8160
E-mail: corpguartc@aol.com

Corporation Service Company
2711 Centerville Road, Suite 400
Wilmington, DE 19805
New Castle County
Tel: 800-927-9800
Tel: 302-636-5400
Fax: 302-636-5454
E-mail: info@incspot.com
Website: http://www.incspot.com

The Corporation Trust Company (CT Corporation System)
Corporation Trust Center
1209 Orange Street
Wilmington, DE 19801
New Castle County
Tel: 302-658-7581
Fax: 302-655-5049
Website: http://www.ctadvantage.com

Corporations & Companies CorpCo)
Suite 300A, Two Greenville Crossing
4001 Kennett Pike
P.O. Box 4477
Wilmington, DE 19807-0477
New Castle County
Tel: 800-318-7407
Tel: 302-652-4800
Fax: 302-652-6760

Delaware Business Incorporators, Inc.
3422 Old Capitol Trail, Suite 700
Wilmington, DE 19808-6192
New Castle County
Tel: 800-423-2993
Tel: 302-996-5819
Fax: 800-423-0423
Fax: 302-996-5818
E-mail: inc_info@delbusinc.com
Website: http://www.delbusinc.com
Website http://www.e-incorporate.com

Del Corp America Inc.
30 Old Rudnick Lane
Dover, DE 19901
Kent County
Tel: 888-736-4300
Tel: 302-736-4300
Fax: 302-736-5620
E-mail: info@corpamerica.com
Website: http://www.CorpAmerica.com

Delaware Corporate Agents, Inc.
4406 Tennyson Road
Wilmington, DE 19802
New Castle County
Tel: 302-762-8637
Fax: 302-762-8643
E-mail: delcorp@delcorp.com
Website: http://www.delcorp.com

Delaware Corporate Management, Inc.
1105 North Market Street, Suite 1300
Wilmington, DE 19801
New Castle County
Tel: 302-427-7650
Fax: 302-427-7663
E-mail: cwatson@wilmingtontrust.com

Delaware Corporate Registry, Inc.
One Commerce Center, Suite 500
1201 N. Orange Street
Wilmington, DE 19801-1140
New Castle County
Tel: 302-655-6500
Tel: 800-655-1480
Fax: 302-655-8500
E-mail: dcr@dellaw.com
Website: http://www.lawyers.com/dellaw

Delaware Corporate Services Inc.
222 Delaware Avenue - 10th Floor
P.O. Box 2306
Wilmington, DE 19899-2306
New Castle County
Tel: 302-888-6839
Fax: 302-888-6989
E-mail: mpowell@dcsdelaware.com

Delaware Corporation Organizers, Inc.
1201 North Market Street, 18th Floor
P.O. Box 1347
Wilmington, DE 19899-1347
New Castle County
Tel: 302-575-7371
Fax: 302-658-3989

Delaware Corporations LLC
800 Delaware Avenue
P.O. Box 8702
Wilmington, DE 19899
New Castle County
Tel: 888-279-9100
Tel: 302-652-7580
Fax: 302-652-8597
E-mail: info@delawarecorp.com

Delaware First Incorporators, Inc.
341 Raven Circle
Wyoming, DE 19934
Kent County
Tel: 302-697-8777

Delaware Incorporating Services, Ltd.
15 East North Street
P.O. Box 1789
Dover, DE 19903
Kent County
Tel: 800-335-2462
Tel: 302-678-3299
Fax: 302-678-3150
E-mail: isl@isl.win.net
Website: http://www.win.net/~isl

Delaware Incorporators & Registration Service, Inc.
Chase Manhatten Centre
1201 Market Street, Suite 1700
Wilmington, DE 19801
New Castle County
Tel: 302-652-5200
Fax: 302-652-7211

Delaware Intercorp, Inc.
113 Barksdale Professional Center
Newark, DE 19711-3258
New Castle County
Tel: 888-324-1817
Tel: 302-266-9367
Fax: 302-266-9940
E-mail: info@delawareintercorp.com
Website: http://www.delawareintercorp.com

Delaware Registered Agents & Incorporators, LLC
411 Jaymar Boulevard
Newark, DE 19702
New Castle County
Tel: 800-346-1117
Tel: 302-571-1117
Fax: 302-571-8115

Delaware Registry, Ltd.
3511 Silverside Road
Suite 105
Wilmington, DE 19810
New Castle County
Tel: 800-321-2677
Tel: 302-477-9800
Fax: 302-477-9811
E-mail: corp@delreg.com
Website: http://delreg.com

Diamond State Corporate Agents, Inc.
1200 North Broom Street
Wilmington, DE 19806
New Castle County
Tel: 302-655-4200
Fax: 302-655-4210

Delaware State Registered Agents, Co.
101 North French Street
Wilmington, DE 19801
New Castle County
Tel: 302-658-1905
Tel: 800-259-1737
Fax: 302-658-1906 or 800-900-7906
E-mail dsra@delaware-agents.com
Website: filings@delaware-agents.com

Diversified Corporate Services Int'l, Inc.
508 Main Street
Wilmington, DE 19804
New Castle County
Tel: 800-433-0773
Fax: 518-434-0943
E-mail: divcorp@aol.com

Donald W. Booker, Esq.
118-A Senatorial Drive
P.O. Box 3587 - Greenville Plaza
Wilmington, DE 19807
New Castle County
Tel: 302-658-9301
Fax: 302-658-9304

Executive Corporation
2207 Concord Pike
Wilmington, DE 19803
New Castle County
Tel: 800-417-0580
Fax: 888-850-9887
E-mail: Info@ExecutiveCorporation.com
Website: http://www.ExecutiveCorporation.com

Executive Offices, Inc.
42 Read's Way
New Castle Corporate Commons
New Castle, DE 19720-1649
New Castle County
Tel: 302-323-8100
Tel: 888-663-3423
Fax: 302-323-8105

First State Corporate Services, Inc.
32 W. Loockerman Street, Suite 109
Dover, DE 19904
Kent County
Tel: 302-736-1777
Tel: 888-736-6398
Fax: 302-736-9883
E-mail kberry@parcelsinc.com
Website: http://www.parcelsinc.com

Genoese, Miller & Associates, Inc.
615 West 18th Street
Wilmington, DE 19802
New Castle County
Tel: 302-655-9505
Fax: 302-655-5105

Global Corporate Services, Inc.
709 Woodside Avenue
Wilmington, DE 19809
New Castle County
Tel: 800-219-9359
Fax: 703-995-0899
E-mail: info@global-inter.net
Website: http://www.global-inter.net

Gregory W. Williams, Esq.
402 Rehoboth Avenue
P.O. Box 739
Rehoboth Beach, DE 19971
Sussex County
Tel: 302-226-3700
Fax: 302-227-3307

Harvard Business Services, Inc.
25 Greystone Manor
Lewes, DE 19958
Sussex County
Tel: 800-345-2677
Tel: 302-645-7400
Fax: 302-645-1280
E-mail: rickbell@delawareinc.com
Website: http://www.delawareinc.com

HIQ Corporate Services, Inc.
15 East North Street
Dover, DE 19901
Kent County
Tel: 800-564-5300
Fax: 410-752-2808

Inc. Plan (USA)
Trolley Square, Suite 26C
Wilmington, DE 19806
New Castle County
Tel: 800-462-4633
Tel: 302-428-1200
Fax: 302-428-1274
Website: http://www.incplan.net

INCORP America, Inc.
30 Old Rudnick Lane
Dover, DE 19901
Kent County
Tel: 800-622-6414
Tel: 302-736-5510
Fax: 302-736-5620
E-mail: info@corpamerica.com
Website: http://www.CorpAmerica.com

Incorporating Services, Ltd.
15 East North Street
Dover, DE 19901
Kent County
Tel: 800-346-4646
Tel: 302-678-0855
Fax: 302-678-3150
E-mail: admin@incorporatingservices.net
Website: http://www.incorporatingservices.net

The Incorporators Ltd.
2979 Barley Mill Road
Yorklyn, DE 19873
New Castle County
Tel: 800-231-5593
Tel: 302-235-5800
Fax: 302-235-5900
Fax: 800-223-3928
Website: http://www.theincorporators.com

Incorporators of Delaware, Inc.
48 The Green
Dover, DE 19901
Kent County
Tel: 302-734-7588
Fax: 302-734-7587

John R. Weaver, Jr., P.A.
913 Market Street, Suite 1001
Wilmington, DE 19801
New Castle County
Tel: 302-655-7371
Fax: 302-655-7374

L. Vincent Ramunno, Esq.
903 North French Street
Wilmington, DE 19801
New Castle County
Tel: 302-656-9400
Fax: 302-656-9344

Leonard L. Williams, Esq.
1214 King Street
Wilmington, DE 19801
New Castle County
Tel: 302-652-3141
Fax: 302-652-3034

Lexis Document Services Inc.
30 Old Rudnick Lane, Suite 100
Dover, DE 19901
Kent County
Tel: 800-634-9738
Tel: 302-736-5510
Fax: 800-457-6299
E-mail: gep@netlds.com
Website: http://www.netlds.com

The Lima Delta Company
4 Penny Lane Court
Wilmington, DE 19803
New Castle County
Tel: 302-765-2577

Nancy J. Wolf, CPA
35A The Commons
3524 Silverside Road
Wilmington, DE 19810-4929
New Castle County
Tel: 302-477-1108
Tel: 302-479-7760
Fax: 302-479-7762
E-mail: nancy@wolfcpa.net
Website: http://www.wolfcpa.net

National Corporate Research, Ltd.
615 South Dupont Highway
Dover, DE 19901
Kent County
Tel: 800-483-1140
Tel: 302-734-1450
Fax: 302-734-1476
E-mail: info@nationalcorp.com
Website: http://www.nationalcorp.com

National Registered Agents, Inc.
9 East Loockerman Street
Dover, DE 19901
Kent County
Tel: 800-767-1553
Tel: 302-674-4089
Website: http://www.nrai.com

Nationwide Information Services, Inc.
15 East North Street
Dover, DE 19901
Kent County
Tel: 800-873-3482
Fax: 800-234-8522

Norman N. Aerenson, Esq.
2213 Concord Pike
Wilmington, DE 19803
New Castle County
Tel: 302-652-2100
Fax: 302-652-8600

Organization Services, Inc.
3411 Silverside Road
103 Springer Building
Wilmington, DE 19810
New Castle County
Tel: 302-478-6160
Fax: 302-478-3667

Paracorp Incorporated
15 East North Street
Dover, DE 19901
Kent County
Tel: 800-533-7272
Fax: 916-447-6091

Parkowski, Noble & Guerke
116 West Water Street
P.O. Box 598
Dover, DE 19903
Kent County
Tel: 302-678-3262
Fax: 302-678-9415

Perry F. Goldlust, Esq.
702 King Street
First Federal Plaza, Suite 600
Wilmington, De 19801
New Castle County
Tel: 302-658-1800
Fax: 302-658-1473

Piet H. Vanogtrop, Esq.
206 East Delaware Avenue
Newark, DE 19711
New Castle County
Tel: 302-368-0133
Fax: 302-368-4587

PJEKS Corporate Services, Inc.
1310 King Street
P.O. Box 1328
Wilmington, DE 19899
New Castle County
Tel: 302-888-6500
Fax: 302-888-6331
E-mail: attorneys@prickett.com
Website: http://www.prickett.com

R. Brandon Jones, Esq.
225 South State Street
Dover, DE 19901
Kent County
Tel: 302-734-7401
Fax: 302-734-5532

Real-Corp Services, Inc.
3200 Concord Pike
P.O. Box 7329
Wilmington, DE 19803
New Castle County
Tel: 302-477-3200
Fax: 302-477-3210

Registered Agents Legal Services, LLC
1220 N. Market Street, Suite 606
Wilmington, DE 19806
New Castle County
Tel: 800-400-6650
Fax: 302-421-5753

Registered Agents, Ltd.
1220 North Market Street, Suite 606
Wilmington, DE 19801
New Castle County
Tel: 800-441-5940
Tel: 302-421-5750
Fax: 302-421-5753
E-mail: corp@dca.net
Website: http://www.incusa.com

RL&F Service Corp.
One Rodney Square
10th & King Streets - 10th Floor
P.O. Box 551
Wilmington, DE 19899
New Castle County
Tel: 302-651-7642
Fax: 302-658-6548

Robert C. Lefton
913 North Market Street - Suite 1011
Wilmington, DE 19801
New Castle County
Tel: 302-656-0703
Fax: 302-656-0704

Schmittinger & Rodriguez, P.A.
414 S. State Street
P.O. Box 497
Dover, DE 19903-0497
Kent County
Tel: 302-674-0140
Fax: 302-674-1830

S.D.M. Robinson Corporate Agents, Inc.
Two Greenville Crossing, Suite 300
4001 Kennett Pike - P.O. Box 3993
Wilmington, DE 19807
New Castle County
Tel: 800-883-4INC
Tel: 302-655-6262
Tel: 302-655-6455
Fax: 302-655-1102

Security Incorporation and Service Inc.
Suite 31B - Trolley Square
Wilmington, DE 19806
New Castle County
Tel: 302-658-4814
Fax: 302-655-2087

Selden Enterprises, Inc.
2055 Limestone Road - Suite 213
Wilmington, DE 19808-5539
New Castle County
Tel: 302-999-1888
Fax: 302-999-9520

Sheldon A. Weinstein, Esq.
Rodney Square North
11th & Market Streets, 11th Floor
P.O. Box 391
Wilmington, DE 19899-0391
New Castle County
Tel: 302-571-6631
Fax: 302-571-1253

Speero Networks Inc.
349 N. Governors Ave.
Dover, DE 19904
Kent County
Tel: 302-242-2879
Fax: 302-736-5200
E-mail: admin@speero.com

Stephen W. Spence, Esq.
1200 North Broom Street
Wilmington, DE 19806
New Castle County
Tel: 302-655-4200
Fax: 302-655-4210

Tunnell & Raysor
South Pine & East Race Streets
Tunnell Building, P.O. Box 151
Georgetown, DE 19947
Sussex County
Tel: 302-856-7313
Fax: 302-856-7329

Twilley & Street, P.A.
426 South State Street
P.O. Box 1366
Dover, DE 19903
Kent County
Tel: 800-253-8488
Tel: 302-735-8400
Fax: 302-735-8417
E-mail: Gstreet@Twilleystreet.com

United Corporate Services, Inc.
15 East North Street
Dover, DE 19901
Kent County
Tel: 800-899-8648
Fax: 914-949-9618

USA Corporate Services, Inc.
15 East North Street
Dover, DE 19901
Kent County
Tel: 800-888-4360
Fax: 518-433-1489

Vance A. Funk, III, Esq.
273 East Main Street - Suite A
Newark, DE 19711
New Castle County
Tel: 302-368-2561
Fax: 302-368-9729

Vanguard Corporate Services, Ltd.
15 East North Street
Dover, DE 19901
Kent County
Tel: 518-436-5616
Fax: 518-436-3964

Whittington & Aulgur
Attorneys at Law
2979 Barley Mill Road
Yorklyn, DE 19736
New Castle County
Tel: 800-441-9459
Tel: 302-235-5800
Fax: 302-235-5900
Fax: 800-231-5593
E-mail: wa@delawarelawer.com
E-mail: info@theincorporators.com
Website: http://www.theincorporators.com

William G. Campbell
902 Market Street
P.O. Box 25130
Wilmington, DE 19899
New Castle County
Tel: 302-655-5000
Fax: 302-658-6395

William S. Hudson, Esq.
225 South State Street
Dover, DE 19901
Kent County
Tel: 302-734-7401
Fax: 302-734-5532

Worldwide Incorporators Ltd.
2530 Channin Drive
Wilmington, DE 19810
New Castle County
Tel: 800-455-8314
Tel: 302-529-5940
Fax: 302-529-5942
E-mail: worldwideinc@dca.net
Website: http://www.worldwideinc.net

XL Corporate Services, Inc.
15 East North Street
Dover, DE 19901
Kent County
Tel: 800-221-2972 ext. 571
Fax: 888-692-9256
Website: http://www.blumberg.com

Yacht Registry, Ltd.
3511 Silverside Road
Suite 105
Wilmington, DE 19810
New Castle County
Tel: 800-321-2677
Tel: 302-477-9800
Fax: 302-477-9811
E-mail: yacht@delreg.com
Website: http://delreg.com/yacht.html

YCS&T Services Corporation
1000 West Street, 17th Floor
Brandywine Building
Wilmington, DE 19801
New Castle County
Tel: 302-571-6600
Fax: 302-571-1253

Appendix C
State Registration Offices

Included in this appendix are the addresses, phone numbers, and web sites of the state offices in which a corporation must be registered. Once you have formed your Delaware corporation, you will need to register it as a foreign corporation doing busines in your home state.

You should contact the office in your state for the latest forms and fee schedule.

Alabama

Secretary of State
Corporate Section
P.O. Box 5616
Montgomery, AL 36130-5616
334-242-5324

Website: http://www.sos.state.al.us

Alaska

Department of Commerce and Economic Development
Division of B.S.C.
Attention: Corporation Section
P.O. Box 110807
Juneau, AK 99811-0807
907-465-2521
Fax: 907-465-2549

Website:
http://www.dced.state.ak.us/bsc/corps.htm

Arizona

Arizona Corporation Commission
1300 W. Washington
Phoenix, AZ 85007-2929
602-542-3135
800-345-5819 (Arizona residents only)
or
400 W. Congress
Tucson, AZ 85701-1347
520-628-6560

Website: http://www.cc.state.az.us/corp/

Arkansas

Secretary of State
Corporation Division
State Capital, Room 58
Little Rock, AR 72201-1094
501-682-5151

Website:
http://www.sosweb.state.ar.us/business.html

California

Office of the Secretary of State
Limited Liability Company Unit
1500 - 11th Street,
P.O. Box 944260
Sacramento, CA 94244-2600
916-653-3795

Website:
http://www.ss.ca.gov/business/corp/corporate.htm

Colorado

Secretary of State
Corporations Office
1560 Broadway, Suite 200
Denver, CO 80202
303-894-2251
Fax: 303-894-2251

Website:
http://www.sos.state.co.us/pubs/business/main.htm

Connecticut

Secretary of State
30 Trinity Street
P.O. Box 150470
Hartford, CT 06106-0470
860-566-4128

Website: http://www.sots.state.ct.us

Delaware

State of Delaware
Division of Corporations
P.O.Box 898
Dover, DE 19903
302-739-3073
Name Reservation: 900-420-8042

Website: http://www.state.de.us/corp

District of Columbia

Department of Consumer and Regulatory Affairs
Corporation Division
941 North Capitol Street NE
Washington, D.C. 20002
202-727-7283

Website:
http://www.dcra.dc.gov/information/build_pla/business_corporations_division.shtm

Florida

Secretary of State
Division of Corporations
P.O. Box 6327
Tallahassee, FL 32314
850-488-9000
850-487-6052

Website: http://www.dos.state.fl.us

Georgia

Secretary of State
315 West Tower
2 Martin Luther King, Jr. Drive
Atlanta, GA 30330
404-656-2817
Fax: 404-651-9059

Website: http://www.SOS.State.Ga.US/

Hawaii

Business Registration Division
Department of Commerce
and Consumer Affairs
1010 Richards Street
P.O. Box 40
Honolulu, HI 96810
808-586-2727

Website: http://www.hawaii.gov/dcca/breg-seu

Idaho

Secretary of State
700 W. Jefferson, Basement West
Boise, ID 83720-0080
208-334-2301

Website: http://www.idsos.state.id.us/

Illinois

Secretary of State
Business Services Dept.
328 Howlett Building, Room 359
Springfield, IL 62756
LLC Division: 217-524-8008
Name availability: 217-782-9520

Website:
http://www.sos.state.il.us/departments/business_services/business.html

Indiana

Secretary of State
Room 155, State House
302 W. Washington, Room E018
Indianapolis, IN 46204
317-232-6576 or
317-232-6531 or
800-726-8000

Website: http://www.state.in.us/sos/business

Iowa

Secretary of State
Corporations Division
Hoover Building
Des Moines, IA 50319
515-281-5204
Fax: 515-242-6556

Website: http://www.sos.state.ia.us/business

Kansas

Secretary of State
Corporation Division
Memorial Hall, 1st Floor
120 SW 10th Avenue
Topeka, KS 66612-1594
785-296-4564

Website: http://www.kssos.org

Kentucky

Commonwealth of Kentucky
Office of the Secretary of State
P.O.Box 718
Frankfort, KY 40602
502-564-2848
502-564-7330

Website: http://www.sos.state.ky.us

Louisiana

Secretary of State
Corporations Division
P.O. Box 94125
Baton Rouge, LA 70804-9125
504-925-4704

Website: http://www.sec.state.la.us/comm/corp-index.htm

Maine

Secretary of State
Bureau of Corporations, Elections, and Commissions
101 State House Station
Augusta, ME 04333-0101
Forms: 207-287-4195
Business answers: 800-872-3838
Fax: 207-287-5874

Website: http://www.state.me.us/sos/cec/

Maryland

State Department of Assessments and Taxation
Corporate Charter Division
301 West Preston Street, Rm. 809
Baltimore, MD 21201
410-225 -1340 or
410-767-1330

Website:
http://www.dat.state.md.us/sdatweb/character.html

Massachusetts

Secretary of the Commonwealth
Corporations Division
One Ashburton Place
17th Floor
Boston, MA 02108-1512
617-727-9640 or 617-727-9440
Citizen Information Service
800-392-6090

Website:
http://www.state.ma.us/sec/cor/coridx.htm

Michigan

Michigan Department of Commerce
Corporation and Securities Bureau
Corporation Division
7150 Harris Drive
P.O. Box 30054
Lansing, MI 48909
517-334-6302

Website: http://www.cis.state.mi.us/bcs/corp/

Minnesota

Secretary of State
Division of Corporations
180 State Office Building
100 Constitution Ave.
St. Paul, MN 55155-1299
612-296-2803

Website:
http://www.sos.state.mn.us/business/index.html

Mississippi

Secretary of State
Business Services Division
P.O. Box 136
Jackson, MS 39205-0136
601-359-1333 or
800-256-3494
Fax: 601-359-1499

Website:
http://www.sos.state.ms.us/busserv/corp/corporations.html

Missouri

Secretary of State, Corporation Division
P.O. Box 778
Jefferson City, MO 65102
573-751-2359 or
573-751-4153

Website:
http://mosl.sos.state.mo.us/bus-ser/soscor.html

Montana

Secretary of State
P.O. Box 202801
Helena, MT 59620-2801
406-444-2034
Fax: 406-444-3976

Website: http://www.sos.state.mt.us/css/index.asp

Nebraska

Secretary of State
Suite 1301 State Capitol
Lincoln, NE 68509
402-471-4079
Fax: 402-471-3666

Website:
http://www.nol.org/home/business.html

Nevada

Secretary of State
Capitol Complex
Carson City, NV 89710
702-687-5203 or
702-687-5105
Fax: 702-687-5071

Website:
http://sos.state.nv.us/comm_rec/index.htm

New Hampshire

Secretary of State
Corporate Division
State House, Room 204
107 N. Main Street
Concord, NH 03301-4989
603-271-3244

Website: www.state.nh.us/sos/corporate/index.htm

New Jersey

Secretary of State
Division of Revenue/Corporate Filing Unit
P. O. Box 308
Trenton, NJ 08625-0308
609-530-6400

Website: http://www.state.nj.us/njbiz

New Mexico

Public Regulation Commission
Corporation Bureau
P.O. Box 1269
Santa Fe, NM 87504-1269
505-827-4511 or 505-827-4504

Website: http://www.nmprc.state.nm.us/corporation.htm

New York

Department of State
Division of Corporations and State Records
41 State Street
Albany, N.Y. 12231-0001
518-473-2492 or 518-474-6200

Website:
http://www.dos.state.ny.us/corp/coprwww.html

North Carolina

Corporations Division
Department of Secretary of State
P.O. Box 29622
Raleigh, NC 27626-0622
919-807-2225

Website: http://www.secretary.state.nc.us/corporations

North Dakota

Secretary of State
Capitol Building
600 East Boulevard Avenue Dept. 108
Bismarck, ND 58505-0500
701-328-2900
Fax: 701-328-2992

Website: http://www.state.nd.us/sec/business/businessinforegmnu.htm

Ohio

Secretary of State
Corporations Division
30 E. Broad St., 16th Floor
Columbus, OH 43215
614-466-3910

Website: http://www.state.oh.us/sos/

OKLAHOMA

Secretary of State-Corporation Division
2300 N. Lincoln Blvd., Room 101
State Capitol Building
Oklahoma City, OK 73105
405-521-3911

Website: http://www.sos.state.ok.us/business/business%20information.htm

OREGON

Secretary of State
Corporation Division
255 Capitol St. NE, Suite 151
Salem, OR 97310-1327
503-986-2200
Fax: 503-378-4381

Website: http://www.sos.state.or.us/corporation

PENNSYLVANIA

Department of State
Corporation Bureau
P. O. Box 8722
Harrisburg, PA 17105-8722
717-787-1057

Website: http://www.dos.state.pa.us/corps/corp.htm

RHODE ISLAND

Secretary of State
100 N. Main St.
Providence, RI 02903
401-222-3040
Fax: 401-277-1309

Website:
http://www.corps.state.ri.us/corporations.htm

SOUTH CAROLINA

Secretary of State
P.O. Box 11350
Columbia, SC 29211
803-734-2158

Website:
http://www.leginfo.state.sc.us/secretary.html

SOUTH DAKOTA

Secretary of State
State Capital
500 E. Capital Street
Pierre, SD 57501
605-773-3537

Website:
http://www.state.sd.us/state/executive/sos/sos.htm

TENNESSEE

Department of State
Division of Business Services
6th Floor, William R. Snodgrass Tower
312 Eighth Avenue North
Nashville, TN 37243
615-741-2286

Website: http://www.state.tn.us/sos

TEXAS

Secretary of State
Corporation Division
P.O. Box 13697
Austin, TX 78711-3697
512-463-5555
To obtain forms: 900-263-0060

Website: http://www.sos.state.tx.us/

UTAH

Department of Commerce
Division of Corporations and Commercial Code
160 E. 300 South, Box 146705
Salt Lake City, UT 84114-6705
801-530-4849

Website: http://www.commerce.utah.gov

VERMONT

Secretary of State
Heritage One Building
81 River Street, Drawer 09
Montpelier, VT 05609-1104
802-828-2363

Website: http://www.sec.state.vt.us/

VIRGINIA

State Corporation Commission
Jefferson Building
P.O. Box 1197
Richmond, VA 23218-1197
804-371-9733

Website:
http://www.state.va.us/scc/division.clk/index.htm

WASHINGTON

Secretary of State
Corporation Division
James M. Dollirer Building
801 Capitol Way South
P.O. Box 40234
Olympia, WA 98504-0234
360-753-7115

Website: http://www.secstate.wa.gov

WEST VIRGINIA

Secretary of State
Building 1, Suite 157-K
1900 Kanawha Boulevard East
Charleston, WV 25305
304-558-8000

Website: http://www.state.wv.us/sos/

WISCONSIN

Dept. of Financial Institutions
P.O. Box 7846
Madison, WI 53707-7846
608-266-3590

Website: www.state.wi.us/agencies/sos

Website for Forms:
http://www.wdfi.org/corp/forms.htm

WYOMING

Secretary of State
State Capitol Building
Cheyenne, WY 82002-0020
Tel: 307-777-7311 or 307-777-7312
Fax: 307-777-5339

Website: http://soswy.state.wy.us/
E-mail: Corporations@missc.state.wy.us

Appendix D
Forms

This appendix contains the blank forms which can be used to form a Delaware corporation or LLC. Be sure to read the text of this book and each form before using it. If a form does not fit your situation, you may want to change it or consult an attorney. You should also consult an attorney if you do not understand the forms.

Forms Used for Both Corporations and LLCs

Forms Used Only for Corporations

State of Delaware - Division of Corporations

FAX **DOCUMENT FILING SHEET**

☐	☐	☐	☐	☐	☐
Priority 1 (Two Hour Service)	Priority 2 (Same Day)	Priority 3 (24 Hour)	Priority 4 (Must Approvals)	Priority 5 (Reg. Approvals)	Priority 6 (Reg. Work)

DATE SUBMITTED ____________
REQUESTOR NAME ____________________
____
____
ATTN ____________________
PHONE ____________________

NAME of COMPANY/ENTITY ____________________

CORPORATION FILE NUMBER/RESERVATION NUMBER ____________

TYPE OF DOCUMENT ____________________

CHANGE of NAME_______ CHANGE of AGENT/OFFICE_______ CHANGE OF STOCK_______

CORPORATIONS	
FRANCHISE TAX YEAR_______	$____________
FILING FEE TAX	$____________
RECEIVING & INDEXING	$____________
CERTIFIED COPIES NO.____	$____________
SPECIAL SERVICES	$____________
KENT COUNTY RECORDER	$____________
NEW CASTLE COUNTY RECORDER	$____________
SUSSEX COUNTY RECORDER	$____________
TOTAL	$____________

METHOD OF RETURN

___ MESSENGER/PICKUP
___ FED. EXPRESS Acct.#____________
___ REGULAR MAIL
___ FAX No. ____________
___ OTHER ____________

COMMENTS/FILING INSTRUCTIONS

CREDIT CARD CHARGES

You have my authorization to charge my credit card for this service:

_ _ _ _-_ _ _ _-_ _ _ _-_ _ _ _ Exp. Date_______

Signature ____________________ Printed Name ____________________

This page intentionally left blank.

REQUEST FOR CORPORATE FORMS

To: Department of Corporate Filings

Please send us any of the following which are available without charge and advise of the cost of any for which there is a charge.

Form for registering a foreign: ☐ corporation ☐ LLC to do business in this state.

Copy of statutes applicable to foreign businesses doing business in this state.

Please send to: ______________________________
Name (Printed or typed)

____
Address

____
City, State & Zip

This page intentionally left blank.

Form **SS-4**

(Rev. December 2001)

Department of the Treasury
Internal Revenue Service

Application for Employer Identification Number

(For use by employers, corporations, partnerships, trusts, estates, churches, government agencies, Indian tribal entities, certain individuals, and others.)

► See separate instructions for each line. ► Keep a copy for your records.

EIN

OMB No. 1545-0003

Type or print clearly.

1 Legal name of entity (or individual) for whom the EIN is being requested

2 Trade name of business (if different from name on line 1) | 3 Executor, trustee, "care of" name

4a Mailing address (room, apt., suite no. and street, or P.O. box) | 5a Street address (if different) (Do not enter a P.O. box.)

4b City, state, and ZIP code | 5b City, state, and ZIP code

6 County and state where principal business is located

7a Name of principal officer, general partner, grantor, owner, or trustor | 7b SSN, ITIN, or EIN

8a Type of entity (check only one box)

- ☐ Sole proprietor (SSN) ______
- ☐ Partnership
- ☐ Corporation (enter form number to be filed) ► ______
- ☐ Personal service corp.
- ☐ Church or church-controlled organization
- ☐ Other nonprofit organization (specify) ► ______
- ☐ Other (specify) ►
- ☐ Estate (SSN of decedent) ______
- ☐ Plan administrator (SSN) ______
- ☐ Trust (SSN of grantor) ______
- ☐ National Guard
- ☐ Farmers' cooperative
- ☐ REMIC
- ☐ State/local government
- ☐ Federal government/military
- ☐ Indian tribal governments/enterprises

Group Exemption Number (GEN) ► ______

8b If a corporation, name the state or foreign country (if applicable) where incorporated | State | Foreign country

9 Reason for applying (check only one box)

- ☐ Started new business (specify type) ► ______
- ☐ Hired employees (Check the box and see line 12.)
- ☐ Compliance with IRS withholding regulations
- ☐ Other (specify) ►
- ☐ Banking purpose (specify purpose) ► ______
- ☐ Changed type of organization (specify new type) ► ______
- ☐ Purchased going business
- ☐ Created a trust (specify type) ► ______
- ☐ Created a pension plan (specify type) ► ______

10 Date business started or acquired (month, day, year) | 11 Closing month of accounting year

12 First date wages or annuities were paid or will be paid (month, day, year). **Note:** *If applicant is a withholding agent, enter date income will first be paid to nonresident alien. (month, day, year)* . . . . ►

13 Highest number of employees expected in the next 12 months. **Note:** *If the applicant does not expect to have any employees during the period, enter "-0-."* . . . . ►

Agricultural	Household	Other

14 Check **one** box that best describes the principal activity of your business.

- ☐ Construction
- ☐ Real estate
- ☐ Rental & leasing
- ☐ Manufacturing
- ☐ Transportation & warehousing
- ☐ Finance & insurance
- ☐ Health care & social assistance
- ☐ Accommodation & food service
- ☐ Other (specify)
- ☐ Wholesale–agent/broker
- ☐ Wholesale–other
- ☐ Retail

15 Indicate principal line of merchandise sold; specific construction work done; products produced; or services provided.

16a Has the applicant ever applied for an employer identification number for this or any other business? . . . . . ☐ **Yes** ☐ **No**

Note: *If "Yes," please complete lines 16b and 16c.*

16b If you checked "Yes" on line 16a, give applicant's legal name and trade name shown on prior application if different from line 1 or 2 above.

Legal name ► Trade name ►

16c Approximate date when, and city and state where, the application was filed. Enter previous employer identification number if known.

Approximate date when filed (mo., day, year)	City and state where filed	Previous EIN

Third Party Designee

Complete this section **only** if you want to authorize the named individual to receive the entity's EIN and answer questions about the completion of this form.

Designee's name	Designee's telephone number (include area code) ( )
Address and ZIP code	Designee's fax number (include area code) ( )

Under penalties of perjury, I declare that I have examined this application, and to the best of my knowledge and belief, it is true, correct, and complete.

Name and title (type or print clearly) ►

Applicant's telephone number (include area code) ( )

Signature ► Date ►

Applicant's fax number (include area code) ( )

For Privacy Act and Paperwork Reduction Act Notice, see separate instructions. Cat. No. 16055N Form **SS-4** (Rev. 12-2001)

Do I Need an EIN?

File Form SS-4 if the applicant entity does not already have an EIN but is required to show an EIN on any return, statement, or other document.[1] **See also the separate instructions for each line on Form SS-4.**

IF the applicant...	AND...	THEN...
Started a new business	Does not currently have (nor expect to have) employees	Complete lines 1, 2, 4a-6, 8a, and 9-16c.
Hired (or will hire) employees, including household employees	Does not already have an EIN	Complete lines 1, 2, 4a-6, 7a-b (if applicable), 8a, 8b (if applicable), and 9-16c.
Opened a bank account	Needs an EIN for banking purposes only	Complete lines 1-5b, 7a-b (if applicable), 8a, 9, and 16a-c.
Changed type of organization	Either the legal character of the organization or its ownership changed (e.g., you incorporate a sole proprietorship or form a partnership)[2]	Complete lines 1-16c (as applicable).
Purchased a going business[3]	Does not already have an EIN	Complete lines 1-16c (as applicable).
Created a trust	The trust is other than a grantor trust or an IRA trust[4]	Complete lines 1-16c (as applicable).
Created a pension plan as a plan administrator[5]	Needs an EIN for reporting purposes	Complete lines 1, 2, 4a-6, 8a, 9, and 16a-c.
Is a foreign person needing an EIN to comply with IRS withholding regulations	Needs an EIN to complete a Form W-8 (other than Form W-8ECI), avoid withholding on portfolio assets, or claim tax treaty benefits[6]	Complete lines 1-5b, 7a-b (SSN or ITIN optional), 8a-9, and 16a-c.
Is administering an estate	Needs an EIN to report estate income on Form 1041	Complete lines 1, 3, 4a-b, 8a, 9, and 16a-c.
Is a withholding agent for taxes on non-wage income paid to an alien (i.e., individual, corporation, or partnership, etc.)	Is an agent, broker, fiduciary, manager, tenant, or spouse who is required to file **Form 1042,** Annual Withholding Tax Return for U.S. Source Income of Foreign Persons	Complete lines 1, 2, 3 (if applicable), 4a-5b, 7a-b (if applicable), 8a, 9, and 16a-c.
Is a state or local agency	Serves as a tax reporting agent for public assistance recipients under Rev. Proc. 80-4, 1980-1 C.B. 581[7]	Complete lines 1, 2, 4a-5b, 8a, 9, and 16a-c.
Is a single-member LLC	Needs an EIN to file **Form 8832,** Classification Election, for filing employment tax returns, **or** for state reporting purposes[8]	Complete lines 1-16c (as applicable).
Is an S corporation	Needs an EIN to file **Form 2553,** Election by a Small Business Corporation[9]	Complete lines 1-16c (as applicable).

[1] For example, a sole proprietorship or self-employed farmer who establishes a qualified retirement plan, or is required to file excise, employment, alcohol, tobacco, or firearms returns, must have an EIN. **A partnership, corporation, REMIC (real estate mortgage investment conduit), nonprofit organization (church, club, etc.), or farmers' cooperative must use an EIN for any tax-related purpose even if the entity does not have employees.**

[2] However, **do not** apply for a new EIN if the existing entity only **(a)** changed its business name, **(b)** elected on Form 8832 to change the way it is taxed (or is covered by the default rules), or **(c)** terminated its partnership status because at least 50% of the total interests in partnership capital and profits were sold or exchanged within a 12-month period. (The EIN of the terminated partnership should continue to be used. See Regulations section 301.6109-1(d)(2)(iii).)

[3] Do not use the EIN of the prior business unless you became the "owner" of a corporation by acquiring its stock.

[4] However, IRA trusts that are required to file **Form 990-T,** Exempt Organization Business Income Tax Return, must have an EIN.

[5] A plan administrator is the person or group of persons specified as the administrator by the instrument under which the plan is operated.

[6] Entities applying to be a Qualified Intermediary (QI) need a QI-EIN even if they already have an EIN. **See Rev. Proc. 2000-12.**

[7] See also *Household employer* on page 4. (**Note:** State or local agencies may need an EIN for other reasons, e.g., hired employees.)

[8] Most LLCs **do not** need to file Form 8832. See **Limited liability company (LLC)** on page 4 for details on completing Form SS-4 for an LLC.

[9] An existing corporation that is electing or revoking S corporation status should use its previously-assigned EIN.

Instructions for Form SS-4

(Rev. December 2001)

Department of the Treasury
Internal Revenue Service

Application for Employer Identification Number

Section references are to the Internal Revenue Code unless otherwise noted.

General Instructions

Use these instructions to complete **Form SS-4,** Application for Employer Identification Number. Also see **Do I Need an EIN?** on page 2 of Form SS-4.

Purpose of Form

Use Form SS-4 to apply for an employer identification number (EIN). An EIN is a nine-digit number (for example, 12-3456789) assigned to sole proprietors, corporations, partnerships, estates, trusts, and other entities for tax filing and reporting purposes. The information you provide on this form will establish your business tax account.

CAUTION *An EIN is for use in connection with your business activities only. Do **not** use your EIN in place of your social security number (SSN).*

File only one Form SS-4. Generally, a sole proprietor should file only one Form SS-4 and needs only one EIN, regardless of the number of businesses operated as a sole proprietorship or trade names under which a business operates. However, if the proprietorship incorporates or enters into a partnership, a new EIN is required. Also, each corporation in an affiliated group must have its own EIN.

EIN applied for, but not received. If you do not have an EIN by the time a **return** is due, write "Applied For" and the date you applied in the space shown for the number. **Do not** show your social security number (SSN) as an EIN on returns.

If you do not have an EIN by the time a **tax deposit** is due, send your payment to the Internal Revenue Service Center for your filing area as shown in the instructions for the form that you are are filing. Make your check or money order payable to the **"United States Treasury"** and show your name (as shown on Form SS-4), address, type of tax, period covered, and date you applied for an EIN.

Related Forms and Publications

The following **forms** and **instructions** may be useful to filers of Form SS-4:

- **Form 990-T,** Exempt Organization Business Income Tax Return
- **Instructions for Form 990-T**
- **Schedule C (Form 1040),** Profit or Loss From Business
- **Schedule F (Form 1040),** Profit or Loss From Farming
- **Instructions for Form 1041 and Schedules A, B, D, G, I, J, and K-1,** U.S. Income Tax Return for Estates and Trusts
- **Form 1042,** Annual Withholding Tax Return for U.S. Source Income of Foreign Persons
- **Instructions for Form 1065,** U.S. Return of Partnership Income
- **Instructions for Form 1066,** U.S. Real Estate Mortgage Investment Conduit (REMIC) Income Tax Return
- **Instructions for Forms 1120 and 1120-A**
- **Form 2553,** Election by a Small Business Corporation
- **Form 2848,** Power of Attorney and Declaration of Representative
- **Form 8821,** Tax Information Authorization
- **Form 8832,** Entity Classification Election

For more **information** about filing Form SS-4 and related issues, see:

- **Circular A,** Agricultural Employer's Tax Guide (Pub. 51)
- **Circular E,** Employer's Tax Guide (Pub. 15)
- **Pub. 538,** Accounting Periods and Methods
- **Pub. 542,** Corporations
- **Pub. 557,** Exempt Status for Your Organization
- **Pub. 583,** Starting a Business and Keeping Records
- **Pub. 966,** EFTPS: Now a Full Range of Electronic Choices to Pay All Your Federal Taxes
- **Pub. 1635,** Understanding Your EIN
- **Package 1023,** Application for Recognition of Exemption
- **Package 1024,** Application for Recognition of Exemption Under Section 501(a)

How To Get Forms and Publications

Phone. You can order forms, instructions, and publications by phone 24 hours a day, 7 days a week. Just call 1-800-TAX-FORM (1-800-829-3676). You should receive your order or notification of its status within 10 workdays.

Personal computer. With your personal computer and modem, you can get the forms and information you need using the IRS Web Site at **www.irs.gov** or File Transfer Protocol at **ftp.irs.gov.**

CD-ROM. For small businesses, return preparers, or others who may frequently need tax forms or publications, a CD-ROM containing over 2,000 tax products (including many prior year forms) can be purchased from the National Technical Information Service (NTIS).

To order **Pub. 1796,** Federal Tax Products on CD-ROM, call **1-877-CDFORMS** (1-877-233-6767) toll free or connect to **www.irs.gov/cdorders.**

Tax Help for Your Business

IRS-sponsored Small Business Workshops provide information about your Federal and state tax obligations. For information about workshops in your area, call 1-800-829-1040 and ask for your Taxpayer Education Coordinator.

How To Apply

You can apply for an EIN by telephone, fax, or mail depending on how soon you need to use the EIN.

Application by Tele-TIN. Under the Tele-TIN program, you can receive your EIN by telephone and use it immediately to file a return or make a payment. To receive an EIN by telephone, IRS suggests that you complete Form SS-4 so that you will have all relevant information available. Then call the Tele-TIN number at 1-866-816-2065. (International applicants must call 215-516-6999.) Tele-TIN hours of operation are 7:30 a.m. to 5:30 p.m. The person making the call must be authorized to sign the form or be an authorized designee. See **Signature** and **Third Party Designee** on page 6. Also see the **TIP** below.

An IRS representative will use the information from the Form SS-4 to establish your account and assign you an EIN. Write the number you are given on the upper right corner of the form and sign and date it. Keep this copy for your records.

If requested by an IRS representative, mail or fax (facsimile) the signed Form SS-4 (including any Third Party Designee authorization) **within 24 hours** to the Tele-TIN Unit at the service center address provided by the IRS representative.

TIP *Taxpayer representatives can use Tele-TIN to apply for an EIN on behalf of their client and request that the EIN be faxed to their* ***client*** *on the same day. (****Note:*** *By utilizing this procedure, you are authorizing the IRS to fax the EIN without a cover sheet.)*

Application by Fax-TIN. Under the Fax-TIN program, you can receive your EIN by fax within 4 business days. Complete and fax Form SS-4 to the IRS using the Fax-TIN number listed below for your state. A long-distance charge to callers outside of the local calling area will apply. Fax-TIN numbers can only be used to apply for an EIN. **The numbers may change without notice.** Fax-TIN is available 24 hours a day, 7 days a week.

Be sure to provide your fax number so that IRS can fax the EIN back to you. (**Note:** By utilizing this procedure, you are authorizing the IRS to fax the EIN without a cover sheet.)

Do not call Tele-TIN for the same entity because duplicate EINs may be issued. See **Third Party Designee** on page 6.

Application by mail. Complete Form SS-4 at least 4 to 5 weeks before you will need an EIN. Sign and date the application and mail it to the service center address for your state. You will receive your EIN in the mail in approximately 4 weeks. See also **Third Party Designee** on page 6.

Call 1-800-829-1040 to verify a number or to ask about the status of an application by mail.

If your principal business, office or agency, or legal residence in the case of an individual, is located in:	Call the Tele-TIN or Fax-TIN number shown or file with the "Internal Revenue Service Center" at:
Connecticut, Delaware, District of Columbia, Florida, Georgia, Maine, Maryland, Massachusetts, New Hampshire, New Jersey, New York, North Carolina, Ohio, Pennsylvania, Rhode Island, South Carolina, Vermont, Virginia, West Virginia	Attn: EIN Operation Holtsville, NY 00501 Tele-TIN 866-816-2065 Fax-TIN 631-447-8960
Illinois, Indiana, Kentucky, Michigan	Attn: EIN Operation Cincinnati, OH 45999 Tele-TIN 866-816-2065 Fax-TIN 859-669-5760
Alabama, Alaska, Arizona, Arkansas, California, Colorado, Hawaii, Idaho, Iowa, Kansas, Louisiana, Minnesota, Mississippi, Missouri, Montana, Nebraska, Nevada, New Mexico, North Dakota, Oklahoma, Oregon, Puerto Rico, South Dakota, Tennessee, Texas, Utah, Washington, Wisconsin, Wyoming	Attn: EIN Operation Philadelphia, PA 19255 Tele-TIN 866-816-2065 Fax-TIN 215-516-3990
If you have no legal residence, principal place of business, or principal office or agency in any state:	Attn: EIN Operation Philadelphia, PA 19255 Tele-TIN 215-516-6999 Fax-TIN 215-516-3990

Specific Instructions

Print or type all entries on Form SS-4. Follow the instructions for each line to expedite processing and to avoid unnecessary IRS requests for additional information. Enter "N/A" (nonapplicable) on the lines that do not apply.

Line 1—Legal name of entity (or individual) for whom the EIN is being requested. Enter the legal name of the entity (or individual) applying for the EIN exactly as it appears on the social security card, charter, or other applicable legal document.

Individuals. Enter your first name, middle initial, and last name. If you are a sole proprietor, enter your individual name, not your business name. Enter your business name on line 2. Do not use abbreviations or nicknames on line 1.

Trusts. Enter the name of the trust.

Estate of a decedent. Enter the name of the estate.

Partnerships. Enter the legal name of the partnership as it appears in the partnership agreement.

Corporations. Enter the corporate name as it appears in the corporation charter or other legal document creating it.

Plan administrators. Enter the name of the plan administrator. A plan administrator who already has an EIN should use that number.

Line 2—Trade name of business. Enter the trade name of the business if different from the legal name. The trade name is the "doing business as" (DBA) name.

CAUTION *Use the full legal name shown on line 1 on all tax returns filed for the entity. (However, if you enter a trade name on line 2 and choose to use the trade name instead of the legal name, enter the trade name on **all returns** you file.) To prevent processing delays and errors, **always** use the legal name only (or the trade name only) on **all** tax returns.*

Line 3—Executor, trustee, "care of" name. Trusts enter the name of the trustee. Estates enter the name of the executor, administrator, or other fiduciary. If the entity applying has a designated person to receive tax information, enter that person's name as the "care of" person. Enter the individual's first name, middle initial, and last name.

Lines 4a-b—Mailing address. Enter the mailing address for the entity's correspondence. If line 3 is completed, enter the address for the executor, trustee or "care of" person. Generally, this address will be used on all tax returns.

TIP *File **Form 8822**, Change of Address, to report any subsequent changes to the entity's mailing address.*

Lines 5a-b—Street address. Provide the entity's physical address **only** if different from its mailing address shown in lines 4a-b. **Do not** enter a P.O. box number here.

Line 6—County and state where principal business is located. Enter the entity's primary **physical** location.

Lines 7a-b—Name of principal officer, general partner, grantor, owner, or trustor. Enter the first name, middle initial, last name, and SSN of **(a)** the principal officer if the business is a corporation, **(b)** a general partner if a partnership, **(c)** the owner of an entity that is disregarded as separate from its owner (disregarded entities owned by a corporation enter the corporation's name and EIN), or **(d)** a grantor, owner, or trustor if a trust.

If the person in question is an **alien individual** with a previously assigned individual taxpayer identification number (ITIN), enter the ITIN in the space provided and submit a copy of an official identifying document. If necessary, complete **Form W-7,** Application for IRS Individual Taxpayer Identification Number, to obtain an ITIN.

You are **required** to enter an SSN, ITIN, or EIN unless the only reason you are applying for an EIN is to make an entity classification election (see Regulations section 301.7701-1 through 301.7701-3) and you are a nonresident alien with no effectively connected income from sources within the United States.

Line 8a—Type of entity. Check the box that best describes the type of entity applying for the EIN. If you are an alien individual with an ITIN previously assigned to you, enter the ITIN in place of a requested SSN.

CAUTION *This is not an election for a tax classification of an entity. See **"Limited liability company (LLC)"** on page 4.*

Other. If not specifically mentioned, check the "Other" box, enter the type of entity and the type of return, if any, that will be filed (for example, "Common Trust Fund, Form 1065" or "Created a Pension Plan"). Do not enter "N/A." If you are an alien individual applying for an EIN, see the **Lines 7a-b** instructions above.

- **Household employer.** If you are an individual, check the "Other" box and enter "Household Employer" and your SSN. If you are a state or local agency serving as a tax reporting agent for public assistance recipients who become household employers, check the "Other" box and enter "Household Employer Agent." If you are a trust that qualifies as a household employer, you do not need a separate EIN for reporting tax information relating to household employees; use the EIN of the trust.
- **QSub.** For a qualified subchapter S subsidiary (QSub) check the "Other" box and specify "QSub."
- **Withholding agent.** If you are a withholding agent required to file Form 1042, check the "Other" box and enter "Withholding Agent."

Sole proprietor. Check this box if you file Schedule C, C-EZ, or F (Form 1040) and have a qualified plan, or are required to file excise, employment, or alcohol, tobacco, or firearms returns, or are a payer of gambling winnings. Enter your SSN (or ITIN) in the space provided. If you are a nonresident alien with no effectively connected income from sources within the United States, you do not need to enter an SSN or ITIN.

Corporation. This box is for any corporation **other than a personal service corporation.** If you check this box, enter the income tax form number to be filed by the entity in the space provided.

CAUTION *If you entered **"1120S"** after the "Corporation" checkbox, the corporation **must** file Form 2553 **no later than the 15th day of the 3rd month of the tax year the election is to take effect.** Until Form 2553 has been received and approved, you will be considered a Form 1120 filer. See the Instructions for Form 2553.*

Personal service corp. Check this box if the entity is a personal service corporation. An entity is a personal service corporation for a tax year only if:

- The principal activity of the entity during the testing period (prior tax year) for the tax year is the performance of personal services substantially by employee-owners, and
- The employee-owners own at least 10% of the fair market value of the outstanding stock in the entity on the last day of the testing period.

Personal services include performance of services in such fields as health, law, accounting, or consulting. For more information about personal service corporations, see the Instructions for Forms 1120 and 1120-A and Pub. 542.

Other nonprofit organization. Check this box if the nonprofit organization is other than a church or church-controlled organization and specify the type of nonprofit organization (for example, an educational organization).

CAUTION: *If the organization also seeks tax-exempt status, you **must** file either Package 1023 or Package 1024. See Pub. 557 for more information.*

If the organization is covered by a group exemption letter, enter the four-digit **group exemption number (GEN).** (Do not confuse the GEN with the nine-digit EIN.) If you do not know the GEN, contact the parent organization. Get Pub. 557 for more information about group exemption numbers.

Plan administrator. If the plan administrator is an individual, enter the plan administrator's SSN in the space provided.

REMIC. Check this box if the entity has elected to be treated as a real estate mortgage investment conduit (REMIC). See the Instructions for Form 1066 for more information.

Limited liability company (LLC). An LLC is an entity organized under the laws of a state or foreign country as a limited liability company. For Federal tax purposes, an LLC may be treated as a partnership or corporation or be disregarded as an entity separate from its owner.

By **default,** a domestic LLC with only one member is **disregarded** as an entity separate from its owner and must include all of its income and expenses on the owner's tax return (e.g., **Schedule C (Form 1040)**). Also by default, a domestic LLC with two or more members is treated as a partnership. A domestic LLC may file Form 8832 to avoid either default classification and elect to be classified as an association taxable as a corporation. For more information on entity classifications (including the rules for foreign entities), see the instructions for Form 8832.

CAUTION: ***Do not*** *file Form 8832 if the LLC accepts the default classifications above.* ***However, if the LLC will be electing S Corporation status, it must timely file both Form 8832 and Form 2553.***

Complete Form SS-4 for LLCs as follows:

- A single-member, domestic LLC that accepts the default classification (above) does not need an EIN and generally should not file Form SS-4. Generally, the LLC should use the name and EIN of its **owner** for all Federal tax purposes. However, the reporting and payment of employment taxes for employees of the LLC may be made using the name and EIN of **either** the owner or the LLC as explained in Notice 99-6, 1999-1 C.B. 321. You can find Notice 99-6 on page 12 of Internal Revenue Bulletin 1999-3 at **www.irs.gov.** (**Note:** If the LLC-applicant indicates in box 13 that it has employees or expects to have employees, the owner (whether an individual or other entity) of a single-member domestic LLC will also be assigned its own EIN (if it does not already have one) even if the LLC will be filing the employment tax returns.)
- A single-member, domestic LLC that accepts the default classification (above) and wants an EIN for filing employment tax returns (see above) or non-Federal purposes, such as a state requirement, must check the "Other" box and write "Disregarded Entity" or, when applicable, "Disregarded Entity—Sole Proprietorship" in the space provided.
- A multi-member, domestic LLC that accepts the default classification (above) must check the "Partnership" box.
- A domestic LLC that will be filing Form 8832 to elect corporate status must check the "Corporation" box and write in "Single-Member" or "Multi-Member" immediately below the "form number" entry line.

Line 9—Reason for applying. Check only **one** box. Do not enter "N/A."

Started new business. Check this box if you are starting a new business that requires an EIN. If you check this box, enter the type of business being started. **Do not** apply if you already have an EIN and are only adding another place of business.

Hired employees. Check this box if the existing business is requesting an EIN because it has hired or is hiring employees and is therefore required to file employment tax returns. **Do not** apply if you already have an EIN and are only hiring employees. For information on employment taxes (e.g., for family members), see Circular E.

CAUTION: *You may be required to make electronic deposits of all depository taxes (such as employment tax, excise tax, and corporate income tax) using the Electronic Federal Tax Payment System (EFTPS). See section 11, Depositing Taxes, of Circular E and Pub. 966.*

Created a pension plan. Check this box if you have created a pension plan and need an EIN for reporting purposes. Also, enter the type of plan in the space provided.

TIP: *Check this box if you are applying for a trust EIN when a new pension plan is established. In addition, check the "Other" box in line 8a and write "Created a Pension Plan" in the space provided.*

Banking purpose. Check this box if you are requesting an EIN for banking purposes only, and enter the banking purpose (for example, a bowling league for depositing dues or an investment club for dividend and interest reporting).

Changed type of organization. Check this box if the business is changing its type of organization. For example, the business was a sole proprietorship and has been incorporated or has become a partnership. If you check this box, specify in the space provided (including available space immediately below) the type of change made. For example, "From Sole Proprietorship to Partnership."

Purchased going business. Check this box if you purchased an existing business. **Do not** use the former owner's EIN unless you became the "owner" of a corporation by acquiring its stock.

Created a trust. Check this box if you created a trust, and enter the type of trust created. For example, indicate if the trust is a nonexempt charitable trust or a split-interest trust.

Exception. Do **not** file this form for certain grantor-type trusts. The trustee does not need an EIN for the trust if the trustee furnishes the name and TIN of the grantor/owner and the address of the trust to all payors. See the Instructions for Form 1041 for more information.

TIP ***Do not*** *check this box if you are applying for a trust EIN when a new pension plan is established. Check "Created a pension plan."*

Other. Check this box if you are requesting an EIN for any other reason; and enter the reason. For example, a newly-formed state government entity should enter "Newly-Formed State Government Entity" in the space provided.

Line 10—Date business started or acquired. If you are starting a new business, enter the starting date of the business. If the business you acquired is already operating, enter the date you acquired the business. Trusts should enter the date the trust was legally created. Estates should enter the date of death of the decedent whose name appears on line 1 or the date when the estate was legally funded.

Line 11—Closing month of accounting year. Enter the last month of your accounting year or tax year. An accounting or tax year is usually 12 consecutive months, either a calendar year or a fiscal year (including a period of 52 or 53 weeks). A calendar year is 12 consecutive months ending on December 31. A fiscal year is either 12 consecutive months ending on the last day of any month other than December or a 52-53 week year. For more information on accounting periods, see Pub. 538.

Individuals. Your tax year generally will be a calendar year.

Partnerships. Partnerships must adopt one of the following tax years:

- The tax year of the majority of its partners,
- The tax year common to all of its principal partners,
- The tax year that results in the least aggregate deferral of income, or
- In certain cases, some other tax year.

See the Instructions for Form 1065 for more information.

REMICs. REMICs must have a calendar year as their tax year.

Personal service corporations. A personal service corporation generally must adopt a calendar year unless:

- It can establish a business purpose for having a different tax year, or
- It elects under section 444 to have a tax year other than a calendar year.

Trusts. Generally, a trust must adopt a calendar year except for the following:

- Tax-exempt trusts,
- Charitable trusts, and
- Grantor-owned trusts.

Line 12—First date wages or annuities were paid or will be paid. If the business has or will have employees, enter the date on which the business began or will begin to pay wages. If the business does not plan to have employees, enter "N/A."

Withholding agent. Enter the date you began or will begin to pay income (including annuities) to a nonresident alien. This also applies to individuals who are required to file Form 1042 to report alimony paid to a nonresident alien.

Line 13—Highest number of employees expected in the next 12 months. Complete each box by entering the number (including zero ("-0-")) of "Agricultural," "Household," or "Other" employees expected by the applicant in the next 12 months. For a definition of agricultural labor (farmwork), see Circular A.

Lines 14 and 15. Check the **one** box in line 14 that best describes the principal activity of the applicant's business. Check the "Other" box (and specify the applicant's principal activity) if none of the listed boxes applies.

Use line 15 to describe the applicant's principal line of business in more detail. For example, if you checked the "Construction" box in line 14, enter additional detail such as "General contractor for residential buildings" in line 15.

TIP *Do not complete lines 14 and 15 if you entered zero "(-0-)" in line 13.*

Construction. Check this box if the applicant is engaged in erecting buildings or other structures, (e.g., streets, highways, bridges, tunnels). The term "Construction" also includes special trade contractors, (e.g., plumbing, HVAC, electrical, carpentry, concrete, excavation, etc. contractors).

Real estate. Check this box if the applicant is engaged in renting or leasing real estate to others; managing, selling, buying or renting real estate for others; or providing related real estate services (e.g., appraisal services).

Rental and leasing. Check this box if the applicant is engaged in providing tangible goods such as autos, computers, consumer goods, or industrial machinery and equipment to customers in return for a periodic rental or lease payment.

Manufacturing. Check this box if the applicant is engaged in the mechanical, physical, or chemical transformation of materials, substances, or components into new products. The assembling of component parts of manufactured products is also considered to be manufacturing.

Transportation & warehousing. Check this box if the applicant provides transportation of passengers or cargo; warehousing or storage of goods; scenic or sight-seeing transportation; or support activities related to these modes of transportation.

Finance & insurance. Check this box if the applicant is engaged in transactions involving the creation, liquidation, or change of ownership of financial assets and/or facilitating such financial transactions;

underwriting annuities/insurance policies; facilitating such underwriting by selling insurance policies; or by providing other insurance or employee-benefit related services.

Health care and social assistance. Check this box if the applicant is engaged in providing physical, medical, or psychiatric care using licensed health care professionals or providing social assistance activities such as youth centers, adoption agencies, individual/family services, temporary shelters, etc.

Accommodation & food services. Check this box if the applicant is engaged in providing customers with lodging, meal preparation, snacks, or beverages for immediate consumption.

Wholesale–agent/broker. Check this box if the applicant is engaged in arranging for the purchase or sale of goods owned by others or purchasing goods on a commission basis for goods traded in the wholesale market, usually between businesses.

Wholesale–other. Check this box if the applicant is engaged in selling goods in the wholesale market generally to other businesses for resale on their own account.

Retail. Check this box if the applicant is engaged in selling merchandise to the general public from a fixed store; by direct, mail-order, or electronic sales; or by using vending machines.

Other. Check this box if the applicant is engaged in an activity not described above. Describe the applicant's principal business activity in the space provided.

Lines 16a-c. Check the applicable box in line 16a to indicate whether or not the entity (or individual) applying for an EIN was issued one previously. Complete lines 16b and 16c **only** if the "Yes" box in line 16a is checked. If the applicant previously applied for **more than one** EIN, write "See Attached" in the empty space in line 16a and attach a separate sheet providing the line 16b and 16c information for each EIN previously requested.

Third Party Designee. Complete this section **only** if you want to authorize the named individual to receive the entity's EIN and answer questions about the completion of Form SS-4. The designee's authority terminates at the time the EIN is assigned and released to the designee. **You must complete the signature area for the authorization to be valid.**

Signature. When required, the application must be signed by **(a)** the individual, if the applicant is an individual, **(b)** the president, vice president, or other principal officer, if the applicant is a corporation, **(c)** a responsible and duly authorized member or officer having knowledge of its affairs, if the applicant is a partnership, government entity, or other unincorporated organization, or **(d)** the fiduciary, if the applicant is a trust or an estate. Foreign applicants may have any duly-authorized person, (e.g., division manager), sign Form SS-4.

Privacy Act and Paperwork Reduction Act Notice. We ask for the information on this form to carry out the Internal Revenue laws of the United States. We need it to comply with section 6109 and the regulations thereunder which generally require the inclusion of an employer identification number (EIN) on certain returns, statements, or other documents filed with the Internal Revenue Service. If your entity is required to obtain an EIN, you are required to provide all of the information requested on this form. Information on this form may be used to determine which Federal tax returns you are required to file and to provide you with related forms and publications.

We disclose this form to the Social Security Administration for their use in determining compliance with applicable laws. We may give this information to the Department of Justice for use in civil and criminal litigation, and to the cities, states, and the District of Columbia for use in administering their tax laws. We may also disclose this information to Federal, state, or local agencies that investigate or respond to acts or threats of terrorism or participate in intelligence or counterintelligence activities concerning terrorism.

We will be unable to issue an EIN to you unless you provide all of the requested information which applies to your entity. Providing false information could subject you to penalties.

You are not required to provide the information requested on a form that is subject to the Paperwork Reduction Act unless the form displays a valid OMB control number. Books or records relating to a form or its instructions must be retained as long as their contents may become material in the administration of any Internal Revenue law. Generally, tax returns and return information are confidential, as required by section 6103.

The time needed to complete and file this form will vary depending on individual circumstances. The estimated average time is:

Recordkeeping	6 min.
Learning about the law or the form	22 min.
Preparing the form	46 min.
Copying, assembling, and sending the form to the IRS	20 min.

If you have comments concerning the accuracy of these time estimates or suggestions for making this form simpler, we would be happy to hear from you. You can write to the Tax Forms Committee, Western Area Distribution Center, Rancho Cordova, CA 95743-0001. **Do not** send the form to this address. Instead, see **How To Apply** on page 2.

BANKING RESOLUTION OF

____

The undersigned, being the

☐ corporate secretary of the above corporation,
☐ member of the above limited liability company,
☐ manager of the above limited liability company

hereby certifies that on the _____ day of __________________, _______ the company duly adopted the following resolution:

RESOLVED that the company open bank accounts with __________________ ____ and that the ☐ officers of the corporation or ☐ members ☐ managers of the limited liability company are authorized to take such action as is necessary to open such accounts; that the bank's printed form of resolution is hereby adopted and incorporated into these minutes by reference and shall be placed in the minute book; that any ____ of the following persons shall have signature authority over the account:

_________________________________ _________________________________

_________________________________ _________________________________

and that said resolution has not been modified or rescinded.

Date: ________________________

____

☐ Corporate Secretary
☐ Member
☐ Manager

This page intentionally left blank.

RESOLUTION TO REIMBURSE EXPENSES
of

____

RESOLVED that the company shall reimburse the following parties for the organizational expenses of the organizers of this company and that the company shall amortize or deduct these expenses as allowed by IRS regulations.

Name	Expense	Amount
______________________	____________	$__________
______________________	____________	$__________
______________________	____________	$__________
______________________	____________	$__________
______________________	____________	$__________
______________________	____________	$__________
______________________	____________	$__________

Date:____________________

____

____

____

____

____

This page intentionally left blank.

BILL OF SALE

The undersigned, in consideration of

hereby grants, bargains, sells, transfers and delivers unto said corporation the following goods and chattels:

To have and to hold the same forever.

And the undersigned, their heirs, successors and administrators, covenant and warrant that they are the lawful owners of the said goods and chattels and that they are free from all encumbrances. That the undersigned have the right to sell this property and that they will warrant and defend the sale of said property against the lawful claims and demands of all persons. IN WITNESS whereof the undersigned have executed this Bill of Sale this ____ day of ____________________, _______.

____

____

____

This page intentionally left blank.

STATE *of* DELAWARE
CERTIFICATE *of* INCORPORATION
A STOCK CORPORATION

- **First:** The name of this Corporation is ______________________________ ____.
- **Second:** Its registered office in the State of Delaware is to be located at _________ _____________________ Street, in the City of ________________________ County of ____________________ Zip Code ________. The registered agent in charge thereof is ______________ ____ ____
- **Third:** The purpose of the corporation is to engage in any lawful act or activity for which corporations may be organized under the General Corporation Law of Delaware.
- **Fourth:** The amount of the total authorized capital stock of this corporation is __________ Dollars ($_______) divided into __________ shares of _________ __________ Dollars ($_______) each.
- **Fifth:** The name and mailing address of the incorporator are as follows:

  Name

  ____

  Mailing Address ____

  ________________________Zip Code___________
- **I, The Undersigned,** for the purpose of forming a corporation under the laws of the State of Delaware, do make, file and record this Certificate, and do certify that the facts herein stated are true, and I have accordingly hereunto set my hand this _______________ day of ______________, A.D. 20_____.

BY:___________________________
Incorporator

NAME:___________________________
(Type or Print)

This page intentionally left blank.

STATE *of* DELAWARE CERTIFICATE *of* INCORPORATION *A* CLOSE CORPORATION *of*

____

- **First:** The name of this Corporation is ______________________________ ____.
- **Second:** Its Registered Office in the State of Delaware is to be located at ________ _________________________ Street, in the City of ___________________ County of _______________ Zip Code _______. The registered agent in charge thereof is ______________________________ ____ ____.
- **Third:** The nature of business and the objects and purposes proposed to be transacted, promoted and carried on, are to engage in any lawful act of activity for which corporations may be organized under the General corporation Law of Delaware.
- **Fourth:** The amount of the total authorized capital stock of this corporation is ___________ Dollars ($_______) divided into ________ shares of _________ ___________ Dollars ($_______) each.
- **Fifth:** The name and mailing address of the incorporator are as follows:

  Name ____

  Mailing Address ____

  ______________________Zip Code___________
- **Sixth:** All of the corporation's issued stock, exclusive of treasury shares, shall be held of record by not more than thirty (30) persons.
- **Seventh:** All of the issued stock of all classes shall be subject to on or more of the restrictions on transfer permitted by Section 202 of the General Corporation Law.
- **Eighth:** The corporation shall make no offering of any of its stock of any class which would constitute a "public offering" within meaning of the United States Securities Act of 1933, as it may be amended from time to time.
- **I, The Undersigned**, for the purpose of forming a corporation under the laws of the State of Delaware, do make, file and record this Certificate, and do certify that the facts herein stated are true, and I have accordingly hereunto set my hand this _______________ day of _____________, A.D. 20_____.

BY:___________________________

Incorporator

NAME:___________________________

(Type or Print)

This page intentionally left blank.

STATE *of* DELAWARE
CERTIFICATE *of* AMENDMENT *of*
CERTIFICATE *of* INCORPORATION

- **First:** That at a meeting of the Board of Directors of ______________________

  ____

  resolutions were duly adopted setting forth a proposed amendment of the Certificate of Incorporation of said corporation, declaring said amendment to be advisable and calling a meeting of the stockholders of said corporation for consideration thereof.

  The resolution setting the proposed amendment as follows:

  Resolved, that the Certificate of Incorporation of this corporation be amended by changing the Article thereof numbered "______" so that, as amended, said Article shall be and read as follows:

  "____

  ____

  ____"

- **Second:** That thereafter, pursuant to resolution of its Board of Directors, a special meeting of the stockholders of said corporation was duly called and held, upon notice in accordance with Section 222 of the General Corporation Law of the State of Delaware at which meeting the necessary number of shares as required by statute were voted in favor of the amendment.
- **Third:** That said amendment was duly adopted in accordance with the provisions of Section 242 of the General Corporation Law of the State of Delaware.
- **Fourth:** That the capital of said corporation shall not be reduced under or by reason of said amendment.

By:______________________________
(Authorized Officer)

Name:______________________________
(Typed or Printed)

This page intentionally left blank.

BYLAWS OF

____

A DELAWARE CORPORATION

ARTICLE I - OFFICES

The principal office of the Corporation shall be located in the City of ________________________ and the State of Delaware. The Corporation may also maintain offices at such other places as the Board of Directors may, from time to time, determine.

ARTICLE II - SHAREHOLDERS

Section 1 - Annual Meetings: The annual meeting of the shareholders of the Corporation shall be held each year on ____________at ____m. at the principal office of the Corporation or at such other places as the Board may authorize, for the purpose of electing directors, and transacting such other business as may properly come before the meeting.

Section 2 - Special Meetings: Special meetings of the shareholders may be called at any time by the Board, the President, or by the holders of twenty-five percent (25%) of the shares then outstanding and entitled to vote.

Section 3 - Place of Meetings: All meetings of shareholders shall be held at the principal office of the Corporation, or at such other places as the board shall designate in the notice of such meetings.

Section 4 - Notice of Meetings: Written or printed notice stating the place, day, and hour of the meeting and, in the case of a special meeting, the purpose of the meeting, shall be delivered personally or by mail not less than ten days, nor more than sixty days, before the date of the meeting. Notice shall be given to each Shareholder of record entitled to vote at the meeting. If mailed, such notice shall be deemed to have been delivered when deposited in the United States Mail with postage paid and addressed to the Shareholder at his address as it appears on the records of the Corporation.

Section 5 - Waiver of Notice: A written waiver of notice signed by a Shareholder, whether before or after a meeting, shall be equivalent to the giving of such notice. Attendance of a Shareholder at a meeting shall constitute a waiver of notice of such meeting, except when the Shareholder attends for the express purpose of objecting, at the beginning of the meeting, to the transaction of any business because the meeting is not lawfully called or convened.

Section 6 - Quorum: Except as otherwise provided by Statute, or the Articles of Incorporation, at all meetings of shareholders of the Corporation, the presence at the commencement of such meetings in person or by proxy of shareholders of record holding a majority of the total number of shares of the Corporation then issued and outstanding and entitled to vote, but in no event less than one-third of the shares entitled to vote at the meeting, shall constitute a quorum for the transaction of any business. If any shareholder leaves after the commencement of a meeting, this shall have no effect on the existence of a quorum, after a quorum has been established at such meeting.

Despite the absence of a quorum at any annual or special meeting of shareholders, the shareholders, by a majority of the votes cast by the holders of shares entitled to vote thereon, may adjourn the meeting. At any such adjourned meeting at which a quorum is present, any business may be transacted at the meeting as originally called as if a quorum had been present.

Section 7 - Voting: Except as otherwise provided by Statute or by the Certificate of Incorporation, any corporate action, other than the election of directors, to be taken by vote of the shareholders, shall be authorized by a majority of votes cast at a meeting of shareholders by the holders of shares entitled to vote thereon.

Except as otherwise provided by Statute or by the Certificate of Incorporation, at each meeting of shareholders, each holder of record of stock of the Corporation entitled to vote thereat, shall be entitled to one vote for each share of stock registered in his name on the stock transfer books of the corporation.

Each shareholder entitled to vote may do so by proxy; provided, however, that the instrument authorizing such proxy to act shall have been executed in writing by the shareholder himself. No proxy shall be valid after the expiration of eleven months from the date of its execution, unless the person executing it shall have specified therein, the length of time it is to continue in force. Such instrument shall be exhibited to the Secretary at the meeting and shall be filed with the records of the corporation.

Any resolution in writing, signed by all of the shareholders entitled to vote thereon, shall be and constitute action by such shareholders to the effect therein expressed, with the same force and effect as if the same had been duly passed by unanimous vote at a duly called meeting of shareholders and such resolution so signed shall be inserted in the Minute Book of the Corporation under its proper date.

ARTICLE III - BOARD OF DIRECTORS

Section 1 - Number, Election and Term of Office: The number of the directors of the Corporation shall be (____) This number may be increased or decreased by the amendment of these bylaws by the Board but shall in no case be less than ____ director(s). The members of the Board, who need not be shareholders, shall be elected by a majority of the votes cast at a meeting of shareholders entitled to vote in the election. Each director shall hold office until the annual meeting of the shareholders next succeeding his election, and until his successor is elected and qualified, or until his prior death, resignation or removal.

Section 2 - Vacancies: Any vacancy in the Board shall be filled for the unexpired portion of the term by a majority vote of the remaining directors, though less than a quorum, at any regular meeting or special meeting of the Board called for that purpose. Any such director so elected may be replaced by the shareholders at a regular or special meeting of shareholders.

Section 3 - Duties and Powers: The Board shall be responsible for the control and management of the affairs, property and interests of the Corporation, and may exercise all powers of the Corporation, except as limited by statute.

Section 4 - Annual Meetings: An annual meeting of the Board shall be held immediately following the annual meeting of the shareholders, at the place of such annual meeting of shareholders. The Board from time to time, may provide by resolution for the holding of other meetings of the Board, and may fix the time and place thereof.

Section 5 - Special Meetings: Special meetings of the Board shall be held whenever called by the President or by one of the directors, at such time and place as may be specified in the respective notice or waivers of notice thereof.

Section 6 - Notice and Waiver: Notice of any special meeting shall be given at least five days prior thereto by written notice delivered personally, by mail or by telegram to each Director at his address. If mailed, such notice shall be deemed to be delivered when deposited in the United States Mail with postage prepaid. If notice is given by telegram, such notice shall be deemed to be delivered when the telegram is delivered to the telegraph company.

Any Director may waive notice of any meeting, either before, at, or after such meeting, by signing a waiver of notice. The attendance of a Director at a meeting shall constitute a waiver of notice of such meeting and a waiver of any and all objections to the place of such meeting, or the manner in which it has been called or convened, except when a Director states at the beginning of the meeting any objection to the transaction of business because the meeting is not lawfully called or convened.

Section 7 - Chairman: The Board may, at its discretion, elect a Chairman. At all meetings of the Board, the Chairman of the Board, if any and if present, shall preside. If there is no Chairman, or he is absent, then the President shall preside, and in his absence, a Chairman chosen by the directors shall preside.

Section 8 - Quorum and Adjournments: At all meetings of the Board, the presence of a majority of the entire Board shall be necessary and sufficient to constitute a quorum for the transaction of business, except as otherwise provided by law, by the Articles of Incorporation, or by these bylaws. A majority of the directors present at the time and place of any regular or special meeting, although less than a quorum, may adjourn the same from time to time without notice, until a quorum shall be present.

Section 9 - Board Action: At all meetings of the Board, each director present shall have one vote, irrespective of the number of shares of stock, if any, which he may hold. Except as otherwise provided by Statute, the action of a majority of the directors present at any meeting at which a quorum is present shall be the act of the Board. Any action authorized, in writing, by all of the Directors entitled to vote thereon and filed with the minutes of the Corporation shall be the act of the Board with the same force and effect as if the same had been passed by unanimous vote at a duly called meeting of the Board. Any action taken by the Board may be taken without a meeting if agreed to in writing by all members before or after the action is taken and if a record of such action is filed in the minute book.

Section 10 - Telephone Meetings: Directors may participate in meetings of the Board through use of a telephone if such can be arranged so that all Board members can hear all other members. The use of a telephone for participation shall constitute presence in person.

Section 11 - Resignation and Removal: Any director may resign at any time by giving written notice to another Board member, the President or the Secretary of the Corporation. Unless otherwise specified in such written notice, such resignation shall take effect upon receipt thereof by the Board or by such officer, and the acceptance of such resignation shall not be necessary to make it effective. Any director may be removed with or without cause at any time by the affirmative vote of shareholders holding of record in the aggregate at least a majority of the outstanding shares of the Corporation at a special meeting of the shareholders called for that purpose, and may be removed for cause by action of the Board.

Section 12 - Compensation: No stated salary shall be paid to directors, as such for their services, but by resolution of the Board a fixed sum and/or expenses of attendance, if any, may be allowed for attendance at each regular or special meeting of the Board. Nothing herein contained shall be construed to preclude any director from serving the Corporation in any other capacity and receiving compensation therefor.

ARTICLE IV - OFFICERS

Section 1 - Number, Qualification, Election and Term: The officers of the Corporation shall consist of a President, a Secretary, a Treasurer, and such other officers, as the Board may from time to time deem advisable. Any officer may be, but is not required to be, a director of the Corporation. The officers of the Corporation shall be elected by the Board at the regular annual meeting of the Board. Each officer shall hold office until the annual meeting of the Board next succeeding his election, and until his successor shall have been elected and qualified, or until his death, resignation or removal.

Section 2 - Resignation and Removal: Any officer may resign at any time by giving written notice of such resignation to the President or the Secretary of the Corporation or to a member of the Board. Unless otherwise specified in such written notice, such resignation shall take effect upon receipt thereof by the Board member or by such officer, and the acceptance of such resignation shall not be necessary to make it effective. Any officer may be removed, either with or without cause, and a successor elected by a majority vote of the Board at any time.

Section 3 - Vacancies: A vacancy in any office may at any time be filled for the unexpired portion of the term by a majority vote of the Board.

Section 4 - Duties of Officers: Officers of the Corporation shall, unless otherwise provided by the Board, each have such powers and duties as generally pertain to their respective offices as well as such powers and duties as may from time to time be specifically decided by the Board. The President shall be the chief executive officer of the Corporation.

Section 5 - Compensation: The officers of the Corporation shall be entitled to such compensation as the Board shall from time to time determine.

Section 6 - Delegation of Duties: In the absence or disability of any Officer of the Corporation or for any other reason deemed sufficient by the Board of Directors, the Board may delegate his powers or duties to any other Officer or to any other Director.

Section 7 - Shares of Other Corporations: Whenever the Corporation is the holder of shares of any other Corporation, any right or power of the Corporation as such shareholder (including the attendance, acting and voting at shareholders' meetings and execution of waivers, consents, proxies or other instruments) may be exercised on behalf of the Corporation by the President, any Vice President, or such other person as the Board may authorize.

ARTICLE V - COMMITTEES

The Board of Directors may, by resolution, designate an Executive Committee and one or more other committees. Such committees shall have such functions and may exercise such power of the Board of Directors as can be lawfully delegated, and to the extent provided in the resolution or resolutions creating such committee or committees. Meetings of committees may be held without notice at such time and at such place as shall from time to time be determined by the committees. The committees of the corporation shall keep regular minutes of their proceedings, and report these minutes to the Board of Directors when required.

ARTICLE VI - BOOKS, RECORDS AND REPORTS

Section 1 - Annual Report: The Corporation shall send an annual report to the Shareholders of the Corporation not later than ______ months after the close of each fiscal year of the Corporation. Such report shall include a balance sheet as of the close of the fiscal year of the Corporation and a revenue and disbursement statement for the year ending on such closing date. Such financial statements shall be prepared from and in accordance with the books of the Corporation, and in conformity with generally accepted accounting principles applied on a consistent basis.

Section 2 - Permanent Records: The corporation shall keep current and correct records of the accounts, minutes of the meetings and proceedings and membership records of the corporation. Such records shall be kept at the registered office or the principal place of business of the corporation. Any such records shall be in written form or in a form capable of being converted into written form.

Section 3 - Inspection of Corporate Records: Any person who is a Shareholder of the Corporation shall have the right at any reasonable time, and on written demand stating the purpose thereof, to examine and make copies from the relevant books and records of accounts, minutes, and records of the Corporation. Upon the written request of any Shareholder, the Corporation shall mail to such Shareholder a copy of the most recent balance sheet and revenue and disbursement statement.

ARTICLE VII- SHARES OF STOCK

Section 1 - Certificates: Each shareholder of the corporation shall be entitled to have a certificate representing all shares which he or she owns. The form of such certificate shall be adopted by a majority vote of the Board of Directors and shall be signed by the President and Secretary of the Corporation and sealed with the seal of the corporation. No certificate representing shares shall be issued until the full amount of consideration therefore has been paid.

Section 2 - Stock Ledger: The corporation shall maintain a ledger of the stock records of the Corporation. Transfers of shares of the Corporation shall be made on the stock ledger of the Corporation only at the direction of the holder of record upon surrender of the outstanding certificate(s). The Corporation shall be entitled to treat the holder of record of any share or shares as the absolute owner thereof for all purposes and, accordingly, shall not be bound to recognize any legal, equitable or other claim to, or interest in, such share or shares on the part of any other person, whether or not it shall have express or other notice thereof, except as otherwise expressly provided by law.

ARTICLE VIII - DIVIDENDS

Upon approval by the Board of Directors the corporation may pay dividends on its shares in the form of cash, property or additional shares at any time that the corporation is solvent and if such dividends would not render the corporation insolvent.

ARTICLE IX - FISCAL YEAR

The fiscal year of the Corporation shall be the period selected by the Board of Directors as the tax year of the Corporation for federal income tax purposes.

ARTICLE X - CORPORATE SEAL

The Board of Directors may adopt, use and modify a corporate seal. Failure to affix the seal to corporate documents shall not affect the validity of such document.

ARTICLE XI - AMENDMENTS

The Articles of Incorporation may be amended by the Shareholders as provided by Delaware statutes. These Bylaws may be altered, amended, or replaced by the Board of Directors; provided, however, that any Bylaws or amendments thereto as adopted by the Board of Directors may be altered, amended, or repealed by vote of the Shareholders. Bylaws adopted by the Shareholders may not be amended or repealed by the Board.

ARTICLE XII - INDEMNIFICATION

Any officer, director or employee of the Corporation shall be indemnified to the full extent allowed by the laws of the State of Delaware.

ARTICLE XIII - CONFLICT

In the event that any of these Bylaws at any time conflict with the General Corporation Law of the State of Delaware, then said law shall control and these Bylaws should be considered revised to comply with said law.

Certified to be the Bylaws of the corporation adopted by the Board of Directors on ___________________, _______.

____
Secretary

This page intentionally left blank.

BYLAWS OF

____

A DELAWARE PROFESSIONAL ASSOCIATION

ARTICLE I - OFFICES

The principal office of the Corporation shall be located in the City of ___________________________ and the State of Delaware. The Corporation may also maintain offices at such other places as the Board of Directors may, from time to time, determine.

ARTICLE II - PURPOSES

The business purpose of the Corporation shall be to engage in all aspects of the practice of ____________________________________ and its fields of specialization. The Corporation shall render professional services only through its legally authorized officers, agents and employees.

ARTICLE III - SHAREHOLDERS

Section 1 - Qualifications: Only persons who are duly licensed and in good standing in the profession by the State of Delaware may be shareholders of the Corporation. Neither the Corporation nor the shareholders may transfer any shares to persons who are not duly licensed. All share certificates of the corporation shall contain a notice that the transfer is restricted by the bylaws of the Corporation. If any shareholder shall become disqualified to practice the profession, he or she shall immediately make arrangements to transfer his or her shares to a qualified person or to the Corporation and shall no longer participate in the profits of the Corporation related to the profession.

Section 2 - Annual Meetings: The annual meeting of the shareholders of the Corporation shall be held each year on___________________________at ___________m. at the principal office of the Corporation or at such other places as the Board may authorize, for the purpose of electing directors, and transacting such other business as may properly come before the meeting.

Section 3 - Special Meetings: Special meetings of the shareholders may be called at any time by the Board, the President, or by the holders of twenty-five percent (25%) of the shares then outstanding and entitled to vote.

Section 4 - Place of Meetings: All meetings of shareholders shall be held at the principal office of the Corporation, or at such other places as the Board shall designate in the notice of such meetings.

Section 5 - Notice of Meetings: Written or printed notice stating the place, day, and hour of the meeting and, in the case of a special meeting, the purpose of the meeting, shall be delivered personally or by mail not less than ten days, nor more than sixty days, before the date of the meeting. Notice shall be given to each Shareholder of record entitled to vote at the meeting. If mailed, such notice shall be deemed to have been delivered when deposited in the United States Mail with postage paid and addressed to the Shareholder at his address as it appears on the records of the Corporation.

Section 6 - Waiver of Notice: A written waiver of notice signed by a Shareholder, whether before or after a meeting, shall be equivalent to the giving of such notice. Attendance of a Shareholder at a meeting shall constitute a waiver of notice of such meeting, except when the Shareholder attends for the express purpose of objecting, at the beginning of the meeting, to the transaction of any business because the meeting is not lawfully called or convened.

Section 7 - Quorum: Except as otherwise provided by Statute, or the by Certificate of Incorporation, at all meetings of shareholders of the Corporation, the presence at the commencement of such meetings of shareholders of record holding a majority of the total number of shares of the Corporation then issued and outstanding and entitled to vote, but in no event less than one-third of the shares entitled to vote at the meeting, shall constitute a quorum for the transaction of any business. If any shareholder leaves after the commencement of a meeting, this shall have no effect on the existence of a quorum, after a quorum has been established at such meeting.

Despite the absence of a quorum at any annual or special meeting of shareholders, the shareholders, by a majority of the votes cast by the holders of shares entitled to vote thereon, may adjourn the meeting. At any such adjourned meeting at which a quorum is present, any business may be transacted at the meeting as originally called as if a quorum had been present.

Section 8 - Voting: Except as otherwise provided by Statute or by the Certificate of Incorporation, any corporate action, other than the election of directors, to be taken by vote of the shareholders, shall be authorized by a majority of votes cast at a meeting of shareholders by the holders of shares entitled to vote thereon.

Except as otherwise provided by Statute or by the Certificate of Incorporation, at each meeting of shareholders, each holder of record of stock of the Corporation entitled to vote thereat, shall be entitled to one vote for each share of stock registered in his name on the stock transfer books of the corporation.

Any resolution in writing, signed by all of the shareholders entitled to vote thereon, shall be and constitute action by such shareholders to the effect therein expressed, with the same force and effect as if the same had been duly passed by unanimous vote at a duly called meeting of shareholders and such resolution so signed shall be inserted in the Minute Book of the Corporation under its proper date.

Section 9 - Proxies: Shareholders may not at any time vote by proxy or enter into any voting trust or other agreement vesting another person with the voting power of his stock.

ARTICLE IV - BOARD OF DIRECTORS

Section 1 Qualifications: Only persons who are duly licensed and in good standing in the profession by the State of Delaware may be directors of the Corporation. If any director shall become disqualified from practicing the profession, he or she shall immediately resign his or her directorship and any other employment with the Corporation.

Section 2 - Number, Election and Term of Office: The number of the directors of the Corporation shall be (____) This number may be increased or decreased by the amendment of these bylaws by the Board but shall in no case be less than one director. The members of the Board, who need not be shareholders, shall be elected by a majority of the votes cast at a meeting of shareholders entitled to vote in the election. Each director shall hold office until the annual meeting of the shareholders next succeeding his election, and until his successor is elected and qualified, or until his prior death, resignation or removal.

Section 3 - Vacancies: Any vacancy in the Board shall be filled for the unexpired portion of the term by a majority vote of the remaining directors, though less than a quorum, at any regular meeting or special meeting of the Board called for that purpose. Any such director so elected may be replaced by the shareholders at a regular or special meeting of shareholders.

Section 4 - Duties and Powers: The Board shall be responsible for the control and management of the affairs, property and interests of the Corporation, and may exercise all powers of the Corporation, except as limited by statute.

Section 5 - Annual Meetings: An annual meeting of the Board shall be held immediately following the annual meeting of the shareholders, at the place of such annual meeting of shareholders. The Board, from time to time, may provide by resolution for the holding of other meetings of the Board, and may fix the time and place thereof.

Section 6 - Special Meetings: Special meetings of the Board shall be held whenever called by the President or by one of the directors, at such time and place as may be specified in the respective notice or waivers of notice thereof.

Section 7 - Notice and Waiver: Notice of any special meeting shall be given at least five days prior thereto by written notice delivered personally, by mail or by telegram to each director at his address. If mailed, such notice shall be deemed to be delivered when deposited in the United States Mail with postage prepaid. If notice is given by telegram, such notice shall be deemed to be delivered when the telegram is delivered to the telegraph company.

Any director may waive notice of any meeting, either before, at, or after such meeting, by signing a waiver of notice. The attendance of a director at a meeting shall constitute a waiver of notice of such meeting and a waiver of any and all objections to the place of such meeting, or the manner in which it has been called or convened, except when a director states at the beginning of the meeting any objection to the transaction of business because the meeting is not lawfully called or convened.

Section 8 - Chairman: The Board may, at its discretion, elect a Chairman. At all meetings of the Board, the Chairman of the Board, if any and if present, shall preside. If there is no Chairman, or he is absent, then the President shall preside, and in his absence, a Chairman chosen by the directors shall preside.

Section 9 - Quorum and Adjournments: At all meetings of the Board, the presence of a majority of the entire Board shall be necessary and sufficient to constitute a quorum for the transaction of business, except as otherwise provided by law, by the Articles of Incorporation, or by these bylaws. A majority of the directors present at the time and place of any regular or special meeting, although less than a quorum, may adjourn the same from time to time without notice, until a quorum shall be present.

Section 10 - Board Action: At all meetings of the Board, each director present shall have one vote, irrespective of the number of shares of stock, if any, which he may hold. Except as otherwise provided by Statute, the action of a majority of the directors present at any meeting at which a quorum is present shall be the act of the Board. Any action authorized, in writing, by all of the Directors entitled to vote thereon and filed with the minutes of the Corporation shall be the act of the Board with the same force and effect as if the same had been passed by unanimous vote at a duly called meeting of the Board. Any action taken by the Board may be taken without a meeting if agreed to in writing by all members before or after the action is taken and if a record of such action is filed in the Minute Book.

Section 11 - Telephone Meetings: Directors may participate in meetings of the Board through use of a telephone if such can be arranged so that all Board members can hear all other members. The use of a telephone for participation shall constitute presence in person.

Section 12 - Resignation and Removal: Any director may resign at any time by giving written notice to another Board member, the President or the Secretary of the Corporation. Unless otherwise specified in such written notice, such resignation shall take effect upon receipt thereof by the Board or by such officer, and the acceptance of such resignation shall not be necessary to make it effective. Any director may be removed with or without cause at any time by the affirmative vote of shareholders holding of record in the aggregate at least a majority of the outstanding shares of the Corporation at a special meeting of the shareholders called for that purpose, and may be removed for cause by action of the Board.

Section 13 - Compensation: No stated salary shall be paid to directors, as such for their services, but by resolution of the Board a fixed sum and/or expenses of attendance, if any, may be allowed for attendance at each regular or special meeting of the Board. Nothing herein contained shall be construed to preclude any director from serving the Corporation in any other capacity and receiving compensation therefor.

ARTICLE V - OFFICERS

Section 1 Qualifications: Only persons who are duly licensed and in good standing in the profession by the State of Delaware may be officers of the Corporation. If any director shall become disqualified from practicing the profession, he or she shall immediately resign his or her directorship and any other employment with the corporation.

Section 2 - Number, Election and Term: The officers of the Corporation shall consist of a President, a Secretary, a Treasurer, and such other officers, as the Board may from time to time deem advisable. Any officer may be, but is not required to be, a director of the Corporation. Any two or more offices may be held by the same person. The officers of the Corporation shall be elected by the Board at the regular annual meeting of the Board. Each officer shall hold office until the annual meeting of the Board next succeeding his election, and until his successor shall have been elected and qualified, or until his death, resignation or removal.

Section 3 - Resignation and Removal: Any officer may resign at any time by giving written notice of such resignation to the President or the Secretary of the Corporation or to a member of the Board. Unless otherwise specified in such written notice, such resignation shall take effect upon receipt thereof by the Board member or by such officer, and the acceptance of such resignation shall not be necessary to make it effective. Any officer may be removed, either with or without cause, and a successor elected by a majority vote of the Board at any time.

Section 4 - Vacancies: A vacancy in any office may at any time be filled for the unexpired portion of the term by a majority vote of the Board.

Section 5 - Duties of Officers: The officers of the Corporation shall, unless otherwise provided by the Board, each have such powers and duties as generally pertain to their respective offices as well as such powers and duties as may from time to time be specifically decided by the Board. The President shall be the chief executive officer of the Corporation.

Section 6 - Compensation: The officers of the Corporation shall be entitled to such compensation as the Board shall from time to time determine.

Section 7 - Delegation of Duties: In the absence or disability of any Officer of the Corporation or for any other reason deemed sufficient by the Board of Directors, the Board may delegate his powers or duties to any other Officer or to any other director.

Section 8 - Shares of Other Corporations: Whenever the Corporation is the holder of shares of any other Corporation, any right or power of the Corporation as such shareholder (including the attendance, acting and voting at shareholders' meetings and execution of waivers, consents, proxies or other instruments) may be exercised on behalf of the Corporation by the President, any Vice President, or such other person as the Board may authorize.

ARTICLE VI - COMMITTEES

The Board of Directors may, by resolution, designate an Executive Committee and one or more other committees. Such committees shall have such functions and may exercise such power of the Board of Directors as can be lawfully delegated, and to the extent provided in the resolution or resolutions creating such committee or committees. Meetings of committees may be held without notice at such time and at such place as shall from time to time be determined by the committees. The committees of the corporation shall keep regular minutes of their proceedings, and report these minutes to the Board of Directors when required.

ARTICLE VII - BOOKS, RECORDS AND REPORTS

Section 1 - Annual Report: The Corporation shall send an annual report to the Shareholders of the Corporation not later than four months after the close of each fiscal year of the Corporation. Such report shall include a balance sheet as of the close of the fiscal year of the Corporation and a revenue and disbursement statement for the year ending on such closing date. Such financial statements shall be prepared from and in accordance with the books of the Corporation, and in conformity with generally accepted accounting principles applied on a consistent basis.

Section 2 - Permanent Records: The Corporation shall keep current and correct records of the accounts, minutes of the meetings and proceedings and membership records of the Corporation. Such records shall be kept at the registered office or the principal place of business of the Corporation. Any such records shall be in written form or in a form capable of being converted into written form.

Section 3 - Inspection of Corporate Records: Any person who is a Shareholder of the Corporation shall have the right at any reasonable time, and on written demand stating the purpose thereof, to examine and make copies from the relevant books and records of accounts, minutes, and records of the Corporation. Upon the written request of any Shareholder, the Corporation shall mail to such Shareholder a copy of the most recent balance sheet and revenue and disbursement statement.

ARTICLE VIII- SHARES OF STOCK

Section 1 - Authorized shares: The Corporation shall be authorized to issue ________________ shares of stock in one class only, each with a par value of $________________.

Section 2 - Certificates: Each shareholder of the Corporation shall be entitled to have a certificate representing all shares which he or she owns. The form of such certificate shall be adopted by a majority vote of the Board of Directors and shall be signed by the President and Secretary of the Corporation and sealed with the seal of the Corporation. No certificate representing shares shall be issued until the full amount of consideration therefore has been paid.

Section 3 - Stock Ledger: The Corporation shall maintain a ledger of the stock records of the Corporation. Transfers of shares of the Corporation shall be made on the stock ledger of the Corporation only at the direction of the holder of record upon surrender of the outstanding certificate(s). The Corporation shall be entitled to treat the holder of record of any share or shares as the absolute owner thereof for all purposes and, accordingly, shall not be bound to recognize any legal, equitable or other claim to, or interest in, such share or shares on the part of any other person, whether or not it shall have express or other notice thereof, except as otherwise expressly provided by law.

ARTICLE IX - DIVIDENDS

Upon approval by the Board of Directors the corporation may pay dividends on its shares in the form of cash, property or additional shares at any time that the Corporation is solvent and if such dividends would not render the Corporation insolvent.

ARTICLE X - FISCAL YEAR

The fiscal year of the Corporation shall be the period selected by the Board of Directors as the tax year of the Corporation for federal income tax purposes.

ARTICLE XI - CORPORATE SEAL

The Board of Directors may adopt, use and modify a corporate seal. Failure to affix the seal to corporate documents shall not affect the validity of such document.

ARTICLE XII - AMENDMENTS

The Articles of Incorporation may be amended by the shareholders as provided by Delaware statutes. These bylaws may be altered, amended, or replaced by the Board of Directors; provided, however, that any bylaws or amendments thereto as adopted by the Board of Directors may be altered, amended, or repealed by vote of the shareholders. Bylaws adopted by the Shareholders may not be amended or repealed by the Board.

ARTICLE XIII - INDEMNIFICATION

Any officer, director or employee of the Corporation shall be indemnified to the full extent allowed by the laws of the State of Delaware.

ARTICLE XIV - CONFLICT

In the event that any of these Bylaws at any time conflict with the General Corporation Law of the State of Delaware, then said law shall control and these Bylaws should be considered revised to comply with said law.

Certified to be the bylaws of the corporation adopted by the Board of Directors on __________________, _______.

____

Secretary

This page intentionally left blank.

Form **2553** (Rev. October 2001) Department of the Treasury Internal Revenue Service

Election by a Small Business Corporation

(Under section 1362 of the Internal Revenue Code)

▶ See Parts II and III on back and the separate instructions.

▶ The corporation may either send or fax this form to the IRS. See page 2 of the instructions.

OMB No. 1545-0146

Notes: 1. *__Do not__ file __Form 1120S,__ U.S. Income Tax Return for an S Corporation, for any tax year before the year the election takes effect.*

2. *This election to be an S corporation can be accepted only if all the tests are met under __Who May Elect__ on page 1 of the instructions; all shareholders have signed the consent statement; and the exact name and address of the corporation and other required form information are provided.*

3. *If the corporation was in existence before the effective date of this election, see __Taxes an S Corporation May Owe__ on page 1 of the instructions.*

Part I Election Information

Please Type or Print		
	Name of corporation (see instructions)	**A Employer identification number**
	Number, street, and room or suite no. (If a P.O. box, see instructions.)	B Date incorporated
	City or town, state, and ZIP code	C State of incorporation

D Check the applicable box(es) if the corporation, after applying for the EIN shown in **A** above, changed its name ☐ or address ☐

E Election is to be effective for tax year beginning (month, day, year) . . . . ▶ / /

F Name and title of officer or legal representative who the IRS may call for more information

G Telephone number of officer or legal representative ( )

H If this election takes effect for the first tax year the corporation exists, enter month, day, and year of the **earliest** of the following: (1) date the corporation first had shareholders, (2) date the corporation first had assets, or (3) date the corporation began doing business . . . . ▶ / /

I Selected tax year: Annual return will be filed for tax year ending (month and day) ▶

If the tax year ends on any date other than December 31, except for an automatic 52-53-week tax year ending with reference to the month of December, you **must** complete Part II on the back. If the date you enter is the ending date of an automatic 52-53-week tax year, write "52-53-week year" to the right of the date. See Temporary Regulations section 1.441-2T(e)(3).

J Name and address of each shareholder; shareholder's spouse having a community property interest in the corporation's stock; and each tenant in common, joint tenant, and tenant by the entirety. (A husband and wife (and their estates) are counted as one shareholder in determining the number of shareholders without regard to the manner in which the stock is owned.)	**K** Shareholders' Consent Statement. Under penalties of perjury, we declare that we consent to the election of the above-named corporation to be an S corporation under section 1362(a) and that we have examined this consent statement, including accompanying schedules and statements, and to the best of our knowledge and belief, it is true, correct, and complete. We understand our consent is binding and may not be withdrawn after the corporation has made a valid election. (Shareholders sign and date below.)		**L** Stock owned		**M** Social security number or employer identification number (see instructions)	**N** Shareholder's tax year ends (month and day)
	Signature	Date	Number of shares	Dates acquired		

Under penalties of perjury, I declare that I have examined this election, including accompanying schedules and statements, and to the best of my knowledge and belief, it is true, correct, and complete.

Signature of officer ▶ **Title ▶** **Date ▶**

Part II Selection of Fiscal Tax Year (All corporations using this part must complete item O and item P, Q, or R.)

O Check the applicable box to indicate whether the corporation is:

1. ☐ A new corporation adopting the tax year entered in item I, Part I.

2. ☐ An existing corporation retaining the tax year entered in item I, Part I.

3. ☐ An existing corporation changing to the tax year entered in item I, Part I.

P Complete item P if the corporation is using the expeditious approval provisions of Rev. Proc. 87-32, 1987-2 C.B. 396, to request **(1)** a natural business year (as defined in section 4.01(1) of Rev. Proc. 87-32) or **(2)** a year that satisfies the ownership tax year test in section 4.01(2) of Rev. Proc. 87-32. Check the applicable box below to indicate the representation statement the corporation is making as required under section 4 of Rev. Proc. 87-32.

1. Natural Business Year ▶ ☐ I represent that the corporation is retaining or changing to a tax year that coincides with its natural business year as defined in section 4.01(1) of Rev. Proc. 87-32 and as verified by its satisfaction of the requirements of section 4.02(1) of Rev. Proc. 87-32. In addition, if the corporation is changing to a natural business year as defined in section 4.01(1), I further represent that such tax year results in less deferral of income to the owners than the corporation's present tax year. I also represent that the corporation is not described in section 3.01(2) of Rev. Proc. 87-32. (See instructions for additional information that must be attached.)

2. Ownership Tax Year ▶ ☐ I represent that shareholders holding more than half of the shares of the stock (as of the first day of the tax year to which the request relates) of the corporation have the same tax year or are concurrently changing to the tax year that the corporation adopts, retains, or changes to per item I, Part I. I also represent that the corporation is not described in section 3.01(2) of Rev. Proc. 87-32.

Note: *If you do not use item P and the corporation wants a fiscal tax year, complete either item Q or R below. Item Q is used to request a fiscal tax year based on a business purpose and to make a back-up section 444 election. Item R is used to make a regular section 444 election.*

Q Business Purpose- To request a fiscal tax year based on a business purpose, you must check box Q1 and pay a user fee. See instructions for details. You may also check box Q2 and/or box Q3.

1. Check here ▶ ☐ if the fiscal year entered in item I, Part I, is requested under the provisions of section 6.03 of Rev. Proc. 87-32. Attach to Form 2553 a statement showing the business purpose for the requested fiscal year. See instructions for additional information that must be attached.

2. Check here ▶ ☐ to show that the corporation intends to make a back-up section 444 election in the event the corporation's business purpose request is not approved by the IRS. (See instructions for more information.)

3. Check here ▶ ☐ to show that the corporation agrees to adopt or change to a tax year ending December 31 if necessary for the IRS to accept this election for S corporation status in the event (1) the corporation's business purpose request is not approved and the corporation makes a back-up section 444 election, but is ultimately not qualified to make a section 444 election, or (2) the corporation's business purpose request is not approved and the corporation did not make a back-up section 444 election.

R Section 444 Election- To make a section 444 election, you must check box R1 and you may also check box R2.

1. Check here ▶ ☐ to show the corporation will make, if qualified, a section 444 election to have the fiscal tax year shown in item I, Part I. To make the election, you must complete **Form 8716,** Election To Have a Tax Year Other Than a Required Tax Year, and either attach it to Form 2553 or file it separately.

2. Check here ▶ ☐ to show that the corporation agrees to adopt or change to a tax year ending December 31 if necessary for the IRS to accept this election for S corporation status in the event the corporation is ultimately not qualified to make a section 444 election.

Part III Qualified Subchapter S Trust (QSST) Election Under Section 1361(d)(2)*

Income beneficiary's name and address	Social security number
Trust's name and address	Employer identification number

Date on which stock of the corporation was transferred to the trust (month, day, year) . . . . ▶ / /

In order for the trust named above to be a QSST and thus a qualifying shareholder of the S corporation for which this Form 2553 is filed, I hereby make the election under section 1361(d)(2). Under penalties of perjury, I certify that the trust meets the definitional requirements of section 1361(d)(3) and that all other information provided in Part III is true, correct, and complete.

Signature of income beneficiary or signature and title of legal representative or other qualified person making the election Date

*Use Part III to make the QSST election only if stock of the corporation has been transferred to the trust on or before the date on which the corporation makes its election to be an S corporation. The QSST election must be made and filed separately if stock of the corporation is transferred to the trust after the date on which the corporation makes the S election.

Instructions for Form 2553

Department of the Treasury
Internal Revenue Service

(Rev. October 2001)

Election by a Small Business Corporation

Section references are to the Internal Revenue Code unless otherwise noted.

General Instructions

Purpose

To elect to be an S corporation, a corporation must file Form 2553. The election permits the income of the S corporation to be taxed to the shareholders of the corporation rather than to the corporation itself, except as noted below under **Taxes an S Corporation May Owe.**

Who May Elect

A corporation may elect to be an S corporation only if it meets all of the following tests:

1. It is a domestic corporation.

Note: *A limited liability company (LLC)* ***must*** *file* ***Form 8832****, Entity Classification Election, to elect to be treated as an association taxable as a corporation in order to elect to be an S corporation.*

2. It has no more than 75 shareholders. A husband and wife (and their estates) are treated as one shareholder for this requirement. All other persons are treated as separate shareholders.

3. Its only shareholders are individuals, estates, exempt organizations described in section 401(a) or 501(c)(3), or certain trusts described in section 1361(c)(2)(A). See the instructions for Part III regarding qualified subchapter S trusts (QSSTs).

A trustee of a trust wanting to make an election under section 1361(e)(3) to be an electing small business trust (ESBT) should see Notice 97-12, 1997-1 C.B. 385. Also see Rev. Proc. 98-23, 1998-1 C.B. 662, for guidance on how to convert a QSST to an ESBT. If there was an inadvertent failure to timely file an ESBT election, see the relief provisions under Rev. Proc. 98-55, 1998-2 C.B. 643.

4. It has no nonresident alien shareholders.

5. It has only one class of stock (disregarding differences in voting rights). Generally, a corporation is treated as having only one class of stock if all outstanding shares of the corporation's stock confer identical rights to distribution and liquidation proceeds. See Regulations section 1.1361-1(l) for details.

6. It is not one of the following ineligible corporations:

a. A bank or thrift institution that uses the reserve method of accounting for bad debts under section 585,

b. An insurance company subject to tax under the rules of subchapter L of the Code,

c. A corporation that has elected to be treated as a possessions corporation under section 936, or

d. A domestic international sales corporation (DISC) or former DISC.

7. It has a permitted tax year as required by section 1378 or makes a section 444 election to have a tax year other than a permitted tax year. Section 1378 defines a permitted tax year as a tax year ending December 31, or any other tax year for which the corporation establishes a business purpose to the satisfaction of the IRS. See Part II for details on requesting a fiscal tax year based on a business purpose or on making a section 444 election.

8. Each shareholder consents as explained in the instructions for column K.

See sections 1361, 1362, and 1378 for additional information on the above tests.

A parent S corporation can elect to treat an eligible wholly-owned subsidiary as a qualified subchapter S subsidiary (QSub). If the election is made, the assets, liabilities, and items of income, deduction, and credit of the QSub are treated as those of the parent. To make the election, get **Form 8869,** Qualified Subchapter S Subsidiary Election. If the QSub election was not timely filed, the corporation may be entitled to relief under Rev. Proc. 98-55.

Taxes an S Corporation May Owe

An S corporation may owe income tax in the following instances:

1. If, at the end of any tax year, the corporation had accumulated earnings and profits, and its passive investment income under section 1362(d)(3) is more than 25% of its gross receipts, the corporation may owe tax on its excess net passive income.

2. A corporation with net recognized built-in gain (as defined in section 1374(d)(2)) may owe tax on its built-in gains.

3. A corporation that claimed investment credit before its first year as an S corporation will be liable for any investment credit recapture tax.

4. A corporation that used the LIFO inventory method for the year immediately preceding its first year as an S corporation may owe an additional tax due to LIFO recapture. The tax is paid in four equal installments, the first of which must be paid by the due date (not including extensions) of the corporation's income tax return for its last tax year as a C corporation.

For more details on these taxes, see the Instructions for Form 1120S.

Where To File

Send the original election (no photocopies) or fax it to the Internal Revenue Service Center listed below. If the corporation files this election by fax, keep the original Form 2553 with the corporation's permanent records.

If the corporation's principal business, office, or agency is located in	Use the following Internal Revenue Service Center address or fax number
Connecticut, Delaware, District of Columbia, Illinois, Indiana, Kentucky, Maine, Maryland, Massachusetts, Michigan, New Hampshire, New Jersey, New York, North Carolina, Ohio, Pennsylvania, Rhode Island, South Carolina, Vermont, Virginia, West Virginia, Wisconsin	Cincinnati, OH 45999 (859) 669-5748
Alabama, Alaska, Arizona, Arkansas, California, Colorado, Florida, Georgia, Hawaii, Idaho, Iowa, Kansas, Louisiana, Minnesota, Mississippi, Missouri, Montana, Nebraska, Nevada, New Mexico, North Dakota, Oklahoma, Oregon, South Dakota, Tennessee, Texas, Utah, Washington, Wyoming	Ogden, UT 84201 (801) 620-7116

When To Make the Election

Complete and file Form 2553 **(a)** at any time before the 16th day of the 3rd month of the tax year, if filed during the tax year the election is to take effect, or **(b)** at any time during the preceding tax year. An election made no later than 2 months and 15 days after the beginning of a tax year that is less than 2½ months long is treated as timely made for that tax year. **An election made after the 15th day of the 3rd month but before the end of the tax year is effective for the next year.** For example, if a calendar tax year corporation makes the election in April 2001, it is effective for the corporation's 2002 calendar tax year.

However, an election made after the due date will be accepted as timely filed if the corporation can show that the failure to file on time was due to reasonable cause. To request relief for a late election, the corporation generally must request a private letter ruling and pay a user fee in accordance with Rev. Proc. 2001-1, 2001-1 I.R.B. 1 (or its successor). But if the election is filed within 12 months of its due date and the original due date for filing the corporation's initial Form 1120S has not passed, the ruling and user fee requirements do not apply. To request relief in this case, write "FILED PURSUANT TO REV. PROC. 98-55" at the top of page 1 of Form 2553, attach a statement explaining the reason for failing to file the election on time, and file Form 2553 as otherwise instructed. See Rev. Proc. 98-55 for more details.

See Regulations section 1.1362-6(b)(3)(iii) for how to obtain relief for an inadvertent invalid election if the corporation filed a timely election, but one or more shareholders did not file a timely consent.

Acceptance or Nonacceptance of Election

The service center will notify the corporation if its election is accepted and when it will take effect. The corporation will also be notified if its election is not accepted. The corporation should generally receive a determination on its election within 60 days after it has filed Form 2553. If box Q1 in Part II is checked on page 2, the corporation will receive a ruling letter from the IRS in Washington, DC, that either approves or denies the selected tax year. When box Q1 is checked, it will generally take an additional 90 days for the Form 2553 to be accepted.

Care should be exercised to ensure that the IRS receives the election. If the corporation is not notified of acceptance or nonacceptance of its election within 3 months of the date of filing (date mailed), or within 6 months if box Q1 is checked, take follow-up action by corresponding with the service center where the corporation filed the election.

If the IRS questions whether Form 2553 was filed, an acceptable proof of filing is **(a)** certified or registered mail receipt (timely postmarked) from the U.S. Postal Service, or its equivalent from a designated private delivery service (see Notice 99-41, 1999-2 C.B. 325 (or its successor)); **(b)** Form 2553 with accepted stamp; **(c)** Form 2553 with stamped IRS received date; or **(d)** IRS letter stating that Form 2553 has been accepted.

CAUTION *Do not file Form 1120S for any tax year before the year the election takes effect. If the corporation is now required to file* ***Form 1120,*** *U.S. Corporation Income Tax Return, or any other applicable tax return, continue filing it until the election takes effect.*

End of Election

Once the election is made, it stays in effect until it is terminated. If the election is terminated in a tax year beginning after 1996, IRS consent is generally required for another election by the corporation (or a successor corporation) on Form 2553 for any tax year before the 5th tax year after the first tax year in which the termination took effect. See Regulations section 1.1362-5 for details.

Part I (*All corporations must complete.*)

Name and Address of Corporation

Enter the true corporate name as stated in the corporate charter or other legal document creating it. If the corporation's mailing address is the same as someone else's, such as a shareholder's, enter "c/o" and this person's name following the name of the corporation. Include the suite, room, or other unit number after the street address. If the Post Office does not deliver to the street address and the corporation has a P.O. box, show the box number instead of the street address. If the corporation changed its name or address after applying for its employer identification number, be sure to check the box in item D of Part I.

Item A. Employer Identification Number (EIN)

If the corporation has applied for an EIN but has not received it, enter "applied for." If the corporation does not have an EIN, it should apply for one on **Form SS-4,** Application for Employer Identification Number. You can order Form SS-4 by calling 1-800-TAX-FORM (1-800-829-3676).

Item E. Effective Date of Election

Enter the beginning effective date (month, day, year) of the tax year requested for the S corporation. Generally, this will be the beginning date of the tax year for which the ending effective date is required to be shown in item I, Part I. For a new corporation (first year the corporation exists) it will generally be the date required to be shown in item H, Part I. The tax year of a new corporation starts on the date that it has shareholders, acquires assets, or begins doing business, whichever happens first. If the effective date for item E for a newly formed corporation is later than the date in item H, the corporation should file Form 1120 or Form 1120-A for the tax period between these dates.

Column K. Shareholders' Consent Statement

Each shareholder who owns (or is deemed to own) stock at the time the election is made must consent to the election. If the election is made during the corporation's tax year for which it first takes effect, any person who held stock at any time during the part of that year that occurs before the election is made, must consent to the election, even though the person may have sold or transferred his or her stock before the election is made.

An election made during the first $2\frac{1}{2}$ months of the tax year is effective for the following tax year if any person who held stock in the corporation during the part of the tax year before the election was made, and who did not hold stock at the time the election was made, did not consent to the election.

Each shareholder consents by signing and dating in column K or signing and dating a separate consent statement described below. The following special rules apply in determining who must sign the consent statement.

- If a husband and wife have a community interest in the stock or in the income from it, both must consent.
- Each tenant in common, joint tenant, and tenant by the entirety must consent.
- A minor's consent is made by the minor, legal representative of the minor, or a natural or adoptive parent of the minor if no legal representative has been appointed.
- The consent of an estate is made by the executor or administrator.
- The consent of an electing small business trust is made by the trustee.
- If the stock is owned by a trust (other than an electing small business trust), the deemed owner of the trust must consent. See section 1361(c)(2) for details regarding trusts that are permitted to be shareholders and rules for determining who is the deemed owner.

Continuation sheet or separate consent statement. If you need a continuation sheet or use a separate consent statement, attach it to Form 2553. The separate consent statement must contain the name, address, and EIN of the corporation and the shareholder information requested in columns J through N of Part I. If you want, you may combine all the shareholders' consents in one statement.

Column L

Enter the number of shares of stock each shareholder owns and the dates the stock was acquired. If the election is made during the corporation's tax year for which it first takes effect, do not list the shares of stock for those shareholders who sold or transferred all of their stock before the election was made. However, these shareholders must still consent to the election for it to be effective for the tax year.

Column M

Enter the social security number of each shareholder who is an individual. Enter the EIN of each shareholder that is an estate, a qualified trust, or an exempt organization.

Column N

Enter the month and day that each shareholder's tax year ends. If a shareholder is changing his or her tax year, enter the tax year the shareholder is changing to, and attach an explanation indicating the present tax year and the basis for the change (e.g., automatic revenue procedure or letter ruling request).

Signature

Form 2553 must be signed by the president, treasurer, assistant treasurer, chief accounting officer, or other corporate officer (such as tax officer) authorized to sign.

Part II

Complete Part II if you selected a tax year ending on any date other than December 31 (other than a 52-53-week tax year ending with reference to the month of December).

Box P1

Attach a statement showing separately for each month the amount of gross receipts for the most recent 47 months as required by section 4.03(3) of Rev. Proc. 87-32, 1987-2 C.B. 396. A corporation that does not have a 47-month period of gross receipts cannot establish a natural business year under section 4.01(1).

Box Q1

For examples of an acceptable business purpose for requesting a fiscal tax year, see Rev. Rul. 87-57, 1987-2 C.B. 117.

In addition to a statement showing the business purpose for the requested fiscal year, you must attach the other information necessary to meet the ruling request requirements of Rev. Proc. 2001-1 (or its successor). Also attach a statement that shows separately the amount of gross receipts from sales or services (and inventory costs, if applicable) for each of the 36 months preceding the effective date of the election to be an S corporation. If the corporation has been in existence for fewer than 36 months, submit figures for the period of existence.

If you check box Q1, you will be charged a user fee of up to $600 (subject to change—see Rev. Proc. 2001-1 or its successor). Do not pay the fee when filing Form 2553. The service center will send Form 2553 to the IRS in Washington, DC, who, in turn, will notify the corporation that the fee is due.

Box Q2

If the corporation makes a back-up section 444 election for which it is qualified, then the election will take effect in the event the business purpose request is not approved. In some cases, the tax year requested under the back-up section 444 election may be different than the tax year requested under business purpose. See **Form 8716,** Election To Have a Tax Year Other Than a Required Tax Year, for details on making a back-up section 444 election.

Boxes Q2 and R2

If the corporation is not qualified to make the section 444 election after making the item Q2 back-up section 444 election or indicating its intention to make the election in item R1, and therefore it later files a calendar year return, it should write "Section 444 Election Not Made" in the top left corner of the first calendar year Form 1120S it files.

Part III

Certain qualified subchapter S trusts (QSSTs) may make the QSST election required by section 1361(d)(2) in Part III. Part III may be used to make the QSST election only if corporate stock has been transferred to the trust on or before the date on which the corporation makes its election to be an S corporation. However, a statement can be used instead of Part III to make the election. If there was an inadvertent failure to timely file a QSST election, see the relief provisions under Rev. Proc. 98-55.

Note: *Use Part III **only** if you make the election in Part I (i.e., Form 2553 cannot be filed with only Part III completed).*

The deemed owner of the QSST must also consent to the S corporation election in column K, page 1, of Form 2553. See section 1361(c)(2).

Paperwork Reduction Act Notice. We ask for the information on this form to carry out the Internal Revenue laws of the United States. You are required to give us the information. We need it to ensure that you are complying with these laws and to allow us to figure and collect the right amount of tax.

You are not required to provide the information requested on a form that is subject to the Paperwork Reduction Act unless the form displays a valid OMB control number. Books or records relating to a form or its instructions must be retained as long as their contents may become material in the administration of any Internal Revenue law. Generally, tax returns and return information are confidential, as required by section 6103.

The time needed to complete and file this form will depend on individual circumstances. The estimated average time is:

Recordkeeping	8 hr., 51 min.
Learning about the law or the form	3 hr., 10 min.
Preparing, copying, assembling, and sending the form to the IRS	3 hr., 27 min.

If you have comments concerning the accuracy of these time estimates or suggestions for making this form simpler, we would be happy to hear from you. You can write to the Tax Forms Committee, Western Area Distribution Center, Rancho Cordova, CA 95743-0001. **Do not** send the form to this address. Instead, see **Where To File** on page 2.

WAIVER OF NOTICE

OF THE ORGANIZATION MEETING

OF

____

We, the undersigned incorporators named in the certificate of incorporation of the above-named corporation hereby agree and consent that the organization meeting of the corporation be held on the date and time and place stated below and hereby waive all notice of such meeting and of any adjournment thereof.

Place of meeting: ______________________________

Date of Meeting: ____________________

Time of meeting: ____________________

Dated: ______________________________

____
Incorporator

____
Incorporator

____
Incorporator

This page intentionally left blank.

MINUTES OF THE ORGANIZATIONAL MEETING OF INCORPORATORS AND DIRECTORS OF

____

The organization meeting of the above corporation was held on __________________ __________________________, ________ at ____ ______________________________ at ____ o'clock __m.

The following persons were present:

______________________________	______________________________
______________________________	______________________________
______________________________	______________________________

The Waiver of notice of this meeting was signed by all directors and incorporators named in the Certificate of Incorporation and filed in the minute book.

The meeting was called to order by ___________________________ an Incorporator named in the Certificate of Incorporation. ________________________________ was nominated and elected Chairman and acted as such until relieved by the president. ________________________ was nominated and elected temporary secretary, and acted as such until relieved by the permanent secretary.

The first order of business was election of directors. The following were duly nominated and elected as director(s) by the incorporator(s).

______________________________	______________________________
______________________________	______________________________

A copy of the Certificate of Incorporation which was filed with the Secretary of State of the State of Delaware on __________________, _______ was examined by the Directors and Incorporators and filed in the minute book.

The proposed Bylaws for the corporation were then presented to the meeting and discussed. Upon motion duly made, seconded and carried, the Bylaws were adopted and added to the minute book.

The election of officers for the coming year was then held and the following were duly nominated and elected by the Board of Directors to be the officers of the corporation, to serve until such time as their successors are elected and qualified:

President: ____________________________
Vice President: ____________________________
Secretary: ____________________________
Treasurer: ____________________________

A corporate seal for the corporation was then presented to the meeting and upon motion duly made, seconded and carried, it was adopted as the seal of the corporation. An impression thereof was then made in the margin of these minutes

The necessity of opening a bank account was then discussed and upon motion duly made, seconded and carried, the following resolution was adopted:

RESOLVED that the corporation open bank accounts with ________________ __________________________________ and that the officers of the corporation are authorized to take such action as is necessary to open such accounts; that the bank's printed form of resolution is hereby adopted and incorporated into these minutes by reference and shall be placed in the minute book; that any ____ of the following persons shall have signature authority over the account:

________________________________ ________________________________
________________________________ ________________________________
________________________________ ________________________________

Proposed stock certificates and stock transfer ledger were then presented to the meeting and examined. Upon motion duly made, seconded and carried the stock certificates and ledger were adopted as the certificates and transfer book to be used by the corporation. A sample stock certificate marked "VOID" and the stock transfer ledger were then added to the minute book. Upon motion duly made, seconded and carried, it was then resolved that the stock certificates, when issued, would be signed by the President and the Secretary of the corporation.

The tax status of the corporation was then discussed and it was moved, seconded and carried that the stock of the corporation be issued under § 1244 of the Internal Revenue Code and that the officers of the corporation take the necessary action to:

1. Obtain an employer tax number by filing form SS-4,

2. ☐ Become an S-Corporation for tax purposes,
   ☐ Remain a C-Corporation for tax purposes,

The expenses of organizing the corporation were then discussed and it was moved, seconded and carried that the corporation pay in full from the corporate funds the expenses and reimburse any advances made by the incorporators upon proof of payment.

The Directors named in the Certificate of Incorporation then tendered their resignations, effective upon the adjournment of this meeting. Upon motion duly made, seconded and carried, the following named persons were elected as Directors of the corporation, each to hold office until the first annual meeting of shareholders, and until a successor of each shall have been elected and qualified.

____

____

____

There were presented to the corporation, the following offer(s) to purchase shares of capital stock:

FROM	NO. OF SHARES	CONSIDERATION

The offers were discussed and after motion duly made, seconded and carried were approved. It was further resolved that the Board of Directors has determined that the consideration was valued at least equal to the value of the shares to be issued and that upon tender of the consideration, fully paid non-assessable shares of the corporation be issued.

There being no further business before the meeting, on motion duly made, seconded and carried, the meeting adjourned.

DATED: ____________________

____

President

____

Secretary

RESOLUTION

of

____

a Delaware Corporation

RESOLVED that the corporation elects "S-Corporation" status for tax purposes under the Internal Revenue Code and that the officers of the corporation are directed to file IRS Form 2553 and to take any further action necessary for the corporation to qualify for S-corporation status.

Shareholders' Consent

The undersigned shareholders being all of the shareholders of the above corporation, a Delaware corporation hereby consent to the election of the corporation to obtain S-corporation status.

Name and Address of Shareholder	Shares Owned	Date Acquired
____________________________________	____________	_______________
____________________________________	____________	_______________
____________________________________	____________	_______________

Date:________________________

____

____

____

____

____

This page intentionally left blank.

OFFER TO PURCHASE STOCK

Date: ____________________

To the Board of Directors of

____

The undersigned, hereby offers to purchase ____________________ shares of the _____________________________ stock of your corporation at a total purchase price of ____.

Very truly yours,

____

- -

Offer to Sell Stock
Pursuant to Sec. 1244 I.R.C.

Date: ______________________

To: _______________________________

Dear

The corporation hereby offers to sell to you __________ shares of its common stock at a price of $_________ per share. These shares are issued pursuant to Section 1244 of the Internal Revenue Code,

Your signature below shall constitute an acceptance of our offer as of the date it is received by the corporation.

Very truly yours,

____

By:____________________________

Accepted:

____

This page intentionally left blank.

Stock Ledger

Certificates Issued						Transfer of Shares				
Cert. No.	No. of Shares	Date of Acquisition	Shareholder Name and Address	From Whom Transferred	Amount Paid	Date of Transfer	To Whom Transferred	Cert. No. Surrendered	No. of Shares Transferred	Cert. No.

This page intentionally left blank.

The shares represented by this certificate have not been registered under state or federal securities laws. Therefore, they may not be transferred until the corporation determines that such transfer will not adversely affect the exemptions relied upon.

Certificate No.

Shares

Organized under the laws of Delaware

This certifies that ______________________________ is the holder of record of ____________________ shares of ____________ stock of

transferable only on the books of the corporation by the holder hereof in person or by attorney upon surrender of this certificate properly endorsed.

In witness whereof, the said corporation has caused this certificate to be signed by its duly authorized officers and its corporate seal to be hereto affixed this ___ day of ____________, _____.

____________________ ____________________

For value received, _____ hereby sell, assign and transfer unto _______________________

____,

____

________ *shares represented by this certificate and do hereby irrevocably constitute and appoint* ____ *attorney to transfer the said shares on the books of the corporation with full power of substitution in the premises.*

Dated ___________________________

____

Witness:

____

The shares represented by this certificate have not been registered under state or federal securities laws. Therefore, they may not be transferred until the corporation determines that such transfer will not adversely affect the exemptions relied upon.

Certificate No.

Shares

Organized under the laws of Delaware ____________

This certifies that ______________________________ *is the holder of record of* ______________________ *shares of* ____________ *stock of*

transferable only on the books of the corporation by the holder hereof in person or by attorney upon surrender of this certificate properly endorsed.

In witness whereof, the said corporation has caused this certificate to be signed by its duly authorized officers and its corporate seal to be hereto affixed this ___ *day of* ____________, _____.

______________________ ______________________

For value received, _____ hereby sell, assign and transfer unto ______________________

____,

____

________ *shares represented by this certificate and do hereby irrevocably constitute and appoint* ____ *attorney to transfer the said shares on the books of the corporation with full power of substitution in the premises.*

Dated ________________________

____

Witness:

____

The shares represented by this certificate have not been registered under state or federal securities laws. Therefore, they may not be transferred until the corporation determines that such transfer will not adversely affect the exemptions relied upon.

Certificate No.

Shares

Organized under the laws of Delaware

This certifies that ______________________________ *is the holder of record of* ______________________________ *shares of* ________________ *stock of*

transferable only on the books of the corporation by the holder hereof in person or by attorney upon surrender of this certificate properly endorsed.

In witness whereof, the said corporation has caused this certificate to be signed by its duly authorized officers and its corporate seal to be hereto affixed this ___ *day of* ________________, _____.

______________________________ ______________________________

For value received, _____ hereby sell, assign and transfer unto ________________________

____,

____

________ shares represented by this certificate and do hereby irrevocably constitute and appoint ____ attorney to transfer the said shares on the books of the corporation with full power of substitution in the premises.

Dated ___________________________

____

Witness:

____

The shares represented by this certificate have not been registered under state or federal securities laws. Therefore, they may not be transferred until the corporation determines that such transfer will not adversely affect the exemptions relied upon.

Certificate No. ______

Shares ______

Organized under the laws of Delaware ______

This certifies that ______ *is the holder of record of* ______ *shares of* ______ *stock of*

transferable only on the books of the corporation by the holder hereof in person or by attorney upon surrender of this certificate properly endorsed.

In witness whereof, the said corporation has caused this certificate to be signed by its duly authorized officers and its corporate seal to be hereto affixed this ___ *day of* ______, ______.

______ ______

For value received, _____ hereby sell, assign and transfer unto ________________________

____,

____

________ shares represented by this certificate and do hereby irrevocably constitute and appoint ____ attorney to transfer the said shares on the books of the corporation with full power of substitution in the premises.

Dated ___________________________

____

Witness:

____

The shares represented by this certificate have not been registered under state or federal securities laws. Therefore, they may not be transferred until the corporation determines that such transfer will not adversely affect the exemptions relied upon.

Certificate No.

Shares

Organized under the laws of Delaware ____________

This certifies that ______________________________ *is the holder of record of* ______________________ *shares of* ______________ *stock of*

transferable only on the books of the corporation by the holder hereof in person or by attorney upon surrender of this certificate properly endorsed.

In witness whereof, the said corporation has caused this certificate to be signed by its duly authorized officers and its corporate seal to be hereto affixed this ___ *day of* ______________, _____.

______________________ ______________________

For value received, _____ hereby sell, assign and transfer unto ______________________________

____,

____

________ shares represented by this certificate and do hereby irrevocably constitute and appoint ____ attorney to transfer the said shares on the books of the corporation with full power of substitution in the premises.

Dated ____________________________

____

Witness:

____

WAVER OF NOTICE OF THE ANNUAL MEETING OF THE BOARD OF DIRECTORS OF

____

The undersigned, being all the Directors of the Corporation, hereby agree and consent that an annual meeting of the Board of Directors of the Corporation be held on the ____ day of ______________, ______ at ___ o'clock __m at ____ ____ and do hereby waive all notice whatsoever of such meeting and of any adjournment or adjournments thereof.

We do further agree and consent that any and all lawful business may be transacted at such meeting or at any adjournment or adjournments thereof as may be deemed advisable by the Directors present. Any business transacted at such meeting or at any adjournment or adjournments thereof shall be as valid and legal as if such meeting or adjourned meeting were held after notice.

Date: ______________________

____
Director

____
Director

____
Director

____
Director

This page intentionally left blank.

MINUTES OF THE ANNUAL MEETING OF THE BOARD OF DIRECTORS OF

____

The annual meeting of the Board of Directors of the Corporation was held on the date and at the time and place set forth in the written waiver of notice signed by the directors, and attached to the minutes of this meeting.

The following were present, being all the directors of the Corporation:

______________________________ ______________________________

______________________________ ______________________________

The meeting was called to order and it was moved, seconded and unanimously carried that ______________________ act as Chairman and that ____________________ act as Secretary.

The minutes of the last meeting of the Board of Directors which was held on __________________, _____ were read and approved by the Board.

Upon motion duly made, seconded and carried, the following were elected officers for the following year and until their successors are elected and qualify:

President:
Vice President:
Secretary
Treasurer:

There being no further business to come before the meeting, upon motion duly made, seconded and unanimously carried, it was adjourned.

____
Secretary

Directors:

____

____

____

____

This page intentionally left blank.

WAIVER OF NOTICE OF THE ANNUAL MEETING OF THE SHAREHOLDERS OF

____

The undersigned, being all the shareholders of the Corporation, hereby agree and consent that an annual meeting of the shareholders of the Corporation be held on the ______ day of ____________________, __________ at ___ o'clock __m at ______________________ ____ and do hereby waive all notice whatsoever of such meeting and of any adjournment or adjournments thereof.

We do further agree and consent that any and all lawful business may be transacted at such meeting or at any adjournment or adjournments thereof. Any business transacted at such meeting or at any adjournment or adjournments thereof shall be as valid and legal as if such meeting or adjourned meeting were held after notice.

Date: ______________________

____
Shareholder

____
Shareholder

____
Shareholder

____
Shareholder

This page intentionally left blank.

MINUTES OF THE ANNUAL MEETING OF SHAREHOLDERS OF

____

The annual meeting of Shareholders of the Corporation was held on the date and at the time and place set forth in the written waiver of notice signed by the shareholders, and attached to the minutes of this meeting.

There were present the following shareholders:

Shareholder	No. of Shares
______________________________	__________
______________________________	__________
______________________________	__________
______________________________	__________

The meeting was called to order and it was moved, seconded and unanimously carried that ____________________ act as Chairman and that ____________________ act as Secretary.

A roll call was taken and the Chairman noted that all of the outstanding shares of the Corporation were represented in person or by proxy. Any proxies were attached to these minutes.

The minutes of the last meeting of the shareholders which was held on ________________, ______ were read and approved by the shareholders.

Upon motion duly made, seconded and carried, the following were elected directors for the following year:

______________________________ ______________________________

______________________________ ______________________________

There being no further business to come before the meeting, upon motion duly made, seconded and unanimously carried, it was adjourned.

____
Secretary

Shareholders:

____

____

____

____

This page intentionally left blank.

WAIVER OF NOTICE OF SPECIAL MEETING OF THE BOARD OF DIRECTORS OF

____

The undersigned, being all the Directors of the Corporation, hereby agree and consent that a special meeting of the Board of Directors of the Corporation be held on the ____ day of ______________, _____ at ___ o'clock __m at ______________________________ ____ and do hereby waive all notice whatsoever of such meeting and of any adjournment or adjournments thereof.

The purpose of the meeting is:

We do further agree and consent that any and all lawful business may be transacted at such meeting or at any adjournment or adjournments thereof as may be deemed advisable by the Directors present. Any business transacted at such meeting or at any adjournment or adjournments thereof shall be as valid and legal as if such meeting or adjourned meeting were held after notice.

Date: ____________________

____
Director

____
Director

____
Director

____
Director

This page intentionally left blank.

MINUTES OF SPECIAL MEETING OF THE BOARD OF DIRECTORS OF

____

A special meeting of the Board of Directors of the Corporation was held on the date and at the time and place set forth in the written waiver of notice signed by the directors, and attached to the minutes of this meeting.

The following were present, being all the directors of the Corporation:

______________________________ ______________________________

______________________________ ______________________________

The meeting was called to order and it was moved, seconded and unanimously carried that ____________________ act as Chairman and that ____________________ act as Secretary.

The minutes of the last meeting of the Board of Directors which was held on ________________, ______ were read and approved by the Board.

Upon motion duly made, seconded and carried, the following resolution was adopted:

There being no further business to come before the meeting, upon motion duly made, seconded and unanimously carried, it was adjourned.

____
Secretary

Directors:

____

____

____

____

This page intentionally left blank.

WAIVER OF NOTICE OF SPECIAL MEETING OF THE SHAREHOLDERS OF

____

The undersigned, being all the shareholders of the Corporation, hereby agree and consent that a special meeting of the shareholders of the Corporation be held on the ____ day of ________________, ______ at ___ o'clock __m at ______________________________ ____ and do hereby waive all notice whatsoever of such meeting and of any adjournment or adjournments thereof.

The purpose of the meeting is

We do further agree and consent that any and all lawful business may be transacted at such meeting or at any adjournment or adjournments thereof. Any business transacted at such meeting or at any adjournment or adjournments thereof shall be as valid and legal as if such meeting or adjourned meeting were held after notice.

Date: ____________________

____
Shareholder

____
Shareholder

____
Shareholder

____
Shareholder

This page intentionally left blank.

MINUTES OF SPECIAL MEETING OF
SHAREHOLDERS OF

____

A special meeting of Shareholders of the Corporation was held on the date and at the time and place set forth in the written waiver of notice signed by the shareholders, and attached to the minutes of this meeting.

There were present the following shareholders:

Shareholder	No. of Shares
______________________________	__________
______________________________	__________
______________________________	__________
______________________________	__________

The meeting was called to order and it was moved, seconded and unanimously carried that ______________________ act as Chairman and that ____________________ act as Secretary.

A roll call was taken and the Chairman noted that all of the outstanding shares of the Corporation were represented in person or by proxy. Any proxies were attached to these minutes.

The minutes of the last meeting of the shareholders which was held on ____________________, ______ were read and approved by the shareholders.

Upon motion duly made, seconded and carried, the following resolution was adopted:

There being no further business to come before the meeting, upon motion duly made, seconded and unanimously carried, it was adjourned.

____
Secretary

Shareholders:

____

____

____

____

STATE *of* DELAWARE
CERTIFICATE *of* INCORPORATION
A NON-STOCK CORPORATION

- **First:** The name of this Corporation is ______________________________________ ____.

- **Second:** Its Registered Office in the State of Delaware is to be located at __________ __________________________________Street, in the City of __________________ County of _________________Zip Code _______. The registered agent in charge thereof is ____ ____ ____

- **Third:** The purpose of the corporation is to engage in any lawful act of activity for which corporations may be organized under the General Corporation Law of Delaware. *(If the corporation is to be a nonprofit corporation, please add: "This Corporation shall be a nonprofit corporation.")*

  ____
  ____

- **Fourth:** The corporation shall not have any capital stock, and the conditions of membership shall be *(In lieu of setting out the conditions of membership in the Certificate of Incorporation, a statement may be inserted that the conditions of membership shall be stated in the By-Laws.)* as follows:

  ____
  ____
  ____

- **Fifth:** The name and mailing address of the incorporator are as follows:

  Name ____

  Mailing Address____

  ________________________Zip Code_____________

- **I, The Undersigned,** for the purpose of forming a corporation under the laws of the State of Delaware, do make, file and record this Certificate, and do certify that the facts herein stated are true, and I have accordingly hereunto set my hand this __________day of _______________, A.D. 20______.

BY: ________________________________
(Incorporator)

NAME: _______________________________
(Type or Print)

This page intentionally left blank.

STATE *of* DELAWARE LIMITED LIABILITY COMPANY CERTIFICATE *of* FORMATION

- **First:** The name of the limited liability company is ______________________________

  ____.

- **Second:** The address of its registered office in the State of Delaware is ____________

  ______________________ in the City of ____________________________________.
  The name of its Registered agent at such address

  ____

  ____.

- **Third:** (*Use this paragraph only if the company is to have a specific effective date of dissolution.*) "The latest date on which the limited liability company is to dissolve is ________________."

- **Fourth:** (Insert any other matters the members determine to include herein.)

  ____

  ____

  ____

  ____

  ____

  ____

  ____

In Witness Whereof, the undersigned have executed this Certificate of Formation of ______________________ this ___________ day of _______________, 20 ________.

By:________________________________
Authorized Person(s)

Name:________________________________
Type or Print

This page intentionally left blank.

Form **8832**

(December 1996)

Department of the Treasury
Internal Revenue Service

Entity Classification

OMB No. 1545-1516

Please Type or Print

Name of entity

...mber (EIN)

Number, street, and room or suite no. If a P.O. box, see instructions

City or town, state, and ZIP code. If a foreign address, enter city, province or state, post...

1 Type of election (see instructions):

a ☐ Initial classification by a newly-formed entity (or change in current classifica... to take effect on January 1, 1997)

b ☐ Change in current classification (to take effect later than January 1, 1997)

2 Form of an entity (see instructions):

a ☐ A domestic eligible entity electing to ne classified as an association taxable as a corporation.

b ☐ A domestic eligible entity electing to be classified as a partnership.

c ☐ A domestic eligible entity with a single owner electing to be disregarded as a separate entity.

d ☐ A foreign eligible entity electing to be classified as an association taxable as a corporation.

e ☐ A foreign eligible entity electing to be classified as a partnership.

f ☐ A foreign eligible entity with a single owner electing to be disregarded as a separate entity.

3 Election is to be effective beginning (month, day, year) (see instructions) . . . . ** ___/___/___

4 Name and title of person whom the IRS may call for more information	5 That person's telephone number

Consent Statement and Signature(s) (see instructions)

Under penalties of perjury, I (we) declare that I (we) consent to the election of the above-named entity to be classified as indicated above, and that I (we) have examined this consent statement, and to the best of my (our) knowledge and belief, it is true, correct and complete. If I an an officer, manager, or member signing for all members of the entity, I further declare that I am authorized to execute this consent statement on their behalf.

Signature(s)	Date	Title

For Paperwork Reduction Act Notice, see page 2. Cat. No. 22598R Form **8832** (12-96)

General Instructions

Section references are to the Internal Revenue Code unless otherwise noted.

Paperwork Reduction Act Notice

We ask for the information on this form to carry out the Internal Revenue laws of the United States. You are required to give us the information. We need it to ensure that you are complying with these laws and to allow us to figure and collect the right amount of tax.

You are not required to provide the information requested on a form that is subject to the Paperwork Reduction Act unless the form or its instructions must be retained as long as their contents may become material in the administration of any Internal Revenue law. Generally, tax returns and return information are confidential, as required by section 6103.

The time needed to complete and file this form will vary depending on individual circumstances. The estimated average time is:

Recordkeeping . . .1 hr., 20 min.

Learning about the law or the form . . .1 hr., 41 min.

Preparing or sending the form to the IRS. . . .17 min.

If you have comments concerning the accuracy of these time estimated or suggestions for making this form simpler, we would be happy to hear from you. You can write to the Tax Forms Committee, Western Area Distribution Center, Rancho Cordova, Ca 95743-001. **DO NOT** send the form to this address. Instead, see **Where To File** on page 3.

Purpose of Form

For Federal tax purposes, certain business entities automatically are classified as corporations. See items **1** and **3** through **8** under the definition of corporation on this page. Other business entities may choose how they are classified for Federal tax purposes. Except for a business entity automatically classified as a corporation, a business entity with at least two members can choose to be classified as either an association taxable as a corporation or a partnership, and a business entity with a single member can choose to be classified as either an association taxable as a corporation or disregarded as an entity separate from its owner.

Generally, an eligible entity that does not file this form will be classified under the default rules described below. An eligible entity that chooses not to be classified under the default rules or that wishes to change its current classification must file Form 8832 to elect a classification, The IRS will use the information entered on this form to establish the entity's filing and reporting requirements for Federal tax purposes.

Default Rules

Existing entity default rule.—Certain domestic and foreign entities that are already in existence before January 1, 1997, and have an established Federal tax classification, generally do not need to make an election to continue that classification. However, for an eligible entity with a single owner that claimed to be a partnership under the law in effect before January 1, 1997, that entity will now be disregarded as an entity separate from its owner. If an existing entity decides to change its classification, it may do so subject to the rules in Regulations section 301.7701-3(c)(1)(iv). A foreign eligible entity is treated as being in existence prior to the effective date of this section only if the entity's classification is relevant at any time during the 60 months prior to January 1, 1997.

Domestic default rule.—Unless an election is made on Form 8832 a domestic eligible entity is:

1. A partnership if it has two or more members.

2. Disregarded as an entity separate from its owner if it has a single owner.

Foreign default rule.—Unless an election is made on Form 8832, a foreign eligible entity is:

1. A partnership if it has two or more members and at least one member does not have limited liability.

2. An association if all members have limited liability.

3. Disregarded as an entity separate from its owner if it has a single owner that does not have limited liability.

Definitions

Business entity.—A business entity is any entity recognized for Federal tax purposes that is not properly classified as a trust under Regulations section 301.7701-4 or otherwise subject to special treatment under the Code. See Regulations section 301.7701-2(a).

Corporation.—For Federal tax purposes, a corporation is any of the following:

1. A business entity organized under a Federal or state statute, or under a statute of a federally recognized Indian tribe, if the statute describes or refers to the entity as incorporated or as a corporation, body corporate, or body politic.

2. An association (as determined under regulations section 301.7701-3).

3. A business entity organized under a state statute, if the statute describes or refers to the entity as a joint-stock company or joint-stock association.

4. An insurance company.

5. A state-chartered business entity conducting banking activities, if any of its deposits are insured under the Federal Deposit Insurance Act, as amended, 12 U.S.C. 1811 et seq., or a similar Federal statute.

6. A business entity wholly owned by a state or any political subdivision thereof.

7. A business entity that is taxable as a corporation under a provision of the Code other than section 7701(a)(3).

8. A foreign business entity listed in Regulations section 301.7701-2(b)(8). However, a foreign business entity listed in those regulations generally will not be treated as a corporation if all of the following apply:

a. The entity was in existence on May 8, 1996.

b. The entity's classification was relevant (as defined below) on May 8, 1996.

c. No person (including the entity) for who the entity's classification was relevant on May 8, 1996, treats the entity as a corporation for purposes of filing that person's Federal income tax returns, information returns, and withholding documents for the tax year including May 8, 1996.

d. Any change in the entity's claimed classification within the 60 months prior to May 8, 1996, was a result of a change in the organizational documents of the entity, and the entity recognized the Federal tax consequences of any change in the entity's classification within the 60 months prior to May 8, 1996.

e. The entity had reasonable basis (within the meaning of section 6662) for treating the entity as other than a corporation on May 8, 1996.

f, Neither the entity nor any member was notified in writing on or before May 8, 1996, that the classification of the entity was under examination (in which case the entity's classification will be determined in the examination).

Binding contract rule.—If a foreign business entity described in Regulations section 301.7701-2(b)(8)(i) is formed after May 8, 1996, under a written binding contract (including an accepted bid to develop a project) in effect on May 8, 1996, and all times thereafter, in which the parties agreed to engage (directly or indirectly) in an active and substantial business operation in the jurisdiction in which the entity is formed, **8** on page 2 is applied by substituting the date of the entity's formation for May 8, 1996.

Eligible entity.—An eligible entity is a business entity that is not included in items **1** or **3** through **8** under the definition of corporation on page 2.

Limited liability.—A member of a foreign eligible has limited liability if the member has no personal liability for any debts of or claims against the entity by reason of being a member. This determination is based solely on the statute or law under which the entity is organized (and, if relevant, the entity's organizational documents). A member has personal liability if the creditors of the entity may seek satisfaction of all or any part of the debts or claims against the entity from the member as such. A member has personal liability even if the member makes an agreement under which another person (whether or not a member of the entity) assumes that liability or agrees to indemnify that member for that liability.

Partnership.—A partnership is a business entity that has at least two members and is not a corporation as defined on page 2.

Relevant.—A foreign eligible entity's classification is relevant when its classification affects the liability of any person for Federal tax or information purposes. The date the classification of a foreign eligible entity is relevant is the date an event occurs that creates an obligation to file a Federal tax return, information return or statement for which the classification of the entity must be determined.

Effect of Election

The resulting tax consequences of a change in classification remain the same no matter how a change in entity classification is achieved. For example, if an organization classified as an association elects to be classified as a partnership, the organization and its owners must recognize gain, if any, under the rules applicable to liquidations of corporations.

Who Must File

File this form for an eligible entity that is one of the following:

- A domestic entity electing to be classified as an association taxable as a corporation.
- A domestic entity electing to change its current classification (even if it is currently classified under the default rule).
- A foreign entity that has more than one owner, all owners have limited liability, and it elects to be classified as a partnership.
- A foreign entity that has at least one owner without limited liability, and it elects to be classified as an association taxable as a corporation.
- A foreign entity with a single owner having limited liability, and it elects to have the entity disregarded as an entity separate from its owner.
- A foreign entity electing to change its current classification (even if it is currently classified under the default rule).

Do not file this form for an eligible entity that is:

- Tax exempt under section 501(a), or
- A real estate investment trust (REIT), as defined in section 856.

When To FIle

See the instructions for line 3.

Where to File

File Form 8832 with the Internal Revenue Service Center, Philadelphia, PA 19255. Also attach a copy of Form 8832 to the entity's Federal income tax or information return for the tax year of the election. If the entity is not required to file a return for that year, a copy of its Form 8832 must be attached to the Federal income tax or information returns of all direct or indirect owners of the entity for the tax year of the owner that includes the date on which the election took effect. Although failure to attach a copy will not invalidate an other wise valid election, each member of the entity is required to file returns that are consistent with the entity's election. In addition, penalties may be assessed against persons who are required to, but who do not, attach Form 8832 to their returns. Other penalties may apply for filing Federal income tax or information returns inconsistent with the entity's election.

This page intentionally left blank.

LIMITED LIABILITY COMPANY
MEMBER-MANAGED OPERATING AGREEMENT OF

____

THIS AGREEMENT is made effective as of _______________, ______ among the member(s) and the company.

1. Formation. A limited liability company of the above name has been formed under the laws of the state of Delaware by filing certificate of formation with the secretary of state. The purpose of the business shall be to carry on any act or activity lawful under the jurisdiction in which it operates. The company may operate under a fictitious name or names as long as the company is in compliance with applicable fictitious name registration laws. The term of the company shall be perpetual or until dissolved as provided by law or by vote of the member(s) as provided in this agreement. Upon dissolution the remaining members shall have the power to continue the operation of the company as long as necessary and allowable under state law until the winding up of the affairs of the business has been completed.

2. Members. The initial member(s) shall be listed on Schedule A, which shall accompany and be made a part of this agreement. Additional members may be admitted to membership upon the unanimous consent of the current members. Transfer or pledge of a member's interest may not be made except upon consent of all members.

3. Contributions. The initial capital contribution(s) shall be listed on Schedule A, which shall accompany and be made a part of this agreement. No member shall be obligated to contribute any more than the amount set forth on Schedule A unless agreed to in writing by all of the members and no member shall have any personal liability for any debt, obligation or liability of the company other than for full payment of his or her capital contribution. No member shall be entitled to interest on the capital contribution. Member voting rights shall be in proportion to the amount of their contributions.

4. Profit and Loss. The profits and losses of the business, and all other taxable or deductible items shall be allocated to the members according to the percentages on Schedule A, which shall accompany and be made a part of this agreement.

5. Distributions. The company shall have the power to make distributions to its members in such amounts and at such intervals as a majority of the members deem appropriate according to law.

6. Management. The limited liability company shall be managed by its members listed on schedule A. In the event of a dispute between members, final determination shall be made with a vote by the members, votes being proportioned according to capital contributions.

7. Registered Agent. The company shall at all times have a registered agent and registered office. The initial registered agent and registered office shall be listed on Schedule A, which shall accompany and be made a part of this agreement.

8. Assets. The assets of the company shall be registered in the legal name of the company and not in the names of the individual members.

9. Records and Accounting. The company shall keep an accurate accounting of its affairs using any method of accounting allowed by law. All members shall have a right to inspect the records during normal business hours. The members shall have the power to hire such accountants as they deem necessary or desirable.

10. Banking. The members of the company shall be authorized to set up bank accounts as in their sole discretion are deemed necessary and are authorized to execute any banking resolutions provided by the institution in which the accounts are being set up.

11. Taxes. The company shall file such tax returns as required by law. The company shall elect to be taxed as a majority of the members decide is in their best interests. The "tax matters partner," as required by the Internal Revenue Code, shall be listed on Schedule A, which shall accompany and be made a part of this agreement.

12. Separate Entity. The company is a legal entity separate from its members. No member shall have any separate liability for any debts, obligations or liability of the company except as provided in this agreement.

13. Indemnity and Exculpation. The limited liability company shall indemnify and hold harmless its members, managers, employees and agents to the fullest extent allowed by law for acts or omissions done as part of their duties to or for the company. Indemnification shall include all liabilities, expenses, attorney and accountant fees, and other costs reasonably expended. No member shall be liable to the company for acts done in good faith.

14. Meetings. The members shall have no obligation to hold annual or any other meeting, but may hold such meetings if they deem them necessary or desirable.

15. Amendment of this Agreement. This agreement may not be amended except in writing signed by all of the members.

16. Conflict of interest. No member shall be involved with any business or undertaking which competes with the interests of the company except upon agreement in writing by all of the members.

17. Deadlock. In the event that the members cannot come to an agreement on any matter the members agree to submit the issue to mediation to be paid for by the company. In the event the mediation is unsuccessful, they agree to seek arbitration under the rules of the American Arbitration Association.

18. Dissociation of a member. A member shall have the right to discontinue membership upon giving thirty days notice. A member shall cease to have the right to membership upon death, court-ordered incapacity, bankruptcy or expulsion. The company shall have the right to buy the interest of any dissociated member at fair market value.

19. Dissolution. The company shall dissolve upon the unanimous consent of all the members or upon any event requiring dissolution under state law. In the event of the death, bankruptcy, permanent incapacity, or withdrawal of a member the remaining members may elect to dissolve or to continue the continuation of the company.

20. General Provisions. This agreement is intended to represent the entire agreement between the parties. In the event that any party of this agreement is held to be contrary to law or unenforceable, said party shall be considered amended to comply with the law and such holding shall not affect the enforceability of other terms of this agreement. This agreement shall be binding upon the heirs, successors and assigns of the members.

21. Miscellaneous. ____

____

____

____

____

____

____

IN WITNESS whereof, the members of the limited liability company sign this agreement and adopt it as their operating agreement this ______ day of ________________________, _________.

______________________________ ______________________________

______________________________ ______________________________

______________________________ ______________________________

LIMITED LIABILITY COMPANY MANAGEMENT OPERATING AGREEMENT OF

____

THIS AGREEMENT is made effective as of ________________, ______ among the member(s), manager(s), and the company.

1. Formation. A limited liability company of the above name has been formed under the laws of the state of Delaware by filing certificate of formation with the secretary of state. The purpose of the business shall be to carry on any act or activity lawful under the jurisdiction in which it operates. The company may operate under a fictitious name or names as long as the company is in compliance with applicable fictitious name registration laws. The term of the company shall be perpetual or until dissolved as provided by law or by vote of the member(s) as provided in this agreement. Upon dissolution the remaining members shall have the power to continue the operation of the company as long as necessary and allowable under state law until the winding up of the affairs of the business has been completed.

2. Members. The initial member(s) shall be listed on Schedule A, which shall accompany and be made a part of this agreement. Additional members may be admitted to membership upon the unanimous consent of the current members. Transfer or pledge of a member's interest may not be made except upon consent of all members.

3. Contributions. The initial capital contribution(s) shall be listed on Schedule A, which shall accompany and be made a part of this agreement. No member shall be obligated to contribute any more than the amount set forth on Schedule A unless agreed to in writing by all of the members. No member shall have any personal liability for any debt, obligation or liability of the company other than for full payment of his or her capital contribution. No member shall be entitled to interest on the capital contribution. Member voting rights shall be in proportion to the amount of their contributions.

4. Profit and Loss. The profits and losses of the business, and all other taxable or deductible items shall be allocated to the members according to the percentages on Schedule A, which shall accompany and be made a part of this agreement.

5. Distributions. The company shall have the power to make distributions to its members in such amounts and at such intervals as a majority of the members deem appropriate according to law.

6. Management. The limited liability company shall be managed by the managers listed on schedule A, which shall accompany and be made a part of this agreement. These managers may or may not be members of the company and each manager shall have an equal vote with other managers as to management decisions. managers shall serve until resignation or death or until they are removed by a majority vote of the members. Replacement managers shall be selected by a majority vote of the members. managers shall have no personal liability for expenses, obligations or liabilities of the company.

7. Registered Agent. The company shall at all times have a registered agent and registered office. The initial registered agent and registered office shall be listed on Schedule A, which shall accompany and be made a part of this agreement.

8. Assets. The assets of the company shall be registered in the legal name of the company and not in the names of the individual members.

9. Records and Accounting. The company shall keep an accurate accounting of its affairs using any method of accounting allowed by law. All members shall have a right to inspect the records during normal business hours. The members shall have the power to hire such accountants as they deem necessary or desirable.

10. Banking. The members of the company shall be authorized to set up bank accounts as in their sole discretion are deemed necessary and are authorized to execute any banking resolutions provided by the institution in which the accounts are being set up.

11. Taxes. The company shall file such tax returns as required by law. The company shall elect to be taxed as a majority of the members decide is in their best interests. The "tax matters partner," as required by the Internal Revenue Code, shall be listed on Schedule A, which shall accompany and be made a part of this agreement.

12. Separate Entity. The company is a legal entity separate from its members. No member shall have any separate liability for any debts, obligations or liability of the company except as provided in this agreement.

13. Indemnity and Exculpation. The limited liability company shall indemnify and hold harmless its members, managers, employees and agents to the fullest extent allowed by law for acts or omissions done as part of their duties to or for the company. Indemnification shall include all liabilities, expenses, attorney and accountant fees, and other costs reasonably expended. No member shall be liable to the company for acts done in good faith.

14. Meetings. The members shall have no obligation to hold annual or any other meeting, but may hold such meetings if they deem them necessary or desirable.

15. Amendment of this Agreement. This agreement may not be amended except in writing signed by all of the members.

16. Conflict of interest. No member shall be involved with any business or undertaking which competes with the interests of the company except upon agreement in writing by all of the members.

17. Deadlock. In the event that the members cannot come to an agreement on any matter the members agree to submit the issue to mediation to be paid for by the company. In the event the mediation is unsuccessful, they agree to seek arbitration under the rules of the American Arbitration Association.

18. Dissociation of a member. A member shall have the right to discontinue membership upon giving thirty days notice. A member shall cease to have the right to membership upon death, court-ordered incapacity, bankruptcy or expulsion. The company shall have the right to buy the interest of any dissociated member at fair market value.

19. Dissolution. The company shall dissolve upon the unanimous consent of all the members or upon any event requiring dissolution under state law. In the event of the death, bankruptcy, permanent incapacity, or withdrawal of a member the remaining members may elect to dissolve or to continue the continuation of the company.

20. General Provisions. This agreement is intended to represent the entire agreement between the parties. In the event that any party of this agreement is held to be contrary to law or unenforceable, said party shall be considered amended to comply with the law and such holding shall not affect the enforceability of other terms of this agreement. This agreement shall be binding upon the heirs, successors and assigns of the members.

21. Miscellaneous. ____

____

____

____

____

____

____

IN WITNESS whereof, the members of the limited liability company sign this agreement and adopt it as their operating agreement this ______ day of ______________________, _________.

______________________________ ______________________________

______________________________ ______________________________

______________________________ ______________________________

SCHEDULE A TO
LIMITED LIABILITY COMPANY
OPERATING OR MANAGEMENT AGREEMENT OF

____

1. Initial Member(s): The initial member(s) are:

2. Capital Contribution(s): The capital contribution(s) of the member(s) is/are:

3. Profits and Losses: The profits, losses and other tax matters shall be allocated among the members in the following percentages:

4. Management: The company shall be managed by:

5. Registered Agent: The initial registered agent and registered office of the company are:

6. Tax Matters: The tax matters partner is:

This page intentionally left blank.

MINUTES OF A MEETING OF MEMBERS OF

____

A meeting of the members of the company was held on ______________________________, at ______________________________.

The following were present, being all the members of the limited liability company:

______________________ ______________________
______________________ ______________________
______________________ ______________________

The meeting was called to order and it was moved, seconded and unanimously carried that ______________________ act as Chairman and that ______________________ act as Secretary.

After discussion and upon motion duly made, seconded and carried the following resolution(s) were adopted:

There being no further business to come before the meeting, upon motion duly made, seconded and unanimously carried, it was adjourned.

____
Secretary

Members:

____

____

____

____

This page intentionally left blank.

CERTIFICATE OF AUTHORITY

for

____

This is to certify that the above limited liability company is managed by its

☐ members

☐ managers

who are listed below and that each of them is authorized and empowered to transact business on behalf of the company.

Name	Address
________________________	________________________
	________________________
________________________	________________________
	________________________
________________________	________________________
	________________________
________________________	________________________
	________________________

Date: ____________________

Name of company:

____

By: ________________________

Position: ______________________

Index

A

B

C

D

E

P

R

S

T

W

Z

Sphinx® Publishing's National Titles

Valid in All 50 States

Legal Survival in Business

The Complete Book of Corporate Forms	$24.95
How to Form a Limited Liability Company	$22.95
Incorporate in Delaware from Any State	$24.95
Incorporate in Nevada from Any State	$24.95
How to Form a Nonprofit Corporation (2E)	$24.95
How to Form Your Own Corporation (3E)	$24.95
How to Form Your Own Partnership (2E)	$24.95
How to Register Your Own Copyright (4E)	$24.95
How to Register Your Own Trademark (3E)	$21.95
Most Valuable Business Legal Forms You'll Ever Need (3E)	$21.95

Legal Survival in Court

Crime Victim's Guide to Justice (2E)	$21.95
Grandparents' Rights (3E)	$24.95
Help Your Lawyer Win Your Case (2E)	$14.95
Jurors' Rights (2E)	$12.95
Legal Research Made Easy (3E)	$21.95
Winning Your Personal Injury Claim (2E)	$24.95
Your Rights When You Owe Too Much	$16.95

Legal Survival in Real Estate

Essential Guide to Real Estate Contracts	$18.95
Essential Guide to Real Estate Leases	$18.95
How to Buy a Condominium or Townhome (2E)	$19.95

Legal Survival in Personal Affairs

Cómo Hacer su Propio Testamento	$16.95
Cómo Solicitar su Propio Divorcio	$24.95
Cómo Restablecer su propio Crédito y Renegociar sus Deudas	$21.95
Guía de Inmigración a Estados Unidos (3E)	$24.95
Guía de Justicia para Víctimas del Crimen	$21.95
The 529 College Savings Plan	$16.95
How to File Your Own Bankruptcy (5E)	$21.95
How to File Your Own Divorce (4E)	$24.95
How to Make Your Own Simple Will (3E)	$18.95
How to Write Your Own Living Will (2E)	$16.95
How to Write Your Own Premarital Agreement (3E)	$24.95
Living Trusts and Other Ways to Avoid Probate (3E)	$24.95
Manual de Beneficios para el Seguro Social	$18.95
Mastering the MBE	$16.95
Most Valuable Personal Legal Forms You'll Ever Need	$24.95
Neighbor v. Neighbor (2E)	$16.95
The Nanny and Domestic Help Legal Kit	$22.95
The Power of Attorney Handbook (4E)	$19.95
Repair Your Own Credit and Deal with Debt	$18.95
The Social Security Benefits Handbook (3E)	$18.95
Social Security Q&A	$12.95
Sexual Harassment:Your Guide to Legal Action	$18.95
Unmarried Parents' Rights	$19.95
U.S.A. Immigration Guide (4E)	$24.95
The Visitation Handbook	$18.95
Win Your Unemployment Compensation Claim (2E)	$21.95
Your Right to Child Custody, Visitation and Support (2E)	$24.95

Legal Survival Guides are directly available from Sourcebooks, Inc., or from your local bookstores.
Prices are subject to change without notice.

For credit card orders call 1–800–432–7444, write P.O. Box 4410, Naperville, IL 60567-4410
or fax 630-961-2168

Find more legal information at: **www.SphinxLegal.com**

SPHINX® PUBLISHING ORDER FORM

BILL TO:		SHIP TO:	
Phone #	Terms	F.O.B. Chicago, IL	Ship Date

Charge my: ❐ VISA ❐ MasterCard ❐ American Express

❐ **Money Order or Personal Check** **Credit Card Number** **Expiration Date**

Qty	ISBN	Title	Retail	Ext.
		SPHINX PUBLISHING NATIONAL TITLES		
____	1-57248-148-X	Cómo Hacer su Propio Testamento	$16.95	____
____	1-57248-147-1	Cómo Solicitar su Propio Divorcio	$24.95	____
____	1-57248-226-5	Cómo Restablecer su propio Crédito y Renegociar sus Deudas	$21.95	____
____	1-57248-238-9	The 529 College Savings Plan	$16.95	____
____	1-57248-166-8	The Complete Book of Corporate Forms	$24.95	____
____	1-57248-163-3	Crime Victim's Guide to Justice (2E)	$21.95	____
____	1-57248-159-5	Essential Guide to Real Estate Contracts	$18.95	____
____	1-57248-160-9	Essential Guide to Real Estate Leases	$18.95	____
____	1-57248-139-0	Grandparents' Rights (3E)	$24.95	____
____	1-57248-188-9	Guía de Inmigración a Estados Unidos (3E)	$24.95	____
____	1-57248-187-0	Guía de Justicia para Víctimas del Crimen	$21.95	____
____	1-57248-103-X	Help Your Lawyer Win Your Case (2E)	$14.95	____
____	1-57248-164-1	How to Buy a Condominium or Townhome (2E)	$19.95	____
____	1-57248-191-9	How to File Your Own Bankruptcy (5E)	$21.95	____
____	1-57248-132-3	How to File Your Own Divorce (4E)	$24.95	____
____	1-57248-083-1	How to Form a Limited Liability Company	$22.95	____
____	1-57248-231-1	How to Form a Nonprofit Corporation (2E)	$24.95	____
____	1-57248-133-1	How to Form Your Own Corporation (3E)	$24.95	____
____	1-57248-224-9	How to Form Your Own Partnership (2E)	$24.95	____
____	1-57248-232-X	How to Make Your Own Simple Will (3E)	$18.95	____
____	1-57248-200-1	How to Register Your Own Copyright (4E)	$24.95	____
____	1-57248-104-8	How to Register Your Own Trademark (3E)	$21.95	____
____	1-57248-118-8	How to Write Your Own Living Will (2E)	$16.95	____
____	1-57248-156-0	How to Write Your Own Premarital Agreement (3E)	$24.95	____
____	1-57248-230-3	Incorporate in Delaware from Any State	$24.95	____
____	1-57248-158-7	Incorporate in Nevada from Any State	$24.95	____
____	1-57071-333-2	Jurors' Rights (2E)	$12.95	____
____	1-57248-223-0	Legal Research Made Easy (3E)	$21.95	____
____	1-57248-165-X	Living Trusts and Other Ways to Avoid Probate (3E)	$24.95	____
____	1-57248-186-2	Manual de Beneficios para el Seguro Social	$18.95	____
____	1-57248-220-6	Mastering the MBE	$16.95	____
____	1-57248-167-6	Most Valuable Bus. Legal Forms You'll Ever Need (3E)	$21.95	____
____	1-57248-130-7	Most Valuable Personal Legal Forms You'll Ever Need	$24.95	____
____	1-57248-098-X	The Nanny and Domestic Help Legal Kit	$22.95	____
____	1-57248-089-0	Neighbor v. Neighbor (2E)	$16.95	____
____	1-57248-169-2	The Power of Attorney Handbook (4E)	$19.95	____
____	1-57248-149-8	Repair Your Own Credit and Deal with Debt	$18.95	____
____	1-57248-217-6	Sexual Harassment: Your Guide to Legal Action	$18.95	____
____	1-57248-168-4	The Social Security Benefits Handbook (3E)	$18.95	____
____	1-57248-216-8	Social Security Q&A	$12.95	____
____	1-57071-399-5	Unmarried Parents' Rights	$19.95	____
____	1-57248-161-7	U.S.A. Immigration Guide (4E)	$24.95	____
____	1-57248-192-7	The Visitation Handbook	$18.95	____
____	1-57248-225-7	Win Your Unemployment Compensation Claim (2E)	$21.95	____
____	1-57248-138-2	Winning Your Personal Injury Claim (2E)	$24.95	____
____	1-57248-162-5	Your Right to Child Custody, Visitation and Support (2E)	$24.95	____
____	1-57248-157-9	Your Rights When You Owe Too Much	$16.95	____
		CALIFORNIA TITLES		
____	1-57248-150-1	CA Power of Attorney Handbook (2E)	$18.95	____
____	1-57248-151-X	How to File for Divorce in CA (3E)	$26.95	____
____	1-57071-356-1	How to Make a CA Will	$16.95	____
____	1-57248-145-5	How to Probate and Settle an Estate in California	$26.95	____
____	1-57248-146-3	How to Start a Business in CA	$18.95	____
____	1-57248-194-3	How to Win in Small Claims Court in CA (2E)	$18.95	____
____	1-57248-196-X	The Landlord's Legal Guide in CA	$24.95	____
		FLORIDA TITLES		
____	1-57071-363-4	Florida Power of Attorney Handbook (2E)	$16.95	____
____	1-57248-176-5	How to File for Divorce in FL (7E)	$26.95	____
____	1-57248-177-3	How to Form a Corporation in FL (5E)	$24.95	____
____	1-57248-203-6	How to Form a Limited Liability Co. in FL (2E)	$24.95	____
____	1-57071-401-0	How to Form a Partnership in FL	$22.95	____

Form Continued on Following Page **SUBTOTAL**

To order, call Sourcebooks at 1-800-432-7444 or FAX (630) 961-2168 (Bookstores, libraries, wholesalers—please call for discount)

Prices are subject to change without notice.

Find more legal information at: **www.SphinxLegal.com**

SPHINX® PUBLISHING ORDER FORM

Qty	ISBN	Title	Retail	Ext.
____	1-57248-113-7	How to Make a FL Will (6E)	$16.95	____
____	1-57248-088-2	How to Modify Your FL Divorce Judgment (4E)	$24.95	____
____	1-57248-144-7	How to Probate and Settle an Estate in FL (4E)	$26.95	____
____	1-57248-081-5	How to Start a Business in FL (5E)	$16.95	____
____	1-57248-204-4	How to Win in Small Claims Court in FL (7E)	$18.95	____
____	1-57248-202-8	Land Trusts in Florida (6E)	$29.95	____
____	1-57248-123-4	Landlords' Rights and Duties in FL (8E)	$21.95	____
		GEORGIA TITLES		
____	1-57248-137-4	How to File for Divorce in GA (4E)	$21.95	____
____	1-57248-180-3	How to Make a GA Will (4E)	$21.95	____
____	1-57248-140-4	How to Start a Business in Georgia (2E)	$16.95	____
		ILLINOIS TITLES		
____	1-57248-206-0	How to File for Divorce in IL (3E)	$24.95	____
____	1-57248-170-6	How to Make an IL Will (3E)	$16.95	____
____	1-57071-416-9	How to Start a Business in IL (2E)	$18.95	____
____	1-57248-078-5	Landlords' Rights & Duties in IL	$21.95	____
		MASSACHUSETTS TITLES		
____	1-57248-128-5	How to File for Divorce in MA (3E)	$24.95	____
____	1-57248-115-3	How to Form a Corporation in MA	$24.95	____
____	1-57248-108-0	How to Make a MA Will (2E)	$16.95	____
____	1-57248-106-4	How to Start a Business in MA (2E)	$18.95	____
____	1-57248-209-5	The Landlord's Legal Guide in MA	$24.95	____
		MICHIGAN TITLES		
____	1-57248-215-X	How to File for Divorce in MI (3E)	$24.95	____
____	1-57248-182-X	How to Make a MI Will (3E)	$16.95	____
____	1-57248-183-8	How to Start a Business in MI (3E)	$18.95	____
		MINNESOTA TITLES		
____	1-57248-142-0	How to File for Divorce in MN	$21.95	____
____	1-57248-179-X	How to Form a Corporation in MN	$24.95	____
____	1-57248-178-1	How to Make a MN Will (2E)	$16.95	____
		NEW YORK TITLES		
____	1-57248-193-5	Child Custody, Visitation and Support in NY	$26.95	____
____	1-57248-141-2	How to File for Divorce in NY (2E)	$26.95	____
____	1-57248-105-6	How to Form a Corporation in NY	$24.95	____
____	1-57248-095-5	How to Make a NY Will (2E)	$16.95	____
____	1-57248-199-4	How to Start a Business in NY (2E)	$18.95	____

Qty	ISBN	Title	Retail	Ext.
____	1-57248-198-6	How to Win in Small Claims Court in NY (2E)	$18.95	____
____	1-57248-197-8	Landlords' Legal Guide in NY	$24.95	____
____	1-57071-188-7	New York Power of Attorney Handbook	$19.95	____
____	1-57248-122-6	Tenants' Rights in NY	$21.95	____
		NORTH CAROLINA TITLES		
____	1-57248-185-4	How to File for Divorce in NC (3E)	$22.95	____
____	1-57248-129-3	How to Make a NC Will (3E)	$16.95	____
____	1-57248-184-6	How to Start a Business in NC (3E)	$18.95	____
____	1-57248-091-2	Landlords' Rights & Duties in NC	$21.95	____
		OHIO TITLES		
____	1-57248-190-0	How to File for Divorce in OH (2E)	$24.95	____
____	1-57248-174-9	How to Form a Corporation in OH	$24.95	____
____	1-57248-173-0	How to Make an OH Will	$16.95	____
		PENNSYLVANIA TITLES		
____	1-57248-242-7	Child Custody, Visitation and Support in Pennsylvania	$26.95	____
____	1-57248-211-7	How to File for Divorce in PA (3E)	$26.95	____
____	1-57248-094-7	How to Make a PA Will (2E)	$16.95	____
____	1-57248-112-9	How to Start a Business in PA (2E)	$18.95	____
____	1-57071-179-8	Landlords' Rights and Duties in PA	$19.95	____
		TEXAS TITLES		
____	1-57248-171-4	Child Custody, Visitation, and Support in TX	$22.95	____
____	1-57248-172-2	How to File for Divorce in TX (3E)	$24.95	____
____	1-57248-114-5	How to Form a Corporation in TX (2E)	$24.95	____
____	1-57071-417-7	How to Make a TX Will (2E)	$16.95	____
____	1-57248-214-1	How to Probate and Settle an Estate in TX (3E)	$26.95	____
____	1-57248-228-1	How to Start a Business in TX (3E)	$18.95	____
____	1-57248-111-0	How to Win in Small Claims Court in TX (2E)	$16.95	____
____	1-57248-110-2	Landlords' Rights and Duties in TX (2E)	$21.95	____

SUBTOTAL THIS PAGE ____

SUBTOTAL PREVIOUS PAGE ____

Shipping— $5.00 for 1st book, $1.00 each additional ____

Illinois residents add 6.75% sales tax ____

Connecticut residents add 6.00% sales tax ____

TOTAL ____

To order, call Sourcebooks at 1-800-432-7444 or FAX (630) 961-2168 (Bookstores, libraries, wholesalers—please call for discount)

Prices are subject to change without notice.

Find more legal information at: **www.SphinxLegal.com**